THE PLANTING OF CHRISTIANITY IN AFRICA

THE PLANTING
OF CHRISTIANITY
IN AFRICA

By

C. P. GROVES

*Formerly Professor of Missions in the Selly Oak Colleges
Birmingham*

VOLUME FOUR
1914–1954

LONDON
LUTTERWORTH PRESS

First published 1958
Reprinted 1964
© C. P. GROVES, 1958

46,309

PRINTED IN THE NETHERLANDS BY DRUKKERIJ HOLLAND N.V., AMSTERDAM

PREFACE

IN THE present volume the story of the third planting of Christianity in Africa is brought up to the contemporary scene. While the terminal date 1954 has been given as marking a round forty years since the outbreak of the First World War, when later developments appeared to demand it they have been, with some temerity, included, for I have not been unmindful of the warning of the poet Horace, that to treat of such near-contemporary events is like walking upon ashes beneath which the embers are still glowing.

It is now fifteen years since the writing of this history was commissioned and many more since the studies that underlie its composition were first commenced. It is with deep gratitude for having been permitted to complete the task assigned that the recorded story is now offered for the service of the Christian Church in Africa, together with the hope that this narrative may be, within its limits, some contribution to the story of the Universal Church.

While in scope and method, as indicated at the outset, there has been some departure from the pattern of my predecessors, yet I remain in heavy debt to them and to all who have left records of work attempted and work done for the redemption of Africa, which would otherwise have fallen into oblivion. The somewhat ample documentation I have ventured to supply bears witness to my debt. Every effort has been made throughout to ensure accuracy of statement and fairness of presentation. For such failures in these respects as my readers may discover I crave their pardon.

J. E. K. Aggrey was accustomed to say that the very shape of Africa was that of a mark of interrogation and betokened the veil of uncertainty that overhung its future. That was a full generation ago, and while none would contend that the veil has yet been lifted, the Christian enterprise in Africa has since his day passed through vicissitudes Aggrey never knew, and, despite the precarious poise of world affairs, the growing Church in Africa has survived and has done so with encouraging increase of vigour. Nevertheless the question mark still stands while peril remains acute in more than one region of the continent.

Once again I record my deep obligation to Dr. Edwin W. Smith who has read the entire first draft of the manuscript of this volume and whose expert knowledge has been most generously placed at my disposal throughout the entire work. To Mr. L. B. Greaves, Secretary for African Affairs of the Conference of British Missionary Societies, who has read the final draft of chapters 4 to 8, I am much indebted. His own extensive experience in Africa and his knowledge of current African affairs I have found a valuable safeguard in navigating many troubled waters. Nevertheless these friends carry no responsibility for such errors of fact or insecurity of judgment as may remain; that responsibility is mine alone.

In the compilation of the Appendix I have received expert help from Professor J. Martin Plumley of the Chair of Egyptology in the University of Cambridge; Professor W. D. McHardy of King's College, University of London; Dr. E. W. Smith, formerly head of the Translations Department of the British and Foreign Bible Society; the Rev. W. J. Bradnock, the present head of that Department, to whom in particular I am indebted for help in resolving various chronological discrepancies between existing authorities; Dr. W. C. Somerville, General Secretary of the National Bible Society of Scotland; and Miss Margaret T. Hills, Librarian of the American Bible Society.

I also tender grateful acknowledgment of the generous assistance which has facilitated the publication of this concluding volume.

Dr. R. Dunkerley has once again given his expert help in the reading of the proofs, and to him I owe my thanks. Mrs. M. Stephenson has earned my gratitude for her unfailing service in preparing the typescript thoughout. The unfailing courtesy and patience of the editorial department of the Lutterworth Press during the years of publication have won my gratitude.

To my wife I have been, throughout the years of execution, more deeply indebted than I can here record.

C. P. GROVES.

August 1957.

CONTENTS

CONTENTS

Permission is acknowledged to the Clarendon Press for the use of the map of Africa in 1914, and to Messrs. George Philip and Son Ltd. for the map of Africa in 1954.

CHAPTER I

WAR OVER AFRICA: (A) EFFECT ON MISSIONS

1914–1918

THE partition of Africa among European Powers bound up forthwith the fortunes of that continent with the destinies of Europe. And with the first decade of the twentieth century the European scene was growing sombre. The Anglo-French rivalry which had marked the eighteen-nineties was, it is true, at last dissolved in the more genial atmosphere of the Entente Cordiale, initiated as a European policy of friendship between the two powers which Edward VII was at much pains to foster. How severe the strain had previously been is indicated by the Fashoda crisis of 1898, which had brought France and Great Britain to the very brink of war over their interests in the Eastern Sudan. This *rapprochement*, however, was anything but pleasing to a watchful Germany, who forthwith proceeded to test the strength of the Entente. It was on African soil that the moves were made.

French influence in North Africa was extending westwards from Algeria to embrace Morocco. A French plan for internal reforms had been presented to the Sultan, who was resisting it. Germany seized the opportunity to intervene : in March 1905 German troops landed at Tangier and promised the Sultan support, while France was bluntly informed that, if she attempted to change the *status quo* in Morocco, Germany would range herself beside the Sultan. A conference was proposed which France perforce had to accept; it met at Algeciras but yielded Germany no advantage she could not otherwise have secured, and meanwhile she had but tightened the bond of the Entente Cordiale.[1] German naval development now set the pace for Europe and threatened the supremacy of Britain on the seas. The British reply was a *Dreadnought* programme of battleships with a heavier armament than had yet been built.

---

[1] J. A. Spender, *Great Britain, Empire and Commonwealth 1886–1935* (n.d.), 238–9, 259–60.

Six years after the Algeciras conference the tender spot of Morocco again became inflamed. In 1911 rebels against the Sultan began marching on his capital of Fez. The French then declared their intention of proceeding to Fez to relieve the Sultan and safeguard Europeans. Germany replied that she would regard the French occupation of Fez as a new situation; in other words, she would require some compensatory advantage. At this stage it was suddenly learned that a German warship had been despatched to Agadir, a small port on the Atlantic coast of Morocco, whose name was then written into history. The British reaction was as prompt as it was unexpected, and the second Morocco crisis brought Europe to the edge of the abyss.[1] There was, however, more behind the abrupt German action than was known at the time; this was nothing less than the intention to acquire German rights in Southern Morocco, prompted by belief in the mineral wealth of the country and its suitability for colonization. When, through the report of its confidential agent, the Wilhelmstrasse was advised that the land was virtually a desert and the idea of accessible metal ore an illusion, the enterprise was hastily abandoned, but the problem then was how to withdraw with honour unimpaired.[2] This led to a prolongation of the crisis which seemed to the outside world to bode the worst, until Germany accepted compensation in the West, a generous slice of the French Congo, 100,000 square miles in extent, being ceded to her. This expansion of the German Protectorate of the Cameroons on the south and east provided for the first time access to the Congo and Ubangi rivers, as well as enclosing Spanish Guinea in German territory and transferring from France the right of its pre-emption. "Those who study history and the map of Africa," writes Sir Charles Lucas, " will realize what strength was added to the Germans in Africa by

[1] *Ibid.*, 401–6. Spender adds: " In the very week in August in which the [British] Government was engaged in its last wrestling with the House of Lords and the whole of public attention was concentrated on that domestic struggle, the German Ambassador himself told me that war between our two countries was a serious possibility before the end of the week."

[2] New light was thrown on the Agadir crisis by the record of moves behind the scenes made public in *Searchlight on German Africa* (1939), a brief historical study by F. W. Pick based on the diaries and papers of Dr. Regendanz, which had been placed at his disposal. Regendanz worked for the Hamburg firms which were interested in the exploitation of Southern Morocco and were in close touch with the German Foreign Office. But the facts as Regendanz found them were shattering: " The land of dreams was a non-existent dreamland. Disappointment without hope was the result of Dr. Regendanz's journey."—*Op. cit.*, 79.

this deal with France and what a potent 'factor was Africa in promoting the Great War." [1]

But the actual firing of the fuse was to take place in Europe within two years. The shots at Sarajevo in July 1914 lit the powder train that led to world conflagration in which Africa was second only to Europe as the scene of war.

(1) *Theatres of Conflict*

Germany alone of the Central Powers had territory in Africa, and with the swelling of the ranks of the Allies her four colonies were soon entirely surrounded, barring the short boundary between Cameroons and Spanish Guinea, by enemy-held frontiers. Indeed, not only was every European Power with territory in Africa, save Spain, speedily involved but the one independent state with a sea frontier—Liberia—also declared in due course for the Allied side. [2] Clearly sea-power would determine in the long run the fate of the African colonies both Allied and German. With the pinning down of the German High Seas Fleet to European waters, the control of the seas remained throughout with the Allies and enabled them to seize the initiative in invading the German colonies. There were thus four theatres of conflict, corresponding to the four colonial claims that had been staked out by Germany in 1884–85 : Togo, Cameroons, South-West Africa, and German East. In the first of these, allied occupation was complete in a matter of weeks, while German forces from the last were still at large when the armistice was signed.

Togo, the smallest of the German African possessions with only thirty-two miles of coastline though expanding inland to an area of some 34,000 square miles, was flanked by the British Gold Coast and French Dahomey. British columns from the south (by sea) and west, and French forces from the east and north, thanks to an African population prepared to welcome them, were soon entering the country, and within a fortnight the campaign was

---

[1] Lucas, *The Empire at War*, IV (1925), 63. This cession increased the area of Cameroons by 50 per cent. The so-called Duck's Beak at the north-east apex of Cameroons, a small triangle of territory, was transferred to France at the same time in order to straighten the frontier.

[2] Liberia entered the war in 1917 on the Allied side at the request of the United States, then a combatant.—E. W. Smith, *Events in African History* (1942), 43. The other independent state, Abyssinia, was almost involved on the German side. Lij Jasu, who on Menelik's death in December 1913 succeeded to the supreme power, disclosed in 1915–16 his Muslim allegiance and pursued a pro-Turkish policy, but this was soon foiled.—Jones and Monroe, *History of Abyssinia* (1935), 153–4, 157–9.

over.[1] Wireless communication was being developed in Togo on the eve of war for strategic reasons, and in July 1914 Africa's largest wireless station was completed at Kamina, some hundred miles north of Lome; it had been designed to communicate with Berlin to the north and with Dar-es-Salaam and Windhuk to the east and south. This the German defenders destroyed before capitulation, a major loss to their prearranged African defence system.[2] The friendly attitude of the African peoples of Togo has been ascribed to more than one cause, but the fact that the frontiers of the country had cut in two various ethnic groups which were now hoping to be reunited must be allowed considerable weight.[3] German merchants and missionaries were not disturbed until 1916 when the former were deported, the missionaries being removed in that and the following year.[4]

The campaign in Cameroons was a vastly different proposition. Here was a territory some 306,000 square miles in extent, exceeding the area of Germany itself by one-third, with its Anglo-German boundary alone running for 1,000 miles; it was characterized by grasslands in the north and east and by dense equatorial forest in the south. This natural division was reflected in the campaign which was more protracted in the difficult southern region. Here British and French forces were again in co-operation, the French being naturally fired with the resolve to recover the territory ceded under duress only three years before. The German defence was capable and stubborn. Of three British columns on the Nigerian frontier, all were worsted, one disastrously. The attack by sea was more successful, Duala, the main port, being in Allied hands by the end of 1914, together with Buea, the official headquarters on Cameroons Mountain, while the one-time British settlement of Victoria had also been occupied. As the campaign advanced the Allies suffered the disadvantage of lengthening communications, while the onset of the rainy season, with its concomitant of increased malaria, further hampered operations. As the main front lay at first in the southern forest region these difficulties were accentuated by the natural obstacles of the country. Eventually a major operation was carried to success in the capture of Yaunde on New Year's Day 1916. The Germans in retreat successfully made their way for more than a hundred miles

[1] Lucas, *op. cit.*, 26–30.
[2] *Ibid.* 26–7, 30.
[3] G. L. Beer, *African Questions at the Paris Peace Conference* (1923), 40–1 ; cf. Lucas, *op. cit.*, 24.
[4] Lucas, *op. cit.* 32.

to the neutral territory of Spanish Guinea where 840 Europeans were interned, soon to be removed to Fernando Po.[1]

South-West Africa was comparable in size to Cameroons, being 322,000 square miles in extent, and likewise having a land frontier of 1,000 miles marching with British territory—the recently set up Union of South Africa. Enjoying a subtropical climate, it had the largest number of German settlers of any of the four colonies, amounting to some 15,000. It is a tribute to British statesmanship in the South African settlement reached in the Act of Union only four years before, thus conferring Dominion status on the country,[2] that the campaign in South-West Africa was conducted under Dutch leadership with a force of Dutch and British troops, unsupported by Imperial aid, and was brought to a successful issue within the year, and this despite a vexatious rebellion of the more extreme Boer elements that had first to be quelled.[3] Ministers of the Dutch Reformed Church were to be found on the rebel side, but the leaders of the Church stood with General Botha, condemning the rebellion as " a faithless breach of the treaty signed at Vereeniging and a positive sin against God." [4] This serious military threat to internal security once disposed of, General Botha, Prime Minister of the Union, in January 1915 took the supreme command of the invasion of South-West Africa, with General Smuts as his brilliant coadjutor. In six months the campaign was brought to a successful conclusion by the German surrender on July 9, 1915. Botha's personal ascendancy, securing a co-operation between Dutch and British that was scarcely to be anticipated, together with his genius as a strategist and his fair human dealing with a defeated enemy, this largely dictated by his own memories of a recent past, did much to secure a speedy termination of the fighting where the nature of the country, the distances to be covered and the strength of the enemy might easily have involved a prolonged and wearisome campaign.[5] The terms of surrender

[1] *Ibid.*, 68–70, 81–4, 108–13.

[2] The Act of Union was passed by the British Parliament in 1909, receiving the Royal Assent in September, and became effective on May 31, 1910.—E. A. Walker, *A History of South Africa* (1947 ed.), 534–5.

[3] The invading force numbered some 50,000 men, of whom about 23,000 were Dutch, mounted for the most part, and 27,000 British, chiefly infantry.—Lucas, *op. cit.*, 437. The rebellion was handled by General Botha himself and a critical phase for South Africa thus safely passed.—Walker, *op. cit.*, 556–60.

[4] Lucas, *op. cit.*, 399.

[5] Walker, *op. cit.*, 560 ; Lucas, *op. cit.*, 438–56; Buxton, *General Botha* (1924), 99–118 ; H. Driessler, *Die Rheinische Mission in Südwestafrika* (1932), 267–70.

were generous: soldiers and officials to be repatriated after the war, but meanwhile officers to retain their arms and live under parole where they might choose, the rank and file to be interned, and reservists to return to their farms under parole. Under these terms some 6,000 were eventually repatriated while 8,000 or so (farmers, traders and others) remained in the country.[1] The administration of the territory, pending future decisions at the peace conference, fell to the Union Government.

The East African campaign by contrast was not completed until the general cessation of hostilities in Europe. German East Africa was bounded on its land frontiers by British East Africa and Uganda on the north, the Belgian Congo on the west, Northern Rhodesia and Nyasaland on the south-west, and Portuguese East Africa on the south. With an area of 384,000 square miles it was the largest of Germany's African possessions. Of its African population of over seven million half were in the states of Ruanda and Urundi in the north-west. Its own position was strategic for securing control of the whole of Central Africa, and Germany was naturally not unconscious of the fact. The greatest asset on the German side in the campaign was the distinguished commander, von Lettow-Vorbeck, who for military capacity and high courage had no German equal outside Europe. True, he had the advantage of internal lines of communication, controlled Lake Tanganyika until December 1915, commanded a force at the outset some 5,000 strong, of whom 260 were Europeans—a force that at its zenith totalled some 20,000 of whom the African askari was excellently adapted to the conditions of the campaign—and had a remarkable stroke of luck in the arrival of a couple of blockade runners with supplies from Germany.[2] Yet the enemy he confronted had control of the sea, were in possession of all land frontiers, were free to import arms and ammunition (replenishment of which was von Lettow-Vorbeck's greatest anxiety), and had an approximate total of 126,000 troops engaged, though the largest number in the field at any one time did not exceed 55,000. That he held them at bay for so long, and remained at large with a considerable force throughout the war, actually working his will on Rhodesian soil at the very last, won the unstinted admiration of friend and foe alike. It was the armistice in Europe that sealed his fate.[3]

[1] Walker, *op. cit.*, 560, n. 3; Lucas, *op. cit.*, 457; Buxton, *op. cit.*, 119, 122–3.

[2] Lucas, *op. cit.*, 154, 158, 161; G. F. Sayers, *The Handbook of Tanganyika* (1930), 79, 81, 83–4, 85.

[3] Sayers, *op. cit.*, 90–1.

Three principal phases in the campaign have been distinguished. In the first, Allied forces were on the defensive and daring German incursions were carried out in the frontier regions of Uganda, the Belgian Congo, Northern Rhodesia, and Nyasaland, while a bid was made to immobilize the railway running from Mombasa to Lake Victoria, a vital British transport link, which was subject to constant raids in the early months. The Government of India then sent an expedition whose leader assumed command of the British forces in the north, but an attempt to capture Tanga was foiled and the first British offensive of the campaign came to nought. The second phase opened with the assumption of the supreme command by General Smuts in February 1916. South African troops, available after the settlement of affairs in South-West Africa, were now arriving with supplies and transport to swell the forces in the field. A major strategy was developed which turned the tide of war and for the first time von Lettow-Vorbeck found himself in slow retreat under Smuts' pressure from the north, supplemented by outflanking movements. In addition, two brigades of African troops from the Congo, under Belgian officers, co-operated from the west, moving through the country between Lakes Victoria and Tanganyika, while a British force from Northern Rhodesia moved north-east between Lakes Tanganyika and Nyasa.

After a year's campaigning, during which the military position had completely changed, Smuts handed over the command. But the campaigning had been costly. Some 12,000 to 15,000 white South African troops had been sent home—malaria was the main enemy to which they capitulated—and African troops from East and West took their place. For the troops the insect vectors of tropical disease and for animal transport the tsetse fly proved elusive and dangerous enemies. With Smuts' departure came the third phase when principally African troops were employed on the Allied side, and von Lettow-Vorbeck was reduced to guerilla tactics and constant evasive action which none the less he conducted with a skill that denied his pursuers the end they sought—his final defeat and capitulation. After withdrawing south of the Rovuma into Portuguese territory he returned to the north of Lake Nyasa and even entered Northern Rhodesia to the no small consternation of the African community, confident hitherto in British protection, while Europeans at danger-points were hastily evacuated. With the communication of the terms of the armistice in Europe, he marched to Abercorn where there was a British garrison and voluntarily laid down his arms on

November 23, 1918, with a surviving force of 155 Europeans and 4,056 Africans of all grades. On the side of the Allies the troops involved from first to last had included (in round thousands) over 52,000 from India, more than 43,000 South African whites, some 3,000 Rhodesians, and 15,000 African troops from East and West Africa with a further 12,000 from the Belgian Congo. The total cost to the British authorities was, by official estimate, put at £72 million.[1]

Before passing from the military and political background to consider the experience of the Christian mission during the war years, it remains to chronicle the movement in Germany for a post-war settlement on the basis of a great German Empire of Central Africa. The Pan-German extremists, who were loudly vocal for a *Mittel-Europa* policy with a Berlin to Baghdad line of advance to the Indian Ocean, were countered by the moderates who argued the case for a *Mittel-Afrika* policy as having most in its favour. Various German publicists presented this with variations in detail, but having in common the proposal that the Belgian Congo, Portuguese Angola, and generous slices of contiguous French and British territories should be welded into a solid German block, extending from the Atlantic to the Indian Ocean and providing invaluable naval bases by which German sea-power could dominate the trade routes from Europe to South America, Southern Asia, and Australia. When it seemed that stalemate had been reached on the Western Front in Europe it was seriously proposed that the return of occupied territory in Belgium and northern France should be conditional on those governments consenting to such a surrender of African territory. Happily the setting up of this invulnerable bastion in Africa, under the control of a single power with confessedly world expansionist aims, was never a matter of serious discussion as a condition of peace.[2]

---

[1] Lucas, *op. cit.*, 155-99, 297-306; Sayers, *op. cit.*, 80-91. General von Lettow-Vorbeck and his officers, in accordance with military tradition in the treatment of a respected and honourable foe, were permitted to retain their swords.

[2] The principal writers whose views were expressed in this direction have been summarized by Edwyn Bevan in his Introduction to a translation of Emil Zimmermann's *Das deutsche Kaiserreich Mittel-afrika als Grundlage einer neuen deutschen Weltpolitik* (Berlin, 1917), under the title: *The German Empire of Central Africa as the basis of a new German World-policy* (London, 1918). Generous extracts from the writers concerned are supplied in the Introduction. See also the chapter on " Germany's Colonial Aims " in G. L. Beer, *African Questions at the Paris Peace Conference* (1923), 46-56. Germany was actually on the point of succeeding in economic penetration of Portuguese Africa on the eve of war. The threat of the mailed fist having

(2) *Elimination of German Missions*

Such an upheaval in the life of the continent as that produced
by the four campaigns already summarized, which involved far
more than German territory, extensive enough as that was in itself,
together with the inevitable far-reaching effects of the death-
grapple on European soil, could not take place without the most
profound effect on the Christian mission. It was barely a generation since the bulk of the German missions had begun to work in
German colonies—undertakings now rudely terminated by the
fortunes of war. Missionaries who were Allied nationals at work
in territory controlled by the Allied Powers were likewise not
exempt from the shock of conflict—this, the first war of global
dimensions in human history. The obvious first effects—reduction
of man-power and restriction of vital supplies—were inevitable
with such a major disruption of international relations. True, the
dominating factor was sea-power, and the Allied control of the
seas permitted continued if much reduced intercourse between
Western Europe and North America on the one hand and Africa
on the other, where German missionaries were denied it and even
Scandinavian neutrals heavily handicapped. Whatever the hope
of German nationals overseas that an ultimate German victory in
Europe would in the end redress the balance now so heavily
against them, the German missions were completely isolated from
the outset. And as the campaigns proceeded the pressure steadily
increased, with sterner measures adopted by the Allies for all
German nationals, missionaries included, until with the armistice
German missions had been almost entirely eliminated from African
colonial territory. It was indeed a major injury to the Christian
cause that after but a single generation's work in their own four
colonies missionaries from the land of Luther—for it was mainly
Protestant missions that were concerned—should be abruptly cut
off and their work left orphaned.

The treatment of the German missions varied from territory to
territory, and passed from a more generous to a sterner policy as
the war went on. In Togo, where the Allied campaign was so
speedily concluded, it was the policy of the Gold Coast Government that was determinative, for the work of the Bremen Mission,
together with the smaller field of the Basel Society in the north of

failed in Morocco there was resort to more peaceful negotiation, and with
Britain's knowledge and Portugal's acquiescence a railway scheme in
Angola and economic expansion that would give Germany practical con-
trol of Portuguese Nyasaland were afoot. For details, see F. W. Pick,
Searchlight on German Africa, 105–36.

the German colony, now fell within the British sphere of occupation.[1] The initial attitude of the British authorities was not ungenerous : in a proclamation at the onset of war the Acting-Governor of the Gold Coast commended the good work of the German missionaries in the country, mainly of the Basel Mission, and called for penalties on any " who seek to molest those who have for many years been amongst us as our good friends and guests." [2] For two years the missionaries remained at work, but the strain of the war told, and these German nationals, human as they were, allowed expression to their natural sympathies which were found to intrude, so it was alleged, into their missionary and educational work. In consequence the Bremen workers were deported in 1916 and those of the Basel Mission in the following year.[3]

In Togo an identical policy was followed after the conquest; the Bremen missionaries who had not been called up for the armed forces, and so had not been taken prisoners of war, were permitted to remain at their posts, with certain restrictions.[4] As an instance of the consideration given to them in their work, two consignments of the revised Ewe Bible, printed in Berlin for the British and Foreign Bible Society but not ready until war had begun, were by special permission of the British Government, despatched to them via Amsterdam and London and received with much joy.[5] But in 1916 the axe fell and under a repatriation order German missionaries of both the Basel and Bremen Societies were removed. In August 1916 the three missionaries on the Basel field in north Togo not long entered, who had been devoting themselves during the war period to linguistic studies, were deported. The last of the Bremen missionaries, with one exception, were

[1] One Bremen station only, Atakpame, fell within the French occupied zone.—J. Richter, *Geschichte der evangelischen Mission in Afrika* (1922), 120.
[2] *International Review of Missions* (henceforth quoted as *I.R.M.*), IV (1915), 41, n. 2. The Basel Mission while nominally a Swiss foundation was represented on the Gold Coast almost entirely by Germans, of whom (including those of the Bremen Mission at two stations in the Gold Coast) there were more than fifty in the actual Colony alone.—Lucas, *op. cit.*, 21.
[3] *I.R.M.*, V (1916), 60 ; VI (1917), 44; VIII (1919), 467; Lucas, *op. cit.*, 21.
[4] Seven of the younger missionaries had been called up for military service in the colony, of whom 6 became prisoners of war in French hands, interned at first in Dahomey. Richter records that of the staff of 17 men and 9 sisters only 11 men and 5 sisters were on the field from the outbreak of war. Richter, *op. cit.*, 120. Cf. *I.R.M.*, VIII (1919), 474.
[5] *The Hundred and Twelfth Report of the British and Foreign Bible Society* (1916), 147.

returned to Germany in October 1917. The exception was Ernst Bürgi, of Swiss nationality, now left to direct affairs. The Gold Coast Government had already taken over the schools so that the religious side of the work alone was a missionary responsibility. Happily there were African helpers in the Bremen field who rendered self-denying service among whom R. D. Baëta, an African minister, played a distinguished part. It was by the self-sacrificial labours of such African leaders that the life of the Church was sustained.[1]

The Roman Catholic prefecture apostolic of Togo had been erected in 1892 and confided to the German Fathers of the Divine Word whose headquarters were at Steyl in the Netherlands. In 1912 they reported the considerable staff of eighty workers.[2] They too were allowed to continue for the time being in the British zone of occupation, but with their enforced repatriation the German Society was in due course replaced by the Society of the African Missions of Lyons, an appropriate change as much of the vicariate (to which the prefecture had been raised in March 1914) now lay within the French occupied sphere.[3]

With the repatriation of the Basel missionaries from the Gold Coast, the Government sought means of continuing the extensive work that had been developed at the educational and religious levels and in the prosperous trading section of the mission. With this in view the Scottish Presbyterians of the United Free Church, whose well-established work in eastern Nigeria had commended them, were approached in September 1916 for their co-operation. An attempt to reconstitute the mission as a purely Swiss enterprise did not succeed; the United Free Church of Scotland then responded to the request to assume direction of the religious and educational side of the work. The trading unit of the mission was dealt with separately; its assets were transferred to the Commonwealth Trust Limited, specially constituted for this pur-

---

[1] J. Richter, op. cit., 121–2; J. Bianquis, Les Origines de la Société des Missions Evangéliques de Paris, III (1935) 371. Happily the Bremen Society had already embarked on the policy of raising up an African ministry, and 6 Ewe pastors had been ordained by August 1914. This was now further developed and a plan put into operation whereby pastors were to be recruited from the ranks of the catechists. In consequence there were already 14 ordained pastors when the missionaries left.— Richter, loc. cit.

[2] These included 44 priests, 14 lay brothers and 22 sisters.—I.R.M., V (1916), 54, n. 1.

[3] Cath. Ency., XVII (1922), 732; Schmidlin, Catholic Mission History (1933), 659 and n. 62.

B 2

pose, on the specific understanding that it was to be operated as far as possible in accordance with the principles of the Basel Mission and for the benefit of the people of the Gold Coast.* A. W. Wilkie, Secretary of the Calabar Mission Council of the United Free Church of Scotland, was called in January 1918 to proceed to the Gold Coast to undertake the responsible task of sustaining the work now laid down by the Basel missionaries. Thus one important orphaned mission was allotted its foster-parent.[1]

In the Cameroons at the outbreak of war three of the four Protestant missions were German—the Basel, the German Baptist, and the Gossner Societies. The American Presbyterians, working in the south of the territory, ranked as neutrals until 1917. The Basel Mission, whose original inheritance was the work transferred by the Baptist Missionary Society at the time of German occupa-tion,[2] had by the outbreak of war developed a network of stations extending into the hinterland with a considerable educational agency: in 1914 there were reported 384 schools with an enrol-ment of 22,818.[3] At the same date, with a Christian community of 15,000, there were forty-six ordained men and nine women on this, the leading mission in the Cameroons.[4] The German Bap-tists, who had arrived to serve those originally Baptist churches that felt the Basel discipline too rigid for their traditional independence, with a Christian community of some 3,000 had in 1913 thirteen men and five women missionaries in service.[5] The third German mission was a recent arrival—the Gossner Society (alternatively known as Berlin II) whose work had hitherto been limited to India. The newly acquired region in eastern Cameroons, ceded by France in 1911, was apparently an attraction, though work had to begin in unoccupied territory to the west of it. The Basel Mission wel-

---

[1] Lucas, op. cit., 21–22; I.R.M., VIII (1919), 467; A. W. Wilkie, "An Attempt to conserve the Work of the Basel Mission to the Gold Coast ", I.R.M., IX (1920), 86–94. When the Basel Mission to the Gold Coast was formally closed as such in December 1917, there were 33 missionaries (55 inclusive of wives) and 29 African pastors (in a total of over 300 African agents), with 11 central stations, more than 12,000 communicants, and an estimated Christian community of 30,000. The schools had an attendance of 8,000 daily.—Ibid., 87.

[2] See Vol. III, pp. 56–7.

[3] W. Schlatter, Geschichte der Basler Mission 1815–1915, III (1916), 319. In 1912, when the Basel Mission reported 13,683 scholars, the Roman Catholic Mission (Pallottine Fathers) claimed 11,534, and the German Baptists 3,087, while the Government operated 4 schools only with an enrolment of 868.—Loc. cit.

[4] I.R.M., VIII (1919), 476.

[5] I.R.M., VIII (1919). 474.

* See page 57 for important additional matter.

comed the new partner for it had no surplus resources of its own permitting it to extend into the new territory. In January 1914 the Gossner Mission commenced operations to the north-east of Yaunde and south of the Sanaga in the region of the Government centres of Dume and Bertua, where a station named Gossnerhöhe was begun. The first missionaries—F. Oksas and Chr. Roszat who were soon followed by H. Fröse and F. Alexander—received fraternal support from both Basel and American Presbyterian neighbours, but had barely got started when war broke out, and hopes were dashed. The American Presbyterians helped the men to the best of their ability until in 1916 Fröse and Alexander succeeded in escaping to Spain, while Oksas and Roszat were interned and did not regain Germany until the end of the war. Meanwhile hostile Africans burnt down their station of Gossnerhöhe.[1] Here was no orphaned mission left behind but just the plaintive sorrow of a stillbirth.

With the capitulation of the German defence in 1915 all German missionaries who had not withdrawn to Spanish Guinea were removed by the Allies, save one who claimed American and one Australian citizenship. This applied equally to the three Protestant Societies and the Pallottine Fathers of the Roman Catholic mission who had been at work since 1890.[2] With the supersession of German rule by French, save for a limited region in the northwest assigned to Britain, the question arose of care for the orphaned missions. Fathers of the Holy Ghost, already operating in neighbouring French territory, replaced the Pallotine Fathers, while the Paris Missionary Society entered the French occupied region, as the Scottish Presbyterians had done in the Gold Coast, to care for the congregations of the Basel Mission. Consultation with the French Governor-designate having proved favourable, three experienced missionaries—Allégret, Œchsner de Coninck, and Bergeret—set out for Cameroons in 1917.[3] This proved to be a permanent responsibility of the Paris Society. That section of the

[1] W. Schlatter, *op. cit.*, III, 303; W. Holsten, *Johannes Evangelista Gossner, Glaube und Gemeinde* (1949), 131; J. du Plessis, *Evangelisation of Pagan Africa*, 172. On the Gossner Society as Berlin II, see Vol. III, p. 73, n. 3.

[2] *I.R.M.*, VI (1917), 48; VIII (1919), 474; J. Richter, *Geschichte der evangelischen Mission in Afrika* (1922), p. 185; *Missionary Review of the World*, XXIX (1916), 463–4.

[3] *Cath. Ency.*, XVII (1922), 430; J. Bianquis, *op. cit.*, III, 371; *I.R.M.*, VII (1918), 44. Allégret had already seen service in Gabon, Œchsner de Coninck in Basutoland, and Bergeret in the Loyalty Islands. Cf. Richter, *op. cit.*, 187–9.

Basel work which fell within the limited British sphere, running north-eastwards from Ambas Bay to within twenty-five miles of the Benue, was left untended.[1]

In South-West Africa the Rhenish Mission easily held pride of place. The Finnish Missionary Society operated in Ovamboland in the extreme north, and Roman Catholic missions existed among both Hereros in the so-called Damaraland [2] and Namaqua Hottentots in the south. The Rhenish Society, with a Christian community of over 25,000, had in 1914 forty-nine missionaries at work in twenty-two stations. Farm and industrial workers among them were mobilized but others carried on their work as far as the vicissitudes of war permitted.[3] With the advance of Union troops a number were temporarily taken prisoner, some of whom were sent to the Union while others were held in South-West Africa. They were soon released and permitted to resume their missionary activity. A number returned to their stations in the latter part of 1915 or early 1916. Their experiences on return aroused mixed feelings : they found that mission property had frequently been plundered by the people and that buildings had not escaped the hazards of war; they nevertheless reported for the most part a heart-warming welcome by their congregations.[4] The exception was significant of the care demanded in missionary relations with the Government among a suspicious people. At the Namaqua station of Rehoboth the missionaries had urged compliance with a German order for the surrender of arms but this was resisted, and in consequence a military detachment moved on Rehoboth. The missionary Blecher went out to meet it to urge clemency of treatment, but unhappily returned riding at the head of it. The people leapt to the conclusion that it was he who had brought the soldiers against them and bitter antagonism was aroused. There followed, when opportunity offered, the looting of both mission houses and a declaration that Rehoboth would have nothing more to do with the Rhenish Mission. In implementation the people

[1] When the writer and his wife visited Victoria and Buea in 1920 they found local African leaders carrying on the work to the best of their ability. A suggestion that the Baptist Missionary Society should resume operations did not prove practicable. Cf. Richter, *op. cit.*, 189.

[2] The Hereros were dubbed Damara by their neighbours, a corruption of the Hottentot " Daman ".—Cd. 9146 (1918), 41, n.

[3] Four Rhenish missionaries crossed the border into Portuguese Angola, where the Society had work among the Ovambos. In 1917 the Portuguese Government expelled them, and this Ovambo field of the Rhenish Mission was then transferred to the Finnish Missionary Society.—*I.R.M.*, VIII (1919), 473.

[4] Driessler, *op. cit.*, 276–8.

invited missionary Weich (son of a Rhenish worker) of the Dutch Reformed Church of the Cape to be their pastor. He sought to soften their asperities and to restore some confidence in the Rhenish missionaries.[1]

While in South-West Africa the missionaries were not banned from the country as being German nationals, thanks to the generous terms of surrender, they then had nevertheless a fundamental issue to face: how could the work now be maintained with all resources from Germany still cut off? From the outbreak of war until hostilities ceased the German Government had borne the cost of salaries, while some supplementary income was available from the mission farms. It was after the surrender that an acute situation arose. The Synod of the Rhenish Mission at the Cape first came to the rescue by securing a loan from the Dutch Reformed Church through a mortgage on the society's property at the Cape. Further requirements were met in South-West Africa by an advance of funds from the post-war administration with the mission farms as security. This procedure met the total cost of the work for something like three years, but the mission's indebtedness had then reached the considerable figure of some £20,000. There was no alternative but to surrender in settlement the mission farms in five areas.[2] With the Treaty of Versailles came a policy of repatriation of German nationals, and four of the surviving Rhenish missionaries received notice to quit, on various grounds.[3]

The two Roman Catholic orders had been at work in South-West Africa for some eighteen years when war broke out, at first under certain restrictions but these were relaxed after 1905. The Oblates of Mary Immaculate, at work among Ovambos and Hereros, were represented by missionaries from the establishment at Hünfeld in Germany. In 1914 they numbered seventy persons, serving a Christian community of 1,000.[4] Austrian members of the Oblates of St. Francis de Sales at work in Namaqualand numbered seventeen, in a Christian community of some 1,500.[5] While these missionaries were granted the same liberty as the Rhenish missionaries to exercise their vocation, they too experienced the same embarrassment of lack of funds from home

[1] Ibid., 278-9.

[2] In Omburo, Otjimbingue, Hoachanas, Anawood and Ousises.—Ibid., 281.

[3] Ibid., 281-2.

[4] I.R.M., V (1916), 55, n. 1. They included 23 priests, 25 lay brothers, and 22 sisters.

[5] I.R.M., V (1916), 55, n. 1. The Salesians consisted of 8 priests and 9 sisters.

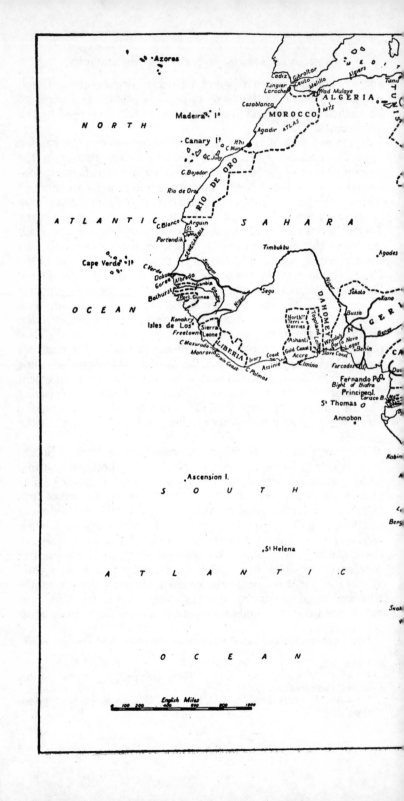

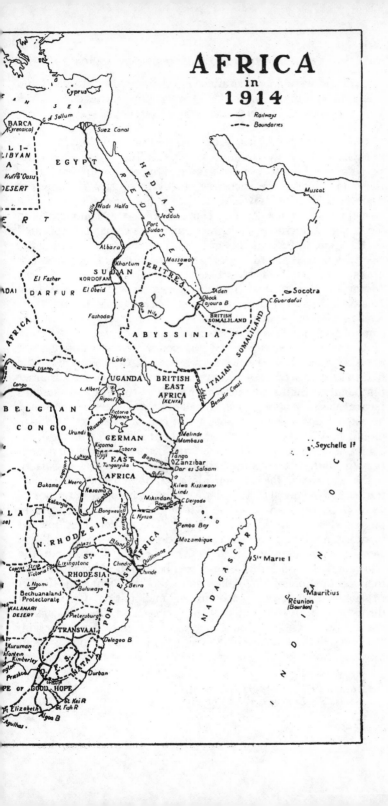

AFRICA
in
1914

— Railways
-- -- Boundaries

sources and were greatly straitened in their circumstances.[1] Thus, while the end of the war found German missionaries still at work in South-West Africa, in comparison with their pre-war prosperity they were now severely crippled.

In German East Africa, as befitted the premier colony, German missions lay heavily committed. The skilfully conducted campaign of von Lettow-Vorbeck accorded them a breathing-space at the outset, but as the encircling enemy forces steadily closed in upon them their fields were invaded, stations evacuated, and work brought to a standstill. The elimination was as complete as in Togo and Cameroons; though, as there, foster-parents appeared on the scene to succour the orphans. The six German Protestant Societies were reported to have, at the outbreak of war, upwards of 150 men in the field.[2] They included the senior Societies : Moravian, Berlin, and Leipzig; together with the Breklum, Neukirchen, and Bethel Missions of later origin. Of the three Roman Catholic orders established in the territory, the Benedictines of St. Ottilien were German in origin.

As naturally determined by the course of the campaign the Societies at work in the northern section of the colony were the first to be displaced. It was from the British East African frontier that General Smuts advanced in March 1916 with the Kilimanjaro area as his first objective. When this was successfully occupied he moved down the Pangani by the end of May and within a month had left behind him the northern railway, running from Tanga to Moshi. By September von Lettow-Vorbeck had been pressed south of the central railway which linked Dar-es-Salaam to the lake, so that the German administration no longer controlled territory to the north of it. Meanwhile, Belgian forces in the north-west successfully advanced into Ruanda in April and were in possession of it by the end of May.[3] These operations covered territory in which four German Societies were at work, and they were correspondingly affected. The Leipzig Mission to the Chaggas, based on Moshi, found itself behind the Allied lines with their occupation of the Kilimanjaro foothills, while the Bethel Mission in Usambara was soon in the same position. Confident in the benevolent attitude of the Allied command, the missionaries did not retire, and this confidence was justified by Smuts' action, reflecting Botha's policy in South-West, in leaving the German missions undisturbed, though naturally this policy could be

[1] *I.R.M.*, VI (1917), 56.
[2] *I.R.M.*, VIII (1919), 472; cf. *I.R.M.*, V (1916), 55, n. 2.
[3] Lucas, *The Empire at War*, IV, 232.

provisional only.[1] The Leipzig Mission was at work in 1914 in
sixteen stations with a staff of twenty-nine missionaries in a
Christian community of 3,700 baptized members with more than
twice that number of scholars in the schools. While by the end of
1917 the number of scholars had fallen by more than half, that of
baptized persons had risen to 5,445, despite the disturbance
occasioned by hostilities.[2]

The Bethel Mission, which had inherited the northern field of
Berlin III, was active in the Usambara country, where it operated
from eight stations with a Christian community of some 2,000.[3] In
the densely populated north-west sector of Ruanda with Urundi
to the south, lying between Lake Victoria and Lakes Kivu and
Tanganyika, Protestant missions had gained a footing only a few
years before the war. The Bethel Mission had entered in 1907
and had eleven stations in being by 1914.[4] For a year and a half
the missionaries continued their work undisturbed without serious
misgiving as to any invasion, though, of course, subject to the
universal German colonial experience in being deprived of supplies
from the home base. But with the British occupation of the Kilimanjaro region in the spring of 1916, Belgian activity to the west
became apparent which soon disclosed itself as a major operation,
and for the first time the evacuation of Ruanda by the German
forces became a disturbing possibility. The majority of the Bethel
missionaries had considered it would be better, if such a situation
developed, to remain at their stations, but in the event official
instructions to leave at once resulted in hurried departures, after
which various stations—Remera, Rubengera, Dsinga, and Rukira
among them—were looted by the pagan populace.[5] Not all could
get away, and one missionary family at least has left a detailed
record of its members' experiences as Belgian prisoners of war.[6]

[1] J. Richter, *Geschichte der Berliner Missionsgesellschaft 1824–1924* (1924),
702.
[2] *I.R.M.*, VIII (1919), 471; J. Richter, *Geschichte der evangelischen
Mission in Afrika* (1922), 597. The missionaries comprised 24 men and
5 single women. The number of scholars reported was 8,500.
[3] *I.R.M.*, VIII (1919), 470. The Bethel was also known as the
Bielefeld Mission from the seat of its headquarters, Bethel bei Bielefeld, in
Germany. In mid-1918 they still had 7 missionaries on the Usambara
stations, while 8 had fallen in the war (7 in Africa) and 18 were interned
overseas.—J. Richter, *Geschichte der evangelischen Mission in Afrika*, 597, n. 1.
[4] E. Johanssen, *Führung und Erfahrung in 40 jährigen Missionsdienst* (n.d.),
II, 181–2.
[5] *Ibid.*, 187–9.
[6] Ernst Johanssen in *Führung und Erfahrung*, II, 189–222. The family
consisted of father, mother, two young daughters, and an infant son.

During the fortnight that Belgian troops were steadily passing through their station of Kirinda they were under close arrest but this was relaxed when the passage of the troops was over.[1] Indeed, Christian outsiders by degrees began attending the family's domestic devotions with their eight African companions, while the Sunday service, which at Whitsuntide even women ventured once again to attend, so swelled in numbers and in power of song, that the guard found it too much of a good thing, and it was at length prohibited. It is a very human story, reflecting the desire of those on both sides, who were subject to all the tensions of a state of war, to behave with decency and moderation. But continued residence at Kirinda was short-lived, and at dawn on July 23, 1916, the little cavalcade sadly set out under guard for the Belgian Congo.[2]

Two missions had only recently arrived in the north-west, the Neukirchen and the Breklum, each of which entered in 1911. The Neukirchen Mission established itself in Urundi where in 1913 five missionaries were reported at three stations.[3] The Breklum Missionary Society, also known as the Schleswig-Holstein Society, had entered the Uha country south of Urundi and work had started at three stations with three missionaries.[4] Once again there were orphaned German missions created by the war. The Neukirchen and Breklum stations, vacated in 1916, could not be provided for and lapsed for the time being. The undertakings of the Bethel and Leipzig Societies, major in comparison, eventually received some parental care. The northernmost Bethel station, at Bukoba in Karagwe on the western shore of Lake Victoria, was in 1917 taken over by the Church Missionary Society, with R. H. Leakey, a senior missionary, in charge. He found nine outstations

---

Johanssen records that they found that when any exchanged Belgian prisoner-of-war had been well treated in Germany, such a Belgian always treated German prisoners well.—*Ibid.*, 191.

[1] The three sentries at the mission house were reduced to one, the missionary's wife was allowed once more to enter her own kitchen, and communication with the eight African Christians (two from Usambara and six from Ruanda), who had elected to remain with the family, was permitted.—*Ibid.*, 191.

[2] *Ibid.*, 194.

[3] *I.R.M.*, VIII (1919), 472. The Neukirchen Missionary Society, as it was sometimes called, was strictly the Neukirchen Mission Institute (Neukirchener Waisen und Missionsanstalt).—Beach and Fahs, *World Missionary Atlas* (1925), 47.

[4] *I.R.M.*, VIII (1919), 472. The official name of the Society was lengthy: Schleswig-holsteinische evangelisch-lutherische Missionsgesellschaft zu Breklum.—Beach and Fahs, *op. cit.*, 47.

that had been begun by the German missionaries, while since their departure the Muganda teacher in charge had opened ten others.[1] The work of the Bethel Mission in Usambara lapsed, but that in Ruanda came under the oversight of the Belgian .Protestants in 1920, while American Lutherans of the Augustana Synod in 1922 accepted responsibility for the Leipzig stations.[2]

In the south the two senior Protestant missionary organizations of the Moravians and the Berlin Society (Berlin I), which had entered side by side in the early 'nineties and settled by mutual arrangement, the Moravians to the west and the Berlin missionaries to the east in the region north of Lake Nyasa, now found themselves still together in the vicissitudes of war. As in the north, so here, von Lettow-Vorbeck's initiative restrained the enemy from spilling over the frontiers in the early months, and mission work in consequence continued undisturbed. With General Smuts' drive over the northern frontier in March 1916, however, a new situation also arose in the south. In May General Northey, who was in command of a Rhodesia-Nyasaland contingent, advanced into the German Nyasa district and by the end of the month had occupied Kondeland, scene of the Berlin Mission's first activity, while in June Kingaland was also invaded. The German missionaries in the south appear to have taken it for granted that the permission for the Leipzig and Bethel Missions in the north to continue for the time being, even when behind Smuts' line of advance, would be repeated in the south. It was therefore a rude awakening to discover that their activity was to be terminated forthwith.[3]

Missionaries of the Berlin Konde Synod were all removed in June 1916, and those of the Hehe Synod soon after. The last Berlin station to fall into Allied hands was Milow, in October 1916. The missionaries and their families were all in due course assembled at Blantyre, the principal Allied military base in Nyasaland,

---

[1] *Proceedings of the C.M.S., 1917–18* (1918), 36–7; *1918–19* (1919), 51.

[2] The respective Societies were: Société Belge des Missions Protestantes au Congo, and Board of Foreign Missions of the Augustana Synod.—Beach and Fahs, *op. cit.*, 22, 44. On the arrangement between the Bethel Mission and the Belgian Protestants, see Johanssen, *op. cit.*, II, 239–42.

[3] Richter has compared Smuts and Northey in this regard, suggesting that Smuts as a Boer appeared not to have lost consideration for the white race in the presence of the coloured, or regard for Christian, in particular German, missions whose work he had known in South Africa, whereas for the English Northey such considerations did not arise.—J. Richter, *Geschichte der Berliner Missionsgesellschaft, 1824–1924* (1924), 702.

to the number of eighty-eight persons half of whom were children.[1] The relations between Alexander Hetherwick, the head of the Church of Scotland Mission at Blantyre, and the internees were not as cordial as they had anticipated would be the case. In their isolation they had remained unaware of the bitter hostility Germany had created by the invasion of Belgium alone, and in consequence they were deeply pained by his judgments.[2] However, they were not long in Blantyre. At the end of October the men were transferred in succession to camps in Mombasa, Tanga, and Egypt whence they reached Germany again at the end of 1919. Meanwhile the wives and children were removed to South Africa in January 1917, and by May 1919 had been repatriated.[3]

The Moravian work was in a similar situation to the Berlin at the onset of hostilities. The oversea missions administration was centralized at Herrnhut in Germany, the British and American boards not yet being independently organized as executive units, so that resources from the home base were at once cut off. Despite this handicap, the work continued with less interruption than might have been expected. But in 1916 the axe fell and the Moravian Nyasa Mission also was deprived of its missionaries. They with their families, sixty-two persons in all, were assembled at Blantyre, and subsequent experiences they shared with the Berlin groups: men were sent to Mombasa, Tanga, and Egypt; women and children first to Pretoria and later to the neighbourhood of Bloemfontein before repatriation in 1919.[4]

Both the Berlin and Moravian Missions had each a second, though less extensive, sphere of operations inherited from Societies that had withdrawn from the districts concerned. The Berlin Society's inheritance in 1903 was the work in Dar-es-Salaam and the Usaramo country to the west of it which had been begun by Berlin III, the rest of whose stations in Usambara to the north had been accepted by the Bethel Mission. The work in Usaramo was

[1] J. Richter, *op. cit.*, 703. Of the total, 23 were men, 21 women and 44 children. Richter complains that though only four of the men had been combatants and one in an ambulance unit, all were treated without distinction as prisoners of war.

[2] Richter alleges that Hetherwick publicly stigmatized the Germans as Huns and expected the missionaries, as Christians, to condemn the acts of their countrymen.—*Ibid.*, 705. Hetherwick was a forthright and spirited man when his moral indignation was aroused. Cf. W. P. Livingstone, *A Prince of Missionaries* (n.d.), 156.

[3] Richter, *op. cit.*, 705-6. Richter is very critical of the treatment meted out to the men.

[4] A. Schulze, *200 Jahre Brüdermission*, II (1932), 615-17, 625-6. Of the 62 persons, 16 were men, 17 women, and 29 children.

limited to four stations in an area rendered unresponsive by the infiltration of Islam from the coast. The Allied occupation of Dar-es-Salaam in September 1916 sealed the fate of this section of the Berlin Society's work. In October missionaries with their families were removed from Maneromango and Kisserawe to Dar-es-Salaam as political prisoners while others from ambulance units were regarded as prisoners of war. At one station—Schlesien near Morogoro—the missionaries were allowed to remain until the setting up of a British administration, but then the final removal took place.[1]

The Moravians had similarly accepted responsibility in 1898 for the London Mission station of Urambo, to the north-west of Tabora (the earlier Unyanyembe), which lay some 350 miles almost due north of their Nyasa mission. The Moravian home directorate had appreciated the significance of a mission centre so near the heart of the territory, and forthwith adopted the policy of a chain of stations that should link this, the Unyamwezi mission, with the original Nyasa enterprise. Within a decade six intermediate stations had been opened, running in a line from north to south.[2] The Belgian advance from the west in 1916, following upon Smuts' invasion from the north, affected the Moravian work in Unyamwezi as it had that of the neighbouring Neukirchen and Breklum Societies. Apart from three unordained men who had been called up for military service, all the missionaries were interned at Tabora in January 1917 and from there

[1] J. Richter, *Geschichte der Berliner Missionsgesellschaft 1824–1924* (1924), 706–7, 708. Schlesien, during its survival as a mission station, became an asylum for German wives and children. The Church Missionary Society offered, in March 1918, to become foster-parent to the Usaramo mission, an offer the Berlin Society was prepared gratefully to accept, with the proviso that the German workers through twenty-seven years should not be forgotten but that the English missionaries should keep their memory green. The shortness of C.M.S. workers, however, did not in the end permit of this help being given.—*Ibid.*, 709; *Proceedings of the C.M.S., 1919–20* (1920), 28–9. A heavy loss to the Berlin Society was that of Martin Klamroth, Superintendent in this field, who died on October 23, 1918, when only 46 years of age. He had arrived in 1900 and was specially gifted for work in this Swahili-Muslim field. He organized the first inter-society conference for a planned, co-operative missionary advance; founded the Swahili paper *Pwani na Bara* (Coast and Interior); and had completed the translation of the New Testament into the Coast dialect of Swahili.— Richter, *op. cit.*, 707–8.

[2] A. Schulze, *200 Jahre Brüdermission*, II (1932), 508–10. The stations in chronological though not in geographical order were: Urambo (1898), Kitunda (1901), Sikonge (1902), Ipole (1903), Kipembabwe (1904), Usoke (1907), and Tabora (1912).—*Ibid.*, II, 512–17.

transferred in separate detachments via the Belgian Congo to the south of France, with few exceptions.[1] Thanks to an arrangement negotiated by the German Government they were at home on German soil once more before the end of the year. The total number interned was forty-two, of whom nearly half were children.[2]

Once more the problem of orphaned missions arose, and in this instance the need of work that had been steadily developed, in the Nyasa area at least, for a full generation and was of some magnitude, could not readily be overlooked. The Berlin Society claimed a Christian community of some 4,000, with a school enrolment of 13,000 throughout its field, while the corresponding Moravian figures were 2,300 and 9,000.[3] Both Berlin and Moravian mission representatives before departure had written to Robert Laws of the Livingstonia Mission, seeking some oversight for the Christian communities they were compelled to leave entirely unshepherded. He responded as best he could, and is credited with the proposal, approved by a conference at Zomba, to share the responsibility among three Nyasa missions: the United Free Church of Scotland Mission to take oversight of Moravian and Berlin stations in the official district of Langenburg; the Church of Scotland Mission, of Berlin stations in the Iringa district; and the English Universities' Mission in that of Songea. The dividing up of work that had hitherto been centralized went sorely against the grain with the Berlin authorities, but most of all they regretted the proposed transfer of a section of their work to the Universities' Mission with whose ecclesiastical outlook they had no sympathy.[4] It was later agreed in international missionary counsel that transfer of German work to a foster-parent must not violate the confessional and ecclesiastical position of the society that had given the mission birth.[5] Nevertheless the Berlin Society found itself

[1] *Ibid.*, II, 626. The exceptions were two married couples with their four children allowed to remain in Tabora, and one mother with two children who joined the Berlin women and children at Schlesien near Morogoro.

[2] *Ibid.*, II, 627. There were 12 men, 11 women, and 19 children.

[3] *I.R.M.*, VIII (1919), 471.

[4] R. Laws, *Reminiscences of Livingstonia* (1934), 198–200; W. P. Livingstone, *Laws of Livingstonia* (1922), 356–8; J. Richter, *Geschichte der Berliner Missionsgesellschaft 1824–1924*, 710–11.

[5] At an international conference, called at the request of national missionary organizations (representative of societies), which met at Crans, near Geneva, in June 1920.—*I.R.M.*, IX (1920), 492–3. As Julius Richter was present at the conference, his account of its findings has first-hand authority.—J. Richter, *op. cit.*, 711.

more in sympathy with the Dutch Reformed Church of the Union alongside which it had always worked happily in South Africa, and so, to avoid the dismemberment of the Nyasa mission, formally requested the General Missionary Committee of that Church to come to their assistance in the supervision of the Nyasa field. This the members of the Dutch Committee were unanimously prepared to do but permission for entry was not then forthcoming as the administration had already confirmed the Zomba conference arrangement.[1]

The total loss to Protestant missionary activity in German East Africa by the removal of all German missionaries was thus severe. It has been estimated that at the outbreak of war there were in all in the territory more than 150 German Protestant men missionaries and 15 single women, serving a Christian community of 12,000, while in the 600 schools maintained some 64,000 pupils were enrolled.[2] The elimination of this effective missionary body, despite the attempts of already overburdened missions to render help in a desperate situation, appeared to leave derelict a field that was passing from blossom-time to harvest. Roman Catholic missions, while less extensive, were more favourably placed for survival. Of the three orders at work, two were French foundations while the third, the Benedictines of St. Ottilien, was of German origin. Its members were therefore removed in 1916 as enemy nationals; they were succeeded in the apostolic vicariate of Dar-es-Salaam by Capuchins from Switzerland, and in that of Iringa by the Consolata Fathers from Turin.[3]

Save in South Africa, there was no extensive work of German missions outside the German colonies. In West Africa the eventual removal of German missionaries from the Gold Coast and the transfer of their stations to Scottish Presbyterians have already been recorded.[4] In British East Africa there were stations of the Leipzig and Neukirchen Societies from which the missionaries were removed as early as 1914 and interned in India.[5] The Leipzig

[1] J. Richter, op. cit., 711.
[2] I.R.M., VIII (1919), 472.
[3] Schmidlin, Catholic Mission History, 658 and n. 61. For Roman Catholic missions, with the central directive of the Congregation of Propaganda to regulate ecclesiastical affairs in missionary countries and with the papal privilege of erecting prefectures and vicariates and entrusting them to particular orders and mission institutes, the problem of orphaned missions, so-called, could not arise as for Protestant Societies working in national and denominational independence.
[4] Vide supra, p. 19.
[5] I.R.M., V (1916), 62, n. 1; VIII (1919), 468. The Leipzig Mission

stations, in pursuance of negotiations begun before the war, were transferred to the Africa Inland Mission. The Neukirchen Society also withdrew from British East Africa, eventually handing over its work to the United Methodist Missionary Society.[1] In Egypt there was also a small German mission enterprise. Karl Kumm, later to be associated more prominently with the Sudan United Mission, had in 1900 founded the Sudan Pioneer Mission at Eisenach, in the expectation that from Aswan as a base there would be advance into the Sudan to the south and west. But the German committee had other ideas and Karl Kumm soon severed his connexion with it. In 1914 the four men and eight single women at work were repatriated.[2] By contrast to such deportations German missionaries in South Africa, where it was estimated there were some 200 at work, were comparatively undisturbed. Naturally reinforcements and support from Germany were cut off but the missionaries were not expelled.[3] True, a number were interned—ten of the Berlin men, for example, for longer or shorter periods—but there was no wholesale removal.[4] Further, in 1917 an official ruling legalized for the Society the raising of loans from time to time to meet the requirements of its work, with the land, of which it was a considerable owner in the northern provinces,

had three stations among the Kambas; the Neukirchen Society had four on the Tana River and one at Lamu.

[1] *I.R.M.*, VIII (1919), 468; *United Methodist Church, Report of the Missions* (1920), 46; *Report* (1923), 52.

[2] I. V. Cleverdon, *Pools on the Glowing Sand: The Story of Karl Kumm* (1936), 36; J. L. Maxwell, *Half a Century of Grace: A Jubilee History of the Sudan United Mission* (1953), 24 and n.; *I.R.M.*, VIII (1919), 466. The Kaiserwerth deaconesses appear to have been permitted to continue their hospital service in Cairo and Alexandria without interruption.

[3] *I.R.M.*, V (1916), 57–58 and n. 3. The 200 missionaries included 180 men and 20 single women. At the outbreak of war the Berlin Society was remitting funds to South Africa at the rate of half a million marks a year.—J. Richter, *op. cit.*, 466.

[4] J. Richter, *op. cit.*, 455. An incident reflecting the more lenient treatment in the Union than generally elsewhere is the following. When missionary Pakendorf was interned in 1914 the church committee of Emmaus, led by the aged African Pastor Gumede, waited on the magistrate when this conversation is reported as taking place: "Where is our minister?" "He is in Maritzburg." "Who has taken him off and what is he doing there?" "He is under arrest." "What has he done?" "He has not done anything but he is a German." "We have never yet heard that a man who has done nothing gets placed under arrest. Besides, it's no crime to be a German. He can't help having been born a German. We must urge our request that at the earliest possible moment he return to us, for he is our father and shepherd." Pakendorf was released!—Richter, *loc.cit.*

as security.[1] In the course of the war the schools in Natal and the
Transvaal, so far as registered, were taken over by the Government, and as straitened financial resources compelled the closing
at the same time of the teacher training and evangelist training
work at Botschabelo the educational arm of the mission appeared
paralysed. But after the war the schools were restored, first in the
Transvaal, then in Natal, and the training courses at Botschabelo
were resumed. As an indication of progress, despite the handicaps
of the time, the Synod of North Transvaal alone reported an increase in membership of 2,250 during the war years.[2]

Similar general conditions affected the Hermannsburg Mission,
the Hanover Evangelical Lutheran Free Church Mission (a secession from Hermannsburg), and the Moravian Brethren. The
Hermannsburg Mission had its internees at different times but
always for brief periods.[3] In respect of finance it was able to
provide for the needs of missionaries by the sale of land to the
Government at the two stations of Beersheba and Bethany, but
resources did not permit of continuing the subsidy to maintain the
teachers and catechists, who now became wholly dependent upon
their own communities.[4] As with the Berlin Mission, the control
of the schools in Natal and the Transvaal was assumed by the
Government and the two Hermannsburg training centres were
also closed. Despite these restrictions of its work there were membership increases here also: some 3,400 in Natal and 8,700 in the
Transvaal.[5] The mission of the Hanover Evangelical Lutheran
Free Church, which appeared in 1892 as a secession from the Hermannsburg Mission, came through the war years with work
unimpaired. It had a few stations in Natal and the south-eastern
Transvaal with a Christian community of some 3,000 and twelve
men to minister to it.[6] The Moravian Brethren, with the undis-
puted honour of having launched the pioneer Christian mission to

---

[1] Richter, *op. cit.*, 467.
[2] Richter, *Geschichte der evangelischen Mission in Afrika*, 525. The
membership of the North Transvaal Synod rose from 13,727 to 15,977 in
the period 1914–18.
[3] At the outbreak of war the Superintendent and twelve missionaries
were interned, but released, the former after a few weeks, the others after
some months. The sole exception was the missionary resident in the
Bechuanaland Protectorate under British rule, who was kept a prisoner for
the four and a half years of the war.—Richter, *op. cit.*, 527.
[4] *Ibid.*, 528.
[5] In Natal from 12,867 to 16,325, and in the Transvaal from 61,230 to
more than 70,000.—*Ibid.*, 528.
[6] *I.R.M.*, VIII (1919), 469; Beach and Fahs, *World Missionary Atlas*
(1925), 48.

South Africa, had at the outbreak of war two fields of work in the Cape Province : in the south-west and in the east adjoining the Kei river. While the work was under the direction of the International Board of the Brethren (only divided into three national executive units after the war), the missionaries in South Africa were for the most part German and so subject to such disabilities as were imposed on enemy aliens. Their experience was much like that of their German neighbours.

In the west there was no incident of note; in the east eight of the fifteen German missionaries were interned for a time. There were inciting causes though not of the missionaries' making : when in September 1914 a rising occurred in the Hlubi tribe the popular idea that Germans must be at the bottom of it led to all Germans beyond the Kei being interned, three Moravian men among them. With the German sinking of the Lusitania in 1915 came another popular outburst, leading to further internments.[1] In this instance the Moravian superintendent, who with two colleagues was subject to the order, successfully contested the case and all three were released.[2] Hampering to the work as even temporary removal of missionaries was bound to be, it was the financial situation that at times pressed most severely. In 1916 all property of enemy nationals came under official control, but in November 1918 the mission was threatened with extinction by a demand for a cash payment equal to the approximate capital value of its property. Happily, through friendly intervention, the exorbitant demand was eventually withdrawn.[3] Thus, even in South Africa, where German missions were at least permitted to survive with a measure of freedom, there were unexpected crises and continual anxieties for those concerned.

The net result of the war years for German missions in Africa was calamitous. In all fields they were completely deprived of reinforcements and resources from the homeland, and in most the missionaries had been removed by 1916-17 for repatriation or internment and the Christian communities left unshepherded, save where devoted African leaders shouldered the burden as best they

[1] A. Schulze, 200 Jahre Brüdermission, II, 440-1.
[2] The superintendent, E. van Calker, produced the original letters from Lord Somerset inviting the Moravians to settle on the eastern frontier in the eighteen-forties, and after some reference to the heavy price they had paid to keep the work going in stormy days on the frontier, pertinently asked whether the promise of a British Governor still held good. The magistrate, having perused the letters, cancelled the missionaries' internment order.— Ibid., II, 441.
[3] Ibid., II, 441-2.

could or already overladen Societies attempted to offer some over-sight. In regions thus denuded of missionaries which at the same time experienced a relaxation of government control there was inevitably a resurgence of paganism accompanied by persecution of the Christian communities, but despite some lapses they were not submerged. In particular where a local African leadership was in being they showed a quite remarkable tenacity. R. D. Baëta was such a leader on the Bremen field in Togo, while in the East African field of the Berlin Mission, Martin Nganischo, receiving ordination in the war emergency, similarly proved his loyalty and capacity in difficult days.[1] Nevertheless the setback was severe. It was the first time that such a gap, so sudden in its appearance and so alarming in its dimensions, had appeared in the ranks of the Christian mission.

(3) Experience of non-German Enterprise

By contrast to the experience of the German missions, those arising from Allied or neutral countries were able to continue without interruption throughout the war years, save for the few at work in German territory or, in the case of East Africa, fringing upon it, where they were subject to von Lettow-Vorbeck's occasional incursions. But they all suffered from restrictions inevit-able in time of war : rationing of supplies, rising costs, heavily reduced transport services aggravated by losses in the submarine campaign, and curtailment of recruits which occasioned lengthened periods on the field without health leave, and some recall of veterans to the service. In respect of foreign missionary staff the American Societies, as was to be expected, suffered less than the British and Continental.[2] A calculation undertaken in 1919 showed nine selected British missions in Africa to have suffered a total reduction of ten per cent in missionary personnel from 1914-18; four non-German Continental Societies (three from neutral countries) less than four per cent; and ten American Societies to have remained all but stationary.[3]

[1] J. Richter, Geschichte der Berliner Missionsgesellschaft 1824-1924 (1924), 709; cf. R. Laws, Reminiscences of Livingstonia (1934), 198-9.
[2] The United States maintained neutrality until, on April 16, 1917, she was brought into the war by the German unrestricted submarine campaign, which had been launched in January of that year in a desperate effort to snatch a victory that at the time seemed to be fast receding.—J. A. Spender, Great Britain, Empire and Commonwealth 1886-1935, 523-5, 527, 544.
[3] For the Societies in question the British totals fell, in the period 1914-18, from 1,108 to 1,006; the Continental group from 414 to 399; while the American ten rose from 388 to 389. The annual reinforcement rate for

In comparison with the work of German Societies that of non-German missions in German territory was small, but such as there was also experienced its vicissitudes. The American Presbyterian Board had extended its work from French Gabon to German Cameroons in 1885 where it had several stations that fell within the field of hostilities. Work at Batanga on the coast was suspended for more than a year; the station at Efulen some fifty miles inland was closed for four months or more; while at Elat, a further seventy-five miles to the east, the German authorities took over the industrial plant for use as an ammunition factory, sending off the missionaries to their station at Metet, a further fifty miles inland to the north-east. Naturally, as neutrals at the time, the Americans were not interned; but with the German withdrawal to Spanish Guinea early in 1916 and the Allied occupation of the country, they were able to resume normal activities at all stations. The fact that these now fell within the French-administered sphere meant that French must replace German as the European language in the schools. Despite the restrictions which a state of war imposed, the missionaries reported that their treatment by Germans, French, and British had been considerate throughout. During this testing time the Church continued to grow; it was estimated that not more than six per cent of the membership lapsed, while at the central station of Elat alone the net increase was twenty-five per cent. The inability of the Home Board to get money into the country was compensated by African generosity in the doubling of local contributions, African evangelists setting the example with a voluntary surrender of fifteen to twenty-five per cent of their slender salaries.[1]

In South-West Africa the Finnish Missionary Society, representative of the Church of Finland, which in 1914 had some 3,000 baptized Christians, with a similar number of adherents and of pupils in the schools, was able to continue unhindered its pioneer work among the Ambos in the north, save that for nearly a year it was isolated from the outside world. Indeed, in the period of the war the missionary force increased from thirty to thirty-six.[2]

In German East Africa two Anglican missions were at work. The

the British nine fell from 54 in 1914–15 to 17 in 1917–18; for the Continental four, from 23 to 21; while for the American ten the figures for the four successive war years were respectively 37, 40, 22, 30, thus reflecting the national situation in relation to the war.—*I.R.M.*, VIII (1919), 480–3, 487.

[1] *The Missionary Review of the World*, XXIX (1916), 325–6; XXX (1917), 337–8; *I.R.M.*, VI (1917), 47–8; VIII (1919), 454.

[2] *I.R.M.*, V (1916), 55 and n. 1, 636; VIII (1919), 487.

Universities' Mission had the more extensive development, both inland from Tanga and in the south towards the Rovuma and Lake Nyasa, which fell respectively within the adjoining dioceses of Zanzibar and Nyasaland. The Church Missionary Society's half-dozen stations lay between these two regions, astride and to the north of the central railway, and were under the jurisdiction of the Bishop of Mombasa. The fourteen missionaries of the Society in this area were assembled in committee at Kongwa when informed by the German officer at Mpwapwa of the outbreak of war. They were directed to remain at their stations but not to pursue their missionary activity—a restriction that was at first unequally enforced but soon effective all round. They were joined at their various stations early in 1915 by twenty-five of the Universities' Mission staff; at the end of May all were assembled at an internment camp at Kiboriani (a few miles to the south-east of Kongwa) where they remained until February 1916. A removal to Buigiri was soon followed by their transfer in April to a camp at Tabora, accommodating 140 internees. Meanwhile members of the Universities' Mission in the south of the territory had all been interned, for the most part at Kilimatinde to the west of Kongwa and Buigiri, some of the men being later transferred to Kiboriani with the C.M.S. group. Eventually the Universities' missionaries, altogether forty-two in number, also found themselves at Tabora. With the capture of this vital point on the central railway by the Belgians on September 19, 1916, the interned missionaries were free once more.

All had suffered, some severely, from the conditions of confinement, and the tasks imposed upon them. The German military hand had proved heavy; the missionaries, whose personal relations with the civil authorities had been friendly before the war, felt that these would have behaved more humanely.[1] Especially resented was the treatment meted out to African Christians, in particular to mission agents as sympathizers with the British side and also in the attempt to get them to incriminate their missionaries.[2] There was some destruction of mission stations, as well as

[1] *Proceedings of the C.M.S., 1916–17* (1917), 34–36; G. H. Wilson, *The History of the Universities' Mission to Central Africa* (1936), 156; *I.R.M.*, VIII (1919), 455–6. For Archdeacon Woodward's diary (U.M.C.A.) of the period of internment, see *Central Africa*, XXXV (1917), 5–16.

[2] *Proceedings of the C.M.S., 1916–17* (1917), 35; G. H. Wilson, *op. cit.*, 157. An African account of internment experiences at Tabora is supplied in " The Story of Martin Kayamba " in M. Perham (ed.), *Ten Africans* (1936), 189–95. Cf. 186, 187–8.

widespread looting, but this is a feature common to both sides in the trail of war. The task of reconstruction was naturally heaviest in the southern region where hostilities had been most prolonged.

The Allied lands abutting on German territory in East Africa did not come through scatheless as did those in the West. In the early months British East Africa suffered various incursions in the German attempt to immobilize the railway from Mombasa to the lake, while border fighting in 1915 in Northern Rhodesia interrupted the work of the Livingstonia Mission at Karonga and Mwenzo, and compelled the London Mission temporarily to withdraw from Kawimbe. In von Lettow-Vorbeck's final raid the Chilubula Mission of the White Fathers was looted, as was the Scottish Mission station at Mwenzo.[1] A more serious because a more persisting dislocation of the work was the call for carriers in British East Africa, which was the principal military base of the Allied campaign, and a similar call in Nyasaland as military operations developed. A certain number of missionaries were also called upon for service, more especially qualified medical men; some were required as chaplains, others in connexion with the carrier contingents.

The effect of the war on missions operating outside the theatres of conflict may be usefully considered, first in respect of so-called Latin Africa (French, Belgian, Portuguese, and Italian territories), and then with some reference to British tropical Africa.

The extensive French domain in Africa, while not seriously the scene of hostilities, was deeply affected by the war. The exemption from military service, normally granted in various countries to ordained ministers of the Churches, was in France, after the separation of Church and State, reduced to vanishing point. This seriously affected those Roman Catholic orders that recruited in France their missionaries for French territories, as also the Paris Missionary Society with its commitments in French Africa, small as these were in comparison with Roman Catholic missions. Age was the only guarantee that a missionary would be allowed to remain at his post; young men were recalled not only from French but also from British colonies. Thus, of the missionaries of the Lyons Seminary for African Missions, which was operating in two French West African colonies (Ivory Coast and Dahomey), two British (Gold Coast and Nigeria), and Egypt, thirty-one priests

---

[1] *Proceedings of the C.M.S., 1914–15* (1915), 54; *I.R.M.*, V (1915), 63; VIII (1919), 457; Lucas, *op. cit.*, 300. In 1913 Chilubula had become the headquarters of the newly constituted vicariate of Bangweolu.—J. Bouniol, *The White Fathers and their Missions* (1929), 284.

were recalled to Europe on mobilization while a further forty-one were called up for local military service.[1] The White Fathers in particular, with their far-flung fields of activity from Kabylia and the Sahara to Uganda, Ruanda-Urundi, and Rhodesia, suffered severe reductions. From Uganda alone thirty-four of the 126 priests were recalled to France for Red Cross service, as well as a number of lay brothers. The total number of priests and brothers in service everywhere in 1923, five years after the armistice, was still less than it had been in 1913.[2] The Paris Missionary Society was similarly affected; from the date of general mobilization (August 2, 1914) men on furlough and at the Mission House were being called day after day to don military uniform, while from its Basuto and Barotse fields under the British flag men were recalled to join their regiments. And those remaining, both Catholic and Protestant, need not expect relief but would have to come through the war as best they could, with expenses cut to the very bone. And they came through, thanks to African generosity and European self-denial, without the surrender of a mission.[3]

Three notable missionary figures in the French African scene during the war years were jointly representative of the vigour and variety of the Christian witness while individually symbolic of three of its principal strands: the monkish recluse in the remote Sahara, faithful to the Roman tradition while witnessing to the Cross amongst nomads of the Crescent; the African prophet, self-directed in response to a divine vocation, evangelizing pagan tribes of the Ivory Coast; the versatile musician, philosopher, and theologian of Protestant conviction, turned medical missionary and ministering in humility to the needy on the edge of the primeval forest of Gabon.

Charles Eugène de Foucauld, born at Strasbourg on September 15, 1858, came of an aristocratic line though not Alsatian. His father, the Viscomte de Foucauld de Pontbriand, was of an ancient

[1] *I.R.M.*, V (1916), 63. The closing down of missionary seminaries in Europe, as at Paris, Lyons, and Steyl, was a further handicap.— *Cath. Ency.*, XVII (1922), 17.

[2] *I.R.M.*, V (1916), 62; VII (1918), 47; cf. J. Bouniol, *op. cit.*, 269–70. Decennial totals for members over a generation were as follows: (1893) 233; (1903) 309; (1913) 549; (1923) 542. But in the next five years the figure had risen once more: (1928) 613.—A. Pons, *La Nouvelle Eglise d'Afrique* (n.d.), 310. Lavigerie had long before laid it down that each mission should aim at self-support, since in the event of a European war home support would be cut off.—Bouniol, *op. cit.*, 104.

[3] J. Bianquis, *Les Origines de la Société des Missions Evangéliques de Paris* III, 369; *I.R.M.*, IV (1915), 40; V (1916), 58 and n. 1.

and noble lineage traceable through a thousand years of French history, his mother a devout member of the Roman Communion. At six years of age Charles lost both his parents. In due course he turned to a military career and was posted to Algeria. Resentful of discipline which his own misdemeanours had evoked, self-will had well nigh proved his ruin when a cause beyond himself reclaimed him : in 1881 through an insurrection in South Oranais he heard the call of France, and through his unconditional submission was permitted to serve with his regiment. At last he had been called out of himself in service and willingness to sacrifice—a harbinger of what was yet to be. The fighting over, he discovered a vocation in learning more of the people of the land, and resigned his commission in order to pursue it by undertaking a journey of exploration in Morocco. Disguised as a Jew, with a Jew as companion (Islam and Judaism were alone the recognized religions in interior Morocco), he carried through an enterprise notable in the annals of North Africa. On his return to Paris his spiritual crisis came, not unconnected with the impression made upon him through the invocation of the name of God by both Jews and Muslims in Morocco; his resort to the Abbé Havelin in Paris, spiritual director of many seeking souls, led to his conversion.[1]

With the whole-hearted devotion of the man, and more than á trace of impetuosity, he decided to seek seclusion from the world among the Trappists.[2] But the experiénce was not finally satisfying. After seven years he was granted a dispensation of release and in 1901 was ordained to the priesthood. Meditating upon where to exercise the sacred office, he turned to North Africa : " In my youth I travelled over Algeria and Morocco. In Morocco, as large as France, with ten million inhabitants, there was not a single priest in the interior; in the Sahara seven or eight times as large as France, are a dozen missionaries! No people seemed to me *more abandoned* than those." [3] The die was cast and in September 1901, negotiations with religious and secular authorities duly completed, Charles de Foucauld found himself in North Africa once more, this time in pursuit of a missionary vocation. He first established himself at Beni-Abbès, an oasis in South Algeria of some seven to eight thousand palm trees on the left bank of the

[1] R. Bazin, *Charles de Foucauld, Hermit and African Explorer* (2nd ed., 1931), 1–4, 10–11, 16–60, 67–71.

[2] De Foucauld entered the novitiate of Notre Dame des Neiges in 1890 and received the tonsure two years later.—Bazin, *op. cit.*, 75, 78–80, 90. The various congregations of Trappists are now united in the single Order of Reformed Cistercians.—*Cath. Ency.*, IX, 35.

[3] Bazin, *op. cit.*, 140–1. Italics in original.

Saura, a junction between the sandy desert of South Oran and the rocky Hamada stretching to the Moroccan frontier. Here he would be, he estimated, 250 miles from the nearest priest. And here, with uttermost self-denial, he devoted himself to his vocation: spiritual father to the little French garrison as required, helper of the poor and needy—slaves, travellers, the sick, the aged —with the daily celebration of mass in the exercise of his priestly office as the overriding concern. More than once he was moved to ransom slaves, but was warned by his prefect to indulge this desire but sparingly or he would be caught in a stranglehold of debt.[1]

Revolt in the desert led de Foucauld in 1905 to go deeper still into the Sahara. After the abortive attack on French outposts in 1903 various groups of Tuaregs—the so-called veiled people of the desert—made submission to France, among them the important Ahaggar people, one of the four main groups into which the race was divided.[2] With the consent of the distinguished desert commander, Laperrine, a fellow-officer of the old days at St. Cyr, de Foucauld established himself at Tamanghasset in the heart of the Ahaggar plateau. Here he was more than 400 miles south of In-Salah, the French headquarters for the desert, and more than twice that distance from Beni-Abbès—an advance guard at a missionary outpost if ever there was one, a lone Christian among Muslim nomads, for, apart from a brief period of three months, he never had a colleague. His hermitage, in a village of only twenty homes, he saw as the centre only of an extensive parish: " This corner of the earth, which is as it were my parish, is 1,250 miles from north to south and 625 miles from east to west, with 100,000 souls scattered over it."[3] Here he gave his Christian witness in life and deed for nearly a dozen years, only thrice broken by brief visits to Europe; though he never won a convert, he gained a far-reaching reputation as a holy man and acquired an unmatched influence over the Ahaggar people and their chief.

It was this, indeed, that led to his tragic end. De Foucauld was from the first under no illusion about the risks he ran: "As long as France has not a European war, we seem to be safe. If there is a European war, there would probably be risings in the whole south

---

[1] *Ibid.*, 148–50, 160–2, 167. His hope of training a few young ransomed slaves as catechumens failed him.—*Ibid.*, 171, 172, 175, 179–80.

[2] F. Rennell Rodd, *People of the Veil* (1926), 17; G. Gorrée, *Les Amitiés Sahariennes du Père de Foucauld* (1946), I, 296–8.

[3] Bazin, *op. cit.*, 257. This was an over-all population figure, including inhabitants of the oases as well as the nomad Tuaregs. Later returns suggest that de Foucauld's figure may have been an over-estimate.— G. Gorrée, *op. cit.*, I, 342.

and here as elsewhere." [1] But while the passage of a decade had reduced the strictly local risks it had done little more, and so when the war came de Foucauld was forthwith a desirable hostage for the desert enemies of France. Germany was well aware of the value to herself of an exploitation of the latent nationalism of North Africa and found an instrument ready to her hand in the Senussi sect, a religious fraternity of Islam that appeared in Cyrenaica in the mid-nineteenth century. With the Italian invasion of the country in 1911 it became identified with nationalist resistance and so acquired a political colour. The war of 1914-18 completed the transformation of a religious sect and missionary order into a political movement. In the course of its extension into the oases Kufra in the Fezzan had become an important centre in 1895.[2] It was in 1915 that Turkish and German officers arrived in Cyrenaica by submarine with arms and supplies, and the Senussi became definitely committed to the side of the Central Powers in the war, though for their own nationalist ends.[3] Associated with them were tribesmen equally eager to expel the European intruder, whether Italian or French. Under these circumstances a raiding party from Ghat and the Fezzan reached Tamanghasset on December 1, 1916. They fell upon de Foucauld's hermitage—he had prepared a little fort and stocked it with arms and supplies, it is said with the protection of his people in view—and secured him intending, it would seem, to hold him as a hostage.[4] But they were startled, while looting the premises, by two stray soldiers from the nearby French fort of Motilynski and forthwith de Foucauld was shot dead by his guard.[5] So fell a

[1] De Foucauld to Livinhac, October 26, 1905.—Bazin, op. cit., 241.

[2] C. G. Seligman, Races of Africa (1930), 245-7; G. Gorrée, op. cit., I, 348-349; E. E. Evans-Pritchard, The Sanusi of Cyrenaica(1949), passim.

[3] Evans-Pritchard, op. cit., 125; G. Gorrée, op. cit., I, 105.

[4] General Laperrine added the following note to the official report (October 20, 1917): " In my opinion the assassination of the Reverend Père de Foucauld is to be connected with the letter found at Agades in the papers of Kaucen, in which a European (Turk or German) advised him, as a first measure, before stirring up the population, to kill or take as hostages Europeans known to have influence over the natives and native chiefs devoted to the French."—Bazin, op. cit., 345.

[5] Bazin, op. cit., 339-41; F. R. Rodd, op. cit., 13-14. As Rodd makes clear, de Foucauld was not the victim of treachery by the people among whom he lived, for the aggressors were a " mixed band of Arabs and Tuareg from another part of the Sahara which had, for generations past, been on terms of raid and counter-raid with the people of Ahaggar."— Loc. cit. And de Foucauld had been politically active, keeping the French authorities fully informed of events, and so was a legitimate object of attack in time of war.

marquis of France, self-dedicated as missionary-monk to the service
of a remote people of the desert, whose Christian witness and
devotion have won for him the title of apostle of the Sahara. If
he handed on no converts to his successors, he at least left them a
legacy of surpassing worth in the inspiration of his life as well as
in his lexicon of the Tuareg language, still accounted the standard
work.[1]

The African prophet of the French Ivory Coast was in all ways
but one in utter contrast to the distinguished Roman priest with
whom he shared the Christian name. William Wadé Harris was
a native of Liberia. Belonging to the Grebo tribe, one of several
groups known collectively as the Kru, his home was at Cape
Palmas where he attended a school of the American Methodist
Mission, and was in due course baptized. His conversion—he
would then be about twenty-one—he ascribed to the preaching of
an African minister of that Church.[2] After several voyages—the
seafaring life calls forth many of the Kru—he served for some ten
years as a teacher in a school of the American Protestant Episcopal
Mission. The Grebos, restless under the yoke of the Liberian
Government, were more than once in revolt, and Harris was
involved with them and imprisoned. On the last such occasion in
1910 he claimed to have received his call as a prophet of the Lord.
With an extensive knowledge of the contents of the Bible he began
to deliver his message in Liberia, was again imprisoned as a
disturber of the peace, and eventually made his way across the
frontier to the French Ivory Coast, apparently in 1913.[3] Here he
continued for a year or so, with a brief excursion to the Apollonia
district of the Gold Coast, until the French Government became
anxious about the mass movement he had started. His equipment
and his message were simple: wearing a long white gown and a
small pectoral cross, he carried a rough cruciform staff and a small
Bible, with a bowl of water to baptize. His message was apparently
confined to the two essentials: there is one God, therefore destroy

---

[1] C. de Foucauld, *Dictionnaire abrégé Touareg Français* (Dialecte Ahaggar),
2 vols. (Alger, 1918–20); *Notes pour servir à un Essai de Grammaire Touaregue*
(Alger, 1920). Among his notes on the people of Ahaggar were collections
of Tuareg poetry and proverbs, some of which are given by Bazin, *op. cit.*,
273–9. Dr. E. W. Smith informs me, on the basis of British and
Foreign Bible Society records, that de Foucauld was said to have
done the Four Gospels into Tuareg, but that the MS. was lost at his
death.

[2] The sermon was on the text: Revelation 2: 4–5.

[3] F. D. Walker, *The Story of the Ivory Coast* (3rd ed., revised, 1930),
13–14; W. J. Platt, *An African Prophet* (1934), 51–3.

the objects of your pagan worship; there is one Saviour who died upon the cross for men, therefore turn to him and be baptized.[1]

And the people did both in their thousands. It was this quiet revolution in the life of the villages that had led the French Government to intervene. But after a personal interview with the Governor, who was soon satisfied that the movement was not political, Harris was once more at liberty to continue his evangelistic crusade. But the liberty was short-lived. The Government was bound to be sensitive about any movement that had possibilities of large-scale disturbance at a time when the pressure of war had seriously reduced the forces of law and order. By April 1915 the Governor decided he could no longer take the risk and Harris was quietly conducted some 300 miles away to the Liberian frontier and forbidden to return.[2] The prophet had been deported, but his baptized converts remained in village after village along the coast, and beyond it; estimates have varied but range from 60,000 to 100,000. They built little churches—at one period these were destroyed by order of an uneasy administration—and secured a Bible for each, which they could not read, confident in the word of their prophet that one day God would send a missionary who would unlock the book. And there for the time being we must leave them. Harris meanwhile lived a quiet life at home, always ready to march, he claimed, if he heard the call again. He had returned as poor as when he left; when gifts were pressed upon him, he would straightway distribute them to the poor around. He was just a prophet of the Word, and found his deep satisfaction in his obedience to his Lord. In contrast in all else to the Roman priest of the desert he was one with him in uttermost obedience to the divine call as he had received it.[3]

[1] F. D. Walker, *op. cit.*, 14–16. When there was danger of the bamboo cross being mistaken for a fetich, he would break it up, throw it away, and make another. His method of baptism is described as follows: "He told the convert to kneel on the ground and made him grasp with both hands the staff of his own bamboo cross. Harris then laid his Bible on the convert's head, saying, ' This is God's Book. You must obey it.' Then, in the name of the Father, and of the Son and of the Holy Spirit, he sprinkled upon the head water from a little calabash." *Ibid.*, 16.

[2] F. D. Walker, *op. cit.*, 17–21. Walker had the incident of the deportation from the Administrator who carried it out.

[3] *Ibid.*, 21–4. References to Harris in contemporary French publications are supplied by W. J. Platt, *op. cit.*, 58–63. Regarding the language used by Wadé Harris, Dr. W. J. Platt informs me: "His preaching, on the Ivory Coast at any rate, was in pidgin English through interpreters. I was friendly particularly with one of his interpreters, Victor Tano, and he had many others. It is possible, however, that in Liberia, where he started his work, he preached in his own native language amongst the

Again in sharp contrast, as if at the third point of a triangle, stands the Protestant scholar, Albert Schweitzer, and once again, as essentially part of that triangle, he shares in full obedience a self-denying vocation. Brilliant interpreter of J. S. Bach, and a foremost scholar in New Testament studies whose interpretations alarmed the orthodox, he yielded to the implicit challenge of his own concluding sentences in *The Quest of the Historical Jesus.*[1] It was in the autumn of 1904 on the threshold of his thirtieth birthday that the call came. He was ready for it. Although at the time Principal of a Theological College he says of himself : " I nevertheless never gave up the hope of finding a sphere of activity to which I could devote myself as an individual and as wholly free." [2] He had been impressed as a boy by the letters of Eugène Casalis of Basutoland, one of the Paris Society's pioneers. When therefore that Society's Director, Alfred Boegner, wrote of the serious understaffing of its work in Gabon, concluding : " Men and women who can reply simply to the Master's call, ' Lord, I am coming ', those are the people whom the Church needs ", Schweitzer knew the hour had come. He comments simply : " My search was over." [3]

His search but not his trials; these came from his friends who were aghast at the mere mention of the brilliant scholar turning jungle doctor : " In the many verbal duels which I had to fight, as a weary opponent, with people who passed for Christians, it moved me strangely to see them so far from perceiving that the effort to serve the love preached by Jesus may sweep a man into a new course of life, although they read in the New Testament that it can do so, and found it there quite in order. . . . I felt as a real kindness the action of persons who made no attempt to dig their fists into my heart, but regarded me as a precocious young man, not quite right in his head, and treated me correspondingly with affectionate

Grebo people. The Bible or parts of it had already been translated into that language by Bishop Auer before Harris' active ministry."

[1] " He comes to us as One unknown, without a name, as of old, by the lake-side, He came to those men who knew Him not. He speaks to us the same word: ' Follow thou me! ' and sets us to the tasks which He has to fulfil for our time. He commands. And to those who obey Him, whether they be wise or simple, He will reveal Himself in the toils, the conflicts, the sufferings which they shall pass through in His fellowship, and, as an ineffable mystery, they shall learn in their own experience Who He is."— *The Quest of the Historical Jesus, A Critical Study of its Progress from Reimarus to Wrede* (English trans. of 2nd ed., 1922), 401. He tells us elsewhere why he ended the book with those words.—Albert Schweitzer, *My Life and Thought, An Autobiography* (English trans., 1933), 71–2.

[2] Schweitzer, *My Life and Thought*, 106.

[3] *Ibid.*, 106–7.

mockery." [1] Desiring to exhibit the religion of love in practice and not offer it in words merely, he had determined on a medical career. While studying medicine he continued his theological lectures, so had the unique experience of being at once teacher and student in his University of Strasbourg. These seven years (1905–1912) were, he admits, a gruelling period of great fatigue. [2]

Then came the formal application to the Paris Missionary Society to serve in Gabon as a self-supporting medical missionary, and the delicate doctrinal situation having thus been by-passed, Albert Schweitzer and his wife sailed for the French Congo in March 1913 and were welcomed by the missionaries to Lambarene at the apex of the Ogowe delta, 130 miles or so from the sea. It was at this station that Dr. R. H. Nassau of the American Presbyterian Board had pioneered in medical work before the mission was transferred to the Paris Society. [3] But the work was barely begun, with the erection of buildings and development of the station that proved necessary, when on August 5, 1914, the Schweitzers heard that war had broken out in Europe, and that very same evening were informed that as Alsatians they were prisoners of war to be held at the Lambarene mission station under African guards. As all intercourse with the people was forbidden, medical work was for the time being at an end. On the second day, therefore, this remarkable man set to work on a subject that had long attracted him : the philosophy of civilization ! But the internment order was temporary only and at the end of November medical work was resumed. Happily a large consignment of medical supplies had been received just on the eve of war. But the respite was limited. In September 1917 the Schweitzers were removed to Europe as prisoners of war and interned in the Pyrenees in the one-time monastery of Garaison, with a transfer in March 1918 to S. Rémy de Provence to a special camp for Alsatians. In July, by an arrangement for exchange of prisoners, they returned via Switzerland to Alsace. It was to be 1924 before the second voyage to Gabon was made. [4] Four and a half years' service to the suffer-

[1] *Ibid.*, 108–9.
[2] *Ibid.*, 119–20.
[3] On Schweitzer's relations with the Paris Missionary Society, see *ibid.*, 115–8, 137–9 ; J. Bianquis, *op. cit.*, III, 367–8. On the American Mission at Lambarene, see Vol. II, p. 242. R. H. Nassau was still alive in the States, and Schweitzer gave him great joy by telling him that his old station was occupied by a doctor once more.—Schweitzer, *op. cit.*, 164. For Schweitzer's own account of the early months, see *On the Edge of the Primeval Forest* (1922), 29–135.
[4] Schweitzer, *My Life and Work*, 171–2, 175, 193–7, 204, 207–10, 238; *I.R.M.*, V. (1916), 63.

ing had been given in Gabon, the major part of it in time of war, and the Christian gospel exhibited in the universal language of loving sympathy.

These three personal records—a life of Christian witness abruptly ended by the war, an episode of evangelism completed within it, and a ministry in the service of suffering barely begun but destined to be long continued—though all under the tricolour may perhaps stand, apart from their more strictly individualist features, as symbolic of prevailing types of missionary service in a wider field. If the extent of French territory in Africa and its comparative proximity to Europe made it of first importance in Latin Africa, that of Belgium in the Congo was second only to it. Unlike France, Belgium was the first to be invaded and had the whole of her territory in German occupation for the duration of the war, being thus entirely cut off from her African domain. This affected severely Roman Catholic missions which were domiciled in Belgium, while the considerable Protestant enterprise in the Belgian Congo from neutral countries (the United States until 1917, and Sweden) enjoyed as unhampered a career as the pressure of a world war would permit. The Roman Catholic occupation of the Belgian Congo was conterminous with the territory which had been divided ecclesiastically into four vicariates and seven prefectures apostolic by 1914, all being entrusted to Belgian houses of the congregations concerned.[1] The news that Germany had invaded and occupied Belgium made every heart heavy with foreboding, but the challenge of their immediate situation brought all Belgians—officials, traders, missionaries—closer together, and by

---

[1] These, with date of erection and community to which entrusted, were as follows: (a) *Vicariates:* Belgian Congo (1888) Fathers of Sacred Heart of Mary, also known as Congregation of Scheutveld; Upper Congo (1895, from mission of 1880) White Fathers; Upper Kasai (1917, from prefecture of 1901) Scheutveld Fathers; Stanley Falls (1908, from prefecture of 1904) Scheutveld Fathers. (b) *Prefectures:* Kwango (1903, from mission of 1892) Jesuits; Katanga (1910) Benedictines of the Belgian Province; Northern Katanga (1911) Fathers of the Holy Ghost; Matadi (1911) Redemptorists; Belgian Ubangi (1911) Belgian Capuchins; Western Welle (1911) Premonstratensians; Eastern Welle (1911) Dominicans of Belgian Province. The Prefecture of Welle had been set up in 1898 and given into the care of the Premonstratensians, but was later divided and apportioned as stated. The vicariate apostolic of the Belgian Congo erected in 1888 was at first comprehensive of the whole territory save for the mission of the White Fathers in the extreme east; from it the various prefectures and vicariates were carved out, and it finally disappeared in 1919 with the setting up of the vicariates of Leopoldville and New Antwerp, each entrusted to the Scheutveld Fathers.

1916 when their forces had reached Tabora in German East there was once more a cheerful courage abroad. The Roman Catholic missionaries were still hard-pressed for essential supplies, often being compelled to rely on their African parishioners for food, but the work went forward and progress was achieved in various directions.

In the vicariate of Stanley Falls over the decade 1911 to 1921 the Scheutveld Fathers reported an increase in baptized members from 7,172 to 22,929, and of catechumens from 10,754 to 20,042.[1] The Jesuit Fathers in the prefecture of Kwango opened four new stations during the war years, and saw the baptized membership rise from 8,200 to 12,500, and those in the catechumenate from 2,600 to 8,000.[2] In the prefecture of Belgian Ubangi where catechumens received six months training at the mission station before baptism, with a further month before being admitted to Holy Communion, the number of members increased from 325 in 1914 to 2,259 in 1918.[3] In the vicariate of the Upper Kasai the important step was taken in 1917 of establishing a seminary for the training of candidates for the priesthood.[4] Lay brothers were naturally recruited for the forces, but if the case of the vicariate of Stanley Falls could be regarded as typical the men members of the staff were not reduced on this account by more than a quarter while the sisters of half a dozen orders continued to serve their schools, homes, and hospitals with customary devotion.[5]

In Protestant enterprise in the Belgian Congo a remarkable development also took place despite the handicaps imposed by war. After a quiescent decade (1900–1910) new Societies began to enter the country so that by 1918 the number had almost doubled, while the work of the earlier entrants began to leap forward.[6] By 1918 seventeen Protestant Societies with more than

---

[1] *Cath. Ency.*, XIV (1912), 247; XVII (1922), 707.

[2] L. Denis, *Les Jesuites Belges au Kwango 1893–1943* (1943), 93.

[3] *Cath. Ency.*, XVII (1922), 748. By 1921 the figure was 4,238.

[4] *Ibid.*, 433.

[5] *Cath. Ency.*, XIV, 247; XVII, 707. Professor Vermeersch of Louvain reported for the Belgian Congo in 1908 sixteen stations staffed by 105 sisters of six orders who were responsible for 13 schools, 9 homes, and 4 hospitals.—*Cath. Ency.*, IV, 237.

[6] Nine Societies at work in 1910 with date of entry were as follows: (a) *British:* Baptist Missionary Society (1882); Regions Beyond Missionary Union (1889); Christian Missions in Many Lands (1894); Westcott Brothers' Mission (1897). (b) *Continental:* Swedish Missionary Society (1886). (c) *American:* American Baptist Foreign Missionary Society (1884);

400 missionaries at some eighty stations were actively engaged.[1]
They were widely representative of the non-Roman world of the
West save that the Anglican communion was not included, and to
their deep regret the Belgian Protestants had been foiled by the
onset of war in the realization of their hope of entry. A Society
for the purpose had been founded in 1910,[2] and in the following
year Henri Anet had visited the Congo in its interest to explore
the situation. The report of his visit, urging the occupation of
territory in the region of the Kasai, was published in 1913, but the
disaster of the German invasion then made action impossible.[3] As
a sample of the growth of the work in the war years, the experience
of the Baptist Missionary Society may be cited : despite a slight
reduction in the men on the field new baptisms exceeded 4,000,
communicant members increased by 2,200 and scholars in the
schools rose from 12,000 to 21,000.[4] Throughout the churches
of the Protestant Missions membership doubled during the war
period.[5]

Portuguese territory suffered more than Belgian. Angola in
the west was immune from invasion, there being no incident on
the southern (German) frontier, but Portuguese East was in due

Christian and Missionary Alliance (1884); Presbyterian Church in U.S.A.
(1891); United Christian Missionary Society (1899).

Eight more had joined them by 1918: (a) *British:* Africa Inland Mission
(1912); Heart of Africa Mission (1913); Congo Evangelistic Mission,
Pentecostal (1915). (b) *Continental:* Two proposed which soon followed,
viz., Swedish Baptist Mission (1919) and Norwegian Baptist Mission (1919).
(c) *American:* Congo Inland Mission, Mennonite (1911); Methodist
Episcopal Church Mission (1911); Methodist Episcopal Church South
(1914); Memorial Baptist Mission; Ubangi-Shari Mission, Brethren
(1918).—*I.R.M.*, VIII (1919), 314–16, maps, 322–3; G. W. Carpenter,
Highways for God in Congo (1952), 20–5; J. du Plessis, *Evangelisation of Pagan
Africa*, 226–7.

[1] *I.R.M.*, VIII (1919), 316.
[2] Société Belge des Missions Protestantes au Congo.
[3] H. Anet, *En Eclaireur, Voyage d'Étude au Congo belge* (1913). I am
indebted to Professor R. Pierce Beaver, of the University of Chicago,
formerly Director of the Missionary Research Library, New York, for this
information.
[4] The men on the staff in the successive years 1915 to 1918 were: 45,
46, 41, 42; the single women remained constant at 9 until reinforced to
12 in 1918. Baptisms for each year 1915 to 1918 were: 772; 998; 1,106;
1,286. Numbers had never before reached the 1,000 mark. Communicant
members rose steadily: 5,165; 5,855; 6,629; 7,353; while scholars leapt
ahead in the earlier years: 12,265; 17,140; 20,978; 21,163.—*B.M.S. Annual
Report, 124th Year* (1916), 199; *125th Year* (1917), 161; *126th Year* (1918),
109; *127th Year* (1919), 111.
[5] *I.R.M.*, IX (1920), 20.

course invaded by von Lettow-Vorbeck's forces and was soon smarting from defeat, with some 300 square miles of its territory overrun by German troops. With stores and ammunition replenished from Portuguese sources, von Lettow-Vorbeck finally emerged into German East Africa once again.[1] Missions, however, were barely affected; on the two occasions on which German forces crossed the Rovuma the Universities' Mission station at Mtonya was raided but with no unhappy result beyond a brief interruption of the work.[2] The bulk of the missions were concentrated in the south in the unexposed districts of Inhambane and Lourenço Marques, and, within the limitations of the customary wartime disabilities, were able to report reasonable progress.[3]

Italian interests lay mainly on the Mediterranean and Red Sea shores. The Italian invasion of Libya in 1911, thus displacing effete Turkish rule, had stimulated the growth of the Senussi brotherhood from a religious to a political movement, with adverse effects during the 1914–18 war.[4] Here Italian Franciscans were engaged on the hard Islamic soil; apart from direct ministration to Catholic immigrants, they were concerned with commending themselves and their mission by works of charity in general and service through schools in particular. The existing prefecture apostolic of Tripoli at the time of the Italian occupation had been superseded in 1913 by the vicariate apostolic of Libya. But with the war ten priests were withdrawn to serve as army chaplains, and the adverse circumstance of internal unrest coupled with the war preoccupation of outside ecclesiastical authorities seriously retarded development in the new vicariate.[5] In Eritrea, lying between the Red Sea and Abyssinia, both Roman Catholics and Protestants were at work. French Capuchins were active in French and British Somaliland and included Eritrea in their sphere of operations. By 1914 Roman Catholics in Eritrea were claimed to be 20,000, mainly converts from the Monophysite form of Christianity, with some 2,700 European immigrants included.[6]

---

[1] C. P. Lucas, op. cit., 197–8, 265–6.

[2] G. H. Wilson, The History of the Universities' Mission to Central Africa, 170.

[3] I.R.M., VI (1917), 56; VII (1918), 50–1.

[4] Vide supra, 44.

[5] Cath. Ency., XVI (1914), 84; XVII (1922), 457; Schmidlin, Catholic Mission History (1933), 587–8.

[6] Schmidlin, op. cit., 587; K. S. Latourette, A History of the Expansion of Christianity, VI, 35. The Italian Trinitarians after patient waiting obtained entry to Benadir or Italian Somaliland in the south of the so-called eastern horn of Africa.—Schmidlin, op. cit., 587, n. 25.

Protestant activity in Eritrea was represented by the Swedish National Missionary Society,[1] which had been established on the Red Sea coast since 1866, when it sought entry to Abyssinia and a mission field among the Gallas. But in the event Eritrea became their principal sphere of operations, with a base at Massawa long in advance of the Italian occupation and development of the port. During the first two years of the war the Swedish missionaries were severely pressed in maintaining their work, but from 1917 the situation was definitely eased.[2]

If the general experience of Christian missions reflected in this survey of Latin Africa was that of " advance through storm ", to borrow Latourette's expressive phrase, and the outlook one of qualified optimism, it was not much otherwise in British tropical Africa. It will suffice to consider in brief the wartime situation in two British territories respectively west and east—Nigeria and the Uganda Protectorate. In each a major political event occurred in 1914. On January 1, the former Governments of Southern and Northern Nigeria were amalgamated under Sir F. D. Lugard as Governor-General, and Nigeria then first appeared on the map as a single political unit.[3] The largely pagan south, with Christian missions making rapid advance, and the predominantly Muslim north were now in double harness. The south itself had a diverse political character east and west of the Niger, so that in reality the unified administration was called upon to deal with three major types of social and political structure, as the eventual transition to self-government, still lying a generation ahead, was to show. In Uganda the coronation of the Kabaka was the outstanding event of the year 1914. Daudi Chwa, for whom three Baganda regents had acted up to his eighteenth birthday on August 8, took his seat for the first time at the head of his Lukiko or Council after that date. On November 7 the formal investiture took place at the traditional site on Budo hill, some eight miles from the capital. As a Christian the Kabaka broke away from all precedent by having as the coronation ceremony a Christian service conducted by the Bishop of Uganda. He had in the previous September taken as wife an educated Christian girl who received formal recognition as his queen consort, again a Christian innovation.[4]

---

[1] Evangeliska Fosterlands Stiftelsen.
[2] *I.R.M.*, V (1916), 224–5, 238; VI (1917), 49; VII (1918), 45.
[3] *Report by Sir F. D. Lugard on the Amalgamation of Northern and Southern Nigeria, and Administration, 1912–1919* (Cmd. 468; 1920), 7–8. The title of Governor-General was personal to Lugard.
[4] *Proceedings of the C.M.S.* (1915), 67.

While the pressure of the general state of war in respect of missionary reinforcements and supplies was common to both, the demands of the local situation were both heavier and longer continued in the east than in the west. By 1916 when the campaigns in Togo and Cameroons were over the first successful Allied drive into German East Africa had just begun. Uganda shared with British East Africa the call for carriers from among the able-bodied men, and for doctors, chaplains, and carrier corps leaders from missionary ranks. In addition leading chiefs with contingents of their fighting men were at the ready for emergency service in the early days. All this had a dislocating effect on organized missionary work in Uganda, both religious and educational, which Nigeria was spared. It was reported, for example, by the C.M.S. in Uganda that in 1917 seven missionaries were actively engaged in war service while practically all pupils over sixteen years of age at the central and high schools had joined the African Native Medical Corps or other units.[1]

In one respect Nigeria enjoyed a phase of development, speeded up by the needs of war, which had considerable social repercussions and opened up at an unparalleled rate a backward and densely populated region. This was the driving of a railway from the coast to the recently located coalfield in the Udi district, whence it was in time to be continued to join the Lagos-Kano line at Kaduna. For the terminus on the coast the new town of Port Harcourt was built during the war years at the head of the Bonny estuary, and in 1916 the first coal trains from Enugu on the Udi coalfield 150 miles away reached the coast to deliver their freight so essential for ocean steamers and colonial railways. This was a vital economic asset both directly and indirectly enabling the Nigerian economy to be maintained at a reasonable level throughout the war.[2] Uganda also came through the war years with a stable revenue and prosperity in trade. A new market for Uganda cotton, the staple export crop, opened up in India and steadily developed, with the effect of stimulating the Uganda growers and multiplying the number of local ginneries. A prosperity unlooked for in time of war smiled upon the country.[3]

[1] *Ibid.* (1915), 64–5; (1916), 54; (1918), 36. When the earlier Uganda Native Medical Corps was demobilized at the conclusion of hostilities in the lake region, the new African Native Medical Corps was formed in March 1917 for service farther afield. The strength speedily reached 1,000 of whom ninety per cent were supplied by Uganda.—C. P. Lucas, *The Empire at War*, IV, 235–6, 239.

[2] *Report by Sir F. D. Lugard* (Cmd. 468), 49. See Vol. III, p. 220, *n.* 2.

[3] Lucas, *op. cit.*, 238–9. "The effect of the war, in short, upon

Against this background of simultaneous development and war demand the missionary situation revealed a state of tension between rapidly arising opportunities and sadly inadequate resources. What have been described as mass movements, though not in the Indian sense of the term as more strictly a group movement, were reported from both fields.[1] They consisted for the most part of young men and the desire for education was evidently as powerful a motive as any impulse to a change of religious faith. But mixed motives are no monopoly of such movements, and even if the lesser good be at first in view the greater may before long rise on the horizon.[2]

The movement was already in existence before 1914 but during the war years numbers increased as if by geometrical progression. In Bukedi (a term used by Baganda for the country south of Busoga) there were in 1909 some 300 under Christian instruction; in 1914 there were 6,000 and 12,000 two years later. An increase in teachers from eight in 1909 to 150 in 1916 fell far behind the demand. In Kavirondo among the Luos there were in 1905 four boys learning to read; in 1916 the " readers " were over 8,000. The increase in the actual war period itself was sufficiently embarrassing: in the Uganda diocese the Christian community (consisting of all the baptized) rose from 98,477 in 1914 to 109,639 in 1918, while the total number of adherents (including those under instruction) increased from 105,232 to 123,820. Yet the African lay agents (to take the largest group of workers) who were 3,388 in 1914 were only 3,775 four years later.[3] Herein lay the tension of the situation. In Nigeria the case was even more spectacular, particularly in the thickly

Uganda, financially, was to produce, in money value, records in trade and revenue and to enable the Protectorate to dispense for the time being with grants from the Home Government."—Loc. cit.

[1] " The distinguishing features of Christian mass movements are a group decision favourable to Christianity and the consequent preservation of the converts' social integration."—J. W. Pickett, Christian Mass Movements in India (1933), 22.

[2] Bishop Pickett's discussion of motives underlying mass movement conversions is very illuminating for the student of missions.—Op. cit., 155–68.

[3] Proceedings of the C.M.S. (1915), xxv; (1917), 36; (1918), 40; (1919), xxv. A census taken in the Buganda Province of Uganda in 1915 showed changes over the period 1911–15 as follows: in 1911 Christians were 46 per cent of the population; in 1915, 55 per cent. The Protestant increase was 6.7 per cent, the Roman Catholic 2.1 per cent. The pagan proportion decreased by 8.7 per cent, the Muslim by 0.1 per cent. The absolute figures for the Christian population of Buganda were 329,285 in 1911 and 374,264 in 1915.—Proceedings (1917), 37–8.

populated provinces east of the Niger in the south. All Societies shared in the rising wave of demand and equally all were inadequately staffed to meet it. The field of the Church Missionary Society may be taken as representative of the area. In the one year 1916 alone the number baptized after a period of instruction was almost exactly 8,000—a figure to which work in non-African fields could offer no parallel.[1] To take, for the war period in the Anglican field, figures comparable with those for Uganda: the Christian community rose from 51,750 in 1914 to 78,189 in 1918, while the total number of adherents increased from 74,686 to 122,238. In this case the African lay agency grew from 784 to 1,432 in the same period. But the tension nevertheless existed between the insistent demand and inadequate supply of African helpers. So much so that impatient chiefs and villagers would employ free-lance teachers to start a school and all too often discover to their discomfiture that they had only been treated as a cow to be milked.[2] It was calculated from the statistics of the leading Protestant Societies at work in the Southern Provinces that whereas in the decade 1896–1906 the number of baptized Christians had increased by 182 per cent, and of adherents by 174 per cent, in the double decade 1896–1916 the increases had been 683 per cent and 923 per cent respectively.[3] Cold as such figures in statistical form may appear, they are nevertheless indicative of a social upheaval, like a heavy groundswell, marking a new epoch in the life of a people. This is not the place to attempt an analysis of a situation in which the African separatist sect and Islam as being also a religion with a book played their part. Suffice it to note the fact, as a measure of missionary opportunity in the war period.

This survey of the effect of the world war on Christian missions in Africa has moved between the two poles of closed fields, deported missionaries, and flocks left shepherdless on the one hand, and on the other, Societies confronted with opportunity for extension and demand for consolidation beyond their power to meet; while between the two extremes have been found missions

[1] *Proceedings* (1918), 21. It was pointed out that in the same year the C.M.S. reported just over 3,700 baptisms in the whole of India and Ceylon (including mass movement areas). The Society in 1916 had 60 British missionaries in Nigeria and 310 in India and Ceylon.

[2] *Proceedings* (1915), xxi; (1919), xxi. In comparing the total C.M.S. figures for Uganda and Nigeria it must be remembered that while in Uganda the C.M.S. as the Protestant pioneer covered the country, in Nigeria its field was delimited in comity with other Protestant missions.

[3] *Proceedings* (1918), 21.

hampered yet surviving, and missionaries faint yet pursuing, despite all the frustrating vicissitudes of war. And through it all the Christian Mission in Africa is now found standing on the threshold of new developments—if not the golden day of promise of the pre-war years, at least a time of keenest challenge, with a new Africa coming to the birth.

AMENDMENT TO PAGES 19–20

To run on from "... the people of the Gold Coast" (*page* 20, *line* 3).

The Basel Mission Trading Co. Ltd. (now The Basel Trading Company Limited) is a Swiss trading corporation which carried on its business in the Gold Coast and elsewhere and has been a separate entity to the Basel Mission. It has been the practice of the Company to make at the free discretion of the Shareholders annual grants to the Basel Mission.

In 1918 the Gold Coast authorities on the instructions of His Majesty's Government seized the properties and assets of the Basel Trading Company in the Gold Coast on the mistaken grounds of pro-enemy activity and transferred them to the Commonwealth Trust Limited, which was created for this purpose. It was subsequently recognized by His Majesty's Government that this action was unlawful and could not be justified. In consequence, His Majesty's Government ordered, in so far as it was possible, the restitution to the Basel Trading Company Limited of its property and assets.[1]

[1] Dispatch from the Secretary of State for the Colonies to the Officer Administering the Government of the Gold Coast, dated 31st July, 1928, Gold Coast No. 657.

CHAPTER 2

WAR OVER AFRICA: (B) IMPACT ON AFRICANS

THE effect of the war on Christian missions in Africa can largely be gauged from records available, both of the missionary organizations through which the work had been promoted, and of the growing Christian communities which were the harvest of their sowing. But another part of the story now claims attention: the impact on Africans of the struggle in their midst between these European giants. This is extremely difficult to assess with accuracy since African spokesmen competent to interpret the outlook of the silent multitude are hard to come by, not to mention the natural reticence of the African in laying bare his inmost thoughts. But with these cautions in mind, some attempt may be made to analyse the effect of a situation without parallel in African annals. It will be useful in the first instance to review the extent to which Africans were themselves involved in the various campaigns, and also to record such expressions of discontent with the European order as the circumstances of the time may have excited.

(1) *Risings at Home*

News of the war was not long in reaching Africans—it spread like wildfire. Indeed, rumour was reporting it in advance of the official declaration.[1]

When through the demands of war the strong arm of internal European administration was apparently weakened or was seemingly—as rumour sometimes had it—about to be withdrawn, it was scarcely to be wondered at that attempts should be made to throw off even the vestige of white control. What was really surprising in such a time of continent-wide conflict (for news travels fast and far in Africa) was not that such attempts were made

---

[1] Martin Kayamba Mdumi, M.B.E., of Zanzibar, stated he first heard on August 2, 1914, that there was war between the British and Germans. Europeans to whom he reported this did not credit it.—M. Perham (ed.), *Ten Africans* (1936), 185.

but that they were comparatively so sporadic and so few. And this, not just because the African was so dazed by the advent of Mars in full panoply—on land, on sea, and in the air, as it came to be— that he was paralysed for action, for he was ready, when called upon, to take an active part in the conflict itself and to do so on a scale unparalleled in history. It was not surprising, then, that some expression of discontent should appear at such a time. For a generation the white man had now imposed his will; his standards, however uncongenial, had largely become determinative, and an adjustment to the new order was gradually being made, for after all were not all white men brothers? And to resist them all was as fatuous to conceive as it would be suicidal to attempt. The white man's rule had stood as a single authority, but now with white men in mutual conflict it was another matter : " If a kingdom be divided against itself, that kingdom cannot stand "—a truth well enough known without recourse to the New Testament for it.[1] The new order that seemed so adamant in its control was cracking after all. For many who were prepared to await the historical issue while nevertheless indulging immediately in a return to such traditional custom as had by European order been forbidden, there were some who impatiently took action to help on its way the now tottering tower of white authority that had been erected in their midst.

In North Africa the Italians had their hands more than full with the fanatical Senussi, a religious brotherhood in origin, rapidly becoming shaped into a formidable machine for nationalist purposes under the hammer-strokes of war; while in the Sahara the French had on their hands the Tuareg nomads for the most part in revolt, in a desert domain of vast distances where the writ of French authority had barely begun to run before the world war started. There was connivance between Senussi sheikhs and Tuareg chiefs, and by December 1916 an important French post of occupation, that of Agades in the French Niger Territory some 300 miles beyond the northern boundary of Nigeria, was besieged. The investing forces had come in part from as far afield as Italian Tripoli, and reports were circulating among them that Germans and Turks had taken Kano—not that they loved German and Turk any more than Italian and Frenchman. But the bubble of their confidence was pricked when some hundreds of Nigerian troops marched into French territory, while French reinforcements advanced through Nigeria to the relief of their encircled

[1] Mark 3: 24.

post. Agades was relieved on March 3, 1917, and by August the Tuareg revolt had been effectively suppressed.[1]

In Nigeria, while the Tuareg rising did not stimulate sympathetic action among their fellow-Muslims of the emirates, there was restlessness apparent among pagan tribes in both the Northern and the Southern Provinces. In the autumn of 1914 the trouble began. In October the people of Kwale staged a revolt, killing over forty persons including seven Africans who were Native Court officers. Despite stiff opposition the rising was suppressed and forty-two individuals charged with murder received a capital sentence before the Supreme Court.[2] In the same month some of the Bassa people, believing all the British to be dead, courteously warned the chief of Koton Karifi that in four days' time they would attack his town. They did and were amazed to be met by a British officer with government armed police![3]

During the year 1915 Lugard reported nine minor military patrols in the Northern Provinces " being necessitated by the unrest caused by the war in the Cameroons and by disturbances and inter-tribal war in many pagan districts, which could not be regularly visited owing to the paucity of political officers ", while the eleven patrols in the Southern Provinces were similarly occasioned : " The majority of these petty risings were due to unrest caused by the War and rumours of the withdrawal of the Government." [4] More serious was a rising of the Egbas in the vicinity of Abeokuta in June 1918, when there were said to be 30,000 rebels in arms. Two full battalions of troops with supporting forces had to be moved in to quell it. It was so well organized that leaders of education and intelligence seem to have been behind it, though reliance on traditional magic and on the help of their pagan deities is said to have inspired their initial confidence. The official report stated that " sections of the railway and the telegraph lines were scientifically destroyed and railway property was

---

[1] C. P. Lucas, *The Empire at War*, IV, 135–6. Troops from Sierra Leone had also moved in to give support but were not required.

[2] *Nigeria Annual Report for 1914* (1916), 28.

[3] *Ibid.*, 29; C. K. Meek, *The Northern Tribes of Nigeria* (1925), I, 301.

[4] *Nigeria Annual Report for 1915* (1917), 23; M. Perham, *Native Administration in Nigeria* (1937), 72–3. Miss Perham quotes Sir Hugh Clifford's vivid figure of the situation, at the outbreak of war, of the so recently unified Nigeria: "Barely seven months earlier Northern and Southern Nigeria had been amalgamated, and the component parts of the vast machine had been too recently assembled for the ship to have had time to find herself ere she was wallowing in the trough."—*Address to the Nigerian Council*, (December 8, 1920), 59.

wrecked and burnt in the most effective manner ". Merchants' stores were looted and the merchants themselves and their employees attacked, one European being brutally murdered. The total killed were estimated at 700. It was not till late August that quiet was so restored that the troops could leave.[1]

The so-called Buta rebellion in Angola, which was not finally settled until 1915, had started before August 1914 and so was not related to the major conflict. It had been caused by continued Portuguese oppression in securing forced labour for the cocoa islands of San Tomé and Principe. Baptist missionaries were concerned in negotiations which were ultimately successful.[2]

In East Africa and Uganda there were but two local disturbances which require notice. Some tribes of South Kavirondo kicked over the traces and succeeded in looting both government stores and mission stations before the outbreak was contained. In the south-west of Uganda lay the Batusi tribe which straddled the frontier with Ruanda in German East Africa. At the call of their paramount chief, the Sultan of Ruanda, they rose in arms against the Uganda Government. The district had to be evacuated until help from the Belgian Congo made it possible to restore the position.[3]

In Nyasaland trouble threatened when the paramount chief of the Ngonis showed himself defiant on a request for carriers for essential services : when sent for he answered that the Resident might come and fetch him if he could; but the news that a company of the King's African Rifles was on the way led him to change his mind. He was deported and the subsidies hitherto paid to him and other insubordinate chiefs were withdrawn, after which firm action by the Government there was peace.[4] In the Shiré Highlands, however, a serious and widespread rising broke out

[1] *Nigeria Annual Report for 1918* (1920), 21, 24; *Proceedings of the C.M.S.* (1919), 28 ; A. C. Burns, *History of Nigeria* (3rd ed., 1942), 241–2; M. Perham, *op. cit.*, 77–8 ; W. M. N. Geary, *Nigeria under British Rule* (1927), 252–3. The immediate occasion of the outbreak was the imposition of direct taxation, its deeper cause the earlier loss of independence.
[2] R. H. Carson Graham, *Under Seven Congo Kings* (n.d.), 136–72; *I.R.M.*, V (1916), 64 and *n.* 4; *Report of the B.M.S.* (1916), 67.
[3] Lucas, *op. cit.*, 231; *Proceedings of the C.M.S.* (1915), 64.
[4] Lucas, *op. cit.*, 260. The inside story of this just-averted punitive expedition is given by Mrs. Donald Fraser. The Chief Chimtunga, when sober (for he had been truculent when in a drunken bout) was truly alarmed at the turn of events, and came along to Donald Fraser for help. He was persuaded to surrender himself to the magistrate, whereupon Fraser urged chiefs and people to meet the needs of Government, and the threat to local peace was removed.—A. R. Fraser, *Donald Fraser* (1934), 226–9.

in January 1915 under the leadership of a certain John Chilembwe. The antecedents were as follows: when Robert Laws of Livingstonia was on a visit to South Africa in 1892 he addressed a meeting in Cape Town on Nyasaland. In the audience was a certain Joseph Booth who maintained the principle of Africa for the African, and decided that Nyasaland would be an admirable sphere for his campaign. In 1892 he appeared at Blantyre with a number of industrial missionaries and informed Alexander Hetherwick of the Church of Scotland Mission that he had come to establish the Zambezi Industrial Mission. He obtained land near to Blantyre and started a coffee plantation, opened a school, and began baptizing by immersion. This was not done without drawing individual Africans from both the Blantyre and Livingstonia missions. The Government was at first complacent, but his characteristic teaching proving subversive he was, according to one account, at length deported. Meanwhile he had taken one of his bright Yao boys, John Chilembwe, to the United States where he pursued a three years' course at a Negro college after which he was ordained. He then returned to Nyasaland, imbued with the same principles as his master, and established himself in the Shiré Highlands, again in the neighbourhood of Blantyre and the Bruce Estates. These had an unfortunate reputation for treatment of African workers, and both school and Christian church, to boot, were prohibited on their extensive lands. Here was fuel for the flame of Chilembwe's ardent campaign which, for all its sincerity, made for racial antagonism. With the coming of the war and the pre-occupation both of the Government and of the unofficial European community with that situation, the real political nature of Chilembwe's cause revealed itself.[1]

On the night of January 23, 1915, the European houses on the Bruce Estates at Magomero were attacked by an armed party some 200 strong, spears being the principal weapons. Three Europeans were killed, another was wounded, and three women and five children carried off. The women and children were well treated

---

[1] W. P. Livingstone, *Laws of Livingstonia* (1922), 259, 339; W. P. Livingstone, *A Prince of Missionaries* (n.d.), 85, 154; J. du Plessis, *The Evangelisation of Pagan Africa* (1930), 309. Booth withdrew from the Zambezi Industrial Mission and founded the Nyasa Baptist Industrial Mission, but subsequently removed to Natal where he gave a stimulus to Ethiopian tendencies. In 1896 he put forward a scheme for a joint-stock company of Africans, but it came to nothing.—*The South African Natives* (1908), 208. The most recent critical study is by G. Shepperson, " The Politics of African Church Separatist Movements in British Central Africa, 1892–1916," in *Africa*, XXIV (1954), 233–45.

and later were safely returned. An attack followed on the African Lakes Corporation store at Blantyre to secure arms and ammunition. On the 26th the principal Roman Catholic centre at Nguludi, seat of the Vicar Apostolic of the Shiré vicariate entrusted to the Marist Fathers, was attacked under cover of darkness and the six large buildings of the mission reduced to ashes. Happily all the Europeans succeeded in escaping, one who was left for dead by the rebels afterwards recovering. Thanks to prompt military action, the revolt was soon suppressed. Chilembwe was intercepted on February 3 when seeking to escape into Portuguese East Africa and, resisting capture, was shot, while many of his following were secured. These were in due course brought to trial.[1] As C. P. Lucas has summarized it : " The movement was designed for the massacre of the whites in the Shiré Highlands, where they are principally congregated, and for the suppression of white rule, and there can be no doubt that it had been in course of preparation for some years by John Chilembwe and the members of the religious fraternity which he had established under the name of the African Baptist Church and Provident Industrial Mission." [2]

That this rising was an expression of the general movement for assertion of African rights known as Ethiopianism seems clear, though it was lamentable that the banner of African claims to a fair deal in their own land should have been carried by such extremists. Robert Laws was of this way of thinking and attributed the growth of the Ethiopian movement in South Africa to the fact that the missions had been too slow in encouraging African leadership and assumption of responsibility within the Church.[3] Be that as it may, an immediate result in Nyasaland was vociferous criticism of the missions for educating the African to such a degree as to make subversive leadership possible. Robert Laws in the Legislative Council called for a Commission of Inquiry; this was appointed, the terms of reference instructing it to inquire " into the effects of mission teaching on the native mind and character ". Alexander Hetherwick presented valuable evidence

---

[1] Lucas, *op. cit.*, 258–9 ; Livingstone, *Laws of Livingstonia*, 352–3 ; *A Prince of Missionaries*, 154–5; G. H. Wilson, *The History of the Universities' Mission to Central Africa*, 164–6; *Cath. Ency.*, XVII (1922), 691. Lucas offers some evidence of Chilembwe having been in correspondence with officials in German East Africa, though why does not seem clear since his campaign was apparently against the European in Africa.—Lucas, *op. cit.*, 259, *n.*

[2] Lucas, *op. cit.*, 259.

[3] Livingstone, *Laws of Livingstonia*, 353.

and offered more than one pungent comment.[1] The Commission's Report was regarded by the Scottish missions as unsatisfactory in its appraisal of mission work, but the recommendations for an Education Department of Government and for official regulation of African labour on European estates were definite gains.[2]

In conclusion to this section it may perhaps be pointed out how local and limited in effect were in general these various risings in so vast a continent, and further, the significance of the African chief in any such situation. Despite the new order imposed by European administrations the chief remained, whether these gave him official recognition or not; and his influence with his people was abiding, none the less effective for being so often unseen. When the chief stood by the administration, no serious trouble need be expected; and it is not too much to claim that where the Christian mission had pioneered among his people, his loyalty to a European suzerain was more deeply rooted still. The paramount of the Basuto, Khama of the Bamangwato, and Lewanika of the Barotse, to take three chiefs officially commended for their unswerving allegiance,[3] were all confessedly indebted to missionaries of the Paris and London Societies, to name only those whose Christian workers had most deeply influenced their peoples. They were called enlightened, but it was not so much a secular cultural as a Christian enlightenment that had reached them. Gifted as they already were with shrewdness and insight into the affairs of their own people, they received from their Christian mentors some standard of valuation for the happenings of the wider world and, beneath the swift stream of current events, ability to appreciate in some measure the deeper issues at stake. The indirect influence

---

[1] Ibid., 354–5; A Prince of Missionaries, 156–7. When the question of Africans not doffing their hats in respect to Europeans was broached, Hetherwick was outspoken: " Sir, the smallest drummer-boy in the Army, if he meets Lord Kitchener in the street and salutes him, may depend upon recognition of the act by the Field Marshal. So here, when the Native salutes a European, let the latter at least give some acknowledgment of the courtesy. Then it will be known that instead of there being only one gentleman, two gentlemen have met."—A Prince of Missionaries, 157.

[2] Livingstone, Laws of Livingstonia, 354–5; A Prince of Missionaries, 158; I.R.M., VI (1917), 51 and n. 4. The Scottish missionaries, who had not only first opened up the country but were still responsible for much the larger part of mission work, were not unnaturally critical of the " distinct partiality for Anglican and Roman Catholic methods " displayed by the Commissioners. The matter reached Colonial Office level before the assurance desired was obtained.

[3] Lucas, op. cit., 283, 348, 352.

of Christian missions in this way, through the personal relations of missionary and chief, in helping to stabilize many a situation where the outbreak of the war rendered local equilibrium an uncertain quantity, has scarcely received that recognition which the facts of the situation would seem to warrant.

(2) *War Service Abroad*

Many thousands of Africans were sucked into the maelstrom of this war of Europeans fought out in part on African soil. There were volunteers and there were pressed men; some served in Africa, some beyond its shores; casualties were heavy whether by act of war or through disease; and those who eventually returned came back different men.

As Spain was the only European power in Africa that remained a neutral, Africans from almost the whole continent were engaged. They served in various capacities : there were fighting men trained in the use of modern weapons in the established colonial regiments, there were scouts and runners and bearers in medical units, while carriers were enrolled in their tens of thousands. The extent of African participation in the conflict may be illustrated from the official records of British territories. Those from West Africa in the armed forces served in the West African Frontier Force under European officers, the Gambia contributing a Company, Sierra Leone a Battalion, and the Gold Coast and Nigeria each a Regiment to it.[1] The Force, which ordinarily maintained a strength of some 7,000 native ranks, rose to nearly 25,000 African combatants during the war.[2] The Cameroons campaign drew heavily upon it, including the whole Gambia Company of 130 rank and file, and the Gold Coast Regiment of some 1,500 (which had already served in Togoland), while of the 5,000 rank and file of the Nigeria Regiment some 4,000 served in Cameroons.[3] There were also African levies from French Equatorial Africa engaged, with a detachment comprising three companies of infantry from Belgian

[1] The West African Frontier Force was first raised in the days of the Royal Niger Company by Lugard, who was sent out in 1897 by the Imperial Government for the purpose. It was later expanded to include the military units in the other West Coast colonies.—F. D. Lugard, *The Dual Mandate in British Tropical Africa* (4th ed., 1929), 574 ; A. C. Burns, *History of Nigeria* (3rd ed., 1942), 173, 236.

[2] C. P. Lucas, *The Empire at War*, IV, 3–4.

[3] *Ibid.*, 6, 37, 119; *Nigeria Annual Report for 1916* (1918), 33–4; W. N. M. Geary, *Nigeria under British Rule* (1927), 251. The Gambia Company increased during the war with a further recruitment of 250.

territory.[1] To this one theatre of war, therefore, were drawn African troops hailing from the Gambia to the Congo.

Even more numerous and varied was the military assembly in German East Africa. With the Togo and Cameroons campaigns concluded, West African troops were drafted to the East Coast. The Gold Coast Regiment was the first to go and the last to return; the total number serving in East Africa (including carriers) was over 4,000.[2] The Nigerian Brigade in East Africa consisted of over 6,000 rank and file, of whom, as in the case of the Gold Coast Regiment, some ten per cent did not live to return.[3] The King's African Rifles was the comprehensive East African Force, with regiments in British East Africa, Uganda, and Nyasaland. These were naturally on active service in German East Africa, the total force, which numbered 2,319 in 1914, having risen to 31,955 African rank and file by the end of the war. There thus came into the field men of varied tribes both east and west—Baganda, Bembas, Ngonis, Yaos, Tongas, Ashantis, Hausas, to name only some of the larger groups, while Sudanese soldiers crossed their own frontiers to serve in British East, Uganda, and French Equatorial Africa.[4]

Impressive as the participation of African combatants in the campaigns is thus seen to have been, even more significant, if only from the standpoint of the numbers involved, were the various Carrier Corps essential to maintain supplies. The military transport problem, in country just in process of being developed with only the beginnings of railways and all-weather roads available, could only be met by head porterage. Here the figures ran into tens of thousands. The Northern Provinces of Nigeria alone provided 25,000 for the Cameroons campaign,[5] and the Union of South Africa 35,000 men from the Bantu tribes for non-combatant duties in German South-West Africa,[6] while the numbers converging on German East Africa from all quarters were amazing : 3,500 from Sierra Leone [7]; 5,700 from Uganda with a further 8,400 as

---

[1] Lucas, op. cit., 69.

[2] Ibid., 41–2. Of these 1,690 became casualties among whom 215 were killed and 270 died of disease.

[3] Ibid., 148; Nigeria Annual Report for 1917 (1919), 25; Report for 1918 (1920), 24. Of the Nigerian Brigade 589 were killed or died.

[4] Lucas, op. cit., 231, 275 and n, 583.

[5] Ibid., 118.

[6] Ency. Brit. (12th ed., 1922), XXXII, 547.

[7] Lucas, op. cit. 18–19. These were attached in East Africa to the Gold Coast Regiment (1,000), and the Nigerian Brigade (2,500) respectively, and saw service in both German and Portuguese East Africa.

66

a Congo Carrier Corps to serve with the Belgians;[1] from Northern Rhodesia nearly 41,000 first line military porters for service in German and Portuguese East Africa during 1916–18;[2] while in Nyasaland in the last year of the war there were recruited 31,800 front line carriers with the troops (the term of engagement often for twelve months), in addition to which a further 34,700 were secured for transport on lines of communication.[3] The Union of South Africa supplied no fewer than 18,000 Bantu for non-combatant duties in East and Central Africa.[4] In addition to these who served in theatres of war, there was much carrier transport internal to the various territories, though the figures, impressive in their totals, are scarcely comparable with the military carrier corps as the larger numbers are partly due to service for shorter periods.

Thus in Nigeria the Cross River column that moved on Cameroons was supported by a carrier force of 12,000 from the Ogoja Province alone;[5] the carrier section of the Uganda Transport Corps totalled 40,000;[6] British East Africa had a force of 7,500 in the early period of the war, but after the formation of the Carrier Corps the figure exceeded 162,000;[7] in Northern Rhodesia, to take the year 1916 alone, 25,000 men may be taken as regularly engaged (it fluctuated between 15,000 and 35,000), the total recruited for war work of all kinds reaching 37,000;[8] while Nyasaland supplied 50,000 in the year 1917–18 for the local transport of food supplies.[9] Deservedly might the field commanders pay them a well-merited tribute and concede that they were indispensable to military victory: "As was frequently admitted by General Smuts and others concerned in the operations

---

[1] *Ibid.*, 238. Fatal casualties in the Congo Carrier Corps were nearly 1,200, of whom 789 died and 402 were reported missing.

[2] *Ibid.*, 309. The period of service was six months but in practice it worked out at nine or ten. Of the 41,000 recruited rather more than 2,300 were reported killed, died, or missing.

[3] *Ibid.*, 270.

[4] *Ency. Brit.* (12th ed., 1922), XXXII, 547.

[5] Lucas, *op. cit.*, 118.

[6] *Ibid.*, 238.

[7] *Ibid.*, 214–15.

[8] *Ibid.*, 295–6. Northern Rhodesia also supplied African runners and cyclists to maintain lines of communication until emergency telegraph lines could be set up. Motor-cycles were tried but were found impossible owing to the state of the roads. The runners, however, beat both cycle and motor-cycle, carrying some messages, by relay with day and night travel, a distance of 450 miles in six days.—*Ibid.*, 287.

[9] *Ibid.*, 270.

against German East Africa, it was the *tenga-tenga* who won the campaign." [1] And they paid the price. Head porterage in time of peace was no easy life in tropical Africa, but at least the length of journey was known, recognized halting-places existed, and there was normal security for life and limb. Not so in time of war; as C. P. Lucas has put it : " In the front lines the carrier had to be ready for work at any moment and not infrequently for long and difficult journeys with the added risk of being wounded or killed. On the lines of communication, there had to be precise organization and regular journeys at stated intervals. With all, there was unusual exposure to wind and rain, cold and heat, for at one time high mountain passes had to be crossed, at another time low-lying fever-stricken swamps. The African native is very susceptible to pneumonic diseases and incapable of much physical resistance to them. Dysentery and malaria are common ailments. That there was considerable sickness and loss of life is not surprising in the circumstances." [2]

Under these conditions it was a genuine humanitarian service to minister to the needs of the Carrier Corps and missionaries were frequently called upon to do so. The situation in British East Africa may be offered as a case in point. As early as November 1914 a Carrier Corps was mobilized there on a volunteer basis, with 7,000 men as the required strength. When the advance into German territory began in 1916 and lines of communication became extended, there was a shortage of volunteers to make up the larger numbers then required. Compulsory recruitment was therefore resorted to, all able-bodied men not in European employ being drafted. Mission adherents, at first exempt, were before long also pressed into service when on their way to school. At this point missionaries of several Societies took the initiative in explaining in the schools the need imposed by the developing campaign; the response was immediate, some 2,000 volunteering for service. With these a Mission Carrier Corps was formed, under the command of Dr. J. W. Arthur of the Church of Scotland Mission, which held together as a Christian group, and won high praise for its efficiency and discipline. Eight of the eleven officers and N.C.O.s of this Kikuyu Missions Volunteer Carrier Corps were missionaries, while of the 2,000 men about half were from the Church Missionary Society stations and half from the Church of

[1] *Ibid.*, 272. *Tenga-tenga*, a Central African term for the carrier service.
[2] Lucas, *op. cit.*, 272. Comprehensive statistics are not available, but in the strenuous year 1917-18 the returns of deaths were at the rate of 40 to 50 per 1,000.

Scotland Mission, the Africa Inland Mission, and the Gospel Missionary Society.[1] But the long absence of so many picked people inevitably affected all the stations for the rest of the war.[1]

Meanwhile the Bishop of Zanzibar had been doing similar service, first in recruiting a carrier corps himself at the time of General Smuts' offensive, and then in leading it for some months with the efficiency and rigid discipline characteristic of the man. Some 600 men were raised in Zanzibar—a mixed company of Christian, Muslim, and pagan. On the mainland the numbers swelled to something like 2,000, though the Christians among them were few. But Frank Weston's personality dominated them for the period of his command, and his evident care for their welfare won their continuing loyalty. General Smuts in a personal letter acknowledged his services.[2] And in less formal ways many a missionary served his people in the very human situation, common to all races, when farewells that might well be the last were being taken. On one such occasion when a company of carriers was being transported from Gabon by steamer for the Cameroons, with the trail of its smoke lost at last in the far distance, Albert Schweitzer stayed behind when the crowd had gone : " On a stone on the river bank an old woman whose son had been taken sat weeping silently. I took hold of her hand and wanted to comfort her, but she went on crying as if she did not hear me. Suddenly I felt that I was crying with her, silently, towards the setting sun, as she was." [3] One touch of nature makes the whole world kin.

It was natural that by far the larger part of the service of Africans, whether as combatants or in auxiliary services, should be given on African soil. But it was not exclusively so. A Sierra Leone detachment served on the Tigris in connexion with water trans-

---

[1] *I.R.M.*, VII (1918), 45–7; *Proceedings of the C.M.S.* (1918), 31–2; H. D. Hooper, "Kikuyu Churches in United Action " in *The Church Missionary Review*, LXX (1919), 15–23. " The men of the Mission Carrier Corps met daily in groups for prayers, and on Sundays united services were held, the order used being that laid down under the Kikuyu federation scheme, while once a month the Holy Communion was administered."—*Proceedings*, loc. cit.

[2] G. H. Wilson, *op. cit.*, 159–60; H. M. Smith, *Frank Bishop of Zanzibar* (1926), 191–201. Smuts' letter ran: " May I thank you for your great services at the head of your Carrier Corps in G.E.A. The Archbishop of Canterbury was much interested in my picture of you marching with an enormous crucifix at the head of your black columns. I told him that, from my point of view, it was better service than Kikuyu controversies."—*Ibid.*, 200. The biographer comments that the " enormous crucifix " was the Bishop's pectoral cross.

[3] A. Schweitzer, *On the Edge of the Primeval Forest*, 169–70.

port;[1] Cape Coloured from South Africa were enrolled to the number of 8,000 in a fighting infantry unit which, after some experience in East and Central Africa, did service in Sinai and Palestine;[2] while 3,600 of them went to Europe to serve in France as drivers, replacing whites required for the forward areas.[3] The African Native Labour Contingent, that served behind the lines in France to the number of some 10,600, was representative of almost every tribe in the Union;[4] while the High Commission Territories of Basutoland, Bechuanaland, and Swaziland made their contributions.[5]

While reliable overall totals are difficult to secure even for the European forces engaged, an estimate, quoted by Lugard, that the African contingents for the war including labourers numbered 700,000, does not seem wide of the mark.[6] But to the British recruits in Africa must be added those from the French colonial Empire and from the Belgian Congo. In the case of France conscription had been established in her African colonies by decree of February 7, 1912.[7] In her dire need in the war colonial troops from Africa for the first time landed on her soil in their tens of thousands : " Arabs and Berbers of the north, Ouloufs and Toucouleurs and Moors and Semitic Peuhls of the west, scarred Bambaras and desert Djermas and Baribas and Gouros of the south." [8] The total

---

[1] Lucas, op. cit., 18.

[2] Ibid., 501.

[3] Ibid., 495.

[4] Ibid., 501; Ency. Brit. (12th ed., 1922), XXXII, 547; E. Hellmann (ed.), Handbook on Race Relations in South Africa (1949), 535–8.   General Botha as Prime Minister paid them tribute : " At no other time have they displayed greater loyalty than they have done in the difficult, dark days through which we are now passing . . . what they have done will redound to their everlasting credit."—Hellmann, loc. cit.

[5] Lucas, op. cit., 349–50, 356–7, 362.   In Basutoland 500 originally volunteered for France, and in 1917 nearly 1,400 more.   Bechuanaland sent 555 volunteers drawn from half a dozen or more tribes.   The Swazis produced only 67 men, alleging " they feared the sea and they did not wish to take part in a war between white men."

[6] F. D. Lugard, The Dual Mandate in British Tropical Africa, 575, n. 1. That this is a reasonable estimate when including carriers is indicated by the fact that the figures of African participation already quoted in this chapter do not fall far short of 600,000.

[7] Lugard, op. cit., 575, n. 1.   " The terms were four years' service between the ages of twenty and twenty-eight, with liability for foreign service."

[8] S. H. Roberts, History of French Colonial Policy (1870–1925) (1929), I, 118; cf. J. Bianquis, Les Origines de la Société des Missions Évangéliques de Paris, III, 370.

number from her African and Asian colonies, Africans preponderating, rose to 1,918,000 of whom 680,000 were actual combatants.[1]

It was natural that much should be claimed at the time, in a glow of patriotic fervour, concerning the loyalty of these African contingents in serving the cause of their respective European overlords, the loyal contingents in the German colonies not being forgotten. Understanding observers, while not minimizing the definite loyalty displayed, were inclined to appraise it in rather different terms from those of simple devotion to the imperial structure of the European Power concerned. Lugard, in an assessment of motive in troops from British territory, wrote : " It would, I think, be untrue to say that they gave their lives to uphold the British Empire, for that was a conception beyond their understanding . . . their chief motives were, I think, personal love of their officers, the terms of pay offered, the decorations they hoped to win, ignorance of the conditions of warfare to which they would be exposed, and their natural courage and love of adventure." [2] Likewise René Bazin warned his French compatriots not to overestimate the motive of the Muslims who came to France from Africa : " Doubtless, during the Great War, thousands of Arabs or Berbers, French subjects, came and fought alongside of our metropolitan troops, and many died for our salvation. In that there is a proof of loyalty which will never be forgotten. But many tribes and nations have made war to uphold causes which were not those of their heart, but rather of their courage, interest, or pride. It would be false, and therefore, dangerous, to believe that, since 1914, the Musulman populations of North Africa have become assimilated to us or simply come near to us, and that between

---

[1] *Ibid.*, II, 605. Roberts points out how this vast colonial assembly for the first time made Frenchmen aware of the reality of their so recently extended colonial empire.

[2] Lugard, *op. cit.*, 575. Miss Perham has warned against exaggerating the positive loyalty of the attitude of the Muslim Emirs of the Northern Provinces of Nigeria in face of the call of their Saharan co-religionists and of the fact that Turkey was aligned with the Central Powers, but concedes that " it indicates at the least a lack of serious latent discontent."—M. Perham, *The Native Administration of Nigeria*, 73. In Basutoland the second recruitment, in 1917, of some 1,400 is said to have consisted " chiefly of men who had passed through the native schools and were anxious to see something of the world, as well as to express their loyalty by acts."— Lucas, *op. cit.*, 350. Dr. E. W. Smith tells me that when Captain A. M. Dale, an administrative officer in Northern Rhodesia under the British South Africa Company, went off to the front, a number of the Ba-ila turned up fully armed with spears and said, " We are going with you."

them and us there are the only durable bonds of understanding, esteem, and friendship." [1]

Mortality among Africans was heavy. The carriers were particularly vulnerable to disease from the conditions of their service, and deserters were not a few. After the formation of the Carrier Corps in the East Africa Protectorate a total of 162,578 were recruited at four principal centres; of these 23,311 or nearly fifteen per cent were known to have died while a further 25,695 were returned as deserted or missing, of whom half might be presumed to have died.[2] Add to this the inevitably large number who died after discharge either on the way to their homes (often at a considerable distance) or after reaching them, and multiply this total by the number of such areas involved, and the overall mortality rate reaches an acutely distressing figure. But even this mortality was exceeded by an enemy that almost everywhere crept up unobserved to their very hearths: the dread scourge of influenza. This epidemic of the so-called Spanish influenza broke out on so colossal a scale in 1918 and 1919 as to merit the term pandemic, and was responsible, so medical authority asserts, for slaying " far more people than perished during the whole course of the Great War." [3]

The conditions in the last months of the war were such as greatly to facilitate its spread and the peoples of Africa were found to be particularly susceptible to it. It swept down the west coast like a prairie fire. Sierra Leone suffered severely in 1918 when it was estimated that five per cent of the population of Freetown was carried off in a month.[4] In Nigeria it took a heavy toll. In the Northern Provinces it was so severe that none could remember its equal, even in the periodic smallpox outbreaks that made their regular ravages; trade was dislocated, and normal activity almost at a standstill. In the Southern Provinces it lashed the denser population mercilessly. Indeed, the mortality, already heavy enough in all conscience, was considerably increased in the Ibibio south-east (some estimates said almost doubled) by the administration of the poison ordeal in the firm belief that the hidden hand of witchcraft was behind it. So serious did this become that a number of arrests of those administering the *esere* bean were made and eighteen persons, found guilty on a

[1] René Bazin, *Charles de Foucauld* (1st ed., 1923), 1943 ed., 192.
[2] Lucas, *op. cit.*, 215.
[3] A. Balfour and H. H. Scott, *Health Problems of the Empire* (1924), 214.
[4] *Proceedings of the C.M.S.* (1919), 24.

capital charge, were publicly executed as a deterrent.[1] Accounts
from the Belgian Congo told the same story of the epidemic : from
the Baptist mission at Wathen it was reported that ninety per cent
of the population were prostrate and that twenty per cent had
succumbed; from Kinshasa, that hundreds were dying and some
3,000 had scattered to their homes in the bush carrying infection
with them, while all business was at a standstill and a near famine
situation existed; and so on.[2] While in Uganda the epidemic was
apparently less severe than elsewhere, in northern Nyasaland there
was a death-roll of 1,400, and the White Fathers in Northern
Rhodesia recorded a mortality rate of twenty per cent in the
population as a whole, beyond which many were victims of the
poison ordeal, as in Nigeria.[3] A government official in a remote
part of Central Africa (not further identified) wrote privately to a
medical correspondent : " I found whole villages of 300 to 400
families completely wiped out, the houses having fallen in on the
unburied dead and the jungle having crept in within two months,
obliterating whole settlements." [4] The Union of South Africa
and South-West Africa did not escape.[5] As the medical authors,
already quoted, summarized the situation : " We were so surfeited
with horrors, so inured to death and suffering, that the true magnitude of the disaster was never appreciated." [6]

(3) New Outlook on a Changing World

For the second time within a generation the white man had
stamped his mark on black Africa, and once again had stamped it
to some purpose. If the first occasion had shown him as a super-
man the second revealed his Achilles' heel : he was vulnerable

---

[1] A. C. Burns, *History of Nigeria*, 251; *Proceedings of the C.M.S.* (1919),
31, 33; W. N. M. Geary, *Nigeria under British Rule*, 253. A colleague of the
author's, who secured permission to visit the condemned on the morning
of their execution, told him that when he repeated the Lord's Prayer
all appeared to join in. They were not recognized as Christian adherents
but at least, as this would seem to show, all had been in contact with the
mission. In attempting to eliminate alleged witches they would regard
themselves as performing a positive social service. Cf. Vol. II, p. 238.

[2] *One hundred and twenty-seventh Report of the B.M.S.* (1919), 31, 33–6.

[3] *Proceedings of the C.M.S.* (1919), 44; W. P. Livingstone, *Laws of
Livingstonia*, 358; J. Bouniol, *The White Fathers and their Missions*, 270.

[4] Balfour and Scott, *op. cit.*, 219.

[5] *Ibid.*, 218; H. Driessler, *Die Rheinische Mission in Südwestafrika* (1932),
281. West Africans returning from the East Africa campaign stopped
off at Cape Town, and " gave most valuable assistance in coping with
the epidemic."—Lucas, *op. cit.*, 18.

[6] Balfour and Scott, *op. cit.*, 218.

after all with his own weapons—as vulnerable when these weapons were in the hands of black men as of white. And the fighting men were the first to find it out. It was a lesson well-learned and not forgotten.

Warfare was anything but new to Africa. The traditional tribal organization based on loyalty to the chief had a military aspect, and under a war lord of personality would produce a formidable fighting force. This could be closely knit and based on an agricultural community as in the case of the kingdom of Dahomey and the confederation of Ashanti, or more loosely organized into raiding regiments mainly devoted to cattle forays, as with the Zulus of the south, their offshoots the Matebele and Ngonis in the Zambezi basin, and the Masai warriors of the East African highlands. Military glory was then the declared goal of youth who were at the service of the chief during their virile years, while marriage and the responsibilities for a family might be postponed until the warrior was released from his obligations. It was a harsh and cruel life and the incoming European was shocked at the barbarity of it. The missionary condemned it and the administration forbad it. Tribal warfare must be eliminated, and any breach of the new rule was severely dealt with by a punitive expedition. So far so good. A considerable social readjustment had to follow, for the man's function as warrior being suppressed, a gap appeared in the respective duties assigned to the sexes. But the white man's development of industry in due course provided a new field in which the youth of mettle could, so to speak, once again win his spurs. But the chief remained. He might be officially reduced in status, or even ignored, but he could not be suppressed. And in his survival as chief to his own people still, lay the latent possibility of military revival.[1]

With the outbreak of the world war the white rulers who had frowned upon the fighting prowess of the tribes now sought the co-operation of the chief in encouraging his young men to enlist.[2] But more : they were to fight, not only against other black men, which was no new thing to them, but against white men too. This was revolutionary and at first went sorely against the grain. To quote the experience of a European who served during the war in

[1] See Malinowski's pertinent discussion of African warfare in B. Malinowski, *The Dynamics of Culture Change* (1945), 84–93.
[2] It was reported from Northern Rhodesia, for example, that one effect of the war was that " the authority of chiefs and headmen had been greatly strengthened . . . in connexion with the enrolment of the populace for the various forms of war work."—Lucas, *op. cit.*, 307.

Togoland, Cameroons, and East Africa, with knowledge of other parts of the continent also : " Our consistent and universal teaching has been that it was sinful to fight. Any transgression of this law by the native has been almost universally followed by punitive measures on our part. Casting this teaching to the winds, and without any reason apparent to him, we have suddenly called upon the native not only to kill his fellow native, but to kill the white man. It was, indeed, with considerable difficulty at the beginning of the war in Africa that the Askari (native soldier) could be induced to fire upon the white. An instance illustrating this occurred in Cameroon when a native patrol, meeting a hostile patrol under a German officer, sent back for ' white man to come shoot white man while black man shoot black man '. The sudden and, to the native, reasonless reversion from our teaching has without question weakened the white man's prestige, while at the same time the native has gained—and justifiably so—the knowledge of his own indispensability to us and his prowess generally as a soldier." [1]

The Bethel missionary, Ernst Johanssen, lamenting the fall in white prestige, records an illuminating incident that took place in his presence at his station of Kirinda, in Ruanda, when the Belgian forces arrived. An African soldier was required by the Belgian lieutenant to disgorge a book he had appropriated, when this outburst occurred : " You Europeans just don't want us to know what is in your books, for once we could read them we should become as bad as you are—even worse—and it would be you who would then have good reason to be afraid of us." The Belgian officer was startled by the retort and gave the man a month's detention. "I can yet picture the scene," says Johanssen, " the trepidation of the officer and the louring looks of the Negroes." [2] It was also somewhat of a turning of the tables for the African warrior, often enough himself stigmatized as a savage and arraigned as a cruel fighter, to turn critic in due course and accuse the white man of not fighting fairly : " With your weapons you shoot from far, far away and do not know whom you are killing : that is unmanly. We prefer to fight man to man. These weapons are too dreadful for us. No one could escape them, not by hiding at the back of caves, nor burrowing under the ground, nor by getting below the water. If the white people must make

---

[1] *The Times*, April 16, 1918. The writer adds: " I could mention cases where black men standing stedfast in a fight have seen white men turn and run", though he admits they were happily very rare instances.

[2] E. Johanssen, *Führung und Erfahrung*, II, 197.

such weapons, let them fight among themselves! It is not a fair way of fighting. No, it is not manly." [1]

With the return of the fighting men these new views of the white man were to be extensively communicated. But meanwhile it was the economic pressure that war brings in its train which most disturbed the villager at home. With the disruption of trade exportable produce often enough lay on their hands, while shortage of stock and loss of shipping inevitably forced up the prices of all imported goods. "The only thing about the war," wrote Schweitzer from Gabon, "which the natives understood at first was that it was all over with the timber trade, and that all commodities had become dearer. It was only later, when many of them were transported to Cameroon to serve as carriers for the active forces, that they began to understand what the war really meant." [2] There were exceptions, Uganda, for example, enjoying an unwonted prosperity through the new cotton market in India; but elsewhere the tendency to a fall in export prices coupled with a definite rise in the cost of articles imported long remained a sore point and often led to a suspicion that the white man was exploiting the situation for his own advantage. So here was a further mark against him. [3] And it might well make the African regret a change of administration with which the higher cost of living became associated. [4]

The self-determination doctrine being preached in the West, more particularly by President Wilson, reached African communities and did not fall upon deaf ears. A growing intelligentsia sat up and took notice, and an already nascent nationalism was further stimulated. Societies of young Africans with some measure of education—clerks and teachers for the most part—would meet in secret conclave as far as Europeans were concerned to discuss the relationship of the races. [5] C. P. Lucas, writing of Nyasaland

[1] Ndansi Kumalo of the Matebele, after a visit to the War Museum in London.—M. Perham, *Ten Africans* (1936), 78–9.

[2] A. Schweitzer, *My Life and Thought*, 171.

[3] In Nigeria "most of the articles in chief demand increased from 150 per cent to 300 per cent"; salt, for example, an indispensable commodity, increased 220 per cent in price.—Lugard, *Report on the Amalgamation of Northern and Southern Nigeria, and Administration, 1912–1919* (1920), 32. Thus even if produce prices had remained stable, the African had to provide so much more to secure the goods he wanted.

[4] When the author had occasion to visit Duala (Cameroons) in July 1919, his two African companions, who mingled with the people ashore, reported that these were saying they wished the Germans were back, as under the French prices had risen so markedly.

[5] The author knew of such a gathering in the Eket District of the Calabar

in 1924, reported: "There are already the awakenings of the
national idea, and all this may have been quickened by the intercourse of the many natives from east and west and north and south
gathered round the camp-fires in the late campaign." [1] Dr.
H. R. A. Philp of Kenya, reviewing the effects of the war on the
African, concluded: "The experiences of the years from 1914 to
1918 were such as to effectively awaken the Kenya native from
the sleep of centuries." [2]

The specific effect of the war on the African attitude to the
Christian religion can only be stated with reserve. Why intertribal
war should be wrong and yet international war should be right
baffled his comprehension.[3] While no easy generalization can be
offered, there are nevertheless various pointers to the African view
of the matter. The reflections of a pastor of the Bremen Mission in
Togo as reported in 1916 led to observations such as these:
Missionaries go to the war like officials and merchants; since
Africans do not know European conditions, they stumble over the
fact that missionaries have to take up arms; European, civilized,
Christian nations fight each other in the land of the heathen.
What can heathendom then think of the Christianity of Europe?
The war has led to mission workers, European and African, being
despised by the pagans and in a measure being persecuted; it has
also increased pagan influence and pagan worship, this being
especially noticeable where there were Christian Churches.[4]

Robert Laws wrote of the effect on thinking young men in Nyasaland: "The conflict has had its lessons for our boys. 'Christian
nations are at war: is that the fault of Christianity?' This question
came to them, and in its answer they learned that there are still
Europeans who do not own allegiance to Christ. That still puzzles
some of them, and troubles some of them; but it also strengthens
them, for it shows them that there is no colour line in the Church

Province in 1920, which one of his African staff was invited to attend. The
invitation was addressed in rather grandiloquent terms to "citizens of
the Oron country". This particular meeting was small and nothing of any
moment was discussed, but it was symptomatic.

[1] Lucas; *op. cit.*, 280.

[2] H. R. A. Philp, *A New Day in Kenya* (1936), 32–3.

[3] It might perhaps be urged that when inter-tribal war was condemned,
there was already an overriding political authority to which appeal for
settlement of a dispute could be made, whereas until some type of world
government is evolved there is no parallel for nations in conflict. But this
was not easy to make clear to peoples with a necessarily limited outlook
on the world, and in any case the problem for the Christian still remained.

[4] *The Missionary Review of the World*, XXIX (1916), 397, based on a
report in the *Allgemeine Missions-Nachrichten*.

of Christ, and that if a man is not necessarily in the Church because he is white of skin, neither is he necessarily outside of the Church because his skin is black." [1] Reports from missionaries in Bechuanaland reflected contrasting attitudes. On the one hand, " The African Christians are at a loss to know what to think of the Christian nations. . . . They say ' Now those who set us free are bound themselves ' ". And on the other, " War was for so long the normal condition in this country that it does not surprise our people. . . . They have never made the mistake of imagining that all white men are Christians." [2] There is evidence that there was fairly widespread an attitude of discrimination between the Christian religion with its message and demands and professing Christians who might be found wanting.[3] It was reported from Uganda, for instance, in the early days that the war happily did not seem to have affected the attitude of the people towards Christianity.[4] And the faith of African Christians sent far from home was strengthened as compared with their pagan neighbours, for the latter's ancestral spirits did not travel while the God of the Christians, as they experienced, was with them everywhere. But the contradiction between precept and practice remained all the same, and those Europeans who were wisest said least. Albert Schweitzer confessed his inability to resolve the problem for them : " We are, all of us, conscious that many natives are puzzling over the question how it can be possible that the whites, who brought them the Gospel of Love, are now murdering each other, and throwing to the winds the commands of the Lord Jesus. When they put the question to us we are helpless. If I am questioned on the subject by negroes who think, I make no attempt to explain or to extenuate, but say that we are in ' front ' of something terrible and incomprehensible. How far the ethical and religious authority of the white man among these children of nature is impaired by this war we shall only be able to measure later on. I fear that the damage done will be very considerable." [5]

[1] W. P. Livingstone, Laws of Livingstonia, 356.
[2] N. Goodall, A History of the London Missionary Society, 1895-1945 (1954), 249.
[3] The author knew of African Christians in south-east Nigeria who said, when they heard after the war that new missionaries were coming who had served in the forces, that if these had killed a man they would not go to hear them preach.
[4] Proceedings of the C.M.S. (1915), 65.
[5] A. Schweitzer, On the Edge of the Primeval Forest, 138. Malinowski noted, as an anthropologist, the factor of African reaction against Christianity and Western civilization (Dynamics of Culture Change, 89) and suggested a self-denying ordinance for nations with colonies: " Would

While what may be called the negative effects of the war, in the heavy slump in white prestige and the unprecedented criticism of the European and his ways, were serious enough in all conscience, this was only one side of the matter. There was a positive aspect in the new African outlook which was nothing less than the reinforcement of African confidence and the will to survive in a changing world. This upsurge of self-assurance, now that the legend of the white man's innate superiority had been exploded by himself, was the index of a new and lively hope. The African had been taken backstage, so to speak, and had himself appeared on the boards to play his part in world events and had played it worthily. He was after all, by any measure, a man. Travel in Africa had brought him into touch with other Africans : his race was more widespread than he had realized. And travel overseas had taken him to Asia and even to Europe itself, and everywhere he had no need to hang his head. His reaction in these new situations was by no means one of blank dismay but rather of lively interest and keen response.[1] If the adaptability that secures survival in a changing environment is biologically a mark of vitality, the Negro as a race can claim to have it.[2]

James Emman Kwegyir Aggrey, with the sure touch of one who knew the way to the hearts of his people, when visiting many parts of Africa in the years following the war, stressed for them this positive aspect of their outlook on a changed world.[3] With the

not one of the first steps on the road to peace consist in agreeing once and for all that the colonies should not be drawn as actual fighting units into European wars ? It seems a foregone conclusion that when there is war in Europe no amount of bloodshed by Africans in Africa will contribute to the final settlement of these issues."—*Ibid.*, 92–3.

[1] It was reported from Northern Rhodesia after the war that a more restless and independent spirit had appeared amongst the younger men, more particularly in districts bordering on the old German East Africa : "There seemed to be a desire to quit the village life and travel to neighbouring countries and ' see life '."—Lucas, *op. cit.*, 307–8.

[2] Perhaps the outstanding instance is that of the Negro in the United States who, despite his servitude, not only survived, but was eager to survive well and to be rated " a 100 per cent American citizen".

[3] J. E. K. Aggrey, born in 1875 at Anamabu in the Gold Coast Colony, first came under the influence of the Wesleyan Mission and notably of the Rev. Dennis Kemp at Cape Coast. In 1898 the African Methodist Episcopal Zion Church, a Negro denomination of the United States dating from 1821, secured a footing on the Gold Coast; Thomas Freeman, son of the Wesleyan pioneer, Thomas Birch Freeman, organized the first church under the authority of Bishop Small. The bishop was a believer in local African leadership and at once set about securing suitable recruits for further training in the United States. Aggrey, at first reluctant, even-

concrete incident and imagery beloved of the African mind he would paint for them a future bright with hope, thus : three French infantrymen in the trenches began discussing their ancestors; two came of ancient and noble lineage and said so; the third sat silent, so they turned to him : " And what of your ancestors? " " I," he answered, " am myself an ancestor " ![1] Aggrey did not proclaim the better day as that which would raise the African to new power and at the same time engulf the European. He preached partnership as the path of hope—witness his famous simile of the black and white piano keys—and drove this home with stories also.[2] But, he would insist, they must grow and develop stature for this to be. This then was their destiny. And now would follow the most famous and uproariously received of all his stories—the story of the eagle.[3]

A certain man went through a forest seeking birds. He caught a young eagle and, bringing it home, put it among the chickens, even though it was the king of birds. Five years later a naturalist called on him and, spotting the eagle, said, " That is an eagle, not a chicken." " Maybe," said the owner, " but I have trained it to be a chicken." " No," replied the visitor, " it has the heart of an eagle still, and I will make it soar into the heavens." " Oh, no," said the owner, " it will never fly "; but he consented to a test. The naturalist held the bird aloft and spoke intensely : " Eagle, thou art an eagle, thou dost belong not to the earth but to the sky; stretch forth thy wings and fly ! " The eagle looked about, then saw the chickens feeding and jumped down again. " I told you it was a chicken," said the owner. The next day the naturalist tried

tually accepted an invitation to go to the States, sailing in 1898 and entering in the same year Livingstone College, Salisbury, N.C., the college of the A.M.E. Zion Church. He did not, however, return to Africa until 1920, and then as a member of the Phelps-Stokes Education Commission—. E. W. Smith, *Aggrey of Africa* (1929), 15–66; C. C. Alleyne, *Gold Coast at a Glance* (1931), 114–15. For an account of the A.M.E. Zion Church in the Gold Coast see Alleyne, *op. cit., passim.* Alleyne was the first resident bishop of the Church in West Africa.

[1] *The Christian Express*, LI (1921), 72.

[2] E. W. Smith, *Aggrey of Africa* (1929), 123. There was, for example, the story of the three monkeys. By a lagoon was a guava tree with one guava left on a branch overhanging the water. A monkey came down the branch but the guava was shaken off and fell into the shallow pool, within sight but out of reach. A second monkey slipped down the branch and over the first monkey—but the guava still lay within sight but out of reach. A third monkey slid down the branch and over the first two monkeys, and reaching down secured the guava. Now, Aggrey would ask, to which monkey did the guava belong?

[3] E. W. Smith, *op. cit.*, 136–7.

again, and again the eagle came to earth. " I told you it was a chicken," said the owner. So the next morning the naturalist rose early, at the moment of the rising of the sun with its first shafts of light piercing the shades of night. He held the eagle aloft and spoke with much intensity : " Eagle, thou art an eagle; thou dost belong, not to the earth but to the sky; stretch forth thy wings and fly !" The eagle looked around, it began to tremble, but it did not fly. Then the naturalist made it look straight at the sun. On the instant it spread its mighty wings, fifteen feet they were from tip to tip, and up it swept into the sky, mounting until lost to sight. Its heart was the heart of an eagle after all.

Aggrey found his people, in those early post-war years, ready for his appeal : " My people of Africa, we were created in the image of God, but men have made us think that we are chickens . . . but we are eagles. Stretch forth your wings and fly !"

CHAPTER 3

ADVANCE IN THE NEW AFRICA
1918–1928

WITH the first world war, nineteenth-century Africa had slipped into history at last and the new Africa of the twentieth century was beginning to emerge. All areas were not moving at the same rate into the new age, but all were moving.[1] A novel feature in the political pattern appeared with the coming into existence of mandated territories under the auspices of the League of Nations, while the growing economic development of the tropics, by European settler and industrialist alike, brought its problems of land and labour with a consequent aggravation of race relations whenever the European secured privilege at the expense of African security. A new era in education was inaugurated by the two Phelps-Stokes Education Commissions whose survey covered the continent south of the Sahara, with the British Government in particular stimulated to some formulation of educational policy for its dependencies in tropical Africa. The Christian mission continued to extend its boundaries and to multiply its variegated agencies, while both centrifugal and centripetal tendencies were exemplified: on the one hand the fragmentation of the Christian community by the alarming rise in the number of African separatist sects, and on the other the coming together for ever-increasing consultation of the major non-Roman missionary agencies. It was a decade which brought many a challenge to the missionary movement, while behind it all lay the unmistakable African claim to a fuller life in the new world.

(1) *The Political Scene*

With the Treaty of Versailles concluded in June 1919 the state of war came to an end and the future of the German colonies in Africa was determined. The last of President Wilson's famous " Fourteen Points ", proposed as the basis of a new world order,

---

[1] As one of the exceptions: " In Uganda the Great War did not, in the same degree as elsewhere, mark off the old world from a new."—Thomas and Scott, *Uganda* (1935), 42.

had required the formation of a general association of nations under specific covenants which would afford mutual guarantees to its members.[1] He succeeded in securing that the Covenant of the newly formed League of Nations should constitute the first part of the Peace Treaty. Article 22 of the Covenant (and so of the Treaty) dealt with the status of the German and Turkish dependencies to be assigned to mandatories on behalf of the League. These dependencies were classified in three categories, to the second of which belonged Togo, Cameroons, and German East Africa.[2] South-West Africa, on the other hand, was given a slightly different status and was to be administered as an integral part of the Union of South Africa to which the mandate had been entrusted.[3] Togo, Cameroons, and German East Africa were each divided for purposes of a mandate : Togo into British and French areas; Cameroons for the most part under French mandate, with a strip of territory adjoining Nigeria under British; and German East Africa into the Belgian mandate of Ruanda-Urundi in the north-west (with approximately half of the total population), and the British Mandate of Tanganyika Territory. Thus the four German colonies now appeared upon the map as seven mandated areas, in each case the forces that had conquered and occupied the land being assigned the mandate. To the cynic's comment, that this was just plain annexation after all, if under another name, there was happily a clear answer : the existence of the Permanent Mandates Commission of the League. This Commission, with members partly drawn from non-mandatory

[1] J. A. Spender, *Great Britain, Empire and Commonwealth 1886–1935*, 865, where the Fourteen Points are given ; also in H. A. L. Fisher, *A History of Europe*, III. (1935), Appendix C.

[2] The relevant section of Article 22 reads as follows: " Other peoples, especially those of Central Africa, are at such a stage that the Mandatory must be responsible for the administration of the territory under conditions which will guarantee freedom of conscience or religion, subject only to the maintenance of public order and morals, the prohibition of abuses such as the slave trade, the arms traffic and the liquor traffic, and the prevention of the establishment of fortifications or military and naval bases and of military training of the natives for other than police purposes and the defence of territory, and will also secure equal opportunities for the trade and commerce of other Members of the League."—*The Covenant of the League of Nations with a Commentary thereon* (Cmd. 151, 1919), 9.

[3] " There are territories, such as South-West Africa . . . which, owing to the sparseness of their population . . . or their geographical contiguity to the territory of the Mandatory, and other circumstances, can be best administered under the laws of the Mandatory as integral portions of its territory, subject to the safeguards above mentioned in the interests of the indigenous population."—Article 22 of the Covenant, *Ibid.*, 9.

F 2

countries, not only received regular reports but could call responsible officials administering the territory before it for interrogation, its own report then going forward to the Council and Assembly.[1] True, it possessed no executive authority, but the publicity secured, which was its only weapon, proved highly effective through reference to world public opinion as the ultimate sanction. This then was the new situation in which any return of German missionaries to the erstwhile German colonies would have to be considered.

The state of public opinion in the Allied countries, particularly in Belgium, France, and Britain, produced by the strain of a ruthless war on land and sea and in the air, was significantly reflected in the harsh and oppressive terms of the Treaty of Versailles, a dictated, not a negotiated, peace. Inevitably severe as was the disappointment of German missionary leaders that their colonies were not to be restored, they experienced further frustration through the embargo on the return of German missionaries anywhere, whether in the former German colonies or in other dependencies; and the inflamed state of public opinion at the time gave no promise of an early reversal of this policy.[2] As if this were not enough to bear, there came in 1923 a shock of a different order that almost proved a knock-out blow—the disastrous inflation when the German exchange came to be counted in millions of marks, with the especially terrible period of some three weeks (October 5 to 26) when the inflation rocketed to a reckoning in billions and the very printing press was left panting in the rear.[3] That mission directors, like heroic captains, stayed on the bridge and rode out the storm won universal tribute to their high courage. Needless to say, they were not left to face the storm alone. In this same year 1923 Protestant missionary organizations on the Conti-

[1] "A permanent Commission shall be constituted to receive and examine the annual reports of the Mandatories and to advise the Council on all matters relating to the observance of the mandates."—Article 22 of the Covenant. *Ibid.*, 9. Not only were members from non-mandatory countries appointed, but no member of the Commission, if belonging to a mandatory Power, could continue to serve if and when he became a member of his country's Government.

[2] Article 119 of the Treaty of Versailles consisted of the German renunciation of title to colonies; while Article 122 conferred on the successor Government authority to repatriate all German nationals, and this was done. Article 438 concerned mission property which was to be handed over to boards of trustees " composed of persons holding the faith of the mission whose property is involved ". For the text of these Articles, see "Acts and Public Documents bearing on the work of Christian Missions " in *I.R.M.*, IX (1920), 593–4.

[3] *Quarterly Notes, Bulletin of the International Missionary Council*, No. 1 (January 1924), vii. Cited in future as *Bulletin of the I.M.C.*

nent of Europe (in Belgium, France, Holland, Scandinavia, and Switzerland), in Great Britain, and in North America contributed for German Missions in Africa and Asia some £150,000, of which approximately one half came from North America.[1] This was good as far as it went—and indeed essential for the future of the missions concerned—but the crux of the matter remained : to secure official permission for the re-entry of German missionaries.

The first move was made by the Conference of British Missionary Societies in relation to the general principle of missionary freedom. Fearing that the tendency during the war to supervise missions of alien nationality might harden into a policy after the war detrimental to missionary interests, the Standing Committee of the Conference sought an opportunity to express their views before any such policy was adopted by the British Government. This was granted and in December 1918 a deputation led by the Archbishop of Canterbury met representatives of the India Office, Colonial Office, and Foreign Office. Criticism of an official proposal already drafted, that all non-British missionaries should be required to secure a licence before entering British territory, led to a modification whereby the general principle of freedom was recognized in that American as well as British nationals were to be exempt from any restriction. The requirement of permits for others then became not the rule but the exception, German missions being excluded " for a period to be defined hereafter ". Such temporary exclusion appeared inevitable for reasons already stated.[2] The general position thus being secured, a further step was taken in 1924, the time then appearing propitious, when the British Con-

---

[1] *Bulletin of the I.M.C.*, No. 3 (July 1924), iv–v. This comprehensive effort to conserve German Missions until such time as German missionaries might return, or to support them as in South Africa, operated in Africa as follows (the Basel Mission in view of its preponderating German personnel being included), the specific source of help being given in brackets: *Gold Coast*, Basel (U.F.C. of Scotland); *Cameroons*, Basel and Baptist (Paris M.S.); *Ruanda*, Bethel (Belgian Evangelical M.S.); *Tanganyika*, Berlin (Church of Scotland and U.F.C.), Leipzig (American Lutherans of Iowa and of Augustana Synods), Moravian (American Moravians), Neukirchen (United Methodists of G.B.); *South Africa*, Hanover (National Lutheran Council of America), Hermannsburg (National Lutheran Council of America and Iowa Joint Synod), Lutheran (Church of Sweden), Moravian (American Moravians).

[2] The memoranda drawn up applied in the first instance to India. In addition to British and American nationals only missionaries of Societies officially recognized by the British Conference and the Conference of North America were to be admitted. For the text of the memoranda, see J. H. Ritson, " The British Government and Missions of Alien Nationality " in *I.R.M.*, VIII (1919), 334–7.

ference approached the Secretary of State for the Colonies with a request that the embargo on German missionaries be lifted. The reply was favourable; on July 1, 1924, it was announced that the discrimination against German missionaries in British colonies, protectorates, and mandated territories would be removed, and that German Societies would be eligible for recommendation by the British Conference equally with other Continental Societies.[1]

Advantage was speedily taken of the new opportunity, though in the nature of the case, the financial position of post-war Germany being what it was, the first attempts at resumption were necessarily slender efforts. But at least the comity of the Christian Mission had proved a reality and German missionaries were apparently the first German nationals to return to their former fields of labour, and did so with the goodwill of the Societies that had served as foster-parents to the orphaned missions. The first four applications of German Societies to return to Tanganyika had been granted by October 1924 but it was another three years before the various local arrangements were completed in all areas.

The Bremen missionaries were the first to return to the Gold Coast and British Togoland sphere, with the Basel workers soon following. This involved an adjustment with the United Free Church of Scotland which had been specially called in by the Government to take charge of the work.[2] It was arranged through mutual consultation that the field should be shared among them, the Bremen Mission to take over the Ewe area, the Basel Mission Ashanti, and the Scottish Presbyterians the remainder of the Basel field. A single Mission Council of Africans, Germans, Scots, and Swiss was formed, the three missions being but sections of one African Church.[3] The Basel Mission was also officially recognized

---

[1] *Bulletin of the I.M.C.*, No. 3 (July 1924), vi; No. 4 (October 1924), vi; K. Maclennan, *Twenty Years of Missionary Co-operation* (1927), 27–8. The India Office took similar action the following year. A further intervention of the British Conference deserves record: compensation for the loss of personal effects and moneys by German missionaries removed from Africa at the beginning of the war. After the necessary investigation, the British Government agreed to indemnify the missionaries to the extent of some £10,000, a cheque for this amount reaching the Basel Mission on Christmas Day 1925 for distribution among the claimants.—K. Maclennan, *op. cit.*, 25.

[2] *Vide supra*, p. 19.

[3] *Bulletin of the I.M.C.*, No. 5 (January 1925), v; No. 8 (October 1925), vii; No. 11 (July 1926), iv. The statesmanship of A. W. Wilkie of the Scottish Mission largely contributed to this happy issue. Eventually the Basel and Scottish Missions co-operated in constituting the Presbyterian Church of the Gold Coast.

for return to the British sphere of Cameroons, where four men were at work by 1926 in co-operation with the Paris Society which had charge of the Basel work in the neighbouring French mandate. At the same time the German Baptists sought re-admission.[1] German missionaries were still excluded, however, from the French sphere of Cameroons.[2]

German East Africa had been the largest field of operations for German Societies, and here the re-admissions were correspondingly greater. The Bethel Mission resumed its work in Usambara in 1925 with missionaries Johanssen and Hosbach, and by 1927 was even back at Bukoba in north-west Tanganyika. Resumption in Ruanda however was not to be enjoyed, the Belgian mandatory of Ruanda-Urundi declining to allow re-entry, so that here the Belgian Protestant Mission continued to care for the work.[3] The Leipzig Society also took up its work again in Kilimanjaro among the Chaggas, two senior missionaries of experience returning in 1925 to a field where they had already won distinction : Johannes Raum and Bruno Gutmann. They were soon reinforced by four colleagues. American Lutherans of the Augustana Synod, who had taken responsibility for this mission in 1922, continued to share the field.[4] The Berlin Society also received recognition in 1925 and by the following year was back in the old Nyasa field with three men in the Konde Synod, for which the United Free Church of Scotland had cared, while the Church of Scotland was waiting to hand over its share of the Hehe Synod as soon as Berlin resources made it feasible. By 1930 the Berlin authorities had so far recovered financially that the resumption of work at Milow could also be contemplated. But here a hitch arose. The Universities' Mission had taken over the Berlin work at this centre in 1923 in good faith expecting to occupy it permanently. Representatives of both sides met in Berlin and an amicable accommodation was arrived at whereby the Universities' Mission would remain at Milow while the Berlin Society would settle on the Yakobi side of the district, the African Christians concerned then being able to seek those whose ministrations they preferred.[5] The

---

[1] *Ibid.*, No. 9 (January 1926), v; No. 11 (July 1926), iv.
[2] *I.R.M.*, XXI (1932), 237.
[3] *Bulletin of I.M.C.*, No. 6 (April 1925), vii; No. 15 (July 1927), v; *I.R.M.*, XXI (1932), 237.
[4] *Bulletin of I.M.C.*, No. 6 (April 1925), vii; No. 8 (October 1925), vii; No. 9 (January 1926), v; No. 11 (July 1926), iv.
[5] *Ibid.*, No. 8 (October 1925), vii; No. 9 (January 1926), v; No. 11 (July 1926), iv; G. H. Wilson, *The History of the Universities' Mission to Central*

Moravian Brethren had had an extensive field stretching from Lake Nyasa to Tabora in Unyamwezi. This had been saved from complete collapse in the Nyasa region by the Livingstonia Mission of the United Free Church of Scotland which had given oversight as generously as resources permitted. In 1923 the Foreign Mission secretary of the Church approached the Moravian Board at Herrnhut with the proposal that they should send out two senior workers who had seen service on that field to co-operate with the Scottish missionaries. But 1923 was the year of the astronomical inflation in Germany and lack of resources made it impossible to respond.

Then came the good news, as unexpected as welcome, that a Scottish friend would defray for three years the cost of Oskar Gemuseus' return. Coupled with this came a suggestion of Mission-Director Knak of the Berlin Mission that the German Societies should tax themselves one per cent of their income in support of the Moravian Brethren. This enabled Ferdinand Iansa to be appointed in due course as a second worker of previous experience. Gemuseus in the first instance worked under the aegis of the Scottish Mission. By 1927 the German Province of the Moravian Church had received recognition as an approved Society and the United Free Church of Scotland had handed back the work in the Nyasa region which it had been supervising.[1] In the northern (Unyamwezi) section a rather different situation existed. The destructive effect of the war was severe, with men engaged on military service, congregations scattered, and all work at a standstill, while there was no neighbouring mission available to extend a helping hand. Happily a Danish missionary of the Church, Nis Gaarde, though at first interned, was permitted to remain when the German nationals were repatriated, and at once set about salvaging what he could of the wreckage. In 1921 Bishop Arthur Ward, the British member of the Moravian Mission Board, visited the region for consultation with Gaarde and a survey of the situation. As German missionaries were still excluded, four Danish workers were secured and under Gaarde's leadership the rebuild-

---

Africa, 241–2. The difficulty of a simple transfer felt by the Universities' Mission was that, many Africans having been trained in the Catholic faith, confirmed and admitted to full communion, some continuing provision must be made " to minister the sacraments and other ministrations of the Catholic Church to those who wished for them".—G. H. Wilson, *op. cit.*, 242.

[1] A. Schulze, *200 Jahre Brüdermission* (1932), II, 489–92; *Bulletin of I.M.C.*, No. 6 (April 1925), vii; No. 11 (July 1926), iv; No. 15 (July 1927), v–vi.

ing of the mission was begun.[1] The Neukirchen Mission became heir to the work initiated by the Breklum Society in the north-west of the territory, and by 1927 had taken up once more its own work on the Tana River in Kenya Colony, which had been cared for meanwhile by the United Methodist Church.[2]

This eventual restoration of German missionaries to so many of their former fields in British colonies and mandated territories was a more impressive demonstration of Christian brotherhood and reconciliation after conflict than much discourse on the subject, and could not fail to have been noted by shrewd African observers of the post-war scene.[3]

If movement on the political stage was mainly concerned with the post-war readjustment of European interests in the continent, it was not entirely limited to this. There was also apparent a stirring of African desire for a larger share in their own affairs, even if voiced by a self-appointed leadership of the intelligentsia through various Congresses convened in the post-war years. Thus the South African Native National Congress, formed in 1912, in December 1918 drew up a memorial to the King in which they drew attention to existing grievances.[4] A Pan-African Congress was in session in Paris during the Peace Conference in 1919, which expressed their aspirations for a larger voice in African affairs. Further conferences were held in London in 1921 and in Lisbon in 1923. At the latter a " charter of rights " was drawn up under seven heads, ranging from advance in self-government to world-disarmament.[5] A West African National Congress also emerged and presented its own petition to the King. Granted that these were the self-appointed leaders of a politically conscious minority and in no way representative of the tribal

[1] A. Schulze, *op. cit.*, II, 524–6; J. E. Hutton, *A History of Moravian Missions* (1923), 508.

[2] *Bulletin of the I.M.C.*, No. 11 (July 1926), iv; No. 15 (July 1927), v–vi; *I.R.M.*, XXI (1932), 237; *United Methodist Church, Report of the Missions for 1926–1927* (1927), 88.

[3] A considerable number of returning German missionaries and candidates spent some months in England before sailing, many of them at Kingsmead, one of the Selly Oak Colleges, Birmingham, at that time the missionary training college of the Friends' Foreign Mission Association. Missionaries of the Basel, Berlin, Bethel, Breklum, Bremen, Leipzig, Neukirchen, and Moravian Missions were in residence during the years 1924–27. The record of the Society of Friends in post-war service made this the religious centre to which most of the Germans were attracted in what were for them still days of deep distress.

[4] *The Christian Express*, XLIX (1919), 152–5. where the full texts of the memorial and the Government reply are given.

[5] *The South African Outlook*, LIV (December, 1924).

masses, they were nevertheless the proverbial straw that showed how the wind was blowing.[1]

(2) *Economic and Social Concern*

The Christian concern for the economic and social conditions of African life is as old as the modern missionary awakening. The abolitionists first gave it authentic expression, and the cause they championed in Britain—in essence the full recognition as persons of peoples of African descent—claimed in Africa men of the order of John Philip and David Livingstone. And many less gifted than such outstanding men have played their part on a smaller stage and with scant recognition, so that Donald Fraser had good reason to declare to an African Conference in 1926 : " As we face questions of land rights, of giving people some share in governing themselves, we should remember that throughout a century and more the missionary has always stood as the African's friend. He has won privileges for the African, has beaten back oppressive legislation, trained him into self-reliance, prepared him not only to claim but to bear responsibility; and all this sometimes in face of hatred and obloquy from men of his own race, who have too often ostracized him for his defence of the black peoples." [2] Two men then living, missionary champions of African rights in the Southern Rhodesia of their day, exemplified his claim : Arthur Shirley Cripps and John White, whose names may stand as representative of that knightly company that sought deliverance for the oppressed and claimed freedom equally for all men.[3] With a quickening of the pace therefore in the economic development of African tropical territories in the post-war years there came a deepening concern for African welfare, and while it was by no means mission circles alone that were sensitive to this situation, they nevertheless made notable interventions from time to time and offered a continuous and thoughtful leadership that served to hold in check such excesses as had in the past too often disfigured the white man's relations with coloured peoples. A further factor to be noted in the post-war situation was the rising concern among Christian people in Europe and North America for economic justice and social welfare, as evidenced in united Christian action on these matters. Thus the C.O.P.E.C. Conference at Birmingham in 1924, with its twelve preparatory commissions on a wide range

[1] D. Fraser, *The New Africa* (1927), 161.
[2] E. W. Smith, *The Christian Mission in Africa*, (1926), 11–12.
[3] A. S. Cripps, *An Africa for Africans* (1927), a book dedicated to John White; C. F. Andrews, *John White of Mashonaland* (1935), *passim*.

of economic and social affairs, comprised all the non-Roman Churches in Great Britain, and was followed up with much local and regional activity.[1] A year later there met at Stockholm the Universal Christian Conference on Life and Work with delegates from the American, British, European, and Orthodox Churches, together with some representation from Africa and Asia—a world conference that proved to be one of the notable steps in the modern ecumenical movement.[2] The effect of these gatherings, with their sequel in the education of their constituencies, was to produce, by however gradual a process, a church membership better informed on the Christian moral ideal and more sensitive to the responsibilities entailed when the white man wielded economic and political power over less advanced peoples.

In the African scene the joint questions of land and labour were of fundamental significance. By his action in these matters the white man would be judged, and in so far as the Christian religion was associated with white men as a race their conduct on these issues could help or hamper the missionary task. " There is no matter," Lord Hailey has written, " in which colonial policy expresses itself so conspicuously as in the use which administrations make of their powers in regard to land, and certainly there is no question which has influenced more critically the attitude of Africans towards the governing power." [3] And second only to it is the problem of labour. This in its incidence falls into two parts : with any alienation of land for European farms or plantations there follows inevitably a demand for workers with consequent resort to various means to induce the often reluctant African to enter the labour field; while the development of large-scale industry, more particularly in the mines, requires a skilled European labour force which then seeks to secure this labour level as its own preserve, thus sharpening a conflict of interests between white and black. Beyond this question of the impact of economic

---

[1] The Proceedings of C.O.P.E.C., being a Report of the Meetings of the Conference on Christian Politics, Economics and Citizenship (1924); C.O.P.E.C. Commission Reports (12 vols., 1924). As an indication of their influence, four impressions of the twelve Reports were called for within nine months of publication.

[2] G. K. A. Bell (ed.), The Stockholm Conference 1925, The Official Report of the Universal Christian Conference on Life and Work held in Stockholm, August 19–30, 1925, (1926); Bulletin of the I.M.C., No. 8 (October 1925), vii–viii.

[3] Hailey, An African Survey (1938), 712. Lugard notes that in savage warfare conquest carries with it the control of land (though often subject to the ancestors' presumed rights), while by contrast " in civilized countries conquest does not justify confiscation of private rights in land".—Lugard, The Dual Mandate in British Tropical Africa (4th ed., 1929), 281 ; cf. 288.

development on race relations, and so indirectly upon the Christian mission itself, there lies the problem of the disruptive social effect of migrant labour upon the African tribal community whose fragile social order is unequal to the stresses and strains produced by the white man's energetic invasion—a problem also demanding in due course some consideration from the Christian standpoint.

In respect of the economic problem typical situations are presented in West, East, Central, and South Africa, in a successive review of which it will be convenient to note in conjunction land policy and labour demand. Further, in any reference to missionary intervention it is not to be assumed that this represents the only effort to safeguard African rights. Such an assumption would indeed be far from the truth as the courageous action of not a few leading officials bears witness, men who are representative of a much larger group. In West Africa generally there has been recognition of African rights in land. The cynic may say that had the climate been more favourable for European settlement a different situation would have arisen. Be that as it may, the tradition was established in the eighteenth century that the European should pay rent to the chief for such land as he occupied.[1] While a new situation arose with the establishment of European governments and the introduction of a western legal system, the right of the people to the land they occupied was recognized by both French and British administrations. The basic assumption of French colonial policy—that French civilization has no peer and all capable of assimilating it may therefore be received as equals—could scarcely grant legal recognition, and so encouragement to survival, to systems regarded as inferior; but in practice African land rights have been respected in French West Africa.[2] In the British West African territories the securing of the land to its African owners was a firm feature of policy in post-war years, with strict regulation of leases and unwillingness to authorize alienation, however benevolent the buyer or eager the seller. In Nigeria in particular even the leasehold of large areas, to permit a plantation system with a view to an improved quality of oil palm products, was refused in the nineteen-twenties. Thus with no alienation of land, the problem of labour for private profit has not arisen. The case of the Gold Coast was different in both respects, but was nevertheless kept under control.[3]

[1] E. C. Martin, *The British West African Settlements, 1750–1821* (1927), 48–9.
[2] L. P. Mair, *Native Policies in Africa* (1936), 189–90, 193–4; Hailey, *op. cit.*, 858–62.
[3] For the situation in Nigeria see F. D. Lugard, *Report on Amalgamation*

In East Africa a more challenging situation appeared which threatened to become acute in Kenya Colony, as the East Africa Protectorate was renamed after the war. Grave developments in the alienation of land and veiled attempts at compulsory labour for private estates occasioned deep misgiving in those who had African interests at heart. By contrast with the West Coast there were in Kenya extensive areas of fertile land at an altitude regarded as favourable for European settlement.[1] Moreover, it was claimed that vast acreages were not in African occupation, though on this point the definition of occupation was the crucial matter : drastic reduction of tribal members by epidemic, periodic rotation of tillage areas to let the land lie fallow, and seasonal migration of pastoral tribes might all leave country temporarily unoccupied but not unclaimed by right of regular if not continuous use. To appreciate the controversial situation that developed some brief reference to the emergence of an official policy of colonization and the conditions controlling it is necessary.

When the Imperial British East Africa Company surrendered its charter in 1895 the Foreign Office took over the territory it had administered. The then existing land regulations were replaced in 1897 but African interests were still safeguarded by a clause in the new regulations which expressly prohibited alienation where such interests would suffer injury. A Crown Lands Ordinance of 1902

---

of *Northern and Southern Nigeria, and Administration, 1912–1919* (1920), 36–7; W. G. A. Ormsby-Gore, *Visit to West Africa during the Year 1926* (1926), 103, 107–8, 130–1; cf. R. Scott, *The Native Economies of Nigeria* (1946), 225,227. In respect of the Gold Coast where mining concessions have been the main concern, see L. P. Mair, *op. cit.*, 160–2, who comments : " The repercussions of land alienation in the Gold Coast have . . . been of a different nature from those which attend a policy of development primarily by European enterprise. It has affected principally the internal political structure of the native States, in creating a cause of serious friction between chiefs and subjects." Ormsby-Gore stated in 1926: " The British Government have again and again laid down that under no circumstances will they undertake to provide compulsory labour for private profit in any British Dependency," and this was scrupulously observed in West Africa.—*Visit to West Africa*, 107.

[1] Highlands lying between 5,000 and 8,000 feet have been regarded as suitable. Some 30,000 square miles were said to fall within this category.— N. Leys, *Kenya* (2nd ed., 1925), 67. A considerable portion of this area, to a distance of some 100 miles east of Lake Victoria, originally lay within the Uganda Protectorate as its Eastern Province. By an Order of March 5, 1902, issued by Lansdowne when Foreign Secretary, it was transferred to the East Africa Protectorate as " the Kisumu and Naivasha Provinces".— McGregor Ross, *Kenya from Within: A Short Political History* (1927), 45.

relaxed the form of this specific safeguard.[1] The pressure of a colonization policy was being felt. This had been stimulated by the completion of the railway from the coast to Uganda in 1901 which for the first time made the highlands readily accessible. A contributory cause was the economic necessity of making the new line, the capital cost of which had been borne by the Imperial Exchequer, a paying proposition. But a colonization policy could only proceed legally, it was felt, if the lands to be disposed of were in the category of Crown lands. Accordingly in 1901 the East Africa (Lands) Order in Council had been issued, claiming all public lands as Crown property, and on this the Ordinance of 1902 had then supervened, seeking to secure settlers by more attractive terms.[2] It succeeded to this extent, that during 1902 and 1903 the number of settlers rose rapidly, but at the cost of depriving Africans of land they held to be their own. As the Hailey *Survey* has judicially expressed it : " Europeans had been permitted to acquire land in a manner that was beginning to cause hardship to the tribes concerned." [3] That the situation did not deteriorate more seriously was largely due to those administrative officers who sought within the limits of their powers to safeguard African interests and so served as a buffer between the land-hungry European and the Africans who owned the land though now without a title recognized in law. In 1905 the administration of the Protectorate was transferred to the Colonial Office, under which a Crown Lands Ordinance of 1915 increased the leasehold period from ninety-nine to 999 years, and defined Crown lands as including " all lands reserved for the use of any native tribe ". This inclusion, intended as a safeguard, assumed that the executive would treat these areas as inviolable, but the executive was con-

[1] W. McGregor Ross, *op. cit.*, 47–51. Whereas by the 1897 Regulations land "cultivated or regularly used" was excluded, this was reduced in 1902 to "land in the actual occupation of natives at the date of the lease".

[2] Hailey, *op. cit.*, 743–4.

[3] *Ibid.*, 745. How loosely the regard for African rights could be interpreted is evidenced by the fact that villages might not only be surrounded by but even included in allotments to Europeans who, if the villagers moved away, might then claim the land.—McGregor Ross, *op. cit.*, 51. McGregor Ross, himself resident for twenty-three years in Kenya (Director of Public Works from 1905, and for six years, 1916–22, an official member of the Legislative Council) has recorded one result: "Under pressure from Government House in East Africa the Home Government had relaxed the standard of trusteeship that had previously prevailed, and, as a result, a large sweep of Kikuyu territory, partially depopulated at the moment as a result of the great famine and smallpox visitation, passed out of native hands."—*Ibid.*, 51.

stantly subject to the strongest pressure from the European settlers, and " the settlers had never accepted the reserve policy as finally debarring Europeans from obtaining grants in the reserves ".[1] Thus matters stood when a new influx of settlers appeared.

In 1919 a soldier settlement scheme was initiated, with 1,300 farms covering some 2,500,000 acres offered to suitable applicants, allotment to be by lottery. The applicants numbered 2,200; 1,031 farms were allotted.[2] But not all were attractive propositions, and the Government sought to placate the complainants by an exchange. For this purpose it was decided to appropriate some 100 square miles of the Nandi reserve; happily the process was checked by a newly appointed Chief Native Commissioner, but not before considerable areas had passed to European ownership for 999 years.[3] Small wonder that the Parliamentary Commission of 1925 reported : " There is probably no subject which agitates the native mind to-day more continuously than the question of their rights in land, both collectively as tribes and individually as owners or occupiers. In this disquiet they are actively supported in their claims by the missionary bodies of all denominations. . . . At every meeting we had with the natives of Kenya Colony there was evidence of a feeling of insecurity as regards the tenure of their lands."[4]

With this notable accession of settlers, directly encouraged by the Government, labour shortage became acute, and the Government was naturally constrained to take steps to relieve it. It did so. On October 23, 1919, there was issued *Labour Circular No.* 1, under the heading : " Native Labour required for non-Native Farms and other Private Undertakings." Among the Governor's " instructions " to his officials were the necessity of using " every possible lawful influence " to induce men to go out as labourers, and even women and children when the farms were near at hand; the insistence on chiefs and headmen accepting it as part of their

[1] Hailey, *op. cit.*, 746–7.

[2] McGregor Ross, *op. cit.*, 81; E. Huxley, *White Man's Country: Lord Delamere and the Making of Kenya* (1935), II, 54–7.

[3] " Much of the tribe's best grazing land was appropriated. Natives were ordered off and were paid five rupees (6s. 8d.) for each of the huts in the villages which were abandoned. It was a drastic clearance. It cost the Government £2,485, which indicates the scale which this forced evacuation of native dwellings reached. This process of allotment of native land to newcomers was still in progress when a new Chief Native Commissioner was appointed . . . Early in his tenure of office about half the area of pirated land was restored to the tribe."—McGregor Ross, *op. cit.*, 81–2.

[4] *Report of the East Africa Commission* (Cmd. 2387, 1925), 28.

duty to encourage their young men to work on plantations; the keeping of a record by District Commissioners of chiefs who were helpful and those who were not and reporting accordingly, with a specific request for any evidence " that any Government Headman is impervious to His Excellency's wishes ".[1] Thanks to immediate missionary protest, the British public was soon informed of what was afoot. In the so-called " Bishops' Memorandum ", issued over the signatures of the Bishops of Mombasa and Uganda and J. W. Arthur of the Church of Scotland, while the urgent need of labour was recognized, exception was taken to the methods proposed for securing it. Allowing that the precise term, forced or compulsory labour, was nowhere used, they asserted that the Circular did in fact introduce such labour. They proceeded to state that under existing circumstances they felt this to be necessary, but wished it openly stated as such and outlined eight conditions under which the power should be exercised. The statement aroused deep misgiving in Britain; if legal compulsion was to be preferred to the existing state of affairs, the situation must indeed be an ugly one.[2] Frank Weston, Bishop of Zanzibar, in his *The Serfs of Great Britain*, was less submissive to the plea of overriding circumstance and roundly rejected forced labour as immoral, anti-social, and cruel.[3] Meanwhile, following a debate on the subject in the House of Lords, Milner the Colonial Secretary stated in a despatch that compulsory labour for private profit was " absolutely opposed to the traditional policy of His Majesty's Government ".

The safeguards, however, on which he relied did not appear such to missionary leaders, and a memorandum over distinguished signatures, urging the appointment of a Royal Commission to cover the whole field of land and labour questions and related African welfare in East Africa, was presented to the Colonial Secretary on December 14, 1920.[4] Before a decision was reached Winston Churchill had succeeded Milner at the Colonial Office and on September 5, 1921, issued his own despatch :

---

[1] The full text is supplied in Leys, *op. cit.*, 395–7; McGregor Ross, *op. cit.* 103–5.

[2] The text of the Memorandum is given in Leys, *op. cit.*, 397–404.

[3] H. Maynard Smith, *Frank, Bishop of Zanzibar* (1926), 247–50.

[4] The personal initiative that led to this action was that of J. H. Oldham. Among the signatures supporting the Memorandum were those of the Archbishops of Canterbury, York, and Armagh, the Moderators of the Scottish Churches, and the heads of the Free Churches. It was officially approved by thirty-one Missionary Societies and had the support of many distinguished public men.—*I.R.M.*, X (1921), 188–94.

Government officials were in future to take no part in recruiting labour for private employment, and compulsory labour for public purposes was to be strictly limited.[1] The part played by missionary leaders in this total situation was notable, and the courage their action demanded was generally conceded.[2] It made clear that in the conditions of the new Africa political questions could no more be ignored by Christian men than in the days of Wilberforce and Buxton, of John Philip and John Mackenzie. The International Missionary Conference at Crans in June 1920 had before it a Report which asserted: " There would appear to be a fatal insincerity at the heart of the missionary undertaking if missions acquiesce without protest in policies which deprive the natives of their rights in land and degrade them to be mere instruments of the white man's gain." [3] Another test of missionary sincerity was soon to emerge in Kenya.

The contact of Indians with East Africa as merchants at Zanzibar and Mombasa had been an early one.[4] Numbers were increased when Indian labour was recruited for the building of the Uganda Railway in the years 1892–1901, there being at one time an Indian labour force of 18,000, a number of whom remained in the country as artisans, traders, and cultivators. In 1921 they numbered 22,822 or 50 per cent of the non-African population, the Europeans totalling 9,651 or 12·1 per cent.[5] The European community became deeply concerned in the years after the war about what they regarded as an Asian threat to their own privileged position in the so-called " White Highlands ", and to their political ascendancy in the country.[6] An Economic Commission, consisting of six settlers and two officials, had been appointed in 1917 and reported two years later. They indulged in much abuse of Indians and demanded the barring of the door

[1] Command Paper No. 1509.

[2] For comments on this from different points of view, see: Leys, *op. cit.*, 194–5; McGregor Ross, *op. cit.*, 105–7; H. M. Smith *op. cit.*, 250–7; E. Huxley, *op. cit.*, II, 63–5; J. H. Oldham in *I.R.M.*, X (1921), 184–8; R. Oliver, *The Missionary Factor in East Africa* (1952), 247–57.

[3] *I.R.M.*, X (1921), 183. The Slavery Commission of the League of Nations placed its judgment on record in 1925: " The Commission considers that forms of direct or indirect compulsion, the primary object of which is to force natives into private employment, are abuses."— *Bulletin of the I.M.C.*, No. 9 (January 1926), v–vi.

[4] See Vol. II, p. 93.

[5] Hailey, *An African Survey*, 335.

[6] There had not been, of course, any grant of representative government, but European members heavily dominated the unofficial minority of the legislative council.—Hailey, *op. cit.*, 164.

against all Indian immigration. Milner in the House of Lords pronounced on their effort as being " purely deplorable ".[1]

The Colonial Secretary might deplore the report produced but the Government of India sat up and took notice. Indians had now become extremely sensitive in the matter of equality of status and claimed the right of fellow-citizenship in the Commonwealth. This was readily conceded at the highest level when, at the meeting of the Imperial Conference in London in 1921, it was declared advisable that the rights of Indians, domiciled in other parts of the Empire, to such citizenship should be recognized.[2] The Convention of settlers' associations in Kenya, which had originated in 1910, was meanwhile actively engaged in anti-Indian propaganda and some of its speakers showed no qualms in importing a religious issue into the controversy. The tender plant of Christianity, they urged, must not be jeopardized; their Africans must be protected from the aggression of rival faiths.[3] A petition to the King made much of the same impending danger.[4] The missionaries must have rubbed their eyes in amazement at this championship of their cause from so unexpected a quarter. But by all accounts some even of them were not too clear on the Christian issue.[5] The reprimand was administered, not by missionary leaders in East Africa, but by the National Christian Council of India, over the signatures of the Metropolitan and S. K. Datta, speaking on behalf of the overwhelming majority of Christians and missionaries in that country : " They hold it to be a gross disservice to Christianity to suggest that it can be extended, maintained, or preserved by doing an injustice to anyone. Kenya Europeans should defend their claims on their merits, not on the ground of the desirability to secure Christianity against the competition of other influences. Such an argument rests on a fundamental misconception of the real nature

[1] *Lords Debates*, July 14, 1920, Col. 161, quoted in McGregor Ross, *op. cit.*, 320; cf. 101.

[2] South Africa was the only dissentient.

[3] McGregor Ross, *op. cit.*, 344–5.

[4] "And they [the petitioners] are fully convinced that Your Majesty, as Defender of the Faith, no empty title, must view with peculiar concern the possibility that the flower of Christian Faith, so recently planted in Eastern Africa, may be choked by the quick growth of other Eastern religions . . . and that the work done in the past by Christian pioneers and missionaries may be lost."—*Ibid.*, 346.

[5] An extreme case was that of a Kenya clergyman who went too far, even for the Convention, which disowned him.—C. F. Andrews in *The East and the West*, XXI (1923), 225–6; McGregor Ross, *op. cit.*, 369–71, 380–1. On the factors involved in the Kenya missionary attitude, see R. Oliver, *op. cit.*, 259–60, and notes.

of Christianity, and assumes that the influences of Kenya Europeans are uniformly helpful to Christianity, which view the recent discussion on forced labour might lead one to doubt." [1]

Despite the hectic fever of the Kenya campaigning, even leading up to threats (and plans) for armed revolt,[2] the settlers did not have their way. The Colonial Secretary, now the Duke of Devonshire, summoned to London representative delegations from both Kenya and India. J. H. Oldham was concerned at the divergent views of missionaries in East Africa and in India; he evolved a policy for which he secured the support of members in both delegations, the core of which was the proposal that African interests should be declared to be paramount, and that a Royal Commission should inquire into the application of the doctrine to Kenya.[3] The proposal was eventually accepted in high quarters and in July 1923 there was issued the White Paper, *Indians in Kenya*, in which the declaration was made : " Primarily, Kenya is an African territory, and His Majesty's Government think it necessary to record their considered opinion that the interests of the African natives must be paramount, and that if, and when, those interests and the interests of the immigrant races should conflict, the former should prevail. . . . As in the Uganda Protectorate, so in the Kenya Colony, the principle of trusteeship for the natives, no less than in the mandated territory of Tanganyika, is unassailable. This paramount duty of trusteeship will continue, as in the past, to be carried out under the Secretary of State for the Colonies by the agents of the Imperial Government, and by them alone."[4] On specific points relating to the status of Indians in Kenya, the legislative council was to include five elected Indian members, a segregation policy in townships as between Europeans and Asians would have to be

---

[1] *The East and the West*, XXI (1923), 290. Canon C. H. Robinson, Editorial Secretary of S.P.G., was equally definite: " Of all the arguments in favour of the exclusion of Indians from East Africa, the weakest and most un-Christian is the plea that the future of Christian Missions is at stake." He further quoted the comment of a Calcutta editor on Delamere's plea, in a memorandum, of the danger to Christianity: " Utterances such as these in which Christianity is dragged into sordid controversies are nothing short of blasphemy."—*Ibid.*, 290.

[2] C. Dundas, *African Crossroads* (1955), 115–16.

[3] R. Oliver, *op. cit.*, 260–2. Roland Oliver, to whom students are indebted for the examination of the archives at Edinburgh House and of missionary material surviving in Kenya, has pointed out that J. H. Oldham had hoped to raise the question of African interests as the overriding problem, in the Royal Commission he sought earlier on the forced labour issue.—*Ibid.*, 255–7.

[4] *Indians in Kenya: Memorandum* (Cmd. 1922, 1923), 9–10.

G 2

abandoned, but the existing practice of retaining the highlands for European settlement would be maintained, though still unprescribed by legal enactment. The official decision thus promulgated, tension became relaxed; neither side had received its claim in full, and the continuance of effective Imperial control had been placed beyond doubt.[1] If the rôle played by missionaries was somewhat confused, at least they were spared the embarrassment of futile controversy among themselves, thanks to the timely intervention of the British Secretary of the International Missionary Council with his statesman-like proposals.[2]

In Central Africa the Independent State of the Congo under Leopold's personal sovereignty had become a byword in pre-war years for the heartless exploitation of its African peoples.[3] When in 1908 the territory was annexed by Belgium there was the promise of a more humane policy but the World War, so soon supervening, delayed the full formulation of a constructive programme of reform. In the post-war years, however, this was put in hand to such good purpose that it could eventually be stated that large-scale enterprise in the Belgian Congo was conducted " with more regard for the welfare of native labour than in most of the other territories in Africa ".[4] The basic law defining the constitution of the Belgian Congo and laying down the determining principles for the control of its affairs was that of October 18, 1908, generally known as the Colonial Charter.[5] The second article repudiated forced labour for private profit.[6] True, the

[1] *Ibid.*, 13–15, 17. At the same time provision was made for the representation of African interests on the legislative council through "a nominated unofficial member chosen from among the Christian Missionaries in Kenya specially to advise on such matters . . . until the time comes when the natives are fitted for direct representation."—*Ibid.*, 14. Delamere had advertised his purpose in visiting England to be to press for the grant of immediate European self-government. His party therefore received no small rebuff in the statement: "His Majesty's Government cannot but regard the grant of responsible self-government as out of the question within any period of time which need now to be taken into consideration."—*Ibid.*, 10.

[2] On the whole question see: Hailey, *op. cit.*, 335–8; N. Leys, *op. cit.*, 344–9; McGregor Ross, *op. cit.*, 318–85; E. Huxley, *op. cit.*, II, 110–66; *The Round Table*, XII (1922), 338–61; *The East and the West*, XXI (1923), 209–43; R. Oliver, *op. cit.*, 259–62. For criticism of the declaration of paramountcy of African interests as an abstract statement of overall policy, see Hailey, 142; Oliver, 263.

[3] See Vol. III, pp. 267–9.   [4] Hailey, *Survey*, 141.

[5] For the full text see: O. Louwers et I. Grenade, *Codes et Lois du Congo Belge* (3me éd., 1927), 11–25.

[6] "Nul ne peut être contraint de travailler pour le compte ou au profit de particuliers ou de sociétés."—*Ibid.*, 12, art. 2.

Belgian Congo had no problem comparable to that of East Africa arising from European settlement in its vast domain, but, as successor to the rule of Leopold with its abuses, the Colonial Government had, inherited a highly distasteful situation in which African suspicion of European intentions would not be readily allayed. Evidence of the sincerity behind the statement of liberal policy was the setting up of a permanent Commission for the protection and welfare of Africans.[1] Such a Commission was peculiar to the Belgian Congo among African colonial territories, and Roman Catholic missionaries were largely responsible for its institution.[2] Despite the fact that the Government, as part of its inheritance from the Leopoldian regime, was itself a large shareholder in commercial companies and found in existence extensive concessions under European control, it sought, within the limits thus imposed upon it, to safeguard the individual and social welfare of its African population. Thus on March 16, 1922, there was issued a Decree determining the nature of the legal contract between labourer and employer which was concerned with the mutual obligations of the parties.[3] A notable effort in the same direction was the setting up of a Commission by the Minister of the Colonies in December 1924 to study the vital question of labour supply. Their report was made available in April 1925.[4]

It courageously proposed certain restrictions in the recruitment of African labour, in the interests of African society, and recommended specific safeguards for the men who were recruited. The proposal to limit recruiting, which was a new idea when other governments were moving in the reverse direction, was expressed for general guidance in a series of percentages of adult able-bodied males in relation to zones at varying distances from the home village; thus: (a) Five per cent could be safely enlisted in work that removed them temporarily far from their home surroundings; (b) a further five per cent could be enlisted for work within some

[1] *Ibid.*, 13, art. 6.
[2] Hailey, *op. cit.*, 210. The Roman Catholic missionaries in the Belgian Congo were members of Belgian provinces or congregations and thus were doubly influential—on national as well as on religious grounds—with the Belgian Colonial authorities. Missions in the Colony were classified as "national" and "foreign", the major test of the former being the requirement that two-thirds of the administering authority be Belgian.—*Ibid.*, 1270.
[3] *Contrat de travail entre indigènes et maîtres civilisés.*—Louwers et Grenade, *op. cit.*, 1725-39.
[4] *Rapport de la commission pour l'étude du problème de la main-d'œuvre au Congo belge* (1925).

two days' march of their village so that family links could be maintained; (c) finally, fifteen per cent could be safely employed in European enterprise locally, such as porterage, agriculture, harvesting of crops, and so forth.[1] There were also recommendations in the interest of recruited labour covering such questions as transport, accommodation, food, medical care, time limit of contract, and free choice of employer.[2] In the same year, 1925, local orders forthwith put into operation this series of permissive percentages, and some districts were temporarily closed to recruitment altogether.[3]

In this the Belgian Government set a standard that was not only in utter contrast to its predecessor in the Congo but that was far ahead of the practice of those other colonies where the problem of both migrant and local labour was a pressing one, The Hailey *Survey* has paid tribute to the initiative in the interests of African welfare displayed by the Belgian policy : " Though the details of the Belgian system may not be capable of general application, its principles commend themselves as worthy of close study. It represents the first attempt to subject the movement of labour to systematic regulation in the interests of native society." [4]

In the complex South African scene in this decade one feature only can be selected for consideration : the so-called Colour Bar legislation of 1926 when for the first time the reservation of certain grades in industrial employment to whites on the ground of colour alone was made fully statutory.[5] Such a determined denial of equality of opportunity on purely racial grounds was so repugnant to the heart of the Christian gospel as understood by the majority of Christian people that here again Church and State (though on this the Churches stood divided) found themselves in conflict. The original discrimination was innocent enough : it was limited to the mines and was based on safety measures. The principal strands in a complex situation were in brief as follows.

An early piece of legislation by the Union after its inauguration was an Act designed to secure the safety of industrial workers, in

[1] Hailey, *Survey*, 645–6; " The Problem of Native Labour in the Belgian Congo " by a Belgian Catholic, in *I.R.M.*, XIV (1925), 537–44.
[2] *I.R.M.*, XIV, 543–44.
[3] Hailey, *op. cit.*, 646. A further Labour Commission of 1930 thought the distinction between classes (a) and (b) unnecessary and therefore recommended that not more than ten per cent should leave the village.— *Ibid.*, 647.
[4] *Op. cit.*, 708–9.
[5] For brief reviews of the South African situation in 1926, see three papers from different points of view in *I.R.M.*, XV (1926), 344–89.

the manner of Factory Acts in general.[1] The Act authorized the issuing of regulations by the Governor-General to carry into effect its central purpose, though it gave no authority for discrimination on the ground of colour. However, a number of skilled occupations, involving the control of machinery and the handling of explosives, were reserved to white men as a safety measure. These occupations were thirty-two in number, and a decade later were reported to contain 7,057 whites.[2] This restriction only operated in the two northern provinces of the Union, the Transvaal and the Orange Free State, and were thought to carry the legal authority of the Act itself. In addition there was in practice the so-called conventional colour bar whereby a further nineteen occupations had, under trade union pressure, also been reserved to white men.[3]

During the decade 1912–22 radical changes had occurred in the situation in the mines, due in part to the pressure of the war years. Thus in 1912 some sixty per cent of the European workers in the mines hailed from the United Kingdom, while in 1922 over seventy-five per cent had been born in South Africa, many of them " merely holders of blasting certificates rather than miners, who had learnt most of what they knew from their own native ' boss-boys ', and who, as even the Pact Mining Regulations Commission of 1924–25 admits, ' frequently and habitually contravened ' the regulations by leaving skilled and semi-skilled work to natives."[4] At the same time a serious rise in the working costs of the mines occurred that led to a survey of the situation by the Low Grade Mines Commission which reported in 1920. This recommended a relaxation of the colour bar, thus reducing costs and keeping mines open, and so averting considerable unemployment.

No action resulted until 1921 when a sudden deterioration in the economic position of the mines led to a proposal to employ African workers in certain semi-skilled trades, thus displacing perhaps some 2,000 whites. But white labour would have none of it; their powerful trade unions resisted to the point of calling the Great Rand Strike of January 1922. Revolutionary elements were before long in control and even sought to arouse the resentment of Africans by calculated and brutal attacks upon them. In March Smuts as Premier declared martial law and within a week the

[1] *Mines and Works Act*, No. 12, of 1911.
[2] As reported in 1920 by the Low Grade Mines Commission.
[3] In 1920 these contained 4,020 persons.
[4] The South African correspondent of *The Round Table*, XV (1925), 831.

rising had been suppressed. It had cost 230 lives.[1] It led to a new political alignment that, as far as Africans were concerned, was ominous for the future : in April 1922 General Hertzog announced that the Nationalist Party and white Labour would combine at the next election.[2] Strange bedfellows in some respects, they at least had this in common : that no policy that undermined the colour bar could be tolerated. The Nationalist stand was well enough known, inherited from the days of the Great Trek. White Labour was no more liberal in its attitude; Sir James Rose Innes has summarized it : " The strike was a struggle by white men for the benefit of their own race. There was no desire to improve the position of the black men, more than 170,000 in number, without whose labour the industry would have collapsed like a pack of cards. The principal object of the strikers was to prevent any weakening of that colour bar . . . which reserved skilled and well-paid work for Europeans." [3]

Two further events brought matters to a climax. In November 1923 a test case came before the Courts to decide the legality of race discrimination based on the Regulations made under the Mines and Works Act of 1911—a colour bar in industry hitherto accepted as legal. The Courts decided that such differentiation was of so drastic a nature that full statutory authority was required; that is, the regulations were to that extent *ultra vires*. The protection of a " legal " colour bar had vanished overnight. In the following year the report of the 1921 Census was issued in

[1] See *Report of the Martial Law Inquiry Judicial Commission* (U.G. No. 35, 1922), and comment in *The South African Outlook* (1922), 258-9.

[2] Hertzog was Minister of Justice in the first Union cabinet under Botha as Prime Minister, but the two were fundamentally divided in their views of the relation of Dutch and British within the Union, and of the Union to the Commonwealth. In a reconstructed cabinet Hertzog, who had declined to resign, was left out. In November 1913 a new " Nationalist party " appeared under Hertzog's leadership. Dr. D. F. Malan was the leader of the new party in the Cape.—Walker, *A History of South Africa*, 542-4; Buxton, *General Botha* (1924), 15-17; J. C. Smuts, *Jan Christian Smuts* (1952), 99, 123, 125-9. The Nationalist-Labour coalition under Hertzog and Cresswell was formally agreed to on April 23, 1923.—J. C. Smuts, *op. cit.*, 267.

[3] B. A. Tindall (ed.), *James Rose Innes: Autobiography* (1949), 285. Sir James Rose Innes was Chief Justice of South Africa for the period 1914-27. He refers to the strikers' unprovoked attacks upon Africans to incite retaliation which could then be hailed as a " Native rising", and to the patient self-control of Africans under this provocation, concluding: " Whatever might have been the rights and wrongs of these disturbances, there can be no doubt that the Bantu mine-labourers came through their ordeal with flying colours".—*Loc. cit.*

which the writer allowed himself, on the basis of population increase in the decade 1911–21, to predict a possible period of twenty-five years, or at the most optimistic, fifty years in which white civilization could establish itself in South Africa. The forecast of such a swift rise in the tide of colour as this assumed (on quite inadequate premises) was alarmist in the extreme, and paved the way for Government action.[1] In February 1925 a single-clause Bill was introduced to give the industrial colour bar a statutory basis. Twice it passed the Assembly, supported by the Nationalist-Labour majority in the House, and twice it was rejected by the Senate. Then, as provided for in the Union Constitution, it was submitted to a joint session of both Houses and was finally passed into law as Act 25 of 1926.[2] It is true that the Act did not introduce a new situation into the mines but simply made statutory an existing one, yet this very fact was daunting enough in itself : now for the first time there appeared in statute law discrimination on the ground of colour alone. Further, the Act made it possible to extend the same discrimination to the Cape and Natal. The Chief Justice described it, in relation to similar legislation on racial issues, as "a darker blot than any of them upon our statute book".[3]

The voice of the Christian community was not silent during these events. In particular, when the amending legislation was before Parliament in 1925 the protest of the Churches—though some Dutch Reformed Church leaders held aloof—was nationwide. Hertzog resented what he regarded as unwarrantable interference.[4] The African verdict in the mouth of a Bantu Christian leader was revealing and severe : "The application of legislative machinery, such as the Colour Bar legislation, by a modern civilized people for the purpose of repressing a backward race must be the despair of the rest of the civilized world. . . . Our last hope lies with the world of the Church and its inculcation of higher ethical standards among the rulers of South Africa, where the underlying belief is that the application of Christianity to economics spells suicide. To believe this is to confess that Christianity is a failure."[5]

[1] The Nationalist-Labour Pact Government had come to power in June 1924 under Hertzog as Prime Minister.
[2] E. Hellmann, *Handbook on Race Relations in South Africa* (1949), 146–7; Walker, *op. cit.*, 583–6, 612–13; *Round Table*, XV (1925), 829–40. Popularly referred to as the "Colour Bar Act" its official title was the Mines and Works Amendment Act.
[3] *James Rose Innes*, 306.
[4] E. H. Brookes, *The Colour Problems of South Africa* (1934), 165.
[5] D. D. T. Jabavu in *I.R.M.*, XV (1926), 588. A major criticism of the

(3) A New Era in Education

Christian missions in Africa had been almost everywhere the pioneers in education.[1] In the nature of the case they had begun at ground level in the so-called bush schools with the vernacular as the medium of instruction. When European governments had settled in they were not inclined to be interested in schools at this level, since the practical problem of securing a junior staff of African clerks tended to govern their views of education. The missions had, it is true, developed a simple type of training institution for teachers for their schools, some of whose products found their way into clerical occupations. An exception to this general pattern in tropical Africa was to be found in the British Colonies of the West Coast where the development of Grammar Schools and High Schools catering for the more advanced people of the towns offered courses usually determined by the demand of external examinations and modelled on those of English secondary schools.[2]

During the war years 1914–18 the high pressure of the pre-war decade on the educational resources of the missions continued and governments began to bestir themselves. A new education ordin-

Act, merely on grounds of expediency, was that it slammed the door on African advance in industry before an opportunity had been opened on the land by placing more acres at African disposal.

[1] Almost, for there were exceptions as in Sierra Leone, where the Company as early as 1793 had 300 children in its schools. In the sixteen years of Company control it spent on education in the settlement from £500 to £1,000 per annum, while the cost of educating Africans in England throughout the period 1791–1807 was upwards of £3,500.—*Report of the Court of Directors of the Sierra Leone Company* (1791), 52; *Special Report of the Directors of the African Institution (1815)*, 23. Schools were also begun in the eighteenth century at certain forts on the Gold Coast—Elmina (Dutch), Christiansborg and Friedensborg (Danish), Cape Coast (English) —though principally for mulatto children.—F. L. Bartels, *Gold Coast Education: Its Roots and Growth*, chap. III, "The Castle Schools; before 1765."

[2] In the main these comprised: (*a*) In Freetown, the C.M.S. Grammar School for boys (1845), the Annie Walsh Memorial School for girls (from a simple beginning, 1845), the Wesleyan Boys' High School (1874), and Girls' High School (1880); (*b*) on the Gold Coast, the Wesleyan Boys' High School at Cape Coast (1876), and Girls' High School (1900), and under Basel Mission auspices schools both for boys and for girls at Akropong, Abokobi, and Odumase; (*c*) at Lagos, the C.M.S. Grammar School for boys (1859), the Wesleyan Boys' High School (1878) and Girls' High School (1879); (*d*) at Calabar, the Hope-Waddell Institute (1895) under Scottish Presbyterians. In addition there were various institutions for the training of teacher-evangelists. There were also Roman Catholic schools for boys and Convent schools for girls.

ance for Nigeria was issued in 1916 with several notable features.[1] Uganda in 1917 saw the first conference in which government and missions jointly considered educational policy, while in Northern Rhodesia an ordinance, not altogether acceptable to missions, was issued in 1918. The outstanding event in South Africa was the opening in 1916 of the South African Native College at Fort Hare, hard by Lovedale.[2] With the coming of the post-war period therefore the time was opportune for an overall survey of the situation. This was undertaken by two Education Commissions in 1920–21 (for West and South Africa) and in 1924 (for East and South Africa) under the auspices of the Phelps-Stokes Fund of New York.[3] As these Commissions were a landmark in the educational history of tropical Africa some further reference to their work and its effects is demanded.

The initiative came from American missionary societies who wished for a survey of the field before developing their educational services in post-war Africa. It was felt that those who had been specially concerned with Negro education in the States might offer valuable suggestions after undertaking such a survey under the leadership of Thomas Jesse Jones, the educational director of the Phelps-Stokes Fund.[4] J. H. Oldham proved an invaluable ally in securing not only the co-operation of British missionary

[1] F. D. Lugard, *Report on the Amalgamation of Northern and Southern Nigeria, and Administration, 1912–1919* (1920), 62–5.

[2] *I.R.M.*, IX (1920), 9–11.

[3] The respective reports, prepared by Thomas Jesse Jones the Chairman in each case, were: *Education in Africa* (1922) and *Education in East Africa* (1925). The Phelps-Stokes Fund had been established for educational purposes in the interests of Negroes in Africa as well as in the United States according to the provisions of the will of Miss Caroline Phelps Stokes.—T. J. Jones, *Educational Adaptations, Report of the Phelps-Stokes Fund 1910–1920* (n.d.), 16.

[4] The question would seem to have been first adumbrated, in relation to the suitability for Africa of the type of education offered at Hampton Institute (Virginia) and Tuskegee Institute (Alabama), at a conference of Mission Boards concerned with Africa held in New York City in November 1917.—*The Christian Occupation of Africa* (1917), 39–40. It was the American Baptist Foreign Missionary Society that first took the matter up through the Committee of Reference and Counsel of the Foreign Missions Conference of North America by whom the approach was made to the Phelps-Stokes Trustees. In November 1919 the Trustees concurred on condition of adequate co-operation by British Missionary Societies being available.—*Education in Africa*, xii–xiii. Dr. T. J. Jones had been for a period director of the research department and Chaplain at Hampton Institute, General Armstrong's famous foundation for Negroes, and had latterly produced a full-scale report on Negro Education in the States.

societies but also of the Colonial Office, while the Belgian official response was likewise gratifying.[1] By their terms of reference the two Commissions were to survey and appraise existing educational work in the light of " the religious, social, hygienic and economic conditions ", and to help to formulate plans for future development.[2] Each Commission was in its composition representative of Africa, America, and Europe. The chairman personally selected as the African member J. E. K. Aggrey whose home was on the Gold Coast but who had lived for some twenty years in the States as student and teacher.[3] Territories visited by the first Commission were Sierra Leone, Liberia, the Gold Coast, Nigeria, Belgian Congo, Angola, and South Africa. The East Africa Commission visited every territory from Abyssinia to the Rhodesias and the South African High Commission Territories. The whole was an epoch-making survey which for the first time envisaged in the light of recognized standards the problem of education in Africa.

While granting generous recognition of the pioneering achievement of missions in the field of education, there were three major criticisms offered as a result of the survey. First, in relation to the far-flung village schools which had been opened in large numbers in response to the pressure of African demand,[4] it was found that these had been multiplied without adequate regard to their supervision and that they were often either futile or potentially dangerous. The Commissions paid tribute to their purpose : "They are the outposts of civilization. With all their defects they have rendered a great service and, in a sense, they are the most important parts of the educational system." [5] But this was not all : " In

[1] *Education in Africa*, xiv.
[2] *Education in Africa*, xvi; *Education in East Africa*, xiii.
[3] The first Commission consisted of T. J. Jones (Chairman), J. E. K. Aggrey, H. S. Hollenbeck (medical missionary of the American Board, Angola), A. W. and Mrs. Wilkie (United Free Church of Scotland, Nigeria and the Gold Coast), and L. A. Roy (Secretary). The second Commission included T. J. Jones (Chairman), J. E. K. Aggrey, J. H. Dillard (a leader in American Negro education), H. L. Shantz (of the U.S. Department of Agriculture), Garfield Williams (Educational Secretary of the C.M.S.), and J. W. C. Dougall (Secretary). Hanns Vischer of the British Colonial Office accompanied this Commission but was not a member of it. C. T. Loram of the South Africa Native Affairs Commission accompanied each Commission during the South African portion of its itinerary. For Aggrey's notable contribution see his biography: E. W. Smith, *Aggrey of Africa* (1929), a best-seller among Africans.
[4] See Vol. III, pp. 235–8.
[5] *Education in East Africa*, 59. For an illuminating interpretation of the significance of the village school, see A. Victor Murray, *The School in the Bush* (1929), 79–97.

their present condition many of them are 'little nothings', neglected, poor and unsupervised. Their buildings are often ugly shacks with no equipment, distinguishable from the Native huts only by their size. A large number of their teachers are ignorant and untrained, 'blind leaders of the blind', either futile as regards community influence, or exercising an influence which has no basis in reality."[1] Improvement in these schools—as basic to the educational system as the base to a pyramid—and their adequate supervision were stressed as a leading priority.

The second principal criticism made by the Commissions concerned the school in its relation to the physical and social environment. They found that with few exceptions education was not integrated into the life of the African community. It appeared as something altogether exotic, bound up with the European and his interests rather than with the basic needs in health, agriculture, and cultural tradition of the people of the land. This was most pronounced in the secondary schools of the West Coast but was not limited to them. One of the methods of the Commissions was to interrogate pupils to discover the educational emphasis of the school, and the results were revealing; A. W. Wilkie reported for the West : " The pupils were asked to sing any song they pleased. . . . The chances were strong that we would hear ' The British Grenadiers !' . . . When they were asked to sing an African song, a boat song, or any chant used in their own plays, a laugh invariably went through the whole class. . . . Similarly, if we asked about history, we soon discovered what happened in 1066, but of their own story—nothing."[2] Small wonder that Gold Coast chiefs, for example, told the Commission that education was the training of their children for the service of the white man.[3] In this matter of the adaptation to the needs of the community of the education offered, the first emphasis of the Commissions was on health. And that this was not unrelated to the religious objective of the missions was indicated by an experience in East Africa. A group of teachers had been questioned about comparative infant mortality rates— in Europe and America at the time, from six to ten per cent, while in African communities ranging from thirty to sixty per cent—and

[1] *Education in East Africa*, 59. Cf. *Education in Africa*, 41.

[2] *Education in Africa*, xix.

[3] Stated at the presentation of an interim report of the first Commission in London in July 1921. The writer once came across the statement, in an African teacher's hygiene examination paper, that the task of Government Sanitary Inspectors was to make the country healthy for Europeans to live in—European self-interest, from the African point of view, again to the fore.

in reference to the high African mortality they had replied, " We should say God has taken them ". " But what would you do about it?" pressed Dr. Jones, and the answer came, " We should pray "— pray God not to take so many more black babies than white.[1] The missionary message of the fatherhood of God was thus being perverted by the hard facts of African experience.[2]

The third major deficiency noted was the absence of any adequate co-operation in the work of education. Missions were showing little concern to co-operate among themselves in the business, governments were found to be carrying a totally inadequate share of the burden, while economic groups, such as trading concerns, and last but not least the people themselves needed to be encouraged to take a worthy part in the enterprise. The significance of the meagre expenditure by governments on African education—ranging from four per cent of total revenue to vanishing point—was that this essential service was being carried almost entirely by missions as voluntary agencies.[3]

With the making available of the findings of the Commissions, by published reports and by conferences, notable effects began to be produced, both at high official levels where government and mission policies were determined, and thereafter in the actual scene of operations in Africa. The first move significant of a new official outlook on education in Africa was the appointment by the British Colonial Office of the Advisory Committee on Native Education in the British Tropical African Dependencies on November 24, 1923. With a distinguished membership it was

[1] Reported at a Conference on the Commissions' work at High Leigh, September 1924.

[2] A Christian doctor with African experience has spoken of the relation of health service to the gospel as " making the love of God credible ".— C. C. Chesterman, *In the Service of Suffering* (1940), 37.

[3] In so far as the expenditure of government on education as a percentage of total revenue is an index of its concern (with some allowance for the war years), the case of Nigeria may be taken: 1·5 per cent (1914), 1·7 per cent (1915), 1·6 per cent (1916), 1·3 per cent (1917), 1·1 per cent (1918), 1·2 per cent (1919)—figures quoted from relevant *Annual.Reports*. If expenditure on health and agriculture were to be included, the Commission calculated that 7 per cent would then be for Nigeria the proportion of total revenue. The corresponding figures for Sierra Leone would be 4 per cent and 13 per cent; and for the Gold Coast, 3 per cent and 10 per cent.—*Education in Africa*, 106, 127, 153. In East Africa relevant figures on the same basis were 3·7 per cent and 16 per cent (Kenya), 2 per cent and 23 per cent (Uganda), under 1 per cent and 13 per cent (Tanganyika), " almost negligible " and 18 per cent (Nyasaland), negligible (for Africans) and 17 per cent (N. Rhodesia).—*Education in East Africa*, 112, 149, 176, 197, 259.

representative of Church and State and of the world of education.[1] The function of this Committee was to advise the Secretary of State on the education of Africans. Its first production was a Memorandum on Education Policy in British Tropical Africa which at once commanded widespread attention and was destined to guide British educational policy in Africa for a generation.[2] The impress of the recommendations of the Phelps-Stokes Commission was plain to see. In particular, the earlier Government attitude which had ignored religion in the school was now replaced by a plea for its inclusion : " The greatest importance must . . . be attached to religious teaching and moral instruction. Both in schools and in training colleges they should be accorded an equal standing with secular subjects. . . . History shows that devotion to some spiritual ideal is the deepest source of inspiration in the discharge of public duty. Such influences should permeate the whole life of the school." [3] An official statement could scarcely go further. A decade later another memorandum on educational policy was issued, which was a revision and expansion of the first in the light of experience in the intervening years.[4] The importance of these two statements is sufficiently indicated in the Report of the Cambridge Conference of 1952 : " The subsequent story of education in Africa is the story of the efforts·that have been made to extend and apply the principles of the memoranda of 1925 and 1935." [5]

Meanwhile missionary interests were being rallied in support of the educational policies which the Commissions had advocated. With this in view a missionary conference with J. H. Oldham as chairman was convened under the auspices of the Conference of

[1] Its ten members included Sir F. D. Lugard, Sir Michael Sadler, two bishops (Anglican and Roman Catholic), and J. H. Oldham as representative of Protestant missionary interests. At a later date the Committee was enlarged to become the Advisory Committee on Education in the Colonies, with correspondingly extended responsibilities. The Committee was established in June 1923 and on July 25 Ormsby-Gore reported to the House of Commons: " We were led to this largely as the result of a most extraordinarily interesting report issued by Dr. Jesse Jones."

[2] Cmd. 2374 (March, 1925). Cf. *African Education, A Study of Educational Policy and Practice in British Tropical Africa* (1953), 3 (Report of the Cambridge Conference of September, 1952).

[3] *Memorandum* (1925), 4–5.

[4] *Memorandum on the Education of African Communities* (Colonial No. 103, 1935). The second memorandum of the Committee, intermediate to those of 1925 and 1935 was: *The Place of the Vernacular in Native Education* (African, No. 1110, May 1927).

[5] *African Education* (1953), 3.

British Missionary Societies in September 1924. It was representative of American, British, and Continental Societies with
several government officials, among whom was Sir F. D. Lugard,
attending as visitors.[1] A memorandum on the elements of an effective education policy for Africa, entitled *An Educational Policy
for African Colonies*, was presented by Dr. T. Jesse Jones and
commended to all societies by the conference. Among the important topics considered were the relation of education to the
African's cultural inheritance and the place of African languages
in the educational programme. A valuable outcome of the
conference arising from these particular discussions was the proposal to form a research organization for these vital questions, and
so was born in due course the International Institute of African
Languages and Cultures, constituted under a triple directorate—
British, French, and German—with missionary organizations as
well as learned societies in active support of its work.[2] A further
subject of importance that came before the conference was the
education of African women and girls. The Reports had called
attention to the low proportion of girls in the schools : thus in the
Gold Coast (a relatively advanced area) the ratio in the Colony
was one girl to five boys, in Ashanti one to nine, and in the
Northern Territories one to twenty.[3] In the East Africa Report a
special chapter was devoted to the subject.[4] This matter was soon

[1] The conference met at High Leigh from September 8 to 13 and was
attended by some 120 people representing 15 British, 7 American, and 7
Continental Societies. The three members of African race were J. E. K.
Aggrey, R. D. Baëta, and Max Yergan. For details of programme and
membership, see *I.M.C. Bulletin*, No. 5 (January 1925), ii; and for three of
the papers presented, *I.R.M.*, XIV (1925), 3–44.

[2] E. W. Smith, "The Story of the Institute. A Survey of Seven Years",
in *Africa*, VII (1934), 1–27. It is now called the International African
Institute.

[3] *Education in Africa*, 130. The writer, in a visitation of some 60 village
schools in South-Eastern Nigeria in 1915, found in a total enrolment of
some 3,700 scholars, less than 40 girls. The above Report comments:
" It is interesting to note that educational facilities in primitive groups
are almost exclusively for boys, but that the advancement of education
results in a rather rapid correction of the disproportion."—*Loc. cit.*

[4] " The Education of Women and Girls ", chap. XVI in *Education in
East Africa*. A notable pioneer institution in South Africa for girls of
European descent, with standards of missionary service, thus indirectly
serving African girls, was the Huguenot Seminary at Wellington in the
Cape. Andrew Murray, inspired by the work for girls of Mary Lyon in
founding Mount Holyoke Seminary in Massachusetts, desired a similar
institution in South Africa as a memorial to the early French settlers. In
1872 he wrote to Mount Holyoke for a graduate. Miss A. P. Ferguson
and Miss A. E. Bliss responded and began the work in 1874. They gave

taken up by J. H. Oldham who convened at Edinburgh House a representative group to discuss the question in all its bearings and so assist the British societies at least to evolve a common policy in the matter that might then receive official approval and encouragement. This group in due course extended its concern to educational affairs in general, and from its deliberations there emerged *The Remaking of Man in Africa*, yet another indirect result of the interest aroused by the Phelps-Stokes Commissions.[1]

If these were results in a field to which the Commissions had first effectively directed attention and official and missionary circles then responded with an initiative of their own, there was a further contribution of importance due to the Phelps-Stokes Trustees themselves. Impressed as they were in the first instance with the fact that American experience in Negro education might have something to say of advantage to Africa, they were confirmed in this by the two reports presented by Dr. T. Jesse Jones. These pointed to the conclusion that the Fund might render yet a further service by making it possible for educators from Africa to visit centres of Negro education in the Southern States and meet directors of the enterprises that had proved their worth in the case of the American Negro. This was generously undertaken until some 250 visitors from Belgian, British, French, and Portuguese Colonies, from Abyssinia, Liberia, and the Union of South Africa—both government and missionary, Roman Catholic and Protestant—had benefited by this experience.[2] Notable among the places visited were the training institutions at Hampton and Tuskegee and community schools on St. Helena Island, South Carolina, and at Calhoun, Alabama, which thus came to play their part, however indirectly, in the African situation. Samuel Chapman Armstrong, who founded Hampton Institute, Virginia, in 1868, was strikingly prophetic in his enunciation of educational principles, offered more by way of addresses, articles, and annual reports than in a formally elaborated theory. That education must include the head, the hand, and the heart and have as its controlling aim the fitting of the pupil for the life he is likely to lead were creative ideas

a lifetime of service, retiring respectively in 1910 and 1920. Meanwhile the institution had grown to University College rank and become affiliated to the University of South Africa. The link with Mount Holyoke was long continued.—G. P. Ferguson, *The Builders of Huguenot* (1927) *passim.*

[1] J. H. Oldham and B. D. Gibson, *The Remaking of Man in Africa* (1931). One appendix contains valuable summaries of educational systems operating in 23 African territories at that date.—*Ibid.*, 151–82.

[2] M. N. Work, *Negro Year Book, 1937–38* (1937), 182. The Fund expended some $40,000 on this service alone.

in his day and made Hampton Normal and Agricultural Institute under his leadership a power for the regeneration of Negro life in the South in the years of frustration that followed the Civil War.[1]

Armstrong's most distinguished pupil, Booker T. Washington, reproduced the master's ideas at Tuskegee in the deep south of Alabama where an institution grew up, entirely under Negro auspices, to become world-famous.[2] No visitor to these residential institutions could fail to be impressed with the fact that the ideal of an education for life was being translated into reality despite the handicap of the social environment of the South where ever-present situations of racial stress might quickly become acute under slight provocation. The contribution of the community schools was of a rather different order where the interests of the adult community were catered for as part of the purpose while their children were educated for this same community, though not without opportunity for the further development elsewhere of special ability.[3] In addition to these established educational centres there was in operation a service as vital as any to the development of the Negro South—the supervision of rural schools. The work of State agents had, from the second decade of the century, been supplemented—indeed rendered effective—by a quite remarkable group of workers: the Jeanes Supervising Industrial Teachers. The Anna T. Jeanes Foundation was established in 1907 by a Quaker lady of that name for the purpose of assisting elementary schools for Negroes in the South. The Principals of Hampton and Tuskegee Institutes were appointed trustees, and along with others evolved, as the plan best calculated to serve the largest number, a system of supervising teachers supported by the Fund, each of whom was responsible for a County-wide area. This scheme, under the direction of J. H. Dillard (a member of the East Africa Commission) had proved its worth in lifting the level of the rural schools through the assistance and encouragement of the Negro teachers instead of remaining content with the hitherto somewhat intimi-

---

[1] E. A. Talbot, *Samuel Chapman Armstrong, A Biographical Study* (1904); F. G. Peabody, *Education for Life, The Story of Hampton Institute* (1919); F. G. Peabody, *Armstrong's Ideas on Education for Life* (1926).

[2] Booker T. Washington, *Up from Slavery* (1900); Booker T. Washington (ed.), *Tuskegee and its People: Their Ideals and Achievements* (1905): E. J. Scott and L. B. Stowe, *Booker T. Washington, Builder of a Civilization* (1917).

[3] For an account of the founder of Calhoun Colored School, Alabama, see: *The Southern Workman*, LVI (1927), 405–12. For Penn School on St. Helena Island, South Carolina, see: Rossa B. Cooley, *Homes of the Freed* (1926); *School Acres: An Adventure in Rural Education* (1930).

dating inspection of the school for official report.[1] J. H. Dillard, who best knew the work of the Jeanes Teachers, paid them tribute : " There have been no nobler pioneers and missionaries than these humble teachers. They have literally gone about doing good." [2] While it was recognized that methods that had proved successful in the Negro South were not necessarily to be transplanted to African soil without some adaptation to the new environment, yet the inspiration of seeing creative ideas in successful operation was a contribution of no mean order to educators in the new Africa.

The effects in Africa of these converging influences from without were not long in appearing, more particularly in the British colonies. Their governments forthwith apportioned a larger percentage of revenue for education, the bulk of which became available to mission schools as grants-in-aid, both for maintenance and for capital development, while missions that had hitherto been reluctant, under the old conditions, to accept official payments, now reconsidered their attitude and modified their policy in this respect, thus sharing in the new opportunity for educational advance. J. H. Oldham had been at some pains to secure that such generous assistance as was now forthcoming should not be utilized merely to relieve an existing financial strain but rather to improve the quality and extend the range of the educational service.[3] The pattern of development in West Africa and in East was slightly different, and in the nature of the case that in the West was the first to get under way.

At the village school level, to which particular attention had been directed by the Commissions, action was soon taken to regularize the situation and governments made clear their interest in educational activity at all levels within their territories, irrespective of qualification for grant-in-aid. Thus, in May 1923 the Government of Nigeria convened a conference of mission authorities operating in the densely populated region east of the Niger, with its hundreds of village schools, where the Government was disturbed, on the ground of public order, at the activities of certain free-lance teachers who battened on ignorant villagers and unsuspecting chiefs when the limited resources of the missions did not

[1] M. N. Work, *Negro Year Book, 1937–38* (1937), 180; Lance G. E. Jones, *Negro Schools in the Southern States* (1928), 137–53. Lance Jones' book is to be commended as a competent survey of the whole field of Negro education in the 'twenties.
[2] Lance G. E. Jones, *op. cit.*, 147.
[3] R. Oliver, *The Missionary Factor in East Africa*, 267.

permit them to respond to urgent appeals. As any extension to this level of the power to close a school would be resisted as an infringement of religious liberty, since school and church were in these cases so intimately connected, the point was not pressed at the time, especially as the disturbing cases referred to were found to be decreasing. It was agreed however that all schools should be registered, and in due course standardized with an educational qualification for the teacher in charge which was acceptable both to the government and the missions. Thus the first step was taken, in respect of these village schools, along the road of a common standardization and of closer relations with the government.

There soon followed a further step in the effort to lift these struggling little schools to a higher plane of activity and influence. The Commission's emphasis on supervision had not passed unnoticed and the Government of Nigeria proposed the appointment of a staff of European supervisors on generous terms—a system soon in operation and amply justified by its results. By 1928 there were fourteen such supervisors giving full-time service in the Southern Provinces.[1] Further, under the Regulations of 1927 religious instruction was to rank as an ordinary school subject in all assisted schools, the voluntary service of missionaries to teach the subject being permissible.[2] These developments all depended in the last resort upon an adequate supply of qualified teachers, and this was the weakest point in the educational structure. In the densely populated region of south-east Nigeria, for example, the Hope Waddell Institute of the United Free Church of Scotland in Calabar was the first to train qualified teachers east of the Niger, an institution that also offered professional training on an apprenticeship system to printers, tailors, and carpenters, giving distinguished service under the principalship for more than a generation of J. K. Macgregor.[3] The latest was the Methodist

[1] New Education Ordinances had been enacted for the Northern Provinces (No. 14 of 1926), and for the Colony and Southern Provinces (No. 15 of 1926). It was in the South that the village school problem was pressing; Ordinance No. 15 therefore included a requirement for the registration of all teachers and authorized the Governor to close schools on the recommendation of his educational advisers. The appointment and duties of supervisors were set out in the Code.—*Education Code : Colony and Southern Provinces* (1927), 6, 22. The 14 supervisors in the South under mission auspices were apportioned as follows: Anglican (C.M.S.), 4; Roman Catholic mission, 3; Wesleyan, 1; Scottish Presbyterian, 1; Primitive Methodist, 4; Qua Iboe Mission, 1.—*A Bulletin of Educational*
[2] *Education Code* (1927), 33–4.   [*Matters*, III (1929), 2.
[3] *Southern Nigeria Annual Report for 1908* (1909), 26; T. J. Jones, *Education in Africa* (1922), 164–5.

Institute at Uzuakoli in Iboland, begun in 1922, which added a Teacher Training Department in 1926, and under the principalship of H. L. O. Williams did notable work in the educational field.[1] The first two Government Training Colleges for Teachers in the Southern Provinces east and west of the Niger were not in operation until 1929.[2]

In East Africa it was the Jeanes teacher on the American model that caught the imagination : the appointment of African teachers, who had already approved themselves, to supervise the village schools of an area with a particular concern for relating the school and its work to the community in whose midst it existed. In Kenya this secured wholehearted support from official and settler alike. Lord Delamere had fully approved of the East Africa Commission's emphasis and gave the Jeanes idea his strongest support. As it was recognized that a course of training would be necessary before the selected teachers could take up their new duties, a Jeanes school was established at Kabete in Kenya for the purpose in 1925.[3] In 1927 the first fifteen qualified Jeanes teachers were sent out to begin their work; by 1931 there were sixty-six men in the field and a further thirty-six in training.[4] The success of the venture was impressive so that Nyasaland, Northern Rhodesia, and Southern Rhodesia soon followed suit. In 1928 these three territories took the matter up and in the following year, again with Carnegie Corporation assistance, a beginning was made : in Nyasaland at Zomba, in Northern Rhodesia at Mazabuka, and in Southern Rhodesia at Domboshawa. In Southern Rhodesia there was an additional venture for the training of women as Home Demonstrators; this was undertaken in a new government school near Bulawayo, attached to the London Mission centre at Hope Fountain.[5] The Jeanes system suitably adapted was meeting the urgent need of African education at

[1] Eighty-third *Annual Report of the Primitive Methodist Missionary Society* (1926), 48.

[2] *Nigeria Annual Report for 1928* (1929), 36.

[3] E. Huxley, *White Man's Country* (1935), II, 181–3. Plans for the school at Kabete were laid in 1924, with generous help from the Carnegie Corporation. The first head was J. W. C. Dougall who had served as secretary to the Phelps-Stokes East Africa Commission.

[4] T. L. Davis, " Digest of Reports on Jeanes Training Schools " in *Report of the Inter-territorial " Jeanes " Conference in Southern Rhodesia, 1935* (1936), 383–4. See further: "An Experiment in African Education in Kenya " in *The Round Table*, XX (1930), 558–72.

[5] *Report of Jeanes Conference, 1935*, 384–6. By 1931 Nyasaland had 18 men in the field and 24 in training; S. Rhodesia had 16 and 17 respectively; Northern Rhodesia had 22 in training.

ground level, and was doing so as a co-operative undertaking between governments and missions. It was a tribute to the responsiveness of both parties to the Commissions' recommendations that so much was done so quickly in both East and West.

But this was not all. In Uganda from the inception of the Christian mission in 1877 education had been left entirely to the missions for well-nigh half a century. A Commission of the Secretary of State in 1937 paid the pioneers high tribute: " It is impossible to praise too highly the devotion, courage, zeal, charity and wisdom with which they performed their task. We doubt indeed whether in the whole history of Christian enterprise there exists a finer chapter than that which tells of the work of these ardent men and women during the formative years of the Protectorate." [1] But once again the Phelps-Stokes Commission pricked government in the heart for its own apparent neglect of duty and in 1924 an Education Department was created, while in 1925 an Advisory Council on African Education was set up, representative of government departments and missionary societies as well as of the African and European communities. A Technical School had already been started in 1921 at Makerere which the following year became Makerere College, where developments were speeded up by the new impulse in education—an institution destined within a generation to attain to University College rank.[2]

Meanwhile the Gold Coast in West Africa was planning development in higher education also looking towards University College status, and doing so under conditions that were the envy and admiration of less fortunate territories. The spectacular prosperity of the African cocoa farmer—for the Gold Coast was producing half the total world consumption—also meant a buoyant revenue from which large schemes could be financed. Coupled with this was a leader suited to the time—a governor of dynamic personality. When Sir F. G. Guggisberg was appointed to the colony in 1919 he placed education in the forefront of his development programme. The impulse contributed by the Phelps-Stokes West Africa Commission two years later still further encouraged this emphasis. In *The Keystone* Guggisberg expounded a sound education as the keystone of progress in a secure economy, while in 1925 he enunciated to his Legislative Assembly fifteen principles of education with an indication of what would be involved in acting upon them.[3] The enterprise,

[1] *Higher Education in East Africa* (Colonial No. 142, 1937), 31.
[2] *Ibid.*, 31–2.
[3] F. G. Guggisberg's *The Keystone* (1924) is inscribed on the title-page:

however, that caught the eye of the outside world was the establishment of the institution known from its location as Achimota, where education was to be provided at both school and college levels. A. G. Fraser was called from Trinity College, Kandy, to be the first principal, with J. E. K. Aggrey as vice-principal.[1] Aggrey's early death in July 1927 suddenly deprived the new institution of the African leadership he had so brilliantly provided. His use of the black and white piano keys as a simile of racial harmony had inspired the distinctive college badge.[2] The provision of secondary education continued to be a direct concern of the principal missions in the Gold Coast : Anglican, Wesleyan, and Roman Catholic. In particular Mfantsipim, the Methodist Boys' School at Cape Coast, started in 1925 on a new career that was to raise it to the front rank of such institutions.[3]

Roman Catholic missions, already receiving privileged treatment in Portuguese and Belgian territories, were soon active participants in these new developments in British Colonies. In 1927 Arthur Hinsley, then Rector of the English College in Rome, was appointed to the newly created post of Visitor Apostolic to Catholic Missions in British African Colonies.[4] His message everywhere was to urge as complete a co-operation as possible with Governments in their forward-looking educational policies; thus at Dar-es-Salaam in 1928 : " Collaborate with all your power; and where it is impossible for you to carry on both the immediate task of evangelization and your educational work, neglect your churches in order to perfect your schools." [5] The formation of the International Institute of African Languages and Cultures, the proposal for which was made at the High Leigh Conference of

" Education is the Keystone of Progress: mix the materials badly, omit the most important, and the arch will collapse; omit character-training from education and progress will stop ". The author paid tribute to the Phelps-Stokes Commission.—*Ibid.*, 17. For the address to the Legislative Assembly see: *The Gold Coast: A Review of the Events of 1924–1925 and the Prospects of 1925–1926*, by Sir F. G. Guggisberg (Accra, February 1925). The fifteen principles are stated on pp. 67–89.

[1] *The Gold Coast, A Review of 1924–1925*, 92–102; *Report of the Committee appointed in 1932 by the Governor of the Gold Coast to inspect the Prince of Wales' College and School, Achimota* (1932), 7–9. The original proposal for a Government Secondary School, from which the project of Achimota began, was made as early as 1920.

[2] E. W. Smith, *Aggrey of Africa* (1929), 278–9.

[3] F. L. Bartels, *Mfantsipim, 1876–1951* (1951), 14–15.

[4] R. Oliver, *op. cit.*, 274.

[5] Quoted from J. Mazé, *La Collaboration Scolaire des Missions et des Gouvernements* (1933), 14, in Oliver, *op. cit.*, 275.

1924 and was thus from the beginning associated with Protestant missions,[1] caught the interest also of Roman Catholic authorities. The Congregation of the Propaganda authorized the formation of a new body representative of all the missionary Congregations at work in Africa and so the Conférence des Missions Catholiques d'Afrique first came into existence.[2]

If this review of the new era in education has been concerned with British territories, it is because in these the most active response was to be found. In so-called Latin Africa with its regional variations—in the wide expanses of French West and Equatorial Africa, the Belgian Congo, and Portuguese Angola and Mozambique—Roman Catholic missions were in the ascendant and the larger part of mission education was therefore in their hands. A Protestant undertaking such as the Phelps-Stokes Commissions could thus scarcely expect to have the same impact on the situation. Moreover, the French and Portuguese policies in education, seeking to draw Africans who have proved their worth and capacity into closer association with the mother country—the acceptance, indeed, of *assimilés* and *assimilados* as fellow citizens —left little room for radical reform.[3] Indeed, the emphasis upon the European language was carried in Portuguese territory to the point that no African vernacular was to be employed save orally in religious instruction or during the early period in teaching Portuguese. No African language was to be used in print save as a parallel version to Portuguese, thus placing upon the missions the burden of bilingual editions. Moreover, the Commission's plea that " international policy requires the recognition of the Native languages as an essential element of Native life " was without effect.[4] The Belgian authorities proved more hospitable and the various recommendations made harmonized with their own liberal and forward-looking policies.[5]

Thus in the post-war decade a new era in education was

[1] *Vide supra*, p. 112.

[2] For details of its origin and functions, see *Africa*, IV (1931), 235–8. The new Conference was granted four representatives on the governing body of the Institute, corresponding to the four allowed to the (Protestant) International Missionary Council.—*Africa*, VII (1934), 7.

[3] W. B. Mumford and G. St. J. Orde-Browne, *Africans Learn to be French* (1936), 27–49. In French territory the Government logically took full responsibility for education and mission participation was negligible.

[4] This was laid down in Article 3 of Decree 77 of December 9, 1921.— T. J. Jones, *Education in Africa*, 233, 246.

[5] *Ibid.*, 258–9, 286–9. By contrast with French territory, in the Belgian Congo the Catholic and Protestant Missions between them enjoyed a virtual monopoly of education.

successfully ushered in with some enthusiasm on the part of both missions and governments and to the deep if inarticulate satisfaction of young Africa. A further decade was to bring home to mission authorities certain embarrassments involved in this re-deployment of their available resources.

(4) Aspects of Missionary Progress

In addition to the weighty political, economic, and social affairs already reviewed, in which the Christian Mission was intimately concerned, there are certain other aspects of missionary development during the decade 1918–28 that demand some notice. First is the extension of missionary agency both by existing societies entering new fields and by new arrivals on the African scene. The restrictions of the war years were only gradually reduced, shortage of passages, for example, due to loss of shipping and heavy demands by both government officials and commercial firms, limiting at first the effort to fill up the missionary ranks. But, these difficulties overcome, the movement once more gathered momentum and missionary occupation in geographical terms began to forge ahead once more. Indeed, in the period 1914–22 alone the number of new Protestant enterprises begun was some twenty per cent of the total number undertaken during the previous century of work,[1] while three-quarters of these belonged to the years 1919–22.

Roman Catholic missions had likewise advanced in the same decade. During the years from 1913 to 1923 more than thirty new vicariates and prefectures had been erected by the division of earlier ecclesiastical units that proved unwieldy as the work developed. These new spheres were distributed over the continent, in West, East, Central and South Africa.[2] As another measuring rod of the expansion of Protestant agency the foreign missionary staff, both men and women, had increased from 4,553

[1] Taking as a unit for purposes of computation one Society's work in one political territory, based on information in the *World Missionary Atlas* of 1925, the comparative figures stand approximately as follows:

Period:	British	American	Continental	African	Total
1820–1914	76	71	32	34	213
1914–1922	10	22	5	3	40

For details by decades of the period 1820–1914, see Vol. III, p. 208. For particulars of advance during the decade 1913–1922 in half a dozen representative fields, see *I.R.M.*, XIII (1924), 493, *n.* 1.

[2] M. Spitz, O.S.B., " Roman Catholic Missions in Africa " in *I.R.M.*, XIII (1924), 369–70.

in 1911 to 6,289 in 1925.[1] A feature of the expansion in the post-war decade was the increasing entry into Belgian, French, and Portuguese colonies. The Belgian Congo, including the mandated territory of Ruanda-Urundi, was the largest beneficiary; indeed, in the two decades between the wars the number of Protestant missions was more than doubled.[2] In 1919 the Norwegian Baptists entered northern Congo; in 1920, the American Mennonite Brethren came to the Kwango area. The Seventh Day Adventists, already established in a dozen African territories, arrived in Congo in 1921, while in the same year the Belgian Protestants entered Ruanda, the Swedish Evangelical Free Church of North America came to the Kivu area, and the Assemblies of God Mission started in northern Congo. In 1922 the Kivu region saw three new arrivals: Norway's Free Evangelical Mission to the Heathen, the Evangelization Society Africa Mission, and the British Pentecostal Union Mission. After the coming of the Ubangi Evangelical Mission in 1923 (first sponsored by the American Evangelical Free Church) there seems to have been a breathing space until 1926. In that year an Anglican mission from Uganda—the Ruanda General and Medical Mission—arrived, the Immanuel Mission of the American Brethren came to northern Congo, and the Canadian Baptists to the Kwango region. Also to the Kwango in 1927 there came the Unevangelized Tribes Mission and the Congo Gospel Mission, while in 1928 the Danish Baptists also entered Ruanda.[3] If the French and Portuguese colonies appeared less welcome to Protestant endeavour, they nevertheless had their accessions in the early post-war years: to French Guinea came the Christian and Missionary Alliance (1918), to the French Sudan the Gospel Missionary Union (1920), to the Upper Volta the Assemblies of God (1921), to Ubangi-Shari in French Equatorial Africa the Council of Baptist Missions of North America (1920), while in the French Mandate of Cameroons the Church of the Lutheran Brethren arrived in 1918, and the Brethren Church Mission of the States in 1920.[4] Portuguese East Africa received in the same period the International Holiness Mission (1921), the Church of the Nazarene Foreign Mission (1922), and the South Africa General Mission (1922).[5]

[1] Beach and Fahs, *World Missionary Atlas* (1925), 76. These totals cover Africa together with Madagascar and neighbouring islands.
[2] G. W. Carpenter, *Highways for God in Congo* (1952), 26.
[3] Beach and Fahs, *op. cit.*, 89; G. W. Carpenter, *op. cit.*, 26–7.
[4] Beach and Fahs, *op. cit.*, 88–9.
[5] *Ibid.*, 90.

Among the territorial extensions of the older established missions the most notable—and indeed spectacular—also occurred in Latin Africa. The appearance of the African evangelist, William Wadé Harris, in the French Ivory Coast on the eve of the World War and his early deportation by the disquieted French authorities have already been recorded.[1] For a decade the range and nature of the response to his appeals remained unknown, and then, almost by accident as it seemed, the veil was drawn from a waiting community numbered by tens of thousands. It happened in this way : trouble had come to a group of Methodists at Grand Bassam, an immigrant community of Fantis from the Gold Coast to whom the Wesleyan Church of the Gold Coast gave pastoral oversight. But the use of Fanti contravened new French regulations of 1922 that religious services must be conducted in Latin, French, or the local vernacular, and in May 1922 the church was closed. W. J. Platt, who with seven years' service in Dahomey had completed his apprenticeship in French territory, was commissioned by the Wesleyan Missionary Society to visit Grand Bassam to resolve the problem. His visit in 1923 was notable not so much for his success in these negotiations as for the great discovery then made : that a multitude of Harris Christians as they came to be called—baptized but still untaught—had been patiently waiting for the past ten years in hope of helpers.

A French lawyer in Grand Bassam and a French official directed his attention to the people's claims. Returning in 1924 to survey the situation he was amazed both at the range of the movement Harris had initiated and at the extent of the transformation he had produced. He was received in village after village with overflowing joy, and their little bamboo churches—only a few were built of stone—were decorated with palm leaves and beflagged, usually containing a desk or table on which an English Family Bible was reverently placed : " We have waited ten years for you," they said. Roman Catholic offers of help had been declined because they would not consent to teach them from the Book. The numbers could not at first be accurately estimated—some 20,000 was suggested—but enough was known to indicate the unparalleled opportunity. The Wesleyan Society, though facing a deficit, courageously answered the call and within a year had eight ordained European missionaries, two women workers, and eight African ministers on the new field. By 1926 reliable figures could be quoted : over 32,000 people had their names on church registers and a Christian community of 40,000 or more could be offered as

[1] *Vide supra*, p. 45.

a conservative estimate. The long and arduous Christian pilgrimage still lay ahead but the setting-out had been propitious; the old pagan religion had faded out in the villages embraced by the movement.[1] The paramount need to conserve the situation, as on a smaller scale in contemporary movements in the Sierra Leone Protectorate and in Ashanti, was that of trained African helpers. To meet this there was started at Dabou a model village where 100 emergency catechists were to be given a one year's course. But the task was colossal.[2]

A further aspect of missionary experience during this first post-war decade was the continued growth of independent African sects. Movements like those of the Ivory Coast under Wadé Harris or under Sampson Opon in Ashanti[3] were very much the exception rather than the rule in that the leaders remained in touch with European missions as friendly if unauthorized collaborators —unauthorized, that is, by European agency, for they unhesitatingly laid claim to Divine authority for their vocation. The rise of independent sects was a widespread phenomenon, and origins were varied though it was the general experience that they grew by drawing off the less mature of mission adherents.

In Uganda the sect of the Malakites proved an embarrassment during the war years. Towards the close of 1913 an African teacher, Malaki Musajakawa, joined a chief, Yosuwa Mugema, in a protest against doctors and the use of medicine, an attitude Mugema had already adopted for many years. This was based on a passage in Deuteronomy where, it was claimed, recourse to a doctor was forbidden.[4] At first adherents were content to protest

[1] W. J. Platt, An African Prophet (1934), 31–9, 66–77; From Fetish to Faith (1935), 86–8; F. D. Walker, The Day of Harvest in the White Fields of West Africa (1925), 71–9; The Story of the Ivory Coast (1926 3rd ed., 1930), 29–42, 59–63; News Notes from French West Africa, No. 1 (January 1926), 1–4; No. 2 (April 1926), 2–3. Polygamy early proved an obstacle; Harris, himself a polygamist, had permitted it while sternly denouncing any extra-marital sexual relations.—The Story of the Ivory Coast, 18; News Notes, No. 1 (January 1926), 4. There were some critics who apparently disapproved of the entry of a Missionary Society, imposing its own standards on a spontaneous movement.—Cf. An African Prophet, 9–10.

[2] News Notes, No. 1 (January 1926), 5; No. 3 (July 1926), 3; F. D. Walker, The Day of Harvest, 16–26, 56–70.

[3] F. D. Walker, The Day of Harvest, 16–18.

[4] Deuteronomy 18: 9–11. In v. 11 the term translated " charmer " in A.V. and R.V. was rendered in Luganda by omusawo, a word also used for doctor; hence their inference. Mugema is said to have held to this attitude for some twenty years, claiming that God was the Healer and recourse to doctors was therefore interference with His purposes. In 1912 he had protested to the Synod against the use of prayers for doctors and

against doctors, remaining in the Church of their baptism, but matters were soon stepped up : they built their own churches, appointed ministers, and began to baptize on an extensive scale. As conditions were easy—no literacy test, no catechetical instruction or examination, no sponsors for their good faith, but a simple acceptance of the " no medicine " formula and an affirmation that God is Almighty—candidates soon rolled up in their thousands; indeed, in one day over 2,000 were said to have been baptized. Both Anglican and Roman Catholic missions suffered from a falling away of their less stable adherents as the new sect got under way.

At first known as the Kitala sect (from Malaki's home) and then as the Malakites,[1] their name for themselves, at first reported to be " The Church which does not drink medicine ", became " The sect of the One Almighty God ".[2] The tolerance of polygamy—monogamy was rejected as not definitely commanded in the Bible—added to the popularity of their baptism. Village churches were half-emptied and something like a landslide of catechumens occurred in outlying districts. A notable accession was that of Semei Kakungulu, sometime paramount chief of Busoga and Bukedi, which was occasioned by what seemed a chance incident. He was proceeding to the Kabaka's coming-of-age celebration in Buganda by way of Jinja where, since there was plague in Jinja, he was informed he must be inoculated before proceeding. He was indignant at the demand and threw in his lot with the Malakites with some enthusiasm. The movement posed a problem for the Anglican diocesan council which wisely decided that " a campaign of instruction and enlightenment is the best method of protecting Christian people, and of winning some of the heathen who have been misled ". This was put into operation with encouraging sucess. Civil authority was in due course compelled to take a hand. Malaki began to visit different districts, ignoring the authorization required by law—a letter showing whence he had come and what he had come for. He was brought before Ham Mukasa, the Sekibobo, and convicted; the Kampala Court confirmed it, and he was restrained from roving about the country. This administered a definite check to the movement which by 1917 appeared to have spent its force. But it persisted for well over another decade until the government was provoked to strong measures. The resistance to vaccination and

medical work in general.—Dr. J. H. Cook in *Church Missionary Review* (1915), 122, quoted in *Proceedings of the C.M.S.* (1915), 65.

[1] *Ba-malaki.*   [2] *Katonda Omu Ainza Byona.*

inoculation by the thousands concerned jeopardized the health of the whole community; the climax came in a murderous attack on a European Sanitary Officer in 1929, after which Malaki was deported, dying a few months later. Sir Albert R. Cook summarized it: "It was indeed nothing less than a parody of Christianity. Its sole creed was to repeat, parrot-wise ' I believe in one God '. The single condition of admission, the repudiation of medical aid, was, as we found in our own hospital work, little observed when they were sick." [1]

Also during the war years a self-styled prophet claiming to be the Second Elijah, in fulfilment of Malachi 4 : 5, appeared in the region of the Lower Niger. Interestingly enough this occurred in the sphere of the Niger Delta Pastorate, an autonomous unit of the Anglican Church, with an African, James Johnson, as bishop who himself described the movement as " a great upheaval in the Niger Delta Church ". Garrick Sokari Braid, as he was called, had been a well accredited member of St. Andrew's Church in the New Calabar district and a trusted evangelist. He had by degrees become noted for dreams and visions of future happenings which the event confirmed, so it was alleged. He also had much success, it was said, in the healing of the sick by his prayers. On declaring himself to be Elijah II he rapidly acquired a remarkable influence in the delta region among Christians and non-Christians alike. Three-quarters of the congregation of St. Stephen's, the cathedral church at Bonny, declared for him; chiefs and headmen would acknowledge him with deep obeisance. He issued two emphatic prohibitions : no medicines should be used or medical help sought from either African or European doctors, and no alcoholic liquor must be taken. The first brought a spectacular drop in visits to doctors, while the second seriously affected commerce and caused European traders deep concern. In his healing ministry he was accustomed to demand confession of sin before attempting to heal. However innocent and sincere in service the movement was in its origin, corrupting influences began to appear. Once more the arm of civil authority was compelled to intervene when his followers, in their iconoclastic zeal (for he denounced all idol worship) invaded private premises. When the prophet laid himself open to arrest on a charge of obtaining money by false pretences, his subsequent imprisonment cooled somewhat the ardour of his following.[2]

[1] *Proceedings of the C.M.S.* (1915), 65–7; (1916), 56–7, 59; (1917), 36; A. R. Cook, *Uganda Memories* (1945), 323–4.

[2] James Johnson, " Elijah II," in *The Church Missionary Review*, LXVII

Soon after the war there was reported from the Lower Congo the appearance of a " prophet movement ", causing widespread disturbance to Protestants and Roman Catholics alike. Again it was begun by one in recognized church connexion and again it was bound up with spiritual healing. It started in May 1921 and within a few months was in full career. Simon Kibangu of the village of Nkamba, himself a member of the Baptist church at Wathen, professed to have had a Divine commission, which at first he resisted, to undertake a ministry of healing. The report that his touch could heal the sick spread like wildfire, mission hospitals were deserted, and Nkamba became a place of pilgrimage to which even the dead were brought. One Baptist missionary said of it : " It spoke to us who looked on of what must have been in the days of the Son of Man. Fetishes and charms were discarded, polygamists put away their extra wives and the services in our villages became crowded." Despite the fact that many claims were dubious—no missionary who inquired into the matter could guarantee any case of healing—numbers still grew. Then others appeared with similar claims—the minor prophets of the movement, both men and women—most of whom had had no church connexion, though some were renegades. They soon began to spring up all over the place. It was an African simile that compared it to the spread of influenza. Features associated with the African diviner began to appear, together with many of the old taboos, until the decisive infiltration of characteristic pagan ideas could no longer be doubted. Yet the name of God was invoked and the doing of His will was claimed. The simmering excitement among the people growing steadily more intense, the civil authority took notice and decided to intervene. Kibangu was arrested, court-martialled, convicted, and given the death sentence. Dr. P. H. J. Lerrigo, who knew the movement at first-hand, regarded him as an innocent neurotic, genuinely subject to the visions he claimed. The missionaries petitioned King Albert on his behalf and he was reprieved. Others were deported with sentences of penal servitude. No evidence was brought forward at the trials to suggest that the movement was in any way politically subversive.[1]

(1916), 455–62; M. T. Pilter, " More about ' Elijah II ' ", in *C.M. Review*, LXVIII (1917), 142–5; *Proceedings of the C.M.S.* (1917), 26–7.

[1] W. B. Frames in *Congo Mission News*, reproduced in *The South African Outlook* (1922), 36–8; P. H. J. Lerrigo, " The ' Prophet Movement ' in Congo " in *I.R.M.*, XI (1922), 270–7; R. H. C. Graham, *Under Seven Congo Kings* (n.d.), 182–194. Graham supplies several verses of the so-called " Prophet's song " which seem innocent enough.

It was in South Africa, however, that the most luxuriant efflorescence of the sects was to be found. The beginning in the eighteen-nineties of the movement known as Ethiopianism, through chafing at European control, has already been noted.[1] But while discontent with the measure of liberty allowed them often enough caused African leaders of ability to secede from the parent body, this was not always the case. Thus, when Halley's comet appeared in 1910, a portent causing considerable alarm among rural people, an African lay-preacher at Bulhoek, near Queenstown, improved the occasion by nocturnal assemblies for hymn-singing, prayer, and preaching at which he declared that the heavenly phenomenon was Jehovah's warning to men to return to their ancient religion, the religion of Israel; the New Testament was but the white man's fiction—had it had any effect on his life? The people were impressed and the church of the *Ama-Sirayeli* or Israelites came into existence. The leader of the movement, Enoch Mgijima, is said to have been a man sincerely given to religious worship, in which he trained his people to spend many hours a day. The reason given for the rejection of Christianity was apparently the true one : it was not, as far as he could see, a religion its professors practised. This was a sect of so-called Zionist type usually associated with pentecostal and faith-healing claims. An annual " passover " was observed by permission from 1918 on common land at Bulhoek. In 1920 the people could not be persuaded to leave, alleging that Jehovah had gathered them together there under his prophet; that they had no wish to disobey the law of the land, but Jehovah's was greater; the end of the world was at hand and they had been brought there to prepare for it. Argument from both African and European to persuade them to move was of no avail. The situation mounted to a climax in May 1921 when 800 armed police, though under strict orders not to fire, were moved up in hope of overawing the deluded people. But the Israelites' reply, who had been assured that bullets would turn to water when fired at them,[2] was fanatical; they " charged like Dervishes and were shot down in scores ". The tragedy of May 1921 was long remembered. A judicial commission declared that the civil authorities had exhausted every means to find a peaceful solution and exonerated them from blame. But this, the only occasion on which a clash occurred between the authorities and a religious sect, inevitably left its scar on Bantu memory. D. D. T. Jabavu pointed the moral to his

[1] See Vol. III, p. 179.
[2] Cf. Vol. III, p. 253.

people : the necessity of an educated, level-headed leadership, and of the wise use of the privilege of religious liberty.[1] The Ethiopian type of independent church was as a rule progressive, with a concern for education and retaining for the most part the liturgical and other practices of the parent body from which secession had sprung. The Zionist churches, on the other hand, were characterized by prophets and a claim to the Bible as chief authority but with little concern for education, and thus became an easy prey to some eloquent exponent of an attractive message.[2]

One result of the Bulhoek tragedy was the appointment of a Commission to inquire into the whole question of the separatist churches. C. T. Loram, a Commissioner for Native Affairs in the Union, writing in 1926 on the basis of this official inquiry, placed the number of independent Bantu churches, on a conservative estimate, as between 120 and 140, ranging, as he put it, from " large and well-known churches, such as the African Methodist Episcopal Church and the African Presbyterian Church, to the many mushroom organizations which spring up and die in the back streets of Johannesburg ".[3] The Commission's forecast that the separatist movement would grow was abundantly justified. J. Merle Davis in 1932 reported 292 separatist churches as registered by the Government of the Union of South Africa, while Edgar H. Brookes obtained a list of 322 as at August 4, 1932.[4] By the time B. G. M. Sundkler published his investigations that total had nearly trebled.[5] To attempt to assign a single adequate cause for so persistent and extensive a development would be an undue simplification of a complex situation, but students of the subject are agreed that the repressive colour bar stands easily first. The Commission above referred to found that there was a widespread feeling in the African community that the " colour bar feeling has

---

[1] *The Christian Express* (1921), 105–6 (D. D. T. Jabavu to Fort Hare students); *The South African Outlook* (1922), 9–11; M. Hunter, *Reaction to Conquest* (1936) 563–5; E. A. Walker, *A History of South Africa* (1947 ed.), 582–3; E. Hellmann, *Handbook on Race Relations in South Africa* (1949), 568. Walker records, as one reverberation of the incident, a request for Bantu representation at the next Imperial Conference, on the ground of a rumour that the Royal veto on Union legislation was to be abolished.

[2] For the characterization of the two types, see: B. G. M. Sundkler, *Bantu Prophets in South Africa* (1948), 53–9; E. Hellmann, *op. cit.*, 565–70.

[3] C. T. Loram, " The Separatist Church Movement " in *I.R.M.*, XV (1926), 476–82.

[4] J. Merle Davis (ed.), *Modern Industry and the African* (1933), 408–14; E. H. Brookes, *The Colour Problems of South Africa, Being the Phelps-Stokes Lectures, 1933, delivered at the University of Cape Town* (1934), 34, 193–201.

[5] B. G. M. Sundkler, *op. cit.*, 317–37.

entered the domain of religion ", so that the separatists say, as one African minister put it, " Come away from the white man, he has no more sincere love for you ".[1] E. H. Brookes found in the separatist church movement a symbol of "the growing distrust and suspicion . . . of the missions and the missionaries ".[2] And the feeling was not without some justification as Sundkler discovered in his researches at a later date.[3] While allowing for such motives as personal ambition and an impatience of European discipline, it was not here that the root of the matter lay; it was in the failure of the white man (as the African saw it) to act in accordance with the demands of the gospel of love which he proclaimed.

There was thus a wide range throughout Africa, from the more ephemeral prophet movements to the formal secessions from mission churches but all giving evidence of an African response, however imperfect, to the teaching of the Christian religion, and claiming an African independence in the formation of their own religious fellowships. According to the tentative interpretation of Miss B. D. Gibson : " The emergence of prophets and the breaking away of native separatist churches may be a sign that Christianity is taking root in Africa." [4]

A third aspect of missionary development in this post-war decade was the steady increase in the taking of common counsel among the Protestant missions, and of organizations to facilitate it. This was to be found at all levels, from the local inter-mission committee charged with delimitation of territory in any contemplated advance, through councils of regional extent with wider purposes, to the highest levels in international consultation where questions of high policy were under consideration. A considerable impulse in this direction had been given by the Edinburgh Conference of 1910, which stimulated further regional conferences in Africa.[5] The world war interrupted but did not terminate this tendency. Sometimes a new beginning was made : thus the Calabar conference of 1911, valuable as was its influence in conditioning the

[1] *I.R.M.*, XV (1926), 478–9. While the Commission did not regard this criticism as justified, they pointed out that they found the view widespread among Africans that the earlier missionaries were free from colour feeling but the later were tainted with it.

[2] E. H. Brookes, *op. cit.*, 161.

[3] E.g., "I have listened to scores of Independent church leaders who have related instances of how they have been turned away from White Church services because of their black skin."—Sundkler, *op. cit.*, 37.

[4] *I.R.M.*, XXI (1932), 222. An estimate of these developments has been offered by R. H. W. Shepherd: "The Separatist Churches of South Africa," in *I.R.M.*, XXVI (1937), 453–63.

[5] See Vol. III, 292–3.

missions east of the Niger for closer relations, was not directly continuous with post-war developments. It was at the Aba conference on educational affairs in 1923 convened by the government, that the Protestant mission representatives adumbrated the proposal which found expression before the year was out in a movement that issued in the Evangelical Union of Eastern Nigeria.[1] On the other hand, the Kikuyu conference of 1913, that occasioned such unhappy controversy, had its direct sequel five years later when a further Kikuyu conference assembled and proposed a working alliance in which the Church Missionary Society, the Church of Scotland Mission, the Africa Inland Mission, and the United Methodist Church Mission would co-operate, with a view to ultimate union. In preparation for this development it was agreed to standardize as far as possible elements of church organization, conditions for admission of communicant members, and the training of African helpers. There emerged the Alliance of Missionary Societies in British East Africa with a Representative Council as its permanent body. It was especially significant for the fact that officials and settlers as well as missionaries were at the conference, and that together they agreed that any policy of separate churches for African and European be abandoned.[2] In 1924 the Alliance secured the formation of a new body, the United Missionary Council, to handle educational and other questions on behalf of the missions in relation to the government, the Alliance itself continuing its existence, with the question of church union as its main concern.[3]

Of the territorial organizations, the two most extensive, which in due course qualified for affiliation to the International

[1] *Vide supra*, p. 115.

[2] *Church Missionary Review*, LXX (1919), 3–4, 6–14; *Proceedings of the C.M.S.* (1919), 7–8, 37–8; *J. du Plessis, The Evangelisation of Pagan Africa* (1930), 347–9. The Bishop of Zanzibar, who was present at the conference, submitted proposals for a united Church as distinct from an Alliance of Missionary Societies, but the non-episcopal representatives were unable to accept them.—*Proceedings* (1919), 37. For a statement of the points at issue in this discussion, and of the general significance of the conference and its decisions, see J. J. Willis, " The Principle of Alliance in Missionary Work " in *C.M. Review*, LXX (1919), 6–14. In 1919 the organizing committee of a fund raised from African sources for providing hospital comforts for Africans on active service in the war, resolved that the balance of some £3,000 should be handed over to the Council of the Alliance for a medical training centre for Africans.—Lucas, *The Empire at War*, IV 221. The money was actually used to establish the Alliance High School, Kikuyu, with vocational training as its objective.—*Kenya Education Department Annual Report, 1926* (1927), 28–30.

[3] *Bulletin of I.M.C.*, No. 6 (April 1925), vii; *I.R.M.*, XIII (1924), 495.

Missionary Council, were those of South Africa and of the Congo. The sixth General Missionary Conference of South Africa was held at Johannesburg in 1925, representative of a score of Churches and Societies, with British, German, French, Swiss and Swedish missionaries present, in addition to those of South African origin. The conference made history in one significant respect : for the first time a paper was read and a discussion opened by Africans.[1] The seventh in the series of conferences met at Lovedale in 1928 and was concerned in particular with the pressure of economic conditions on the life of the African in the Union. In this connexion Clements Kadalie, Secretary of the (African) Industrial and Commercial Workers' Union (known as I.C.U.) was invited to address the conference.[2] At the eighth conference in 1932 a new constitution was asked for, from which emerged the General Missionary Council of South Africa in affiliation with the International Missionary Council.[3]

Protestant missions in the Congo were quick to respond to the influence of the Edinburgh Conference of 1910, and in 1911 the Congo Continuation Committee was set up by the Congo General Conference of that year. A valuable activity, keeping the member missions in touch with one another, was the publication from 1912 of the quarterly *Congo Mission News*, which continued to appear throughout the war years. The Congo General Conference of 1924 took the further step of merging the Congo Continuation Committee in the Congo Protestant Council of which Emory Ross became the first secretary. This organization proved of the highest value for enabling American, British, and Continental missions to take common counsel over a wide range of affairs that intimately affected their work.[4] This Council and that of South Africa were for many years the only two in the continent that were affiliated members of the International Missionary Council.[5] Roman Catholic missions in the Congo, though manned for the most part by Belgians yet varied in the congregations and orders at work,

[1] *Bulletin of I.M.C.*, No. 8 (October 1925), iv–v; *The South African Outlook*, LV (1925), 179–81; LVI (1926), 83–4.
[2] *Bulletin of I.M.C.*, No. 20 (October 1928), iv–v. For the rise and fall of the I.C.U. see *Handbook on Race Relations in South Africa* (ed. E. Hellmann), 492, 521. By 1926 it had achieved an African membership of over 100,000.
[3] *Bulletin of I.M.C.*, No. 36 (October 1932), iv; No. 37 (January 1933), v.
[4] *Ibid.*, No. 8 (October 1925), v.; G. W. Carpenter, *Highways for God in Congo*, 35–6, 37.
[5] *Bulletin of I.M.C.*, No. 65 (January 1940), iv–v. Egypt was included in the Near East Christian Council for Missionary Co-operation.

likewise were in need of some co-ordinating agency, though in
their case it naturally took the form of a hierarchical appointment
rather than the setting up by common consent of an open forum.
On April 27, 1930 the apostolate of the Belgian Congo received
its first apostolic delegate in the person of Dellepiane.[1]

The Rhodesias also had their missionary conferences. That
of Southern Rhodesia was affiliated to the General Missionary
Conference of South Africa.[2] In Northern Rhodesia an unusual
extent of co-operation was experienced. Beginning as the Conference of North-Western Rhodesia in 1914 under Edwin. W.
Smith as its first President, with its next session in 1919 at the close
of the war, it became in 1922 the General Missionary Conference
of Northern Rhodesia, with subsequent meetings in 1924, 1927,
1931, and 1935. The comprehensiveness of its membership was
remarkable : in 1922 there were represented the Brethren in
Christ, the Dutch Reformed Church, the London Mission, the
Paris Mission, the Primitive Methodist Mission, the Seventh Day
Adventists, the South Africa Baptist Mission, the United Free
Church of Scotland, the Universities' Mission, the Wesleyan
Methodist Mission, and the Jesuit Fathers of the Prefecture of the
Zambezi.[3] This comprehensiveness happily was long maintained.
In 1927 the Mission of the White Fathers was represented, and
in 1931 Capuchins and Franciscans were also present as full members. The hope of the first President seemed not ill-placed : " In
the deepest experience of our hearts Catholic and Protestant are
one : the living presence of the risen, glorified Christ is, thank
God, our common possession . . . working together and praying
together we shall grow into a larger unity." But ' thus far and no
farther ' came the fiat from above : in 1933 the Secretary was
informed by higher Roman authority that Roman Catholic
missionaries might no longer remain in full membership. As
associate members however they were still welcomed. Meanwhile
the Conference had grown in membership with accessions from
newly entered Protestant missions. It was nevertheless a notable
Christian witness in the heart of Africa that for twenty years

[1] Schmidlin, *Catholic Mission History*, 654, *n.* 44. It was in the same
year that Arthur Hinsley was appointed the first apostolic delegate for
Africa with residence at Nyeri, as East Africa was his chief concern. *Ibid.*,
739.
[2] Beach and Fahs, *World Missionary Atlas*, 56. The Natal Missionary
Conference and the Transvaal Missionary Association were likewise
affiliated to the General Conference.
[3] *Proceedings of the General Missionary Conference of Northern Rhodesia, 1922,*
(1923), 1-2.

Catholic and Protestant had sat side by side as full members of a conference in taking common counsel.[1]

At the continental level a conference on the Christian Mission in Africa met at Le Zoute in Belgium in September 1926. It was international in character, its 221 members, nationals from America, Europe, and Africa, being representative of some seventy Protestant missionary societies and organizations. It was the first time a conference devoted to missionary affairs in Africa had been convened on such a continental scale. And its subjects of discussion were equally comprehensive : preaching the gospel and building the Church were inevitably on its programme as the very *raison d'être* of the Christian mission; but there were included questions of health and population, of land and labour, and of education with experts present from the American Negro field as well as the Phelps-Stokes Commissioners.[2] Recommendations and resolutions of the conference on these and kindred topics had a profound effect on missionary policies.[3] As but one instance of this, there was set up in 1929 the International Committee on Christian Literature for Africa whose first Secretary, Margaret Wrong, initiated and largely directed, as expert consultant, a continent-wide movement for the provision of books for Africa, in which government bureaux, thanks to her stimulating visits and well-planned objectives, began to play their part.[4]

Meanwhile preparations were in hand for a further world missionary conference, for which it was felt the time was opportune, though not on the scale of Edinburgh 1910. Developments of

[1] *Proceedings, 1924* (1925), 5; *Proceedings, 1927*, 9–10; *Report of the General Missionary Conference of Northern Rhodesia, 1931*, 4–5, 149–50; *Report, 1935*, vi–vii, 3–4. For other inter-mission conferences see Beach and Fahs, op. cit., 56.

[2] E. W. Smith, *The Christian Mission in Africa: A Study based on the work of the International Conference at Le Zoute, Belgium, September 14th to 21st 1926* (1926), *passim*. Papers in preparation had been published in the *International Review of Missions.—I.R.M.*, XV (1926), 323–590.

[3] E. W. Smith *op. cit.*, 108–26. A Roman Catholic comment on the concern of the conference with social and economic questions was to the effect that the Protestant missionary " now tries to create an environment rather than to save individual souls. World evangelism requires a change of sanitation quite as much as a change of heart ".—Quoted in R. Oliver, *The Missionary Factor in East Africa*, 276, n. 2.

[4] E. W. Smith, *op. cit.*, 118. *Books for Africa*, the Quarterly Bulletin of the Committee, was first issued in January 1931. While the original proposal of such an appointment was a recommendation at Le Zoute, the Committee, as a sub-committee of the I.M.C., was actually constituted at a meeting of the Council in Williamstown, U.S.A., in July 1929.—*Books for Africa*, I (1931), 1.

organization in the post-war years determined its form. In June 1920 the first international post-war meeting was held at Crans by Lake Geneva, representative of missionary organizations in North America, Great Britain, the Continent of Europe, and South Africa. Here proposals for an international missionary Council were brought forward and a draft constitution recommended to the national organizations. Approval was given, and in October 1921 the first International Missionary Council came into being at Lake Mohonk in New York State. A second meeting was held at Oxford in July 1923.[1] When the desirability of another world conference was clear, it was agreed that it should take the form of an enlarged meeting of the International Missionary Council. This meeting took place in April 1928 at Jerusalem. Its total membership of 231 was less than a quarter of that at Edinburgh, but in one significant feature it showed a marked advance: fifty-two of its members, or nearly one-fourth of the Conference, repre-sented the Younger Churches as they were now called.[2]

The topics discussed at Jerusalem also reflected the new concerns of missions.[3] It was but natural that the situation in Africa should not be to the fore at the meeting since at Le Zoute two years earlier an international conference had been devoted exclusively to the affairs of that continent. But in two of the sub-jects for discussion Africa was particularly concerned: the papers presented on race conflict included a delineation of the South African situation by Dexter Taylor of the American Board; Max Yergan of South Africa addressed the conference on the subject; while D. D. T. Jabavu pointed out the stark situation: " One of the great difficulties in the way of black people in South Africa building up their own Church is the feeling that even under Christian missions there is no equality in Church or State. Islam

---

[1] *I.R.M.*, XV (1926), 68–70; W. Richey Hogg, *Ecumenical Foundations* (1952), 195–210.

[2] I owe this figure to Professor R. Pierce Beaver, formerly Director of the Missionary Research Library, New York, who has made a careful assessment of the available evidence. Africa was represented by four Africans and five Westerners.—*I.R.M.*, XVIII (1929), 37. The sequence of international Christian conferences at this time was indicative of the activity of the ecumenical movement: Stockholm (1925), Le Zoute (1926), Lausanne (1927), Jerusalem (1928).

[3] These topics were: (1) The Christian Message in relation to non-Christian Systems; (2) Religious Education; (3) The Relation between the Younger and Older Churches; (4) The Christian Mission in the Light of Race Conflict; (5) The Christian Mission in relation to Industrial Problems; (6) The Christian Mission in relation to Rural Problems; (7) International Missionary Co-operation.

is gaining more adherents because of the attitude on this question." [1] In the consideration of the Christian Mission in relation
to growing industrialism Africa stood with Asia as a principal
theatre involved. Not only was the conference fortunate in the
presence of H. A. Grimshaw, Chief of the Native Labour Section
of the International Labour Office at Geneva, but it reached the
conclusion that an adequately staffed Bureau of Social and
Economic Research and Information should be set up in connexion with the International Labour Office as well as with
appropriate Christian organizations. In the event the Bureau's first
major piece of field research was concerned with the Copperbelt
then developing in Central Africa.[2]

The years 1918–28 were for Christian missions in Africa a
crowded decade. Emerging from the sombre shadows of an intensive four years' war, hope soon revived that the interrupted progress
might be resumed. And in a sense it was, but in an Africa that had
now begun to move into a new day almost at breakneck speed, so
that, for example, Africans of the Congo, who had never seen an
engine until the railway reached Katanga in 1910, were in 1926
driving locomotives and handling railway signals.[3] If on the one
hand a more acute situation in race relations loomed ahead through
the hustling European's temptation to exploit the African as one
of Africa's resources, yet on the other governments were at last
awake to their responsibilities in education and the missions no
longer bore almost the total burden. And whereas the multiplica-
tion of African Christian sects was an ominous sign of the times,
reflecting a deep discontent with the white man's behaviour as a
superior even in Christian relations, yet the steady pull throughout
the decade towards co-operation and international consultation
was a counter-balancing source of strength.

On the whole, then, the sky was clearing, and a brighter day
might reasonably be expected, despite the impoverishment by war
of the major nations of Europe both in material resources and in
the natural leaders of the future.[4] But once again the African sky
was to be overcast by threatening cloud from Europe.

[1] *Jerusalem Meeting Report* (1928), IV, 93–141, 217–20, 223.
[2] *Ibid.*, V, 78–87, 146–56, 191–2.
[3] E. W. Smith, *The Golden Stool* (1926), 52.
[4] Cf. T. Tatlow, *The Story of the Student Christian Movement* (1933),
xii–xiii.

CHAPTER 4

A DIFFICULT DECADE
1928–1938

THE second decade of the post-war period dawned over Africa less cheerfully than had been hoped, and by the time it closed warnings of world war were once again flashing from the European horizon. The decade was ushered in with an economic depression which rapidly assumed world dimensions and became so severe among the industrialized peoples of the West as to warrant its description as an economic blizzard. A spectacular business collapse in the United States in 1929–30 was followed by the financial crisis in Great Britain in 1931. Thus the two major creditors of the post-war debtor nations were both seriously incapacitated and could no longer advance loans to enable their clients to maintain the façade of regular repayment. In Africa the fall in world prices affected both the peasant producer of raw materials and the colonial revenue derived in the main from customs dues on imported goods. The missions in general were thus subject to a threefold financial constriction: depleted funds from the home authorities, severely straitened resources in their local constituency, and drastically reduced grants for education from falling government revenues.

Coupled with the economic handicap came steady deterioration in international affairs. Upon a scene where so much to inspire hope and renew courage had already begun to appear—notably in the valiant efforts to make the League of Nations an effective instrument for international collaboration [1]—there now

---

[1] While the provisions for dealing with threatening political situations were negative to the extent that their purpose was the prevention of war, there were collateral organizations whose object was co-operation with the positive purpose of improving existing world conditions, such as the World Health Organization and the International Labour Office. Both of these had begun to serve African interests admirably across existing political frontiers. Cf. *The International Labour Organization of the League of Nations*, No. 96 of League of Nations Union issues (1922); *The World's Health and the League of Nations*, No. 174, L.N.U. (1925); C. A. Macartney, *Refugees: The Work of the League* (1931), and other issues.

came down, as the decade advanced, heavy clouds of fear and foreboding. A shaft or two of light on rare occasions led incurable optimists to think the sky was still clearing but the realities of the situation grew steadily darker. Dictators in Europe were on the move and to all appearance were having things much their own way, with Abyssinia an early victim. With a not unnatural prefer- ence to realize their expansionist programmes without open con- flict, they were nevertheless clearly prepared to go to war if the auspices proved favourable, and made no bones about their armed preparedness. And the decade was barely out before the event happened and the mightiest death-grapple in human history had begun.

If for Africa there were thus troubles without there were also stresses within. The racial situation grew more acute in south and east with an expressed European determination to maintain cultural supremacy by means of political power, while the African reaction was a keener nationalism among the more politically minded, tempered with a realization that the yoke of Europeans on the spot, with all their faults, was to be preferred to the mailed fist of a scornful dictator. Together with this racial tension was the fast mounting tempo of social change in African communities with the many problems of readjustment that were involved.

It was under such conditions that the Christian mission pursued its task and pursued it with purpose : the young Churches that had begun to appear were nurtured, some re-orientation to the African cultural heritage was increasingly accepted together with the necessity of ministering to the pressing need of a sorely disordered society, while the steady drawing together of the non-Roman missions, as in Christian Councils and co-operative undertakings, found expression at the end of the decade through a more effective sharing than heretofore in a world conference—the Tambaram Meeting of December 1938.

(1) *Dictators on the Move*

The dictatorships that arose in Italy and Germany were both actively concerned in African affairs : Italy in developing her holdings in North and East Africa and in acquiring control of Abyssinia; Germany in the recovering of her lost African colonies, at least as a first step. In both cases there were repercussions on missionary work : in Abyssinia in the elimination of non-Roman missions; and in colonial areas where German missionaries were established, their eventual removal for the second time within a generation.

The Italian dictator was the first to come to power and the first to plot an aggressive advance. Benito Mussolini established in 1919 an unofficial organization of " blackshirts " whom he named the Fascisti as reminiscent of the ancient Roman symbol of authority, the lictor's *fasces*. On October 30, 1922 he marched on Rome and assumed control of the State. Liberalism was submerged in the rising tide and Mussolini was soon *Il Duce* throughout the land. For a decade he devoted himself to the resuscitation of his country from its baleful post-war depression, and won both enthusiastic devotion at home and reluctant admiration abroad by the almost Roman splendour of his achievement. A powerful buttress to the régime was secured in 1929 by the Concordat with Pius XI whereby the acute differences between Church and State surviving from Garibaldi's day were at last allayed and the miniature political unit of the Vatican State came into existence. The home front being thus made secure, attention could more readily be given to adventure overseas.[1]

Italian colonial ambitions were long-standing : " It was in 1838 that Mazzini claimed North Africa for Italy—for the Italy that was not yet in being; and ever since the idea has lain at the back of every Italian statesman's mind." [2] With the French occupation of Tunis—to the intense chagrin of Italy—and the British control of Egypt, Italian attention was directed to Tripolitania as her share of the North African littoral. In the end she declared war on Turkey in September 1911.[3] By October 1912 the war was over, though Arab resistance still continued, and Italy had once more set foot on territory that was strewn along the coastline with ruins of imperial Rome.[4] But the World War interrupted the process of pacification which was thus not finally complete until 1929.[5] In due course 18,000 Italian settlers crossed the Mediterranean to a new home. Within ten years, by 1939, there were some 35,000 Italian colonists, in what was henceforth described as Libya, with Tripolitania and Cyrenaica as constituent provinces. This influx of Italian colonists in their tens of thousands naturally brought the Roman Catholic constituency in Libya to a higher level, but the increase was balanced by a corresponding fall in Italy itself. As far as any advance among the Muslim Arabs

[1] H. A. L. Fisher, *A History of Europe*, III (1935), 1193–5.
[2] W. K. McClure, *Italy in North Africa: An Account of the Tripoli Enterprise* (1913), 4.
[3] For antecedent diplomatic exchanges and the real reasons behind the invasion, see McClure, *op. cit.*, 19–37.
[4] For the campaign and its sequel, see McClure, *op. cit., passim.*
[5] *Vide supra*, p. 52.

was concerned, this was farther off than ever through their deep resentment at the Italian invasion.[1]

With the new colony at last pacified and on the way to organization and development, attention could be directed more freely to Italian interests in East Africa. Here the first establishments had been made in the 'eighties, with the Italian colony of Eritrea appearing in 1890, together with some control of the coast of what later became Italian Somaliland. In the attempt to establish by force a protectorate over the independent Kingdom of Abyssinia, Italy had courted disaster: events moved swiftly to a climax of catastrophe for Italian arms at Adowa in 1896.[2] The humiliation was deep and was not forgotten. This is not to say that Mussolini had planned a dramatic military *coup* to seize Abyssinia when the time was opportune, but the determination to make the country an Italian dependency was not in doubt. However, in the post-war scene there was a new factor in the international situation : the League of Nations with headquarters at Geneva. Abyssinia had applied for membership and been admitted in 1923.[3] The Regent, Haile Selassie, on whose initiative the step was taken, was crowned Emperor in 1930. His confidence in the League, as a guarantee of security for his country's independence against Italy's pretensions, was sadly misplaced. The first major blow to the League's authority in the political field was the uncensured invasion of Manchuria by Japan—a signal to an alert dictator that, despite the League, aggression could succeed. The fact that in 1928 Italy had taken the initiative in concluding a Treaty of Amity with Abyssinia need be no hindrance.

On October 3, 1935 the undeclared war began with the advance of an Italian army from Eritrea on Adowa, while a second advance was attempted from Italian Somaliland. On October 7 the Council and on October 11 the Assembly of the League named Italy as an aggressor, and the question of the application of economic sanctions was then set for consideration. In the upshot they were never applied to oil—the only article still vital to Mussolini's campaign—and the indispensable transport of troops and munitions through the Suez Canal was left unhindered. To its weaker members this became a test case of the authority and effectiveness of the League in a political crisis. Why France and Great Britian, already well apprised of Italian intentions, should

---

[1] C. Hollis, *Italy in Africa* (1941), 84–91.
[2] See Vol. III, p. 42.
[3] France had proposed the nomination and Italy supported. Great Britain opposed.

have deliberately practised benevolent neutrality (for export of weapons and munitions of war to Abyssinia was banned strictly enough) was due to, though not condoned by, a complexity of causes of which the rise of Hitler to armed power in Germany was not the least.

The advance of the well-equipped Italian armies against Abyssinian levies, still trusting pathetically to their nineteenth-century weapons, could not be withstood, nor indeed even delayed. For all their native courage the Abyssinians were at the mercy of the bomber planes, and when poison gas was sprayed upon them they were blistered into agonizing dispersion. Within seven months the Italians were in Addis Ababa and Haile Selassie went into exile.[1]

While admirers of Fascism lauded an Italian conquest, others were repelled, not to say horrified, by the callous cruelty of the Italian attack upon a brave people defending their homeland from invasion. Vittorio Mussolini, the Duce's son, even found it a jest.[2] De Bono, in command of the first advance from Eritrea, had waged a relatively humane war. Under his successor, Badoglio, came an intensive ferocity expressed not only in indiscriminate bombing but in the use of poison gas. The Geneva Convention of 1925, to which Italy was a party, had prohibited its use, but this was no deterrent. The date was Sunday, December 22, 1935: " For the first time in the history of the world, a people supposedly white used poison gas upon a people supposedly savage. Some were blinded. When others saw the burns spread upon their arms and legs and felt the increasing pain . . . they broke and fled. . . . Experiments in the burning of Ethiopians from the air were opened on all fronts." [3] On Tuesday May 5, 1936 Marshal Badoglio entered Addis Ababa at the head of the victorious Italian army and in due course the Italian Empire of Ethiopia was proclaimed.[4]

[1] For the detailed story of a war correspondent see G. L. Steer, *Caesar in Abyssinia* (1936), *passim;* and for the whole story, from preliminary political moves to final occupation, G. T. Garratt, *Mussolini's Roman Empire* (1938), 9–121. Steer was correspondent of *The Times*, Garratt of the *Manchester Guardian*. Documents relevant to the Italian aggression will be found in: S. Heald (ed.), *Documents on International Affairs, 1935*, II (1937).

[2] " One group of horsemen gave me the impression of a budding rose unfolding as the bomb fell in their midst and blew them up. It was exceptionally good fun." Quoted from Vittorio Mussolini's *Flying over Ethiopian Mountain Ranges* in Garratt, *op. cit.*, 102 *n.*

[3] Steer, *op. cit.*, 233; cf. 279, 283.

[4] *Ibid.*, 399–403.

The continued presence of Christian missions in Abyssinia was now no longer dependent on the goodwill of Haile Selassie but on the consent of the Italian authority. That the Roman Church should seek to occupy the country in force was to be expected, a country where earlier efforts in the seventeenth and nineteenth centuries had only met with humiliating frustration.[1] A Roman Catholic writer commented on the attitude of Pius XI to the Abyssinian adventure: " He could not have wanted war, and he said so as clearly as possible. It is true that he kept silent—many people think for far too long a time. It is equally true that he wanted to see the spread of Catholicism in Abyssinia, and he felt that would only be possible with the support of Italy." [2] While the Pope did not himself bless the Italian armies, " he raised no finger to stop Italian bishops up and down the country from going on Fascist platforms and doing everything possible to support the Italian arms ".[3] After the conquest, however, he declared the pleasure of the Vatican in " the triumphal happiness of a great and good people ".[4] Roman Catholics outside Italy seem to have been generally favourable to Italian action but there were some critical comments.[5] The opportunity presented by the conquest however was welcomed with enthusiasm; Cardinal Tisserend was reported in October 1936 as declaring: " The work of the Catholic missionary will nobly go hand in hand with the civilizing actions which Italy, under the Fascist government, has already begun in order to restore to the people the civilization of Rome." [6] The same month the advance guard of Italian missionaries left Italy for Abyssinia—members of the Sacred Heart of Verona.[7]

The position of the non-Roman missions by contrast appeared

[1] See Vol. I, 138–42; II, 85–90, 291–2; III, 172–3.

[2] W. Teeling, *The Pope in Politics: The Life and Work of Pope Pius XI* (1937), 128–9, quoted in Garratt, *op. cit.*, 106.

[3] Teeling, *op. cit.*, 129, quoted in Garratt, 106. Some ten Italian archbishops, along with other prelates, aligned themselves with Mussolini in approving the invasion as a beneficent enterprise, the Cardinal Archbishop of Milan claiming that the Italian armies were opening " the doors of Ethiopia to the Catholic Faith and the civilization of Rome."—A. J. Toynbee, *Survey of International Affairs, 1935*, II (1936), 104.

[4] A. J. Toynbee, *Ibid.*, 105.

[5] As in the magazine of the Belgian university missionary movement known as *Aucam* (=*Academica Unio Catholicas Adjuvans Missiones*).—*International Review of Missions*, XXV (1936), 97.

[6] *I.R.M.*, XXVI (1937), 60.

[7] *Ibid.*, 100. " Italian missionaries," said Cardinal Tisserend, " will gradually be substituted for former missionaries of non-Italian nationality." —*Ibid.*, 60.

at the time somewhat precarious to say the least. The Vatican view, as reported to have been expressed by the Pope to a meeting of cardinals convened to discuss church organization in Abyssinia, was to the effect that the two main obstacles to be confronted were " the activity of numerous Protestant sects ' which prevents souls from reaching the truth ' and the activity of Islam ".[1] The fact that religious toleration was declared to be the policy of the Fascist state led some to hope for continuance, but in the event most evangelical missionaries had to leave. Some half-dozen missions had been at work in the country with the approval of the Emperor —Swedish, American, Canadian, British, and German. The Evangelical National Missionary Society of Sweden had begun work in Eritrea in 1866,[2] moving into the north of Abyssinia in 1870. In 1903 they had opened work in Harar in the south. In both Harar and Addis Ababa their educational work was notable for its influence on many who were destined for the public service of their country. With the Italian occupation in 1936 they received notice to quit.[3] Missionaries of the Swedish Bibeltrogna Vänner mission were also ordered to leave.[4] The American United Presbyterians had pioneered in western Abyssinia and then begun work in Addis Ababa in 1922 where they opened the second hospital to be established in the capital.[5] Haile Selassie had presented the site and encouraged both hospital and schools.[6] Under the Italian authorities the hospital was at first allowed to continue under Presbyterian auspices, but when they proceeded to expropriate it the American missionaries were compelled to leave. Those at work at Goré and Soya in western Abyssinia were also expelled and Roman Catholic workers took over their premises. The 300 communicants of the mission with four times that number of adherents then built their own church and supplied five preaching stations.[7]

The Sudan Interior Mission had also given educational and medical service for which Haile Selassie granted all facilities.[8] A

[1] *I.R.M.*, XXVII (1938), 103.   [2] See Vol. II, p. 292.
[3] C. Sandford, *Ethiopia under Haile Selassie* (1946), 63–4, 68: *I.R.M.*, XXVI (1937), 59. Two Swedish missionaries, however, were allowed to remain in Eritrea.—*I.R.M.*, XXX (1941), 60.
[4] *I.R.M.*, XXVI (1937), 59.
[5] The Menelik Hospital was the first, begun under the auspices of the Russian Red Cross in the late nineteenth century.—Sandford, *op. cit.*, 64.
[6] *Ibid.*, 65, 68.
[7] *I.R.M.*, XXVI (1937), 59; XXVII (1938), 63; XXVIII (1939), 53; XXIX (1940), 67.
[8] The S.I.M., which had its headquarters in Toronto, was first organized as such in 1901 though its pioneer work in the Sudan had begun in 1893.— Beach and Fahs, *World Missionary Atlas* (1925), 18.

medical centre for the treatment of leprosy, in charge of a Canadian surgeon with twelve nurses, was started in 1934. With the change of régime in 1936 the leader of the mission took up Italian citizenship, and the work continued for a couple of years; twenty missionaries were still at work in 1937, but in 1938 property was expropriated and compensation paid but further sites refused, so the remaining seven missionaries then withdrew.[1] The Seventh Day Adventists, who had entered the country as early as 1907, had also been welcomed for their medical work, and especially the Zauditu Memorial Hospital under the patronage of the empress, which was opened under their auspices in 1934. They too soon shared the fate of other Protestant workers.[2] The Germans of the Hermannsburg mission were at first also compelled to withdraw, but after three years two of their number returned to find the work had been well maintained in their absence.[3] The Bible Churchmen's Missionary Society had been one of the last to commence operations before the Italian invasion.[4] First entering in 1933, by the end of the following year the Society had twelve British missionaries in the country. In contrast to the policy of the other Protestant Societies in working among pagan, Muslim, and Jewish sections of the population, they followed the earlier policy of the Church Missionary Society in Egypt and Abyssinia in seeking to reform and revivify the ancient national Church.[5] For this reason they described themselves as Helpers of Ethiopia, and to avoid any suggestion of proselytizing they had no ordained Anglican amongst them. With headquarters in the capital, the next station was begun at Asbe Tafari, half-way mark on the railway to Jibuti, and a third at Fiche in the mountains, sixty miles north of Addis Ababa. For barely four years the work went on, when in 1937 the blow fell with the expulsion of British missionaries from the country.[6]

[1] Sandford, op. cit., 65–6; I.R.M., XXVI (1937), 59; XXVII (1938), 63; XXVIII (1939), 53.

[2] Sandford, op. cit., 65, 68.

[3] I.R.M., XXVI (1937), 59; XXIX (1940), 66–7; Bulletin of the I.M.C., No. 58 (April 1938), vi.

[4] The Society had its origin in 1922 as a secession from the Church Missionary Society on doctrinal grounds, more particularly with reference to the authority of the Bible. See W. S. Hooton and J. Stafford Wright, The First Twenty-five Years of the Bible Churchmen's Missionary Society (1922–47), 3–14. Alfred B. Buxton, who with C. T. Studd had pioneered the Heart of Africa Mission, had joined the B.C.M.S. and served as a missionary of the Society in Abyssinia during 1934–6.—N. P. Grubb, Alfred Buxton of Abyssinia and Congo (1942), 85–6, 132–55.

[5] See Vol. I, p. 309.   [6] Hooton and Wright, op. cit., 107–12.

The British and Foreign Bible Society was able to continue its establishment in the capital despite various vicissitudes. In the period of riot and looting in Addis Ababa between Haile Selassie's departure and the arrival of the Italian advance-guard on May 5, 1936 there was destruction of property and stock exceeding £600 in amount. In July the British agent was ordered to leave, but his wife was permitted to remain in charge until March 1938 when an Italian agent—a Baptist pastor—arrived to take control. As required by Italian law, the centre became a sub-agency of the Bible Society office in Rome. While therefore the agency continued to function, it was much hampered by the fact that the various Protestant missionaries, through whom distribution of the Scriptures had taken place, had now almost all left the country. The total circulation, including portions, fell from 17,333 in 1936 to 5,306 in 1938.[1]

The national church of the country was not left without some attention from the new rulers. The *abuna* was traditionally appointed by the Patriarch of Alexandria.[2] When the new *abuna*, Qerillos V, came to the office in 1929 five Ethiopian monks were consecrated as suffragans on condition they did not themselves proceed to consecrate bishops. Two of these were executed by the Italians on political grounds, but they did not wish to commit themselves to a policy of persecution. J. S. Trimingham has summarized Italian policy as the attempt " at one and the same time to undermine the Church's influence and to win it over to accept the fact of Fascist control ".[3] In this connexion the *abuna* Qerillos was invited to Rome to consider terms of separation of the national Church from the Patriarchate of Alexandria. These he refused and being therefore not permitted to return, retired to Cairo. The Italians replaced him by Abraham, one of the surviving suffragans, who was forthwith excommunicated by the Patriarch of Alexandria. On Abraham's death in 1939 his successor Mikhail, another of the suffragans, was likewise excommunicated. As these two are said to have consecrated some dozen bishops who in their

---

[1] *The Hundred and Thirty-third Report of the British and Foreign Bible Society* (1937), 125–6; *The Hundred and Thirty-fourth Report* (1938), 27; *The Hundred and Thirty-fifth Report* (1939), 25–6. Of the 1936 total 5,048 were free grants to Ethiopian soldiers.

[2] " Until recent years the Ethiopians accepted as genuine an apocryphal decree of the Council of Nicaea which constituted Ethiopia a single bishopric of the Patriarchate of Egypt."—J. S. Trimingham, *The Christian Church and Missions in Ethiopia* (1950), 17.

[3] Trimingham, *op. cit.*, 19.

turn ordained about 2,000 priests, the affairs of the Church were brought into some confusion.[1]

In pursuit of its declared policy of religious liberty the Italian Government encouraged the Waldensian Church of northern Italy to send its ministers to Abyssinia. Two were serving as chaplains by 1939 and in the following year the Waldensian mission was reported to have organized four churches in Addis Ababa with regular services conducted in Italian and Amharic.[2]

If these were the direct effects of the occupation on the Christian mission, the indirect effects, though less susceptible of precise statement, were of no less moment to the Christian cause on a wider front. The Italian action, claiming to be a mission of civilization with Divine countenance, was at the least embarrassing and often enough distressing to the Christian enterprise. One instance of the claim was the pamphlet by Badoglio, copies of which were dropped on Addis Ababa on April 27, 1936 : " People of Shoa, listen ! I am the head of the victorious Italian Army, and will enter Addis Ababa with the help of God. . . . These leaflets should be a greeting to the Ethiopian people. I do not want the Christian Ethiopian people to be destroyed. We bring peace and civilization. But if you destroy our roads or try to oppose the advance of my Army, then the Italian Army will destroy and kill without pity, the aeroplanes will massacre from the air and destroy everything that exists." [3] And after the experience of blasting harmless villagers from the air, of spraying poison gas, and of bombing Red Cross hospitals and transport, this threat of frightfulness was known to be no idle boast. Such news is not slow of foot in Africa. Throughout the continent the Italian achievement was bruited and its manner duly noted. Refugees seeking asylum in Kenya and in French and British Somaliland were firsthand reporters.[4] From the highly developed peoples of the Gold Coast, where it was reported that events in Abyssinia had seriously discredited western Christendom in the eyes of the educated, to the more restricted Bantu of the Union of South Africa, where groups of

[1] I.R.M., XXX (1941), 60; Trimingham, op. cit., 19–20.
[2] I.R.M., XXIX (1940), 67; XXX (1941), 60. A decade earlier, in 1930, the Italian Government, while severely restricting Swedish missionaries in the neighbouring Eritrea, had invited Waldensians to enter to the number of nineteen.—I.R.M., XIX (1930), 46; XX (1931), 48.
[3] G. L. Steer, Caesar in Abyssinia, 8–9.
[4] Some 10,000 refugees had entered Kenya by 1938. Their interests were cared for by the Bible Churchmen's Missionary Society, which did the same for groups in French and British Somaliland.—I.R.M., XXVII (1938), 70; XXVIII (1939), 61; Hooton and Wright, op. cit., 112.

Zulu warriors on the one hand and of Bantu students on the other sought to offer for service in the war, the story was the same.[1] It was a grave event in African history—whether for the tortuous political evasions at Geneva or the callous and horrific use of the resources of " civilization " during the campaign—a grave event for the Christian Church of Western Europe to outlive. In Africa memories are long.

The German dictator's intervention in African affairs during the decade was less direct but none the less definite. The claim for restoration of the African colonies lost in the World War found in him a spokesman who commanded universal attention, while a policy of steady Nazi infiltration sought to prepare the way for a resumption of German rule under National Socialist auspices.

Adolph Hitler, surveying his country laid low in defeat, had dedicated himself to raising it once again to power. He has been described as " a tough, resentful, visionary figure, half crazy with anti-Semitism . . . but disinterested, patriotic, and charged with Teutonic pride ".[2] His National Socialist brownshirts, currently termed Nazis,[3] with a fanatical faith in the fatherland, failed in 1923 in their bid for power by a revolutionary outbreak. Hitler was now in prison and used his enforced leisure to write the Nazi classic, *Mein Kampf*. He emerged, a hero to many, with a determination to secure power by more constitutional means though not foregoing gangster methods. He made amazing progress : by 1933 he was Chancellor of the Reich, and, when the aged President von Hindenburg died in August 1934, was finally approved by the German people—an overwhelming majority was claimed— as their national leader. *Der Führer* now matched his erstwhile

[1] *I.R.M.*, XXVI (1937), 63, 76. A French observer wrote: " Tous les noirs la suivent avec passion "; and an Englishman, that Africans were waiting to see " whether the Church will use its influence to secure that the black man has a fair deal ".—*Ibid.*, 76. A. J. Toynbee, after noting Muslim and Hindu sympathy with Christian Abyssinia in her distress, has reviewed the immediate unhappy reactions in Africa, and among peoples of African descent elsewhere.—A. J. Toynbee, *Survey of International Affairs, 1935*, II (1936), 108–112.

[2] H. A. L. Fisher, *A History of Europe*, III (1935), 1195–6.

[3] Dr. Konrad Braun informs me that as Sozi was a common nickname for Socialists, being a convenient abbreviation of Sozialisten, so Nazi was formed by analogy for National-sozialisten, though the term was not recognized by the party but only used by their critics and opponents. It was in use from 1920 when the swastika as the party badge first appeared. Mass meetings were organized in Munich from 1921.

model *Il Duce*. He was at last firmly seated in the saddle as master of a German totalitarian state.[1]

Hitler had not commended himself to Africans by his disparaging references in *Mein Kampf* to the Negro race. The effort expended on "primitive and inferior" people by Christian missionaries, "annoying the negroes with missions which they neither wish nor understand", would be far better spent, he had contended, on the superior and capable European. He charged it as "a criminal absurdity to train a born half-ape until one believes a lawyer has been made of him", and denounced as a sin against the Creator neglect of the race of highest cultural standard "while Hottentots and Zulu Kafirs are trained for intellectual vocations. For it is training, exactly as that of the poodle, and not a ' scientific ' education ".[2] While the anti-Semitic animus of Hitler lay in a different category, yet his policy with regard to Jews made plain enough how the master race would treat those it despised when once in its power.

The mandated territory of South-West Africa, by reason of its larger German population than those of the other ex-German colonies in Africa, received special attention. Nazi activities first started in 1929, but with Hitler's rise to the first stage of power in 1933 they were intensified, Nazi organizations in South-West Africa being closely linked with the party in Germany. In the closing months of 1934 the Administrator of the territory banned both the Hitler Youth movement and the Nazi movement as subversive organizations.[3] A South-West Africa Commission, appointed by the Union Government to inquire into constitutional and other issues, reported that Nazi activities were continuing much as before, though not under their name.[4] On the basis of evidence submitted to them it was alleged that "the Germans of South-West Africa have been successfully seduced from their allegiance to the mandatory Power ".[5] The Union Government determined to take firm action on this issue and in April 1937 a drastic proclamation clamped down on political activities that involved disloyalty to the mandatory authority. There were at that very time some 600 young Germans from the territory, under

[1] H. A. L. Fisher, *op. cit.*, III, 1195-1206.
[2] Adolf Hitler, *Mein Kampf* (complete and unabridged translation, Reynal and Hitchcock, New York, 1939), 607-8, 640. Cf. 90, 244, 385.
[3] *The Round Table*, XXV (1935), 425-8.
[4] *Report of the South-West Africa Commission* (Union Government 26 of 1936).
[5] The South Africa correspondent of *The Round Table*, XXVI (1936), 780.

oath of fealty to Hitler, known as the "South-West African National Group", who were receiving so-called "vocational training" in Germany. They were engaged in organizing a "Corporation of Patriots" which was to be the core of a Germanic community in the territory. The whole procedure was bluntly described as conspiracy.[1] And despite the Union's proclamation the activity continued so that in July 1938 it was reported that "the greater part of the German population, naturalised and unnaturalised, has been regimented into an elaborate system of cells and groups, with their *Führers*, in ascending ranks, under the ultimate leadership of the appropriate division of the German Foreign Office".[2] If Berlin bestowed its greatest attention on South-West Africa it did not neglect its interests elsewhere. Indeed, the whole Nazi campaign for the restoration of colonies provoked a sharp refusal from France to surrender these points of vantage for air bases, which would in effect deliver the whole of Africa north of the Zambezi into the hands of the two dictators.[3]

German missionaries in the colonies were thus put to the test as to their loyalties. While the outside world was deeply shocked at the "blood-bath" of June 30, 1934 when leading terrorists who were Hitler's comrades were ruthlessly liquidated, and at the murder of the Austrian President, Dollfuss, at Nazi instigation, in Germany those who felt the shame of it were overborne by the wave of nationalist enthusiasm that acclaimed a great deliverer, if not indeed a veritable Messiah. "These atrocities," wrote H. A. L. Fisher within a year of the events, "reminiscent of the Roman Empire in the third century, were condoned. It was sufficient that Hitler, the wild hero of Wagnerian opera, stood for a Germany proud, united, and defiant. When in the spring of 1935 he suddenly restored conscription in breach of the Versailles Treaty, an hysterical paroxysm of delight shook the country." [4] Those missionaries who were not pacifist by conviction not unnaturally shared for the most part their countrymen's enthusiasm, and were often enough devoted admirers of their *Führer* as a deliverer raised up for the resuscitation of the German people. They pointed to his social policies at home—care for the unemployed, Winter Help campaigns, the rescue of German youth from the frustrations

[1] *The Round Table*, XXVII (1937), 863–6.
[2] *Ibid.*, XXVIII (1938), 853–4.
[3] See pamphlet, *Non! nous ne livrerons pas les clefs de l'empire*, with text and two maps in colour by General Tilho, Vice-President of the Academy of Colonial Sciences. This appeared in the issue of *Monde Colonial Illustré* for December 1, 1938.
[4] *Op. cit.*, III, 1206.

of the post-war years—and would reiterate that he cared nothing for himself but always was at the service of the German people. And if it was suggested, for example, that what was euphemistically termed the Jewish elimination was scarcely Christian, this objection was brushed aside with appeal to the distinction between the individual ethic and the state ethic, so that the citizen as citizen could endorse as necessary what his conscience for himself as individual would not approve. If the older German missionaries were for the most part grave and disquieted at the course of events, the younger in all sincerity not infrequently shared the newborn enthusiasm of their generation. And there were those who, having gone abroad before the more brutal persecutions began, were disinclined to believe such news which naturally was not purveyed through the official German sources. It was therefore scarcely to be wondered at that, with the coming of another war, colonial governments made no exception of missionaries when promptly interning German nationals.

(2) *Entrenching Racial Privilege*

While the political drive of the European dictators, acting with mutual understanding as the Axis, was from without an embarrassment to the Christian mission, from within the continent race relations between African and European presented their own peculiar challenge. The earlier emergence of these situations of strain, within what were in due course to be described as multiracial communities, has already been reviewed. It only remains to consider certain developments during the present decade.

In South Africa General Hertzog as Prime Minister boldly grasped the nettle of Bantu status in the Union and in 1926 put before Parliament four related Bills for consideration. These dealt respectively with parliamentary representation, the creation of a Native Council, the provision of land, and the status of the Cape Coloured group in respect to the franchise.[1] The first set out to abolish the existing franchise of the Bantu (never granted in the Free State and the Transvaal and only actual to any extent in the Cape) and to substitute seven constituencies for the whole Union with European representatives for the Assembly, elected on a strictly limited franchise. The second proposed to set up a body authorized to legislate for the Bantu alone in local affairs. The

---

[1] The four were named: The Representation of Natives in Parliament Bill; The Union Native Council Bill; The Natives Land Act, 1913, Amendment Bill; and The Coloured Persons Rights Bill.

third was designed to make more land available for Bantu purchase, while the fourth proposed to extend the franchise in due course to Coloured (half-caste) people throughout the Union. The four Bills were presented as interdependent.[1] It was a sincere attempt to deal with the pressing problem of European-Bantu relations, though from the definitely Nationalist position of race discrimination. In the desire to lift the measures above mere party debate, Hertzog took the unusual course of referring them to a Select Committee of the House in advance of the second reading, in order that a measure of agreement might be reached. But the rock of offence was the determination to abolish the Cape franchise which the Bantu had enjoyed since 1853.[2] Africans in the Free State and Transvaal made it clear that, totally unenfranchised as they then were, they wanted no vote of any kind at the expense of the disappearance of the Bantu franchise in the Cape—a symbol to Africans throughout the Union of equality of citizenship for black and white. Moreover, the Cape franchise for the Bantu was safeguarded in the South Africa Act of the British Parliament, and could therefore only be modified by a two-thirds majority of both Houses in joint session. At such a joint sitting in February 1929 the Bill failed to secure this majority. At the following general election in the same year, with its Native policy as a principal plank in its platform, the Nationalist Party was returned to power with a clear majority.[3] But the campaign had done a deep disservice to race relations; as a competent local observer put it : " It has broadcast among the native peoples the impression that the white man lives in fear of them as a menace to his existence, and that his only remedy is a policy of repression." [4]

Domestic affairs in the Union before long led to a coalition between the two major parties, Nationalist and South African, in 1933 with Hertzog as Premier and Smuts second-in-command. D. F. Malan remained a dissident Nationalist but willing to serve on his own terms. Meanwhile procedure with the Native Bills was not to be pressed. It was 1936 before the Native Bills, now reduced to two dealing with franchise and land respectively, were

[1] *The Round Table*, XVII (1927), 389–401; E. H. Brookes, " The South African Race Problem in the Light of General Hertzog's Proposed Legislation ", in *I.R.M.*, XVI (1927), 182–91.
[2] While parliamentary institutions had been granted to the Colony in 1853, the first Cape Parliament did not meet until 1854. On the franchise, see E. A. Walker, *A History of South Africa* (1947 edition), 252, *n.* 1.
[3] *The Round Table*, XVIII (1928), 878–80; XIX (1929), 647–51; XX (1930), 416–19.
[4] *Ibid.*, XIX (1929), 873.

on the programme for the session.[1] The Franchise Bill was the contentious measure and it required the statutory two-thirds majority in a joint session. This was secured : the third reading was passed on April 6, 1936 by 169 votes to 11.[2] For a decade the proposed legislation, with modifications, had been before Parliament and was finally enacted by the European in his own favour.

The blow to Bantu aspiration was severe. The so-called Colour Bar Act of 1926 [3] had, it is true, made statutory discrimination in industry on the ground of race alone, but in practice it was not a new departure. Now, on the contrary, a much treasured right which had been enjoyed for upwards of eighty years and was enshrined in the Act of Union itself [4]—a symbol of a possibly wider egalitarian franchise—was taken away. Happily Christian leaders had not remained silent under the threatened injustice but had from time to time registered their protest. At the outset of the struggle there were fearless European spokesmen for Bantu rights.

Sir James Rose Innes, Chief Justice of South Africa 1914–27, has recorded his own reaction : " The proposal was unique in constitutional history. It roused indignation and alarm, not only among the Africans of the Cape Province, but among their fellows throughout the Union. Nor was there lack of European opposition. A manifesto drafted by Professor Freemantle, the Right Hon. Henry Burton, and myself, in consultation with that champion of liberal opinion, the Rev. Mr. Balmforth, became the basis of the Non-Racial Franchise Association formed to oppose any race or colour differentiation between franchise rights in the Cape Province, and to promote the adoption of civilisation as a franchise qualification throughout the Union." [5] He concluded a wise and carefully reasoned statement, delivered at the first meeting under the Association's auspices, with the moral implications of South Africa's choice : " South Africa stands at the parting of the ways. She may take the path of repression, easy at first with its downward

[1] The Coloured Voters' Bill had been dropped and the remaining three resolved into two (the Representation and Council Bills in one and Land in the other) by the joint committee to which they had been referred and which issued its report in May 1935.

[2] The Round Table, XXV (1935), 722–34; XXVI (1936), 535–9.

[3] The Mines and Works Amendment Act, No. 25 of 1926.

[4] E. A. Walker, De Villiers, His Life and Times (1925), 446–7, 470, 471. There were in 1935 some 900,000 voters in the Union of whom some 11,000 were Bantu resident in the Cape Province. In Natal, which nominally admitted non-European voters, only one of African race was reported. The Free State and the Transvaal had never granted the franchise to non-Europeans.—The Round Table, XXV (1935), 725.

[5] B. A. Tindall (ed.), James Rose Innes, Autobiography (1949), 304.

grade, but it leads to the abyss—not in our time, but in the time of our descendants, whose interests it is our sacred duty to guard. Or she may take the path of liberty, rugged and steep and full of difficulty, but it leads to the mountain tops." [1] Three years later, at a National European-Bantu Conference meeting at Cape Town in February 1929, men and women of all races who were assembled recorded their protest against " any alteration of the law which would result in depriving the Natives of the Cape Province of the franchise in its present form ".[2] And at the final contest in Parliament itself there were found at least one Senator and one Minister —Senator F. S. Malan and J. H. Hofmeyr, Minister of the Interior —in the liberal tradition of W. P. Schreiner,[3] to speak the noblest words to be heard in the final debate. Hertzog, with that candour for which the Bantu respected him despite his policies, had frankly stated European self-preservation as the motive,[4] while Smuts, perhaps rather more diplomatically, saw in the new Native Advisory Council " a model for native administration for the continent of Africa ".[5]

F. S. Malan and J. H. Hofmeyr spoke effectively and trenchantly against the measure. And it was a moral and profoundly Christian appeal to fundamental principle that they made, condemning recourse to the argument of self-preservation. The Senator, deprecating the fear of being swamped by the black vote, declared : " There is the golden rule : Do justice and the rest will take care of itself "; while the Minister did not hesitate to quote the Master's words : " Whosoever will save his life shall lose it." [6] These forthright appeals did credit to the Christian name, and, as the Bantu understood it, disclosed honest men who in a crisis were Christian not in word only but in deed and truth.

While this was a major issue of the decade and the government action one which the Bantu most deeply resented, there were also

[1] *Ibid.*, 327. The speech is printed verbatim in Appendix A.

[2] *Bulletin of the I.M.C.*, No. 23 (July 1929), ii.

[3] E. A. Walker, *W. P. Schreiner, A South African* (1937), *passim*.

[4] " The native, whatever his rights, has no claim on us to give him anything that is inconsistent with our own existence."—*The Round Table*, XXVI (1936), 540.

[5] *Ibid.*, 541. The Bantu had been bitterly disappointed at Smuts, as they saw it, deserting their cause, and he became for them " Slim Jan ".

[6] *The Round Table*, XXVI. (1936), 543-4, whose South African correspondent commented: " The fervour and appeal to first principles that informed the speeches of Senator Malan and Mr. Hofmeyr have hardly been heard in our Parliament since the late W. P. Schreiner thundered against the Union franchise compromise and the Native Land Bill of 1913. Even the serried ranks of Tuscany could scarce forbear to cheer."

other occasions when the Christian voice was raised in protest from the European side.[1] And the establishment of the Institute of Race Relations in 1929 was a positive contribution to better racial understanding second to none in its long-term significance. Beginnings are traceable to Dr. J. E. K. Aggrey's visit to South Africa when a member of the Phelps-Stokes Commission, as a result of which inter-racial Councils were set up on the model of inter-racial committees in the Southern States.[2] By 1928 there were some eighteen such councils in South Africa of which the Johannesburg Joint Council was outstanding. When in 1927 the Phelps-Stokes Fund agreed to support an organizer of inter-racial work for a limited period and in 1928 the Carnegie Corporation of New York took a similar step, the Committee under which they proposed to take joint action resolved itself into the South African Institute of Race Relations, of which J. D. Rheinallt Jones became first secretary, a distinguished worker in the field of race relations to which he devoted his life.[3] The influence of the Institute, through its periodical and other publications, in radiating the light of informed reason where all too often the blindness of prejudice had determined decisions, can scarcely be calculated.

[1] As, for example, the Native Service Contract Bill of 1932, which gave Bantu squatters on European farms the choice between becoming vagrants (with the pains and penalties that involved) or serfs-at-will without the security of tenure enjoyed by serfs in a feudal system. It was vigorously attacked by two ex-Chief Justices, James Rose Innes of the Union and Clarkson Tredgold of Southern Rhodesia, " and by the heads of nearly every Christian denomination in the country . . . the whipping clause drew forth a protest from the Missionary Conference of the Dutch Reformed Church ".—*The Round Table*, XXII (1932), 669–72.

[2] *Missions and Race Conflict* (Jerusalem Meeting Report, IV), (1928), 82–92; *The South African Outlook* (April 1934), 71. While the Institute sprang from the Joint Council movement the Councils were not superseded by it, but continued to function locally in useful co-operation with it.

[3] *Ibid.*, IV, 134–5; *Bulletin of I.M.C.*, No. 25 (January 1930), i–ii. Rheinallt Jones arrived in South Africa in 1905 and at once became actively concerned with social welfare. In the decade 1919–29 he was involved in the establishment and development of the University of the Witwatersrand where he lectured on race relations. For five years (1937–42) he was a Senator representing African interests. With the extensive gold mining developments in the Orange Free State, in which the Anglo-American Corporation had large interests, Sir Ernest Oppenheimer invited Rheinallt Jones to become full-time adviser on African welfare for this large group of mines. He accepted the appointment, welcoming the opportunity and the full freedom allowed him to plan for the social welfare of African mineworkers in a new undertaking. He died on January 30th, 1953.—*The Times*, January 31, 1953.

In 1930, the year following the Institute's establishment, came a new Christian adventure in race relations : the Bantu-European Student Christian Conference. There came together from forty-two universities, colleges, and training institutions one hundred and thirty Bantu students, sixty European students, and one hundred and fifty senior people, Bantu and European. It was no extravagance to describe the Conference as unique in its field : the discussion by students of both races in South Africa of the fundamentals of the Christian Faith and their social implications. The mere fact of the Conference was significant, and experience at it a revelation of the possibilities of human relations in a Christ-centred society. The gathering at the Lord's table, in its racial variety yet ecumenical unity, was declared to be memorable as perhaps the first really South African communion service.[1] The World's Student Christian Federation, set up in 1895 under the leadership of John R. Mott,[2] had given, at the Peking Conference of 1922, a larger place than before to the African student field. It was then determined to make a comprehensive investigation of this field, to foster African student movements, and to seek to remove difficulties in the way of American Negroes serving in Africa as Christian missionaries.[3] Max Yergan, the American Negro Secretary of the Bantu Student Christian Association of South Africa, had himself been elected in 1924 a member of the W.S.C.F. Executive Committee, the first person of African descent to be so honoured.[4] It was Max Yergan whose labours brought into being the Bantu-European Conference, with the W.S.C.F. Chairman himself as one of the overseas visitors who came to the Conference from America, Asia, and Europe. Thus the major South African problem was increasingly becoming of interest to the Christian students of the world.

One further strand in the political situation requires mention. There were, embedded in or adjoining Union territory, three British areas, the High Commission Territories of Basutoland, Bechuanaland, and Swaziland. On economic and general grounds it would seem obvious that they should be incorporated in the Union, with the proviso that Bechuanaland, adjoining both the Union and Southern Rhodesia, might on geographical grounds be

---

[1] *The South African Outlook* (August 1930), 146–63; *Christian Students and Modern South Africa*, A Report of the Bantu-European Student Christian Conference, Fort Hare, June 27th-July 3rd, 1930 (1930).
[2] See Vol. III, p. 206.
[3] R. Rouse, *The World's Student Christian Federation (1948)*, 278–9.
[4] *Ibid.*, 298.

assigned in part to each.[1] The Act of Union of 1909 had retained these Territories under the United Kingdom Government, but at the same time had provided for possible transfer at some future date by stipulating conditions designed to safeguard existing African rights.[2] When the Bill was before the British Parliament pledges were given that " Parliament should have the fullest opportunity of discussing and, if they wished, disapproving any proposed transfer of these Territories and also that the wishes of the inhabitants would be ascertained and considered before any transfer took place ".[3] These pledges were re-affirmed on various occasions. The question of transfer was first raised in 1913 and pressed by the Union Government on various subsequent occasions. Meanwhile the Statute of Westminster of 1931 had so far modified the situation that the Union Government was now competent to amend the Schedule to the Act of 1909, but this in no way affected the pledges of the British Government concerning the conditions to be fulfilled before transfer could take place. From 1934 to 1939 General Hertzog steadily pressed the Union case, but the native policy he had been pursuing was not calculated to win the assent of the inhabitants of the Territories, and British opinion was far from reassured as to the possible future actions of the Union Government.[4] In 1938 there was appointed a standing Joint Advisory Conference to " study openings for co-operation . . . and to consider matters of joint concern ".[5] With

[1] On the earlier history of Basutoland see Vol. II, 147–52, 269–70; of Bechuanaland, Vol. II, 159–61; Vol. III, 31–2, 104–5. An exhaustive survey of the financial and economic position of all three Territories was undertaken in 1931–34 by A. W. Pim as Commissioner for the purpose appointed by the Secretary of State for Dominion Affairs. *Financial and Economic Situation of Swaziland*, Cmd. 4114 (1932); *Financial and Economic Position of the Bechuanaland Protectorate*, Cmd. 4368 (1933); *Financial and Economic Position of Basutoland*, Cmd. 4907 (1935).

[2] In the South Africa Act, 1909, Section 151, and the Schedule to the Act. For the text see: *Basutoland, The Bechuanaland Protectorate and Swaziland, History of Discussions with the Union of South Africa, 1909–1939*, Cmd. 8707 (1952), 118–20. The inhabitants of the Territories had in 1909 asked that they should not be included in the proposed Union.—*Ibid.*, 5.

[3] *Ibid.*, 6.

[4] *The Round Table*, XXIV (1934), 785–801; XXV (1935), 746–53; " Memorandum prepared by the Parliamentary Committee for studying the Position of the South African Protectorates ", Supplement to *Journal of the African Society*, October, 1934; M. Perham and L. Curtis, *The Protectorates of South Africa, The Question of their Transfer to the Union* (1935), *passim;* "A Reply to the Propaganda for the Incorporation of the Bechuanaland Protectorate within the Union " by Chief Tshekedi, in *The South African Outlook* (May 1935), 92–5.

[5] Cmd. 8707, 9, 89, 90–8.

the outbreak of war however in September 1939 the whole question of transfer remained in abeyance. When it was taken up again in the post-war period it was in a greatly changed situation.[1]

How far these profoundly disturbing developments, pinning down the Bantu of the Union to a position of permanent inferiority, encouraged the separatist sects—for in this religious sphere at least the Bantu could manage their own affairs—it is scarcely possible to measure, but they certainly continued to increase, expand, and flourish, proud in their independence of the white man's leadership.[2] And for the religious situation in general it has come as a judgment on the discrepancy between the Christian ideal proclaimed and white Christians' practice—all too glaring, alas, in such situations as we have reviewed—that Bantu Christians have followed suit. W. M. Eiselen, writing in 1934, at the close of a discussion of the matter framed the indictment : " It seems to follow that contact with a population of white Christians has raised the quantity and has lowered the quality of Bantu Christians. They have certainly grasped the fact that the missionary's Christian theory and the Europeans' Christian life are two quite different matters; and they are becoming increasingly indifferent to the essentials of Christianity. Native Christians are now following the white man's example in being good Christians when convenient only. From our urban people they have learned that you may be a church member and yet shirk all the responsibility and all the obligations that arise from such membership. From the rural population they have learned that it is possible to distinguish clearly between your Christian duties towards those within your own racial group and towards those outside it." [3]

While in South Africa there was a settled European community with a total history of nearly three centuries, in East Africa European immigrants were new-comers with barely a generation

---

[1] L. B. Greaves, *The High Commission Territories* (1954), *passim*. *Vide infra*, p. 265.

[2] B. G. M. Sundkler has discussed the relation of the colour bar to the rise and development of these independent churches.—B. G. M. Sundkler, *Bantu Prophets in South Africa* (1948), 32–7, 290–1, 295.

[3] W. M. Eiselen, " Christianity and the Religious Life of the Bantu " in I. Schapera (ed.), *Western Civilization and the Natives of South Africa* (1934), 73–4. B. G. M. Sundkler endorses the indictment, and finds the discrepancy most pronounced in the observance of the colour bar within the Christian Church.—*Op. cit.*, 36–7.

to their credit. Yet here also the settlers in the so-called White Highlands of Kenya, or at least the vocal section of them, aspired to make secure their privileged position by obtaining a grant of self-government so that with political power in European hands there would be no risk of repressive interference from Whitehall in developing the territory as a white man's country. On another point than that of length of occupation there was also wide disparity between East and South. Of the South, where the ratio of European to Bantu was approximately 1 to 3, James Rose Innes declared : " South Africa never has been and never can be a white man's country in the literal sense." [1] What then of the claim for Kenya where the ratio of European to African was less than 1 to 200? [2] True, it was the white highlands that were to be kept exclusive, but black labour was essential to success, and so the claim was made, by an active and articulate minority at least, that " there was no solution except to get control of the Colony in our own hands ".[3] The first concrete demand from the settlers for the grant of self-government without undue delay was contained in a memorandum of Delamere's presented to the Colonial Office at the time of the Indian controversy.[4] The Government reply was definite and discouraging.[5] There had followed in 1924–25 the East Africa Commission which had been instructed to include in its purview Northern Rhodesia, Nyasaland, Tanganyika, Uganda, and Kenya. They reported that federation was opposed by African and Indian opinion, in so far as expressed, and was under suspicion by Kenya Europeans, and therefore concluded that any attempt at federation would be premature.[6]

In 1927 there was appointed a Commission specifically to inquire into the desirability of federation or some alternative form of closer union in both Eastern and Central Africa; and to make appropriate recommendations.[7] The personnel consisted of Sir

[1] B. A. Tindall (ed.), op. cit., 319.

[2] In 1929 the Europeans numbered 12,529 and the Africans were estimated at 2,549,300.—Cmd. 3234 (1929), 315.

[3] The Hon. Captain Coney, elected Legislative Councillor, as reported in East African Standard, February 16, 1926. The context is quoted in W. Macgregor Ross, Kenya from Within, 117; cf. 171.

[4] E. Huxley, White Man's Country (1935), II, 153–5. Delamere conceded that African affairs might be reserved to the Secretary of State. Vide supra, p. 100.

[5] Indians in Kenya, Cmd. 1922 (1923), 10.

[6] Report of the East Africa Commission, Cmd. 2387 (1925), 3, 9–10. The chairman of the Commission was W. Ormsby-Gore, later Lord Harlech.

[7] The terms of reference were contained in a White Paper, Future Policy in regard to Eastern Africa, Cmd. 2904 (1927).

E. Hilton Young as chairman, Sir Reginald Mant and Sir George Schuster both with Indian experience, and J. H. Oldham, Secretary to the International Missionary Council—the first time that such an appointment representative of missionary interests had been made. Their report is a document of first-rate importance in the recent history of East Africa, and the sequel was the occasion of further controversy.[1] In a preliminary chapter of fifty pages on the general principles governing the relations between native and immigrant communities, they concluded : " There can be no question of responsible government in these territories until the natives themselves can share in the responsibility, because, until that stage is reached, the Imperial Government will be under obligations of trusteeship which cannot be discharged without reserving a right to intervene in all the business of government." [2] Into the more detailed recommendations of the Commission this is not the place to enter : suffice it to say that the point of view from which they were considered was that of a liberal policy of development for the African peoples while at the same time seeking the economic and general welfare of all other communities.[3] The report was less favourable to the Colonial Secretary's policy than he had anticipated; he now despatched his chief permanent official, Sir Samuel Wilson, to East Africa to discuss the Hilton Young Commission's recommendations with local governments and communities.[4] But on his return a new Government was in office with Lord Passfield as Colonial Secretary. Wilson's report was therefore issued with a disclaimer, and in 1930 Passfield made public his own policy in

[1] *Report of the Commission on Closer Union of the Dependencies in Eastern and Central Africa*, Cmd. 3234 (1929).

[2] *Ibid.*, 83–4; cf. 87. There was thus no encouragement to hope for self-government on a basis of European franchise only, which would in effect be an oligarchy masquerading in the guise of democracy. For a critical view of the Commission and its Report, see E. Huxley, *op. cit.*, II, 223–32.

[3] As an alleged instance of concessions in a public service in the interests of one community, the commissioners reported that African-grown cotton from Uganda was conveyed to the coast 20s. per ton cheaper by rail through Tanganyika than on the much shorter rail haul through Kenya, and added: " Critics of the Nairobi management say that high rates have to be charged on native cotton from Uganda in order to enable the railways to carry maize produced by Kenya settlers at less than cost price ".— *Report*, 63.

[4] *Report of Sir Samuel Wilson on his Visit to East Africa, 1929*, Cmd. 3378 (1929). Elspeth Huxley's frank comment is apposite: " Mr. Amery lost no time in trying to pull his federal baby out of the fire before it was too badly burned to survive. He despatched . . . Sir Samuel Wilson . . . His task, in fact, was to tone down the commission's findings to a pitch to which local agreement could be secured ".—*White Man's Country*, II, 232.

two simultaneous White Papers: *Memorandum on Native Policy in East Africa*, which caused more than a flutter in the European dovecotes by its insistence on the paramountcy of African interests when these and those of European immigrant communities were in conflict; and a statement of the course the Government proposed to pursue in the appointment of a Joint Committee of both Houses before which any interested parties could appear.[1]

The sittings of the Joint Committee lasted from December 4, 1930 to September 30, 1931, and secured wide publicity. On the declaration, made both in 1923 and in 1930, that in Kenya the interests of Africans must be paramount, they pointed out that " this broad statement of native rights " was qualified in subsequent paragraphs which stated that the interests of other communities must severally be safeguarded—a qualification made both in 1923 and 1930.[2] On the political issue of African representation the Committee stated they had been much impressed by the ability of the Africans who had given evidence before them and added that " the time may well come, if the unitary system of government is maintained, when the most suitable representation for the African will be by members of their own community ".[3] Meanwhile they urged a more rapid development of Native Councils, particularly in Kenya, to enable Africans of ability to be trained for such duties. They added that they attached " special importance, in the case of Kenya, to the handing over, at the earliest practicable moment, of new functions, in proportion to the advance in interest and in capacity made by any particular council ".[4]

[1] *Memorandum on Native Policy in East Africa*, Cmd. 3573 (1930); *Statement of the Conclusions of His Majesty's Government in the United Kingdom as regards Closer Union in East Africa*, Cmd. 3574 (1930). When it was pointed out that the statement on paramountcy of African interests was simply repeated from the Duke of Devonshire's White Paper of 1923, it was retorted that Passfield's reproduction was unnecessarily harsh and provocative in tone.

[2] *Joint Committee on Closer Union in East Africa*, Vol. I, Report, No. 156 (1931), 29–30. Mr. L. B. Greaves writes to me that M. Pierre Ryckmans (an ex-Governor-General of the Belgian Congo), stated to the Fourth Committee of the United Nations Organization in reply to criticisms made by its members of Belgian Colonial rule : " The Charter declares that the interests of the inhabitants of the territory are paramount. I believe that this text should be understood to mean that the interests of the territory are paramount over those of the metropolitan country where these two interests should come into conflict, rather than that the interests of one category of inhabitants should prevail over those of other elements of the population."

[3] *Joint Committee on Closer Union in East Africa*, Vol. I—*Report*, No. 156 (1931), 42.

[4] *Ibid.*, 43. An authoritative missionary comment on the Report ran:

The question that loomed largest in African discontents was that of land. The Hilton Young Commission had assigned priority to land in their discussion of "essential native interests" because they regarded it as of dominating importance.[1] On this issue the Joint Committee recommendation stated: "In view of the nervousness among the native population as regards the land question, a full and authoritative enquiry should be undertaken immediately into the needs of the Native population, present and prospective, with respect to land within or without the reserves," and that pending such survey no further alienation of land should take place.[2] With commendable promptitude the Kenya Land Commission, under the chairmanship of Sir Morris Carter, was appointed in April 1932 with generous terms of reference which included consideration of all claims advanced by Africans, whether to land already alienated or not yet alienated and to recommend adequate settlement of claims admitted. It was a thorough inquiry with visitation of all the provinces and hearing of 736 witnesses, of whom 487 were Africans. The Report was completed in September 1933 and issued as a Command Paper in May 1934.[3] Its recommendations were at once comprehensive and fundamental and for the first time offered an adequate policy for the treatment of land questions in Kenya. Concurrently with the publication of the Report the Government issued a White Paper outlining the more important features and indicating the Government's intentions.[4]

Meanwhile, however, an extremely disconcerting situation had arisen. The Hilton Young Commission had declared: "The question of title is in itself of dominating importance. When in any territory it becomes necessary to fix the boundaries of what are to be reserved as native areas, then it is absolutely essential that the title of the natives to their beneficial occupation should be indefeasibly secured. Native confidence in the justice of British rule is jeopardised by even a suspicion that the complete inviolability of their beneficial rights is in any circumstances whatever

"Its declarations and recommendations, so far as they go, are in the main reassuring to those who desire to see Native interests adequately protected and the principle of trusteeship maintained unimpaired."—*I.R.M.*, XXI (1932). 221–2.

[1] For their discussion and recommendations, see Hilton Young *Report*, 42–56.

[2] *Joint Committee on Closer Union in East Africa, Vol. I—Report*, 44.

[3] *Report of the Kenya Land Commission*, Cmd. 4556 (1934).

[4] *Kenya Land Commission Report: Summary of Conclusions reached by His Majesty's Government*, Cmd. 4580 (1934).

liable to infringement or modification."[1] This question of security was handled without delay and an Ordinance of 1930 (a revision of a less satisfactory proposal of 1928) was passed by the Government of Kenya, placing the reserves under a Native Lands Trust Board and declaring that they were " set aside for the benefit of the native tribes for ever ".[2] Scarcely had this happened when a severe test was imposed on European sincerity in honouring it.

Gold was discovered at Kakamega in the Kavirondo Reserve, which until now had not been disturbed. Mineral rights were already reserved to the Crown. The question that now arose was that of surface control and disturbance for the purpose of winning the minerals. In 1932 a Native Lands Trust Amendment Ordinance was passed, relaxing the conditions of the 1930 Ordinance and thus modifying what was in the nature of a public pledge to the African tribes. This produced widespread uneasiness in Britain which found expression both in Parliament and the Press. The Archbishop of Canterbury and Lord Lugard in the Lords and Sir Robert Hamilton, an ex-Chief Justice of Kenya, in the Commons took the lead in giving the matter full publicity, while *The Times* in a leading article declared, anent the new provision permitting compensation of expropriated Africans with cash instead of with land : " Such a course, however immediately convenient, is plainly at variance with the recent declaration made by the Governor to the natives concerned, and with the terms of the Land Trust Bill, which, less than three years ago, was passed to give the natives a sense of absolute security in the possession of their reserves. . . . The Kenya ordinance was left as a local ordinance, with possibilities of amendment, on the explicit and declared understanding that, if land was to be taken away from the natives, they must receive equally extensive and not less valuable land somewhere else. That is the safeguard which is now in jeopardy."[3] This situation was overtaken by the Carter Commission's total findings and action

[1] Hilton Young *Report*, 51.

[2] Hailey, *An African Survey* (1938), 749.

[3] *The Times*, January 4, 1933. The Morris Carter Commission, before whose arrival prospecting had already begun, were consulted about the passing of the amending ordinance and they " raised no objection to it as a temporary measure ". In their *Report*, however, they insisted that land must be given for land.—*Kenya Land Commission Report*, 298–9. Dr. Mair is forthright on the issue: " The possible alternative of leaving the natives undisturbed seems to have occurred to no one; still less the consideration, which in relationships between Europeans is axiomatic, that the possibilities of dealing with a given situation are limited by obligations previously undertaken."—L. P. Mair, *Native Policies in Africa* (1936), 87. Cf. Psalm 15: 4.

upon them, but damage had already been done in confirming African distrust of local European intentions. Two principal recommendations of the Commission, both accepted by the British Government, concerned additional land for tribal use,[1] and the definition of boundaries of both the European highlands and the reserves which was to be declared by Order in Council, thus making any local amending ordinance impossible in the future— a final safeguard not resorted to hitherto.[2]

The case of land alienated to missions within what was claimed as Kikuyu territory received separate attention. The total area involved was found to be 7,939 acres enjoyed by some six missions of which three were Roman Catholic and the remainder Protestant.[3] Distinguishing between land essential to the purposes of a mission, whether for educational use, agricultural instruction, or residence for staff and African adherents on the one hand, and what the Commission termed endowment land on the other—land intended to be farmed at a profit to provide funds for the mission (and in some instances sold or sub-leased in part)—they assessed the former at 2,300 acres, and recommended that for the balance of 5,639 acres " equal compensation must be found for the Kikuyu in return for the land lost ".[4]

With this comprehensive settlement of land claims in Kenya a period of more normal development seemed at last to be on the horizon. African rights had been securely safeguarded, opportunity for African economic progress provided (as in coffee growing, for long a European monopoly),[5] and a hope that a better day might dawn had now appeared. Indeed, a survey of Christian missions in the country in 1936 was entitled *A New Day in Kenya*.[6]

[1] African claims were investigated with care and an additional 1,474 square miles recommended in satisfaction of them, while a further 1,155 square miles were proposed for present and future economic needs, together with 939 square miles as a further reserve but not allocated.—Cmd. 4556, 383–4; Cmd. 4580, 2–4.

[2] Cmd. 4556, 534–5; Cmd. 4580, 5. On the significance of Order in Council in an earlier episode at the Cape, see Vol. I, p. 254, *n*. 1.

[3] Cmd. 4556, 127, 560.

[4] *Ibid.*, 127. On the method of tenure for school and church plots in the Kikuyu Reserve and the attitude of the Kenya Missionary Council in the matter, see pp. 568–71.

[5] *The Times*, October 2, 1936. For the success of the Chagga in coffee growing on the slopes of the neighbouring Kilimanjaro, see C. Dundas, *African Crossroads* (1955), 124–5.

[6] H. R. A. Philp, *A New Day in Kenya* (1936). The author was for many years a medical missionary of the Church of Scotland in Kenya. In addition to a comprehensive account of the missions he has a fair and balanced comment on the European community.—*Ibid.*, 109–18.

But far sharper experiences for the European community lay ahead than the most farsighted among them had yet imagined. Meanwhile the proposal of an East African federation was stillborn. The Africans of Uganda would have none of it, and Tanganyika, with Sir Donald Cameron at the helm, had already set out on a more liberal course than Kenya settlers could find agreeable.[1]

The central territories of Nyasaland and Northern Rhodesia also came within the purview of the Hilton Young Commission. They were divided in their recommendations, but both reports felt compelled to take the position of Southern Rhodesia also into consideration. The majority report considered six courses, two of which were federation and amalgamation. Federation between such unequal partners as two Protectorates and a Colony possessing responsible government they felt could scarcely succeed, while amalgamation involving control of a large black population by a small white community would be premature.[2] The *Memorandum on Native Policy in East Africa* [3] provoked a lively reaction among Europeans in Northern Rhodesia who then advocated amalgamation with Southern Rhodesia in order to escape Colonial Office control. The British Government, however, declined to encourage such a policy at that time. But the issue was kept alive and at the instance of Southern Rhodesia a meeting of representative European leaders from both territories was held at the Victoria Falls in January 1936, when there was unanimity in the demand for complete self-government for an amalgamated Colony of Rhodesia. Again the British Government indicated it could not then entertain such a proposal. Further discussions, however, led to the decision to appoint a Royal Commission under the chairmanship of Viscount Bledisloe to survey the whole question and submit recommendations. In March 1938 the Commission was appointed and within a year its Report was presented to Parliament.[4]

[1] For the attitude in Uganda, see *Joint Committee on Closer Union in East Africa*, Vol. I, *Report*, 15–16. Cameron, nurtured in the more liberal policies of the West Coast under Lugard in Nigeria, while recognizing alienated areas which were an inheritance from the German regime, was at pains to secure African interests in any future development.—D. Cameron, *My Tanganyika Service and Some Nigeria* (1939), *passim*.

[2] Cmd. 3234, 281–6. They pointed out that the ratio of white to black in Southern Rhodesia of 1:19 would be increased to 1:65 in the proposed amalgamation.—*Ibid.*, 283. The Commission's recommendations are given on pp. 295–7 of their *Report*.

[3] Cmd. 3573 (1930).

[4] *Rhodesia-Nyasaland Royal Commission Report*, Cmd. 5949 (1939), For the historical summary of the Closer Union movement, see pp. 107–16. The

In brief, the Commission could recommend neither federation nor amalgamation and the reason was the same in both cases : the disparity between the native policy pursued in self-governing Southern Rhodesia and that of the Colonial Office in the Protectorates. It was not denied that Southern Rhodesia was in some ways more liberal in expenditure on African welfare services than was the case in the Protectorates to the north, but segregation and the colour bar were tolerated to a degree that proved, the Commission felt, restrictive of African development. That the policy was more liberal than that of the Union to the south was conceded, but the conception of " parallel development " did not commend itself to the Commission as entirely equitable. True, when Southern Rhodesia had been granted responsible government, together with the reservation of foreign affairs to the Imperial Government had gone the right of veto on legislation affecting Africans. But the right had never been exercised even when the much disliked pass system for Africans was introduced, there being a natural reluctance to intervene, save at a crisis of supreme moment, in the affairs of a self-governing territory.[1] Federation as a form of closer union was therefore rejected by the Commission on the ground of the wide disparity between the proposed partners in both social and political development.[2] Amalgamation as the form of closer union was regarded more favourably, though not immediately desirable. Here the question of native policy was to the fore, and a cautious though definite judgment was expressed : " While Southern Rhodesia, along her own course, has progressed furthest in the provision of certain social and development services, that course is in some respects restrictive and will, if persisted in, limit the opportunities open to Africans, as they gradually emerge from their present backward condition." [3] They found European opinion in both Southern and Northern Rhodesia anticipating that the existing constitution of Southern Rhodesia

Report stands with that of the Hilton Young Commission as an important document on African affairs.

[1] It is claimed that the mere existence of the right may well have exercised restraint in the type of legislation brought forward.

[2] Ibid., 213.

[3] Ibid., 215. They instanced the virtual exclusion of Africans from skilled employment in certain vocations, and the limitation of opportunity for their employment in clerical and other occupations in the central government service. On the comparative educational, medical, and agricultural services in the three territories, including relevant grants to missions, cf., 83–106. The Commission paid tribute to the service of missions.— Ibid., 95.

would apply to the combined territory, while many in Northern Rhodesia were eager for speedy emancipation from " Colonial Office control ". African opinion, in so far as ascertainable, they found to be in the Protectorates solidly opposed to closer union through dislike of the policies of Southern Rhodesia.[1] Thus matters stood at the end of the decade, and thus they remained for a decade more, for in March 1939, when the Bledisloe Report was presented to Parliament, Adolf Hitler had marched into Prague and the Munich agreement lay in fragments.

Such in briefest outline were the attempts made by resident Europeans during the decade to secure their position of racial privilege by the use of political power or the gaining of it. At bottom it was a moral problem, involving the right of every human being to enjoy justice and liberty consistently with his acceptance of normal social obligation. And herein lay the significance for the Christian mission which could scarcely proclaim its message were the denial of justice and liberty to be condoned. A wise student of African affairs, writing in 1927 on " The New Problem of Africa," stated the issue : " It is necessary to realise that the early relations between white and black, in which the white is the apex of the social, economic and political pyramid and the native is the base, cannot be permanent. They will inevitably change. Any attempt to perpetuate the relations which are appropriate when civilisation and barbarism first come into contact, by legislation or otherwise, is bound not only to prove unjust to the native, but to be fatal to the moral foundation on which alone white leadership can rest, and in the long run to end in violence, revolution, and failure. The only principle to follow is that of justice and liberty for every individual." [2]

(3) Upheaval in African Society

Concurrently with the external political movements and the internal political pressures already noticed, came a third factor of major importance in the situation to complicate the task of the missionary—an unprecedented upheaval in African society under the impact of rapid economic developments. There had, of course, already been influences at work producing a measure of social disintegration, but these had operated more gradually than

[1] *Ibid.*, 217–18. For a concise review of native policy in Southern Rhodesia in 1932, see *The Round Table*, XXIII (1933), 214–19.
[2] *The Round Table*, XVII (1927), 462. The whole article deserves attention, pp. 447–72.

the economic drive which was now bringing almost cataclysmic change.

The direct intervention of the Government in African social affairs had been on a limited scale. African customary law had been generally recognized, save where it conflicted with the dictates of humanity and natural justice.[1] Thus the death penalty was reserved to the supreme authority with a consequent curtailment of the power of the chief, and the status of slavery, an agelong institution in Africa, was no longer tolerated with the advent of a civilized government. Nevertheless even here the process of disallowing a social institution was only gradually carried through. Domestic slavery survived well into the twentieth century. F. D. Lugard, writing of his action in Northern Nigeria in 1901, stated : "The sudden abolition of the institution of domestic slavery would have produced social chaos, and the wholesale assertion of their freedom by slaves was therefore discouraged."[2] The permissive freedom, which the abolition of the legal status of slavery bestowed, was therefore a first stage towards general emancipation.[3] It was not until 1916 that the Slavery Ordinance was passed, abolishing the legal status of slavery throughout the Protectorate of Nigeria.[4] A decade later the continued existence of domestic slavery in the Protectorate of Sierra Leone startled the Christian public, all the more since the original settlement was begun as a home for liberated Africans. True, domestic slavery was a mild institution, and the Government, while not oblivious of its undesirability, had hoped to eliminate it by gradual measures.[5] In the upshot an Ordinance to abolish the legal status of slavery in the Protectorate was passed in 1927, to become effective the following year.[6] These two instances afford evidence of the reluctance of the Governments concerned to force an issue at the cost of social disruption when there was reasonable expectation of gradual reform which would permit of social readjustment.

[1] F. D. Lugard, *The Dual Mandate in British Tropical Africa* (4th edition, 1929), 312, 550–1. For the judicial system in French territory, *ibid.*, 568–9.
[2] *Report by Sir F. D. Lugard on the Amalgamation of Northern and Southern Nigeria, and Administration, 1912–1919*, Cmd. 468 (1920), 43.
[3] For the distinction between the abolition of the legal status of slavery and general emancipation, see F. D. Lugard, *The Dual Mandate in British Tropical Africa* (4th edition, 1929), 368.
[4] *Report by Sir F. D. Lugard on Amalgamation*, etc., Cmd. 468, 44; *Correspondence relating to Domestic Slavery in the Sierra Leone Protectorate*, Cmd. 3020 (1928), 37.
[5] *Correspondence relating to Domestic Slavery in the Sierra Leone Protectorate* Cmd., 3020, *passim*.
[6] *Ibid.*, 74–8.

The influence exerted by Christian missions, while inevitably contributing in the long run to social upheaval, was nevertheless also gradual in its first effects. Where refusal of initiation rites and rejection of so-called bride-price as the mechanism of the marriage contract were required of converts, a serious loosening of social obligation was certainly introduced, while the demand for monogamy as the only valid form of marriage had wider repercussions than for the individual concerned.[1] Ancestor worship, as the core of the traditional religion, was replete with social significance, yielding perhaps the most effective sanction for good social behaviour. Its unconditional rejection involved once again a disruption of the existing social order through a weakening of the ties of family and clan.[2] Such negative injunctions, when accepted, were bound to contribute steadily to the disintegration of existing society. But a positive factor of no small significance was the unremitting extension by missionary agency of western education. Pert youngsters with that dangerous modicum—a little learning—began to think their illiterate elders of less account and a dangerous rift began to appear between the generations. The Christian mission, then, had its share of responsibility to bear for

---

[1] *Vide infra.* Initiation rites, pp. 213–17; bride-price, pp. 218–20; polygamy, pp. 344–7. For a concise statement of the pros and cons of polygamy, see Lugard, *Dual Mandate*, 588–9.

[2] Malinowski has expressed his view as a social anthropologist: "Ancestor worship seems to me in many ways the crucial problem and the touchstone of missionary work. . . . For the principle of ancestor worship itself is as sound a theoretical principle as the Fourth Commandment. To work it gradually into a subordinate position, to make it an outcome of monotheism—in short, to harmonize it completely with the Christian attitude of filial piety and reverence to ancestors—would achieve the same end in a slow and much more effective way. In such a compromise may be found the common factor between Christianity and ancestor worship ".— B. Malinowski, *The Dynamics of Culture Change* (1945), 69. Persuasive as the plea may appear, the missionary is beset on the other hand with warnings as to the perils of syncretism. The spontaneous reactions of African Christians in this particular context are often illuminating. Thus Dr. S. T. Pruen records his experience in East Africa: " Others, besides myself, have been struck by one of the first acts of native converts when they come to the knowledge of the truth. They pray for their relations who never heard the good news, and died long ago in ignorance ".—S. T. Pruen, *The Arab and the African* (1891), 265–6. More recently African Christians in Uganda were reported to have taken the initiative in thanking God for their ancestors in public ceremony at the graves.—*Congrès International des Sciences Anthropologiques et Ethnologiques, Londres, 1934* (1934), 213. The strong group feeling shared by Africans is expressed by E. W. Smith, *African Beliefs and Christian Faith* (1936), 46–7. For the ideal of regard for elders, see T. Cullen Young, *African Ways and Wisdom* (1944 ed.), 11–12.

the weakening social ties, a result in part inevitable from the very nature of its message, but in part avoidable where ruthless prohibition was premature to say the least.

This earlier situation of social change by comparatively slow degrees was now rudely disrupted by the advancing tide of economic expansion on the grand scale. While only the more remote regions of the continent were relatively placid and undisturbed, the social dislocation was most intense in areas supplying manpower in the mines : to the Rand from all parts of the Union, from Basutoland, Portuguese East Africa, and farther afield; while with the development of the deep but rich copper deposits in Northern Rhodesia there came a spectacular enlargement of the copperbelt beyond the Belgian Congo boundaries with heavy demands for labour once again. The material reward was an adequate incentive and the attraction of urban centres had its own magnetic power, so young men trekked from home—far from home —at the sore expense of the little village communities they left behind them. The personal problems of the migrant labourers were a further aspect of the situation, while the growth of urban centres through these new accessions from the African hinterland presented its own social and religious challenge.

The plight of the village, deprived of a large proportion of its manpower, was often pitiable. The idea, at one time propagated in defence of large-scale labour recruitment, that in any case the women did the work of the village, has been exploded by those students of African tribal life whose monographs are authoritative. A traditional allocation of duties between the sexes is universal, with the man bearing a not unworthy share, though the nature of the distribution is often enough a contrast to that known to western societies.[1] Whatever the relative percentage (40 per cent for the men and 60 per cent for the women has been suggested in some cases), when a majority, it may be, of able-bodied males were away for contract periods of several years, some never to return, family and village life became sadly disrupted with the delicate equilibrium of reciprocal obligations thus rudely disturbed. So serious did the situation become that in Nyasaland, to take a case in point, a committee was appointed in June 1935 with the following terms of reference : " To report on the conditions now prevailing with regard to the exodus of natives from the Protectorate for work outside, the effect on village life and the probable future effect on the Protectorate." They submitted their findings in December of the

[1] H. A. Junod, *Life of a South African Tribe* (2nd ed., 1927), I, 340–1, *n.*; *Africa*, I (1928), 289–319; N. Leys, *Kenya* (2nd ed., 1925), 39–40.

same year.[1] This quick report was due to the sense of emergency which their discovery of the situation had created: " As our investigations proceeded we became more and more aware that this uncontrolled and growing emigration brought misery and poverty to hundreds and thousands of families and that the waste of life, happiness, health and wealth was colossal." [2] They estimated the total exodus as in the neighbourhood of 120,000 which represented a quarter of the adult male population of the Protectorate. And the emigrants were scattered far afield over the Union, Southern Rhodesia, Northern Rhodesia, the Belgian Congo, and Tanganyika.[3] Not more than five per cent, it appeared, were accompanied by their wives, but other women ventured abroad with the unhappiest social results.[4] It was a tragic finding that from 25 per cent to 30 per cent of the emigrants never returned and were designated by their relatives " the lost ones ".[5]

The effect of such a serious dislocation on family and village life is not easy to conceive. The actual additional burden on the women as wives, as mothers, and as supporters of the home led the Committee to state : " The most pathetic effect of emigration is that it is responsible for the tragic lot of tens of thousands of women." [6] Traditional ideas of the binding nature of the marriage contract suffered serious invasion, and the consequent moral peril of men at the mines and women left at home is not difficult to imagine. W. Y. Turner, a medical missionary of the Church of Scotland, wrote from a wide experience : " Many stand with an amazing chastity beyond all praise, but it is little wonder that in the absence of the age-long sanctions of native life, there is a loosening from the fine morality which characterises tribal life in its really primitive condition." [7] Further, it was the age-group

---

[1] *Report of the Committee appointed by His Excellency the Governor to enquire into Emigrant Labour, 1935* (Zomba, 1936). W. P. Young of the Livingstonia mission was the missionary member of the Committee.

[2] *Ibid.*, 7.

[3] *Ibid.*, 15.

[4] " The number of unmarried women emigrants is small, but has apparently been increasing of late to the dismay of Native Authorities and of the older villagers. Of the unmarried women who do go, only a few go to marry, the remainder are either women who follow men in order to avoid obligations which are imposed by marriage or those who go to become prostitutes; the latter appear to be increasing in number."— *Ibid.*, 16; cf. 27.

[5] " *Machona* is used throughout the Protectorate to denote those who are lost through emigration."—*Ibid.*, 16 *n*.

[6] *Ibid.*, 32.

[7] *Ibid.*, 32.

of those who went away that was significant. While the exodus was estimated to involve some quarter of the total adult male population, it represented in a third of the districts from 30 per cent to 60 per cent of the able-bodied men equal to the vicissitudes of emigrant life.[1] Thus the main prop of the village community was steadily whittled away. Let a summary statement of the Committee conclude the survey of this aspect of the problem : " It is easy to criticise the old order—to say that it subordinated the individual to the community to an undue extent, that it provided little incentive to endeavour and that it resulted in stagnation. But it worked : the community was stable and responsibilities were counterbalanced by rights. There was a give and take. Emigration, which destroys the old, offers nothing to take its place, and the family-community is threatened with complete dissolution." [2]

If this was the case at the rural end, at the other a new urban problem was created. True, on the Rand it had already appeared, but now it was reaching more alarming dimensions. The drift to the towns was all too often becoming for the young almost a torrent, with rapidly mounting problems in the racial readjustment of the detribalized. Questions of health and housing, of education and recreation, of juvenile delinquency and the hardened criminal, all pressed for attention and not least on those committed to the service of Christian missions. The Rand had already been recognized as a mission field of a new order, and the copperbelt now made similar claims.[3] The first field study of the Bureau of Social and Economic Research and Information, established under the auspices of the International Missionary Council as a result of the Jerusalem Meeting of 1928, was concerned with the copperbelt in Central Africa.[4] The economic recession of the early 'thirties slowed up mining development, and

[1] Ibid., 36.
[2] Ibid., 35–6. A collateral study was that by I. Schapera, " Labour Migration from a Bechuanaland Native Reserve " in Journal of the African Society, XXXII (1933), 386–97; XXXIII (1934), 49–58. Care for the migrant labourer increasingly became a concern of Colonial Governments. For a comprehensive statement of the situation in the 'thirties, with a summary of colonial legislation on the subject, see G. St. J. Orde Browne, The African Labourer (1933), passim.
[3] J. Dexter Taylor, " The Rand as a Mission Field ", in I.R.M., XV (1926), 647–61. An authoritative factual study of the situation on the Rand was by R. E. Phillips, The Bantu in the City: A Study of Cultural Adjustment on the Witwatersrand (1938); see also E. Hellmann, Rooiyard: A Sociological Survey of an Urban Slum Yard, Rhodes-Livingstone Papers, No. 13 (1948), passim.
[4] J. Merle Davis (ed.), Modern Industry and the African (1933).

missions, as we have already noted, were straitened in their resources at the time. But by the mid-'thirties the wheels of industry were turning more rapidly and missionary societies concerned had evolved a joint policy. The United Missions in the Copper Belt came into being in 1936 with six societies co-operating in support, the only missions finding themselves unable to participate being those of the Roman Catholic Church and the Dutch Reformed Church of South Africa.[1]

This challenging situation of social disequilibrium, found in greater or less degree in all parts of the continent, had been produced by the resounding impact of western civilization upon the small scale societies of Africa with their simple resources. The introduction of a cash currency, for example, proved revolutionary. It introduced a money economy with social repercussions difficult to exaggerate. In the old African society the sharing of resources, on the basis of reciprocal obligations and privileges, was a fundamental rule. Money was now shattering it. Food from the farm or the herd or the hunt would always be shared, but not so now when bought with money. Dr. A. I. Richards, in a study of food and society among the Bembas of Northern Rhodesia, reported of the Bemba housewife: " Where she buys her supplies with money, at any rate for part of the year, she considers herself free of all the tribal rules of division. . . . I have seen a young couple eat meat alone while almost starving neighbours looked on. They shrugged their shoulders when questioned, and said, ' We bought this meat with money '." [2]

Other aggravating factors new to the scene, interestingly enough again connected with money, were taxation and a wage system, both providing stress and strain in readjustment from the old order and occasions of disturbance in the new. To illustrate from the decade under review, in 1929 a serious outbreak occurred among the women of Eastern Nigeria who had been stirred to violence by the belief that they were to be taxed. In

[1] The co-operating Missions were the Church of Scotland, London Missionary Society, Methodist Missionary Society, South African Baptist Mission, United Society for Christian Literature, and Universities' Mission to Central Africa.—*United Missions in the Copper Belt, First Annual Report, 1936–7* (1938), 2–3. The U.M.C.B. continued for twenty years but in 1955 it was superseded by another organization.—*Vide infra*, p. 310.

[2] A. I. Richards, *Land, Labour and Diet in Northern Rhodesia* (1939), 153. After offering examples of family budgets where food is bought, Dr. Richards comments: " Thus inequality as between family and family much more nearly resembles conditions in our own society and appears to be the necessary result of the adoption of a money economy."

172

1926 men in the Districts concerned had been enumerated (without disclosure of the reason) and then had been taxed; when therefore an enumeration of women was included in a total count in 1929, the women were convinced they too would be taxed. As they were already contributing to existing taxation they resented the injustice of the action they ascribed to the Government and took the law into their own hands so effectively that troops had to be called out to support the overwhelmed police. There was already widespread discontent among the women at the fall in prices for produce while high prices were still maintained for imported goods—a situation traceable to the economic blizzard that had begun to sweep the West, but which had no parallel in the internal system of African markets.[1] Taxation again was the occasion of serious disturbances in the copperbelt in 1935. An increase in the rate of poll tax for mine workers led to their going on strike at three mines in succession and to consequent disturbances, with troops again involved. Predisposing causes were alleged to be discontent with wages and rations, and the breakdown of tribal custom and control, on which point the finding of the Commission of Inquiry ran: " The commission consider that the choice lies between the establishment of native authority, together with frequent repatriation of the natives to their villages; or, alternatively, the acceptance of definite detribalisation and industrialisation of the mining population under European urban control." [2]

Such situations serve as pointers to the continuing vigour of Africans in seeking adjustment to a new environment, and their determined refusal, within the limits of their powers, to be engulfed in the swirling vortex of social change. But they also stress the

[1] *Report of the Commission of Inquiry appointed to Inquire into the Disturbances in the Calabar and Owerri Provinces, December 1929* (Lagos, 1930), 93, 121. Women of the Ibo and Ibibio tribes were concerned. The rising revealed a hitherto unsuspected capacity of the women for united action. For an account of their various organizations, as far as known, see *Memorandum as to the Origin and Causes of the Recent Disturbances in the Owerri and Calabar Provinces*, Secretary, Southern Provinces, Annexure I to above *Report*. Also C. K. Meek, *Law and Authority in a Nigerian Tribe* (1937), 331-2.

[2] *Report of the Commission appointed to enquire into the Disturbances in the Copperbelt, Northern Rhodesia, October 1935*, Cmd. 5009 (1935), *passim*. The increase in taxation of mine workers was fully counter-balanced by a reduction in tax payable in their home villages, though this had unhappily not been explained to them at the time. In deference to a resolution of the General Missionary Conference of Northern Rhodesia criticizing the composition of the Commission of Inquiry as unsatisfactory a new Commission was appointed.—*Report of Proceedings of Seventh Conference, 1935*, 19; *I.R.M.*, XXV (1936), 67.

necessity of sympathetic understanding on the part of Europeans in authority of any kind, that wise guidance may be given, which is so sorely needed at such times of threatening conflict. It was therefore from this very angle a matter for profound satisfaction that, coincidentally with these changes, a scientific study of African society was proceeding and a reorientation of the missionary attitude to the African's social heritage was progressively taking place. The illuminating approach of the functional school in social anthropology, under the stimulus of Radcliffe-Brown and Malinowski, did much to inspire a new generation of field workers whose researches were to lay bare in yet greater detail the functioning organism of simple human societies. And coupled with the professional anthropologists were missionaries of note whose pioneer contributions had blazed the trail for their successors. In the forefront among them has been Edwin W. Smith of whose *The Ila-speaking Peoples of Northern Rhodesia*, written in collaboration with Captain A. M. Dale,, it has been said : " It founded modern anthropological research in British Central Africa." [1] In *The Golden Stool, Some Aspects of the Conflict of Cultures in Modern Africa* (1926) he produced the classical statement of the case which for a generation has widely influenced cadets and candidates designated for African service. His election by the members of the Royal Anthropological Institute as their President—the only missionary to receive the honour —was recognition of sterling service to African studies.[2] And further, it should never be forgotten that it was to missionaries and the friends of missions that the foundation of the International African Institute was due, an enterprise that led to the financing of research, the training of researchers, the publication of a series of standard studies, and the undertaking of comprehensive ethnographic and linguistic surveys.[3]

---

[1] E. Colson and M. Gluckman (ed.), *Seven Tribes of British Central Africa*, (1951), ix.

[2] Of the eighteen or more volumes to his credit dealing with African affairs there may be mentioned in this connexion: *African Beliefs and Christian Faith* (1936); *Knowing the African* (1946); and *African Ideas of God* (1950), a symposium to which he contributes an Introductory Survey and the essay on the idea of God among South African Tribes. It may, perhaps, be added that his *The Religion of Lower Races* (1923) was given, without his consent, a title which he disowns.—See E. W. Smith, *The Way of the White Fields in Rhodesia* (1928), 23 *n*. 3. Cf., also the Presidential Address, "Anthropology and the Practical Man" in *Journal of the Royal Anthropological Institute*, LXIV (1934), xiii-xxxvii.

[3] *Vide supra*, p. 112.

Under the stimulus of such advocacy, together with the shock to the missionary of an unprepared-for encounter with a disintegrating society, social anthropology became increasingly recognized as an indispensable element in missionary training, though it is true that only a minority of those committed to a missionary vocation were as yet being introduced to the discipline in any effective way.[1] It must be regretfully confessed that all too often the Western missionary, however unwittingly, was still inclined to look somewhat superciliously upon African society as from a superior vantage ground, failing to find, as appreciation of the positive values in it would have enabled him to do, that fullness of respect for its members which was needed to enable him to fulfil his missionary vocation among them at the deepest level.

(4) *Increasing Concern for African Welfare*

It was but natural in such a situation that Christian missions should modify existing types of social service and engage in new ones, prompted by a better understanding of current needs and in response to the demands of changing times. The growing concern for African health was reflected in significant action at a high level, national and international. In 1931 an International Conference on African Children was convened at Geneva by the Save the Children International Union. The Africans, Americans, and Europeans who comprised the 180 members of the Conference were fully representative of the interests involved: medical officers, missionaries, representatives of governments, and anthropologists. Four questions were before the Conference, on which preliminary papers by qualified and experienced writers had been prepared. Of the nineteen papers presented eleven were by missionaries or former missionaries.[2] With the new emphasis on preventive medicine in Africa the question of nutrition now received con-

[1] A notable contribution was made by W. C. Willoughby, when Professor of Missions in Africa in the Kennedy School of Missions, Hartford, Conn., in his *Race Problems in the New Africa* (1923), *The Soul of the Bantu* (1928), and *Nature-Worship and Taboo* (1932). Two Anglican contributions to be noted, having more particular regard to the Eastern and Southern Bantu, were: W. V. Lucas, "The Christian Approach to Non-Christian Customs" in E. R. Morgan (ed.), *Essays Catholic and Missionary* (1928); D. W. T. Shropshire, *The Church and Primitive Peoples: The Religious Institutions and Beliefs of the Southern Bantu and their Bearing on the Problems of the Christian Missionary* (1938).
[2] The four questions were: (1) Still-birth and infant mortality from the pathological point of view; (2) Still-birth and infant mortality from the social and economic point of view; (3) Education in regard to the preparation of children for life; (4) General conditions of work for children and adolescents and the protection of children at work. Each was reported on

siderable attention. An investigation under the auspices of the British Medical Research Council was conducted in the Kikuyu and Masai Reserves in Kenya,[1] while the Government of Tanganyika made a survey of the tribes of the Territory with the customary diet of each and notes on the food deficiency they revealed.[2]

The British Colonial Office appreciated the importance of the questions at issue and a Committee on Nutrition in the Colonial Empire carried through a full-scale investigation.[3] The natural sequel was to stress the fundamental importance for African welfare of agriculture in the African economy, and the need for scientific methods of cultivation to be applied when the local conditions had been adequately studied. The Phelps-Stokes Education Commissions had already directed attention to this,[4] and the Jerusalem Meeting of the International Missionary Council in 1928 had as one of its main topics the Christian Mission in relation to rural problems though considered predominantly from an Asian angle.[5] There sprang into being the Agricultural Missions Foundation which, through its periodical and other publications, made available experience on a world-wide front for workers in the rural field.[6] The social anthropologists also took a hand in studying the sociological aspects of food in African society.[7] For Christian missions the immediate practical concern necessarily broadened into a spiritual objective : the promotion of a Christian rural civilization, as the Christian Rural Fellowship expressed it [8];

from five regions: West, East, Central, North, and South, save that (2) had no North Africa report—hence the total of 19 papers. For the Report of the Conference see Evelyn Sharp, *The African Child* (1932), *passim*.

[1] J. B. Orr and J. L. Gilks, *Studies of Nutrition: The Physique and Health of Two African Tribes* (1931).

[2] R. C. Jerrard, *The Tribes of Tanganyika, Their Districts, Usual Dietary and Pursuits* (1936).

[3] *Nutrition in the Colonial Empire*, Cmd. 6050 (1939); *Summary of Information regarding Nutrition in the Colonial Empire*, Cmd. 6051 (1939).

[4] In the second Report, *Education in East Africa* (1925), a chapter on "Agriculture in East Africa" was contributed by H. L. Shantz of the U.S. Department of Agriculture.

[5] *The Christian Mission in relation to Rural Problems*, Jerusalem Meeting Report, VI (1928).

[6] For the comprehensive service of this Foundation after a decade of activity, see *The Economic Basis of the Church*, Tambaram Madras Series, V (1949), 486.

[7] A. I. Richards, *Hunger and Work in a Savage Tribe* (1932) was the pioneer study. See also: R. Firth, "The Sociological Study of Native Diet" in *Africa*, VII (1934), 401–14.

[8] The Christian Rural Fellowship, with rural communities in the United States primarily in view, issued the first number of its Bulletin in June 1935.

more precisely, the leading of village folk to regard the normal use of the land as co-operation with God, and the focusing of the occupational and recreational pursuits of an enlightened and literate rural community in the Christian worship of God as a satisfying destiny. The realization of such a policy, together with the encouragement of technical proficiency in agriculture, demanded an educational programme for the purpose. Colonial Governments were actively interested in such provision, and in America and Britain training facilities for assisting missionaries of urban origin (the great majority) to become more rural-minded began to appear.[1]

Another aspect of African welfare that now engaged the interest of Christian missions to a far greater extent than before was the need of the leper, to which governments were also alert. In this the British Empire Leprosy Relief Association gave valuable help. It was stated in 1927 that on a conservative estimate there were 90,000 lepers in Nigeria and 5,000 in the Gold Coast, of whom sixteen per cent and four per cent respectively were receiving treatment.[2] In British territory in East and Central Africa there were estimated to be at least 60,000 of whom 5,000 were under treatment.[3] A pioneer venture was that of Dr. A. B. Macdonald of the Church of Scotland general hospital at Itu on the Cross River in south-east Nigeria. In 1926 a leper appeared seeking help. The drug required was received in three months' time. In six months 400 lepers were under treatment. By 1928 there were 800 (the Government now giving liberal help); by 1931 there were 1,100 patients in residence. This was the pioneer settlement where all sides of the leper's life were cared for: industries from weaving to blacksmithing, school for the children, a daily market, recreational facilities, and the church for worship, adorned by the patients with beautiful clay carvings.[4] In Nigeria Itu was but a beginning; other missions followed suit, inspired by the success at Itu. In 1932 the Methodist Mission established a leper colony at Uzuakoli in Iboland, with liberal help from the Native Administration of Owerri Province. The settlement was soon accommodating

[1] In 1930 the New York State College of Agriculture at Cornell University held the first annual school for missionaries on furlough working in rural areas. In 1931 the Selly Oak Colleges in England offered the first vacation course on the Christian Mission in Rural Areas, held at Avoncroft, a college for rural workers.

[2] *Report of the British Empire Leprosy Relief Association for 1927* (1928).

[3] F. Oldrieve, Secretary of B.E.L.R.A., in *The Times*, October 6, 1927.

[4] A. B. Macdonald, *Can Ghosts Arise? The Answer of Itu* (1946), *passim.*

1,000 lepers.[1] By 1938 there were leper colonies in which missions and government co-operated in Northern Nigeria—in Bornu under the Sudan United Mission, and in Zaria under the Church Missionary Society.[2] Meanwhile another partner had appeared in the Toc H movement which sent out five workers in 1935.[3]

By 1936 there were sixteen leper settlements under the auspices of the various missions in Nigeria.[4] The attraction of lepers to these colonies provided a new basis for estimating the number in the country. Dr. E. Muir of B.E.L.R.A. estimated 200,000 in 1936 while in 1938 the estimates offered ranged from three to ten per cent. of the population of twenty million.[5] In the northern (Muslim) zone of the Anglo-Egyptian Sudan the Government erected a leper home with accommodation for ninety patients and placed it under the direction of the hospital in Omdurman of the Church Missionary Society.[6] In the southern Sudan Dr. Kenneth Fraser took the initiative in 1926 in starting a leper colony for fifty patients; by 1929 there were 150. Help from the Sudan Government, B.E.L.R.A., and the Mission to Lepers established the work more firmly.[7] In Uganda the Church Missionary Society, famed for its medical service, soon had three centres in action : a leper hospital for children at Kumi in 1929, a leper colony on Bwana Island in 1930, and another at Ongino in 1934.[8] In Tanganyika the Church Missionary Society had established two leper settlements, at Kilimatinde and Berega respectively, again with assistance from B.E.L.R.A. and the Mission to Lepers.[9] The Benedictines of St. Ottilien were responsible for two considerable settlements at Ndanda and Peramiho respectively in the Southern Provinces.[10] All these and others under mission auspices received support from the Government of Tanganyika. The aim of all these mission settlements was to provide the patients with as natural a life as possible, making available occupations that lay within their powers and cultivating social and religious interests in the community. In addition clinics for treatment only were

---

[1] *The Methodist Recorder*, April 8, 1937.
[2] *I.R.M.*, XXVIII (1939), 57.
[3] A. B. Macdonald, *op. cit.*, 19; E. B. Worthington, *Science in Africa* (1938), 547.
[4] E. B. Worthington, *op. cit.*, 487.
[5] *West Africa*, July 25, 1936; *I.R.M.*, XXVIII (1939), 57.
[6] W. W. Cash, *The Changing Sudan* (1930), 36.
[7] E. Fraser, *The Doctor Comes to Lui* (1938), 60, 63, 66.
[8] Thomas and Scott, *Uganda* (1935), 331.
[9] G. A. Chambers, *Tanganyika's New Day* (1931), 51.
[10] E. B. Worthington, *op. cit.*, 548.

maintained by missions—a dozen such, for example, in Nyasa-land.[1] In French colonies the care of the leper was primarily the task of the Government.[2] In the Belgian Congo the Croix Rouge du Congo was active in providing villages for leper patients.[3] The American Baptist Mission at its medical training centre at Sona Bata in the Lower Congo started a leper colony in 1938, with help from the American Mission to Lepers.[4] The full magnitude of the problem became further revealed as facilities increased. It could be stated authoritatively by 1938: "About half a million cases of leprosy are already known in Africa, so the real number cannot be less than a million."[5]

Christian missions continued to carry large responsibilities for schools throughout most of Africa. At village level—the first meeting-place of the old and the new—the missions were almost the only providers. In the complex situation of accelerated social change the education of the young became supremely significant. The missionary attitude to tribal education through traditional puberty rites—an education that, whatever its limitations had proved effective in preparation of the adolescent for adult responsi-bilities at the tribal level—is discussed below.[6] Strictures passed by the Phelps-Stokes Commissioners on the western type of education they found currently offered by the missions have already been reviewed.[7] Between these two extremes there were various attempts by alert-minded men and women to meet the challenge of changing times. In the education of girls a notable develop-ment in Northern Rhodesia was that of the London Mission at Mbereshi.[8] The aim from the beginning was to preserve a respect for the African way of life as far as consistent with Christian discipleship, expressed as loyalty to the Great Chief, thus prepar-ing eager youth with their roots still in African soil to be faithful members of the Christian fellowship under the strains and stresses of the new Africa. The decade 1930–40 saw a large achievement

[1] *Ibid.*, 548.
[2] *Ibid.*, 495–6.
[3] *Ibid.*, 549–50.
[4] P. H. J. Lerrigo, *All Kindreds and Tongues* (1940), 247–8; *I.R.M.*, XXVIII (1939), 59.
[5] E. B. Worthington, *op. cit.*, 546.
[6] *Vide infra*, pp. 213–17, where Christian adaptations of the rites are also considered.
[7] *Vide supra*, pp. 109–10.
[8] The work of the Mbereshi team is best known through the writings of Miss Mabel Shaw who retired in 1940 after twenty-five years' service. Her earlier books, presenting the ideals and actualities of this educational venture were: *Dawn in Africa* (1927) and *God's Candlelights* (1932).

of this aim in the lives of Christian women : over sixty trained teachers had come from the Teachers' Training Department begun in 1930; old girls were to be found resident, as wives and mothers, from Jadotville in the Belgian Congo to Salisbury in Southern Rhodesia, while others were engaged in Christian service as nurses and deacons.[1] The Christian influence radiating from this one educational centre would be difficult to compute. In Northern Nigeria an educational programme, utilizing familiar local material on the basis of an appreciation of the positive values in the African heritage, was put into operation by the Brethren Mission among the Bura people.[2] The venture was successful in linking up the school with local craftsmen and community needs, thus helping to bridge the gap between the generations that threatened to appear when self-confident literate youngsters were tempted to resent control by their illiterate elders.[3]

Education policy was the subject of considerable inquiry and discussion during the decade. A standard study which exercised much influence was A. Victor Murray's *The School in the Bush*, which expounded the subject against the general background of political and economic life and theological belief, based on an extensive tour of South, Central, and West Africa.[4] Coincidentally the British Colonial Office through its relevant Committee [5] recommended in 1928 that a professional biologist should visit Africa and advise on the place of biology in the curriculum. It was arranged that Julian Huxley should carry out this commission, and in 1929 he accordingly visited Zanzibar, Tanganyika, Kenya, and Uganda for this purpose. His recommendations were embodied in a Report to the Colonial Office.[6] The necessity of some guiding principle in

---

[1] *Decennial Report of Women's and Girls' Work, Mbereshi, 1930–1940*, 4–7. The Sunday Bible Class for young women at Mbereshi had 220 members in 1940.—*Ibid.*, 5. In the boarding school during 1939–40 there were received into the catechumenate 27 girls, while 22 were baptized.— *Report of Educational Work among Girls at Mbereshi, 1939–1940*, 3.

[2] A. D. Helser, *Education of Primitive People* (1934), *passim*.

[3] Thus one project was concerned with the local blacksmith, inculcating respect for his skill as smelter and smith; while the local medicine man was co-opted in a vaccination campaign, his co-operation at once making it acceptable to the community.—*Ibid.*, 49, 267–72.

[4] A. Victor Murray, *The School in the Bush: A Critical Study of the Theory and Practice of Native Education in Africa* (1st edition, 1929).

[5] The Colonial Office Advisory Committee on Native Education in Tropical Africa.

[6] *Biology and the Biological Approach to Native Education in East Africa*, Report by Professor *Julian Huxley, M.A.* African (East), No. 1134 (April 1930); *Biology and its Place in Native Education in East Africa. Report by Professor Julian Huxley, M.A.* African (East), No. 1134, Revised Edition (June

the organizing of a curriculum was accepted, and it was argued that biology could best be the central core in the conditions to be found in East Africa.[1] In 1936 a Commission on higher education in East Africa was appointed by the Colonial Secretary, with special reference to the future of Makerere College in Uganda. The Commissioners were agreed that in primary education there should be an agricultural bias and a biological approach.[2] While recognizing the value of the missionary contribution to education, they noted that further expansion in provision of schools must be at government expense; nevertheless mission schools should not be supplanted but " regulated, enhanced, and carefully controlled ".[3]

The Protestant missions had at this time an education adviser who stated the case for mission schools from the mission side.[4] He admitted a subtle threat to Christian education from various factors affecting the efficiency of mission schools, and proposed as a corrective the sharing of responsibility with the growing African Church (having first trained leaders for this purpose), and an improved co-operation between missions which would make it possible to replace the denominational by the community area as the unit for school purposes.

In West Africa by far the weakest country educationally was Liberia. The Phelps-Stokes Commissioners had recorded the outstanding defects in the administration of education there.[5] The missionary societies at work in the country then requested their Boards in the United States, together with the Colonization Society and the Phelps-Stokes Fund, to nominate an educational adviser to reorganize their schools. James L. Sibley, with eighteen years' experience of Negro education in Alabama and Georgia, was appointed in 1925, and after an extensive survey of the field

1931). A popular account of the tour with his observations on East African affairs was provided by Julian Huxley in *Africa View* (1931). Chapter 18 was devoted to " The Education of the African ".

[1] He commented on this central core: " With our present ideas about education, which are based on religious tolerance, it cannot well be religious: if, as now, the different religious bodies are to be permitted to teach their respective views, there cannot be a single agreed religious basis ". (Original, p. 11; Revised, p. 9). But cf. *infra*, p. 283, for more recent Gold Coast experience. Other possibilities were also rejected.

[2] *Higher Education in East Africa: Report of the Commission appointed by the Secretary of State for the Colonies.* Colonial No. 142 (1937), 41.

[3] *Ibid.*, 31, 35, 36, 53. On the place of religion in secondary education, see p. 54.

[4] J. W. C. Dougall, *Missionary Education in Kenya and Uganda: A Study of Co-operation* (1936).

[5] T. J. Jones, *Education in Africa* (1922), 316.

settled down in 1927 to his task. In 1928 he was appointed Director of Education to the Liberian Government. In 1929 he died, a victim of yellow fever. It was a heavy loss.[1] His successor had to contend with serious difficulties : the situation revealed by the Christy Commission in 1931 in respect of slavery and forced labour, in particular the recruiting and shipment abroad of labourers under " conditions not distinguishable from slave-raiding and slave-trading " with the connivance of high officials [2]; and the near bankruptcy of the Negro Republic in finance and administration that produced a crisis in 1933.[3] The deliberate policy of the American Negro bureaucracy in intimidating the interior tribes naturally deprived these of all opportunity for progress, so that the Christy Commission could speak of " the lack of means of education in the provinces and its total absence in the Hinterland, except where a few missionaries are installed ".[4] Some further relief was brought to this tragic human situation when the Firestone Tyre Company of the United States began to develop welfare services on its large rubber-growing concession. Meanwhile the missions kept alive in the Hinterland the flickering flame of hope for a brighter day of opportunity for its peoples.

In sharp contrast was the situation in the Gold Coast, where Government-assisted and non-assisted schools were numerous. Thus in 1935 there were in the Gold Coast Colony and Ashanti nineteen Government primary schools with an enrolment of 3,969 boys and 1,346 girls, while the number of mission-assisted schools was 361, the non-assisted being reported as 259.[5] Of the three secondary schools two were mission establishments receiving grants-in-aid, while of the four training colleges for men teachers

[1] *West Africa*, September 24, 1927; July 6, 1929. J. L. Sibley was a white man from the Southern States who had found his vocation as a layman in the service of the Negro. He had collaborated with Professor Westermann of Berlin in a book on the country: J. L. Sibley and D. Westermann, *Liberia Old and New* (1928). In chapters 10 and 11 Sibley outlined his educational policy and programme for Liberia.

[2] *The Times*, January 12, 1931. The International Commission, under the auspices of the League of Nations, consisted of Dr. Cuthbert Christy (nominee of the League of Nations), Dr. Charles S. Johnson, the American Negro sociologist (United States nominee), and ex-President Barclay (nominee of Liberia). The principal destination of the forced labour shipments was Fernando Po.

[3] *The Times*, March 17, 1932; May 30, 1933.

[4] *The Times*, January 12, 1931. Some 15,000 American settlers of African descent tyrannized over the 2,000,000 hinterland inhabitants.

[5] *Annual Report on the Social and Economic Progress of the People of the Gold Coast, 1934-35* (1936), 55.

three were mission institutions : Akropong (Presbyterian), Wesley (Methodist), and St. Augustine's (Roman Catholic). The mission girls' schools frequently held classes for training women teachers.[1] If the mission contribution to education in terms of schools and colleges, scholars and students, was thus the preponderating one, yet with liberal assistance from the State it was essentially a co-operative enterprise. And here as in East Africa there was a limit to the contribution missions could continue to make, as a national system with compulsory primary education began to come into view.

In the Union of South Africa, where African education was a Provincial responsibility, the missions, which had pioneered here as elsewhere, still provided the major part of the service. It was felt, however, in the 'thirties that the time had come for an overall survey, and in 1935 a Government Committee was duly appointed which reported in the following year.[2] Under its terms of reference it made two principal recommendations in respect of administration. The first was that the Provinces should relinquish the control of African education which should then be vested in the Union Government; and further, that it should be associated not with the Native Affairs Department, but be placed under the Union Education Department.[3] The second recommendation had reference to the place of missions in the system. The Committee recognized the duplication of effort that existed, with some twenty-eight denominations in rivalry not always friendly, but found this being corrected by increasing co-operation in united or amalgamated mission schools. They found many African teachers restive under mission direction and advocating Government control of all schools similar to that existing in the case of European education. Despite the arguments advanced the Committee stated that " all responsible witnesses agreed that in a civilized Christian State religious instruction—not denominational teaching—must have a place in the curriculum of the school, even if it be a Government school ", and concluded : " There are weighty considerations in favour of retaining the direct influence of the missionaries in a South African system of Native education." [4] The first recommendation involved change and was not acted upon : control of

[1] *Ibid.*, 57. The number of students in residence at the end of 1934 stood as follows: Akropong, 124; Achimota (Government), 85; Wesley, 83; St. Augustine's, 54.

[2] *Union of South Africa: Report of the Inter-departmental Committee on Native Education, 1935-1936.* U.G. No. 29/1936 (1936).

[3] *Ibid.*, 58.

[4] *Ibid.*, 68-9.

African education remained with the four Provincial administrations. The second endorsed the retention of mission schools, and these continued as before to be the overwhelming majority. Thus in 1946 the total number of State schools for Africans in the Union was 232 as against 4,335 State-aided schools.[1] But within a couple of decades these were to be almost entirely absorbed in a State system.

In Latin Africa, so-called, the place accorded to Christian missions in the educational system continued during this decade with little change. In French territory education was a Government responsibility and was strictly secular. As two qualified observers, who toured the seven territories embraced in French West Africa in 1935 for this purpose, expressed it : " The triumph of reason and the ' moral conquest of civilisation ' through education is to France a spiritual end, and its pursuit is carried on with a definite religious fervour." [2] In the Belgian Congo the preferential advantages accorded to Roman Catholic missions as ' national ' missions continued to operate, the only Protestant mission qualifying on the basis of Belgian nationality being the Société Belge des Missions Protestantes. The effect was virtually to limit recognition and State subsidy to Roman Catholic schools.[3] In Portuguese colonies a serious limitation on schools was imposed in respect of language. In Angola in 1921 by Decree 77, schools were forbidden to teach African languages or to print books in them.[4] In 1929 the use of vernaculars in Portuguese East Africa was similarly prohibited by Decree 168; while instructions for its enforcement made in the following year granted some relaxation in other respects, it was reasserted that " reading and writing must be taught in Portuguese alone ".[5]

Thus, while during the decade the preponderant share of missions in the task of education remained undisturbed, there were

[1] E. Hellmann (ed.), *Handbook on Race Relations in South Africa* (1949), 364. The respective numbers in the four Provinces as at June 1946 were: Cape, 15 and 2,057; Natal, 216 and 756; Transvaal, 1 and 1,060; O.F.S., none and 482.
[2] W. B. Mumford and G. St. J. Orde-Browne, *Africans Learn to be French* (n.d.), 39; cf. 68–9.
[3] *I.R.M.*, XXI (1932), 231, 377–8; XXIV (1935), 73; H. Anet, "Protestant Missions in Belgian Congo," in *I.R.M.*, XXVIII (1939), 415–25.
[4] For the text of the Decree see T. J. Jones, *Education in Africa* (1922), 232–4.
[5] *I.R.M.*, XIX (1930), 50; XX (1931), 55; XXI (1932), 240. For the text of the Decree and the later Instructions, see E. Moreira, *Portuguese East Africa* (1936), 92–3, 96–7.

signs on the horizon of a coming change : Governments were becoming increasingly alert, with a concern for education at all levels, and showing every intention of expanding a system of State schools even where a policy of grants-in-aid already existed, if and when the missions proved unable to shoulder additional burdens. On the side of the missions misgiving was growing as to the amount of effort the expanding educational service now required, which was often felt to be expended at the cost of evangelistic enterprise and pastoral care of the growing Church. This situation was to become yet more acute.

A pioneer enterprise of some importance was undertaken in 1935 by the International Missionary Council, through its Department of Social and Industrial Research, in the Bantu educational cinema experiment. The purpose was to discover the value of the cinema as an instrument for helping Africans to understand and adapt themselves to the demands of social change, to preserve the worthy elements in the African inheritance offering them as such, to assist in popularizing health and agriculture programmes, and to supply entertainment of a suitable character. The experiment was made possible by the Carnegie Corporation of New York with the sympathetic co-operation of the British Colonial Office and the British Film Institute. It achieved its purpose in demonstrating the possibilities of this aspect of visual education, as also the intelligent interest aroused in African audiences.[1]

Meanwhile the grave disturbance of much of African tribal society, with the problems attendant on urban life that faced many young Africans, produced among its undesirable results the social problem of juvenile delinquency. In Nigeria juvenile offenders might be committed under mandate to a Boys' Industrial Home at Yaba near Lagos, with accommodation for fifty boys, maintained by the Salvation Army with a government subsidy. The boys were taught trades for the practice of which they received equipment on discharge.[2] In Johannesburg the problem was of major proportions : in the year 1936–37 the Juvenile Court had before it 833 male and 117 female African offenders. Excluding statutory

[1] *Quarterly Notes. Bulletin of the I.M.C.*, No. 46 (April 1935), ii–iii; No. 49 (January 1936), vi; No. 54 (April 1937), v; *I.R.M.*, XXV (1936), 68, 89. The experiment was fully reported by its field directors in *The African and the Cinema* by L. A. Notcutt and G. C. Latham (1937). Cf. *I.R.M.*, XXVII (1938), 267–9. The Committee on education in South Africa took note of it: *Report of the Inter-departmental Committee on Native Education, 1935–1936* (1936), 119–20.
[2] *Annual Report on the Social and Economic Progress of the People of Nigeria, 1935* (1936), 66.

offences not applying to Europeans (Pass Laws, etc.), theft, house-breaking, and robbery accounted for 70·23 per cent of offences by males and 56 per cent of those by females. Next came assaults (16·74 per cent and 16·08 per cent), and then (in the case of males) gambling at 9·34 per cent. Sexual offences of males were 8 out of a gross total of 833. The first hostel for juvenile delinquents was begun by the Salvation Army in Sophiatown; the second was organized by a missionary of the American Board Mission, with municipal activity soon to follow.[1]

Such were some of the activities and interests on which missions were invited to spend themselves in a period of unprecedented social change. It was clear however that for the most part such responsibilities would in due course have to be discharged by municipalities and governments on the one hand and by the African churches themselves on the other. Meanwhile the missions were not altogether oblivious of their primary task of evangelization and of nurturing the infant Church.

(5) The Continuing Outreach of Missions

The variegated picture the decade presents includes not only the promotion of new and modified types of service designed to serve the current age, but also consolidation and extension in terms of geographical occupation. Despite the varying political, economic, and social handicaps of the time, the period witnessed an uninterrupted extension of missionary operations together with a further accession of missionary agencies. As some of these did not observe the principle of comity, which the older missions had now for the most part long respected, their coming was not always an unmixed advantage to the cause.[2] The Roman Catholic expansion was impressive, particularly in the wide zone of equatorial Africa; while African separatist sects not only continued to flourish in the Union but sprang up in what might have been thought the less fertile soil of the equatorial region.

In East Africa Kenya had now been in the political limelight since the early 'twenties, presenting the complex problem of a multi-racial society. African needs were well served by some six-teen Societies of which the South Africa General Mission was the latest to arrive.[3] A competent observer, after a careful survey of the situation in the mid-'thirties, concluded: "There is no need

[1] R. E. Phillips, *The Bantu in the City* (1938), 184–5, 243.
[2] Cf. *I.R.M.*, XXVII (1938), 67.
[3] H. R. A. Philp, *A New Day in Kenya* (1936), 149; *I.R.M.*, XXIV (1935), ; XXV (1936), 66.

for more societies or more missionaries." [1] On the other hand the considerable Indian community domiciled in Kenya had been sadly neglected. When the Salvation Army came to the country in 1921 there were those who hoped that, with its considerable experience of work in India, it might undertake this evangelistic task, but the service of the African absorbed its energies. [2] In 1933 the National Missionary Society of India had before it a proposal to send Indian missionaries to evangelize their fellow-nationals in Kenya but this did not mature. [3] In 1934 the British and Foreign Bible Society appointed an Indian as colporteur for work among Indians in Kenya. [4] A new arrival of a different order was the African Orthodox Church, officially registered in the Union of South Africa, whose Archbishop Alexander came to Kenya in 1936 and proceeded in Kikuyu to train candidates for ordination. He was said to be in touch with the independent schools which had seceded from the Church of Scotland, the Church Missionary Society, and other missions during the female circumcision controversy. [5]

In the neighbouring Protectorate of Uganda, where Anglican and Roman Catholic missions were the pioneers, with the Africa Inland Mission (1922) and the Seventh Day Adventists (1927) much later arrivals, there came the Salvation Army in 1931 and the Bible Churchmen's Missionary Society in 1933, the latter undertaking pioneer work among the Karamojong by arrangement with the Anglican Upper Nile diocese. [6] In Tanganyika Territory there were at work in 1930 sixteen Societies: two Anglican, four Lutheran, five other Protestant bodies, and five Roman Catholic Orders. The estimated number of adherents of the Roman missions was 211,000 and of the non-Roman 91,000. [7] The Anglican diocese of Masasi (Universities' Mission) was separated from that of Zanzibar in 1926, while that of Central

[1] H. R. A. Philp, *op. cit.*, 143.

[2] *Ibid.*, 107.

[3] *Missionary Review of the World* (1933), 517. The National Missionary Society of India was founded in 1905 by seventeen leaders of the Church in India who were deeply concerned for the evangelization of their people. Cf. C. E. Abraham, *The Founders of the National Missionary Society of India* (1948), *passim*. Dr. C. E. Abraham informs me that Rai Bahadur A. C. Mukherji prepared a draft plan and received offers of service in response to his appeal, but the necessary financial support was not forthcoming.

[4] *I.R.M.*, XXIV (1935), 76.

[5] *I.R.M.*, XXVI (1937), 67. *Vide infra*, p. 215.

[6] Thomas and Scott, *Uganda* (1935), 336-7; *The Salvation Army Year Book* (1953), 68.

[7] G. F. Sayers, *The Handbook of Tanganyika* (1930), 386.

Tanganyika (Church Missionary Society) was formed in 1927, the Anglican Church in Australia assuming responsibility for it.[1] These organizational developments set the stage for Anglican advance. The Roman Catholics had in 1930 nine vicariates and prefectures of which four were entrusted to the White Fathers.[2] In 1933 the Salvation Army entered the territory, to be followed by two Pentecostal missions, the Swedish Glad Tidings mission, and the Eastern Mennonite mission.[3]

In West Africa from Sierra Leone to Nigeria there were steady developments. Mendeland in the Protectorate of Sierra Leone was the scene of evangelistic outreach by Anglicans, British Methodists, and the United Brethren of America, with the opening in 1933 of a new Union College at Bunumbu for training the much needed teachers and evangelists in which the three denominations co-operated.[4] The Worldwide Evangelization Crusade, whose policy, as the name of its original unit, the Heart of Africa Mission, implies, was to penetrate beyond the existing missionary frontier,[5] found new fields in West Africa at this time. In 1935, permission having been granted by the French authorities, their missionaries began work among tribes in the Ivory Coast. In 1938 a group of seven entered Liberia with unevangelized tribes as their objective, while in the same year a party reached the Gold Coast and established themselves in the north-west in a district adjoining the Ivory Coast.[6] A separatist church countenancing polygamy, the African Universal Church, developed up-country in the Gold Coast in 1935. It was not an importation from South Africa but rather a symptom of growing nationalist feeling in the country.[7]

In Nigeria the four missions constituting the Evangelical Union in the south-east were all reaching northwards towards the Benue. The Methodist mission entered the Idoma country to the north of Iboland in the mid-'twenties where an unwritten language confronted it but by the early 'thirties Biblical translations were appearing. The Church Missionary Society faced a similar task in its pioneer outreach to the Egedde people, where an African catechist undertook the language work.[8] The Qua Iboe mission

[1] G. A. Chambers, *Tanganyika's New Day* (1931), 3.
[2] G. F. Sayers, *op. cit.*, 387.
[3] *The Salvation Army Year Book* (1953), 68; *I.R.M.*, XXVI (1937), 69
[4] *I.R.M.*, XXV (1936), 61.
[5] See Vol. III, p. 230, *n.* 4.
[6] *I.R.M.*, XXV (1936), 61; XXVIII (1939), 55, 56.
[7] *I.R.M.*, XXV (1936), 61-2.
[8] *I.R.M.*, XXVI (1937), 65.

also bestirred itself; in 1931 a deputation visited the Igala country in the Kabba Province south of the Benue, as a result of which work was begun. Five years later the Benue was crossed and the outpost pushed forward to the Bassa and Igbirra tribes, again with language work awaiting.[1] A less happy experience was the secession from the Qua Iboe mission of the Ibesikpo tribe who thereupon invited the Lutheran Synodical Conference in the United States to receive them. At the request of the Qua Iboe mission their Methodist and Presbyterian neighbours sought a solution that would obviate the entry of a new denomination into an adequately provided area, but decisions had been taken and the Lutheran mission accepted its new responsibility in 1936.[2] The followers of an African prophet, Joseph Babalola, in Southern Nigeria in the early 'thirties became separated into two streams : one of several thousands flowed into the existing churches; the other remained distinct as the African Apostolic Church under the encouragement of Europeans of a revivalist sect.[3] The most significant development however for Nigeria in this decade was the new opportunity for entry to the Muslim north. The early policy of Lugard, which restricted missionary entry to cases where the emirs had expressed their approval, had, it was felt, become hardened under his successors into a formula of rigid prohibition.[4] In 1927 the Governor of Nigeria gave an assurance to mission representatives that it was the aim of the Government to encourage among the emirs the recognition of the principle of religious toleration. He further agreed that in certain circumstances opportunity for missionary entry might be given. Long deferred hopes were at last to be realized : in 1931 the Church of the Brethren mission was granted entry to the Biu division of the north-east Bornu Province. The Church Missionary Society was able, after a full generation at Zaria, to advance from that outpost into Sokoto Province in the north-west; while the Sudan Interior Mission was by 1936 becoming established in the four northern Provinces of Sokoto, Katsina, Kano, and Bornu, in all of which it had been granted openings.[5]

In Muslim North Africa there was characteristically little movement of the Christian cause. The effect of the Italian conquest

[1] From the Qua Iboe to the Benue (n.d.), 20–2; I.R.M., XXVI (1937), 65.

[2] I.R.M., XXVI (1937), 65.

[3] I.R.M., XXVIII (1939), 57. This appears to be independent of the Separatist Church of the same name in South Africa. Cf. B. G. M. Sundkler, Bantu Prophets in South Africa (1948), 317.

[4] See Vol. III, pp. 260–1.

[5] I.R.M., XXI (1932), 239; XXIII (1934), 66; XXVI (1937), 64.

upon Roman Catholic fortunes in that region has already been noted.[1] Anglican interests were consolidated by the formation in 1936 of a new diocese of North Africa comprising Morocco, Algeria, and Tunisia together with the Portuguese and Spanish islands off the Atlantic coast.[2] The Methodist Episcopal mission of the States withdrew from its commitment in Tunisia but maintained its Algerian work in which the M.E. Church of Norway now co-operated.[3] In 1934 the Salvation Army joined the missions at work in North Africa, and two years later it entered Egypt.[4] The Anglo-Egyptian Treaty of 1936, which gave recognition to Egypt as an independent state and opened the way for her membership of the League of Nations, did not, for the moment at least, affect the status of missions in the country.[5]

There were still regions of the continent, remote in terms of accessibility, awaiting missionary occupation. Two enterprises, typical of the hard pioneering such spheres still required, belong to the period. In the southern zone of the Anglo-Egyptian Sudan some 1,000 miles up the Nile from Khartoum were the pagan Dinkas to whom the Church Missionary Society came in 1906, while 120 miles to the west lay the Moru country. To Lui, a strategic centre for the tribe, came Dr. and Mrs. Kenneth Fraser in 1920. With the formation of the Upper Nile diocese in 1926, comprehending the pagan section of the Sudan and the Elgon Mission in the north of the Uganda Protectorate, more attention could be given to the needs of this vast region.[6] In 1926 the first converts were received when eight Moru boys were baptized. In 1930 the first Christian women of the tribe, five in number, received the rite. By 1934 there were 125 baptized members of the church with a total Christian community of 414. Biblical translation was carried forward, so that the infant church was before long provided with the Gospel of St. Mark (1928), the Gospel of St. Luke and the Acts of the Apostles (1931), and the Gospel of St. John (1934).[7] Fraser's policy was far-sighted : " The doctor's idea was to have eventually a school and dispensary every fifteen miles along the roads in every direction. He always stressed the importance of decentralization, of getting out into the distant

[1] *Vide supra*, p. 139.   [2] *I.R.M.*, XXVI (1937), 61.
[3] *Ibid.*, 61.
[4] *The Salvation Army Year Book* (1953), 32.
[5] *I.R.M.*, XXVII (1938), 60–1.
[6] W. W. Cash, *The Changing Sudan* (1930), 48–51, 68–70, 71. Cf. Vol. III, p. 258.
[7] E. Fraser, *The Doctor Comes to Lui: A Story of Beginnings in the Sudan* (1938), 37, 39–40.

parts of the district and using Lui primarily as a training ground for that purpose." [1] Moreover, dispensary, school, and church were to be one, and to this end the two African workers sent to each centre—a teacher and a dispenser trained as such and each an evangelist—were to co-operate, the teacher helping in the dispensary and the dispenser sharing in the school. By 1938 there were sixteen such centres at distances from Lui varying from seven to 185 miles and serving a population of 65,000 in an area of 15,000 square miles.[2]

In the south of the continent, in the Anglican diocese of Damaraland in South-West Africa, an enterprise of the South African dioceses of George and Cape Town was begun in Ovamboland, with the friendly approval of the neighbouring Finnish mission.[3] The people were the Ovakuanjama settled astride the frontier with Angola, of whom some 25,000 in the mandated territory constituted the prospective field. It lay some 240 miles beyond the railhead, 100 miles of this journey being across the " thirst belt " of desert. Transport was naturally a major problem. The first station, St. Mary's Mission, was begun in 1924. A second centre thirteen miles to the east, Holy Cross Mission, was started in 1927. Outstations sprang up around each centre—some half dozen attached to St. Mary's and three to Holy Cross. In the early 'thirties an outstation was begun some thirty-six miles southwest of St. Mary's among a section of the Oukuambi tribe who had settled there. The successful sinking of a well by the teacher, at a point directed in a dream, was a triumph of note in a desert country and greatly enhanced his prestige. Here also medical work (there was a hospital at St. Mary's), bush schools, and evangelism were the three strands in missionary service, with permanent churches at the two European stations for daily worship.[4]

---

[1] Ibid., 52.

[2] Ibid., 52, 55, 69; cf. P. L. Garlick, The Wholeness of Man: A Study in the History of Healing (1943), 169–70. Dr. Fraser's memorial is in the Moru Country, but a tablet in Khartoum Cathedral commemorates him: " Give thanks to God for Kenneth Fraser, M.D., physician and evangelist, by whose skill in healing and godliness of living, Christ's light has shone upon the darkness of the Moru people. He was born in 1877, and died at Lui 10th January, 1935. Thy word, O Lord, healeth all things.— Wisdom, xvi, 12."

[3] The work of the Finnish mission in Ovamboland received high commendation from Lord Lugard at the session of the Permanent Mandates Commission of the League of Nations in 1932 for the excellence of its work in the territory.—Quarterly Notes, Bulletin of the I.M.C., No. 38 (April 1933) viii.

[4] E. M. Wolfe, Beyond the Thirst Belt: The Story of the Ovamboland Mission (1935), 28–9, 76, 87, 90–2.

In the Belgian Congo both Protestant and Roman Catholic missions registered notable advance. The Baptist Missionary Society in 1931 added a further European station to its chain along the Congo—Tshumbiri, south of Bolobo—while the index of baptisms (2,868 in 1937, 3,908 in 1938) represented " a very great extension of the area of evangelization and a corresponding addition to the responsibility for teaching and shepherding the converts and their families ".[1] The American Baptist Foreign Mission Society reported 2,907 baptisms in 1938, with a total church membership in 1939 of 34,498, compared with 21,340 in 1931 and 5,361 in 1921.[2] These two Societies, which had long co-operated in training African pastors and teachers at Kimpese in the Ecole de Pasteurs et d'Instituteurs (formerly known as the Kongo Evangelical Training Institution), were now joined by the Swedish Missionary Society which in 1938 decided to co-operate in this work.[3] In the decade 1921–31 many new missions of American, British, and Scandinavian origin entered the Belgian Congo, so that Henri Anet could report that " the Congo may be said to be now fully occupied, in the sense that there are no longer great tracts where no mission has ever been ".[4] Nevertheless in 1934 the Salvation Army established its first corps in Leopoldville, and in 1937 crossed the Congo into French Equatorial Africa with, in due course, a considerable extension of its activities in both territories.[5] In 1934 a recrudescence of the so-called Prophet Movement in the Lower Congo was experienced. Teachers and church members were drawn into highly emotional and intensely excited gatherings at night with more of pagan practice than Christian demeanour. As one missionary observer expressed it : " We had the opportunity to see the wildest orgies strangely enacted under the name of Christian ecstasy, divine inspiration and guidance "— yet another warning of the perils confronting the Church in Africa.[6] In the neighbouring mandated territory of Ruanda-Urundi administered by Belgium, to which German missions had not been permitted to return, the Church Missionary Society and

[1] *The Baptist Missionary Society, 147th Annual Report* (1939), 18, 78.

[2] P. H. J. Lerrigo, *All Kindreds and Tongues: An Illustrated Survey of the Foreign Mission Enterprise of Northern Baptists* (Fourth Issue, 1940), 244; *I.R.M.*, XXI (1932), 224.

[3] P. H. J. Lerrigo, *op. cit.*, 246; *I.R.M.*, XXVI (1937), 66.

[4] *I.R.M.*, XXI (1932), 225.

[5] *The Salvation Army Year Book* (1953), 54–5.

[6] K. Alden, " The Prophet Movement in Congo ", in *I.R.M.*, XXV (1936), 347–53. *Vide supra*, p. 127.

the Danish Baptist Mission now began work.[1] In 1936 an Alliance of Protestant Missions in the area was formed, and this was in due course affiliated to the Congo Protestant Council.[2]

Roman Catholic missions have shown a remarkable buoyancy in tropical Africa. It has been alleged that the Roman authorities regarded North Africa as too deeply committed to Islam for any hope of success within measurable time, and South Africa as so largely Protestant that the prospect was not encouraging (though in Basutoland Roman Catholic missions have made striking headway), whereas the equatorial belt offered unparalleled opportunity for advance.[3] Whatever the high strategy involved, there is no doubt about the impressive expansion of their missions. In the seven years 1922–29 the number of vicariates in Africa rose from ninety-two to 115 with a corresponding increased facility for evangelistic work.[4] Central Africa was the region of most rapid growth, with the Belgian mandated territory of Ruanda-Urundi the most spectacular. Thus in the vicariate of Ruanda in a single year (1933–34) the number of baptized persons rose from 97,959 to 142,549.[5] Elsewhere the increase was substantial if not quite so overwhelming; thus in French Cameroons, a mandated territory, the 26,000 baptized persons of 1914 had become 170,000 in 1937.[6] It is not surprising that by 1939 it was reported that in Central Africa—Ruanda, Urundi, and Uganda in particular— the missionary personnel was becoming quite insufficient for the dual task of pastoral and missionary duty, and this despite the steady increase in priests and sisters.[7] Thus in Uganda the total number of priests increased from 173 (31 African) in 1927 to 302 (77 African) in 1939; in Tanganyika from 213 (14 African) in 1927 to 498 (41 African) in 1939; and in the Belgian Congo from 547 (29 African) in 1927 to 1,233 (78 African) in 1939.[8] Such progress within a dozen years was without parallel. Against this

[1] I.R.M., XXI (1932), 225.
[2] I.R.M., XXVII (1938), 70. Five missions were concerned: Belgian, C.M.S., Danish Baptist, Friends' African Gospel Mission, and Free Methodist.
[3] H. R. A. Philp, op. cit., 138.
[4] I.R.M., XXI (1932), 378.
[5] I.R.M., XXIV (1935), 111.
[6] R. Delavignette, Freedom and Authority in French West Africa (first published as Service Africain, 1946; English translation, 1950), 99.
[7] I.R.M., XXVIII (1939), 97.
[8] International Fides Service, October 1, 1949. Corresponding statistics for sisters were: Uganda, 251 (171) to 613 (382); Tanganyika, 267 (89) to 566 (145); Belgian Congo, 559 (111) to 1,631 (175).—I.F.S., October 8, 1949.

background it is the less surprising that there were claimed in 1937 a total of 2,826,354 Roman Catholics and 1,440,328 catechumens in Africa.[1]

If then the second decade between the wars presented what was in certain respects a somewhat sombre if not sinister environment for the Christian movement in Africa, yet the environment did not master it. This was no new experience in the history of the Christian Church, and once again the tenacity of the Christian mission and the vitality of the growing Church were maintained despite the gathering cloud around.

[1] Albert Hublou, S.J., in *I.R.M.*, XXVII (1938), 525.

CHAPTER 5

THE EMERGING CHURCH

COUPLED with the tenacity of the Christian mission during dangerous days, which for the most part was a foreign agency still, was the fact of the emerging Church slowly becoming rooted in African soil. It was a far cry from Bickersteth's injunction to the Church Missionary Society's devoted pioneers in Sierra Leone, after a dozen years of work, to make evangelism their first priority; from Krapf and Rebmann's pioneering journeys in the 'forties; from the dramatic turn in the whole story when David Livingstone lifted the veil from Central Africa; from George Grenfell's explorations of the interlacing waters of the Congo at the close of the century; and the patient and laborious, often heartbreaking, Christian service of many more. But their labour was not in vain in the Lord. That for which they toiled was now coming slowly into being : a fellowship of Christian disciples of African descent that might be as salt in their own community and a shining light among their people.

(1) *The Coming of the Church*

To herald the coming of the Church in Africa is not to claim that communities of spotless Christians were beginning to appear —even Paul who addressed " the church of God which is at Corinth . . . called to be saints " [1] was far from claiming that they were immaculate—but that groups of believers, sincerely committed to the Christian faith and way of life, with however imperfect a practice of it, were living in community, as expressed in corporate worship, in some regular edifying fellowship, and in unselfish service of their fellows, as inspired by the command : " Thou shalt love the Lord thy God with all thy heart, and with all thy soul, and with all thy strength, and with all thy mind; and thy neighbour as thyself." [2] It is true that a difference of emphasis was to be found according as the comprehensive or the gathered church was the ideal, but the experience of Christians growing in community was shared by both.

[1] I Corinthians 1 : 2.
[2] Luke 10: 27.

The picture of the Church thus scattered through the continent was, in the nature of the case, a variegated óne with the two main streams of traditional and reformed Christianity flowing side by side, and with the emerging Church found at different stages of its' growth, from the slender blade peeping above the earth to the ear with its promise of a harvest, though barely producing yet the full corn in the ear. While a comprehensive survey would scarcely be possible or indeed desirable, certain selected situations may nevertheless with fairness be presented, not only in their own right but as in some respects samples of a larger whole.

The Roman Catholic Church had long recruited Africans to the priesthood and religious orders, including establishments specifi-cally for those Africans who were conscious of such a vocation.[1] The raising up of a native priesthood for the regular celebration of mass marks for the Roman Catholic a vital stage in the coming of the Church. With characteristic foresight and statesmanship an Encyclical of 1926, *Rerum Ecclesiae*, which greatly stimulated missionary enterprise, singled out for particular attention the urgent necessity of bringing into being everywhere an indigenous priesthood to serve the faithful in the uncertain days ahead. Ten years later the Pontifical Society of St. Peter the Apostle for the Native Clergy decided to establish branches in all lands.[2] These acts did but serve to intensify an existing concern in Africa. In Uganda, a pioneer field of the White Fathers, a junior seminary had been begun in 1893, which, together with a senior course, in time comprehended eighteen years of study. It was accordingly 1913 before the first two African priests were ordained. In 1921 there were nineteen, and by 1939 seventy-seven African priests had been ordained, or half the total of 152 for all British Africa at that date.[3] In the Belgian Congo the two African priests of 1921 had become seventy-eight by 1939, the majority being in eastern Congo. The first in western Congo was ordained in 1934; his first mass in his native village is said to have been so enthusiastic an occasion that a congregation of 20,000 assembled.[4] Tangan-yika with one African priest in 1921 had forty-one by 1939.[5]

In West Africa the growth of the priesthood was less rapid :

[1] See Vol. II, p. 215; *I.R.M.*, XXVII (1938), 106. A new congregation of African nuns, the Handmaids of the Holy Child, received its first novices in West Africa in 1937.

[2] *I.R.M.*, XXVI (1937), 100–1.

[3] Thomas and Scott, *Uganda* (1935), 333; *International Fides Service*, October 1, 1949.

[4] *International Fides Service*, October 1, 1949: *I.R.M.*, XXIV (1935),111.

[5] *I.F.S.*, October 1, 1949.

Nigeria in 1921 had one African priest, in 1939 ten; the Gold
Coast none and three in the same years; while in French West
Africa the four of 1921 had only become five by 1939. In French
Equatorial Africa by contrast the increase over the same period had
been from eight to twenty-two.[1] The total number of African
priests, small compared with Asian fields had almost reached 500
by 1938, though no African bishop had then been consecrated in
modern times.[2] Nevertheless the number of seminarists in training
and the growing number of ordinations offered tangible assurance
for the future African leadership of the Church. A further step
had been taken by the development of the hierarchy in Africa. In
1922 the first Apostolic Delegate, Gijlswijk, had arrived in South
Africa where a new ecclesiastical arrangement had appeared, and
in 1924 the first Roman Catholic Synod of South Africa was held.[3]
In 1930 the first Apostolic Delegate, Dellepiane, was appointed
for the Belgian Congo, while in the same year Arthur Hinsley,
later Cardinal Archbishop of Westminster, took up his duties as
first Apostolic Delegate for Africa. As East Africa was his more
particular concern he resided at Mombasa in Kenya.[4]

As with the Roman Catholic Church so with the various Protestant Churches, each for the most part reproduced in Africa its own
particular pattern of ecclesiastical organization. The American
Board of Commissioners for Foreign Missions had pioneered its
work in Natal in 1835. A generation later, in 1869, the Board
declared its aim to be the establishment of independent churches
with a ministry recruited from among them, and added : " If its
missionaries appear to be over-cautious in devolving responsibilities upon native organizations and a native ministry, they are
encouraged to the exercise of a stronger faith and to bolder action
in this regard." [5] The secretary, Nathaniel Clark, applied more
than a little judicious pressure to secure these developments and
by degrees ordained Zulu pastors were placed in charge of
churches, thus releasing the American missionaries for more

[1] *Ibid.*, October 1 and 8, 1949.
[2] *I.R.M.*, XXVII (1938), 520. Commenting on the relatively small
number of African priests, Albert Hublou, S.J., has explained this by
reference to " the rules of the Roman Catholic Church as regards the
literary education and celibacy of its priests. The training of a European
priest takes at least six years of philosophical and theological studies, in
addition to the classical humanities, and these rules are strictly maintained
with regard to coloured priests."—*Loc. cit.*
[3] Schmidlin, *Catholic Mission History* (1933), 739.
[4] *Ibid.*, 739.
[5] *The Missionary Herald* (A.B.C.F.M.), LXV (1869), 363.

aggressive evangelism.[1] In due course there was prepared a Constitution of the Congregational Churches of the American Board, federating the various congregations in an organization comprising an annual assembly with executive committee, a pastors' conference, and a board of trustees to hold church property. The relation of the Board to the churches found expression in the office of supervisor to which specific functions were assigned.[2]

A neighbouring church of independent status was the Bantu Presbyterian Church of South Africa, the fruit of the labours of Scottish Presbyterians. The Free Church of Scotland and the United Presbyterians had in the eighteen-forties each inherited work among the Xhosa-speaking peoples, resulting from the pioneer service of the Glasgow Missionary Society.[3] When a union of the Free Church and the United Presbyterians in South Africa was contemplated—a union that matured in 1897 in the formation of the Presbyterian Church of South Africa—the relation of the African to the European congregations provoked some debate. In the issue the missions of the United Presbyterians entered the new Church while the missions of the Free Church retained the direct connexion with Scotland, the local African congregations constituting the Synod of Kaffraria. The anomaly of this situation was pressed home when the two parent Churches in Scotland entered into union in 1900, issuing in the United Free Church of Scotland.

In the Plan of Union the overseas policy of the Church was declared to be the formation in each country of an independent Church. The application of such a policy to South Africa still presented the old dilemma : integration of the African and European sections despite differences of language, tradition, and experience; or a distinct organization where African congregations with their own church courts could develop independently though with as much co-operation from the European missionary as might be desired. The second course was adopted and in 1923 the Bantu Presbyterian Church of South Africa came into being with the inauguration of its first General Assembly at Lovedale on July 4—significant date ! The new Church comprised some

---

[1] The initial course of development is given in E. W. Smith, *The Life and Times of Daniel Lindley* (1949), 396–404. Daniel Lindley wrote of these proposals, which he welcomed: " If we carry out his suggestions we shall hardly know ourselves. It will seem as if the white folks had become black and the black folks white ".—*Ibid.*, 397.

[2] For the full text of the Constitution, see *The Younger and Older Churches*, Jerusalem Meeting Report, III (1928), 327–33.

[3] See Vol. II, p. 136, *n.* 1.

forty-five congregations organized in seven presbyteries with a communicant membership of over 22,000 and 7,000 candidates in
preparation for membership, these all being confided to the pastoral
care of forty-eight ordained European and African ministers, for
the missionaries accompanied their congregations into the new
Church with as full powers as the African ministers, no colour
bar being even tacitly admitted. Indeed, the first Moderator to
be elected was an honoured veteran missionary of forty-two years'
service.[1] The constitution of the Church naturally preserved a
Presbyterian polity, with presbyters or elders and deacons as the
two recognized orders, and included a statement of doctrine in
eight principal articles. The independence of the Church was
formally recognized in the constitution : " This Church has the
inherent right, under the safeguards . . . which it itself has provided, to frame and adopt its subordinate standards, to revise and
alter the same . . . to interpret its statement of doctrine, to modify
or change its constitution. . . ." [2]

The formation of the Baptist Union in South Africa in 1881
had been followed in 1892 by the establishment of the South
African Baptist Missionary Society.[3] The African congregations
resulting from the Society's labours were granted the first stage
of independent status in 1927 with the inauguration of the Bantu
Baptist Church. The independence was limited since the powers
of the assembly of the new Church were advisory only, the Society
retaining executive control, but a free forum was now provided
for African debate such as had not before been available. European
missionaries joined with African ministers and delegates in the
annual deliberations. It was specifically stated at the inauguration
that the continuance for the time being of European control was
" not because of racial difference but of stored experience . . . that
under our leadership you may share more clearly in shaping your
destiny ".[4]

In Nyasaland the Scottish Presbyterians also proceeded towards
devolution, though this involved a union of the Livingstonia
(United Free Church) and Blantyre (Church of Scotland) Presbyteries in a Synod which became the Supreme Court of a united
Church—the Church of Central Africa (Presbyterian). The functions of the new Synod were stated in the constitution, while the
respective Presbyteries continued as before. It was an interesting

---

[1] *The South African Outlook*, LIII (1923), 127–8, 174–6.
[2] For the full text, see *The Younger and Older Churches*, 333–6.
[3] See Vol. III, p. 176.
[4] *The South African Outlook*, LVIII (1928), June 1.

provision that " as far as possible the rights of the native language shall be maintained in the Church courts ". A short doctrinal statement was also included.[1] A third Presbytery, that of Mkhoma under the Dutch Reformed Church of South Africa, adhered to the union, while at the close of our decade negotiations were proceeding for the Church in Rhodesia established by the London Missionary Society to accede to it also.[2] The original proposal for a united Church for the growing Christian community had been made at the Conference of Federated Missions of Nyasaland, meeting at Mvera in 1910, and the Scottish Presbyterians were the first to take action upon it.[3]

In Basutoland the Paris Missionary Society, like the American Board in Natal, had entered in the eighteen-thirties, and passed through many vicissitudes incidental to the political turmoil of the time.[4] The aim of the Society had been the establishment of an independent African Church and this was in due course realized. Like the American Board, the Society took the first step forward in the 'sixties and then admitted laymen to the mission Conference in 1865. But the time was stormy and progress was delayed. However, in 1872 an important step was taken in setting up local councils in conformity with tribal organization. Each outstation had its council under a catechist analogous to the village *lekhotla* under its headman, while a central council, corresponding to the chief's *lekhotla*, consisted of some sixty members. The method of conducting business in the *lekhotla* was followed and council members thus received a valuable training in shouldering their share of responsibility for church affairs. It was to be the 'nineties before the next notable advance was made. Then, in 1894, under the inspiring leadership of Adolph Mabille, a central fund was set up to which all congregations were required to contribute, and the first Synod was held.[5] In 1898 came the crown of his labours when the *Seboka* or Assembly was established in which the Basuto themselves now jointly held the reins : " The Seboka, or Assembly, was to be composed of European missionaries and the Basuto ordained

[1] For the text, see *The Younger and Older Churches, Ibid.*, 336–8.
[2] *The Growing Church*, Tambaram Madras Series, II (1939), 31–2.
[3] The original name proposed, in view of the intention, was therefore simply " The Church of Central Africa," but " as the organization of the Church was, in fact, Presbyterian, and it was felt that brethren of the Anglican communion might misunderstand the motives which lay behind the use of the name adopted, it was decided to add the descriptive term ".— *Ibid.*, 31.
[4] See Vol. II, pp. 147–52.
[5] E. W. Smith, *The Mabilles of Basutoland* (1939), 137, 210, 347.

pastors, on terms of equality, with various lay representatives, and was to have jurisdiction in all affairs of the Church—discipline, finance, the creation of parishes, the primary, Bible and Theological Schools. All business was to be conducted in Sesuto." [1] The year 1898 may therefore be regarded as the date of birth of the Church of Basutoland. The Constitution, Rules, and Regulations as eventually adopted and revised were issued in 1927 in a series of nineteen chapters covering all aspects of the life and work of the Church.[2] As with Nyasaland so with Basutoland there was a steady migration beyond the territory, and as Johannesburg was the lodestar for many, the Paris Society included the city within its purview. In 1938 on four urban locations with a population of 60,000 Africans, 20,000 were from Basutoland.[3]

In Bechuanaland the growth of the organized Church was a slower process. Under the auspices of the London Mission the individual churches that began to appear were naturally of the Congregational order. The District Committee, in which missionary authority constitutionally resided, took the first step in 1906 by setting up Native Advisory Councils for each of the two areas under the Committee's jurisdiction, and from 1909 these became active bodies. A Native Ministers' Committee was the next development, emerging from a series of African ministers' conferences. This Committee in 1932 sought a clarification of the position of the African ministry, with helpful results; but it was not until 1943 that the South Africa Mission Council was to appear, on which Africans both ministerial and lay shared the membership with European missionaries. " The late development of an organized church ", says Norman Goodall, " and the numerical weakness of the African ministry suggests that in Bechuanaland capacity for self-government in matters ecclesiastical was slow to show itself." [4] A material factor appears to have been the unwillingness of the chiefs to tolerate the growth of a self-governing Church, which to their way of thinking was bound to involve serious risks to the authority of the chieftainship.[5]

In Tanganyika an African Church of Lutheran persuasion appeared under the auspices of the Leipzig Evangelical Lutheran

[1] *Ibid.*, 360.
[2] A summary is given in *The Older and Younger Churches*, Jerusalem Meeting Report, III, 319–27.
[3] *Basuto and Barotse News* (January 1939), 24–6.
[4] Norman Goodall, *A History of the London Missionary Society, 1895–1945* (1954), 282–4.
[5] *Ibid.*, 285–7. Dr. E. W. Smith tells me that at one time the Basuto chiefs likewise regarded with suspicion the Church as organized, as if it

Mission. It was the recognized policy of the mission to tread the middle way between an uncompromising prohibition of African social custom and deliberate attempts at Christian adaptation, by giving recognition to a permissive survival pending further enlightenment of Christian converts through education.[1] But for one missionary at least this was not enough. A distinguished member of the mission, Bruno Gutmann, made an intensive study of the Chagga among whom the mission worked, and proposed that the organization of the Church should not be a repetition of the German Lutheran model but should reflect in its pattern the Bantu social structure, while the sanctions operative in tribal life should be employed as far as possible.[2] Development on these lines in the post-war years led to the holding of the first Synod of the Church in 1930 when a constitution was completed. The responsibility, accepted by individual congregations, for sending and supporting teacher-evangelists in new areas was before long resulting, as reported in 1938, in an annual accession of some 1,500 to 2,000 baptized members.[3]

In Uganda the beginnings of the little Christian community had been characterized by a courage and fidelity, under the merciless fires of persecution, second to none in the continent. And as the early years passed by progress was such that " readers " were numbered in their tens of thousands, though it is true that enrolment as a reader did not necessarily imply a desire for baptism.[4] Under wise leadership in the Anglican mission African teachers and clergy were multiplied until the far-sighted Bishop Tucker decided the time had come to devolve more responsibility for their own affairs upon the Africans of the diocese.[5] On his arrival in the

were the setting up of a rival authority to their own. In earlier days in Calabar, Eyo Honesty II, for all his support of the Scottish mission, had shown similar sensitiveness. See Vol. II, p. 39, n. 1.

[1] *I.R.M.*, XXVI (1937), 501.

[2] In 1925 Gutmann's *Gemeindeaufbau aus dem Evangelium, Grundsätzliches für Mission und Heimatkirche* expressed his principles. His works that made him the recognized authority on the Chagga included: *Das Recht der Dschagga* (1926), and *Die Stammeslehren der Dschagga* I (1932), II, (1935), III (1938). Gutmann offered a brief exposition of his views in "Aufgaben der Gemeinschaftsbildung in Afrika ", in *Africa*, I (1928), 429–45. Two valuable commentaries are provided in: " Dr. Gutmann's Work on Kilimanjaro: Critical Studies of his Theories of Missionary Method " by Otto Raum and Günter Wagner in *I.R.M.*, XXVI (1937), 500–13.

[3] J. Richter, *Tanganyika and its Future* (1934), 20–2; *The Economic Basis of the Church*, Tambaram Madras Series, V, 481–2.

[4] See Vol. III, p. 97.

[5] A. R. Tucker, *Eighteen Years in Uganda and East Africa* (1908), I, 114–15, 235–7.

country in 1890 he found a Church Council already in existence; it became his policy to strengthen it and develop its functions as far as possible. He wrote to a leading colleague as early as January 1891 : " It will be our wisdom to develop the Church Council, and to make its members realise that theirs is the responsibility, the work of organising the Church, and of evangelising their fellow countrymen. Let us consult them in everything and make their meetings times of real conference, one with the other, on the pressing questions of the day." R. H. Walker, later Archdeacon of Uganda, was the colleague and proved a most willing and able collaborator in the bishop's policy.[1] Tucker realized that if the missionary body held aloof from the councils of the native Church, content to act through their own organization, Africans would be quick to see that decisions in the missionary body were those that mattered and would lose interest in their own Church organization.[2]

By 1897 Tucker decided the time had come to prepare and submit a constitution for the Church which embodied the representative principle, hitherto lacking. A collateral question that proved obdurate of solution was the relation of the missionaries to such a church organization on a representative basis as was proposed. Tucker felt strongly that they should find their place within the Church, sharing with Africans in its government. But the missionary body felt it better to remain outside as an advisory group. In 1899 as much of the constitution as was agreed to— which was three-fourths of it, providing for parochial and district councils and representation to the Central Council, together with the establishment of a central fund—became the working rule of the Church. A further step forward was taken in 1907 with the establishment of an annual Synod. But it was not till 1909 that the full constitution received unanimous support, with missionaries accepting their position within it, to Tucker's deep joy. The constitution provided for an African majority in the House of Laity, and one in the House of Clergy as soon as African clergy were in the majority among the ordained men of the diocese. This gave the Church of Uganda complete self-government under an African majority, modified only by the standards of faith and doctrine enshrined in the constitution and by the bishop's veto so long as he remained a European.[3]

[1] Ibid., I, 238–9, 240.   [2] Ibid., I, 241; II, 148.
[3] Ibid., II, 202–3, 341, 348; A. P. Shepherd, Tucker of Uganda (1930), 84–5, 119, 146–7, 175, 181–2, 187; R. Oliver, The Missionary Factor in East Africa (1952), 219–22.

In the Belgian Congo, with its forty-five Protestant missions at work, the ideal had been fostered since 1934 of the Church of Christ in Congo. It was admitted that the foreign missionary had long dominated the situation so that a working partnership with African leaders had been the rare exception. By encouraging regional conferences in which Christians of varied evangelical missions might share, with Congo-wide gatherings in due course, it was hoped to realize in progressive stages the ideal of the name, the common use of which the missions encouraged. " The unity of the Church ", writes G. W. Carpenter, " has been conceived in terms of fellowship, not of organization, and rightly so. It is unlikely that the missionaries, representing many backgrounds and preoccupied with many tasks, will discover the full meaning of the unity of the Congo Church. But it is imperative that the Christians of Congo should do so." [1]

A Church in process of attaining autonomy, in fellowship with sister Churches in L'Église du Christ au Congo, was that in the Kasai region under the auspices of the Presbyterian Church in the United States, more briefly known as the Southern Presbyterians. Commencing operations in 1891 it was twenty years before any considerable expansion could be reported, but by the mid-'twenties the foreign staff numbered sixty-four, the African helpers exceeded 1,900, and the communicant membership was 21,000 with a further 22,000 under instruction.[2] By 1938 there were nearly 900 outstations grouped around the seven principal centres. Such developments demanded some suitable form of church organization; to meet the need the *Book of Church Order* was issued in 1931. This presented the results of earlier experience and discussion in this field, both co-ordinating existing practice and providing a larger opportunity for African participation in church affairs. The session, a church court found at the main stations, consisted of African elders with the pastor sitting as moderator while the foreign missionary attended as adviser only. For the two higher courts vernacular names were chosen. The *Tshihangu* (place where a palaver is held) or presbytery met quarterly and was composed of all ordained Africans and Europeans, with representatives from the African elders, the African majority being at least ten to one. The *Moungilu* (place where people confer or covenant together) corresponded to the annual Synod in Presbyterian polity; here there was still an African majority of not less

[1] G. W. Carpenter, *Highways for God in Congo* (1952), 82.
[2] Beach and Fahs, *World Missionary Atlas* (1925), 89, 110.

than three to one.[1] The purpose in view was the eventual integration of the church organization into a Congo-wide Christian fellowship : " It is sincerely hoped that our present organization, stripped of all non-essential details, may fit into the framework of the Église du Christ au Congo." [2]

In the Portuguese territory of Angola the churches of the Congregational order had taken the lead in Protestant effort. The American Board entered the country in 1880, and in 1886 the Foreign Missionary Society of the Congregational Churches of Canada (in 1924 merged in the United Church of Canada) joined in support of the work which was in the districts of Benguella and Bihé.[3] Progress was such that by 1933 the American Board reported a staff of 715 African workers paid and voluntary, while the United Church of Canada reported 853—together 1,568 out of the Protestant total of 2,854. The Church in Angola, under the auspices of these two missions, claimed in 1938 a Christian community of some 100,000. As in Basutoland and among the Chagga, so here the existing system of village government became the model for church government, with such modifications as the difference of function required. The paid workers—fourteen ordained pastors, ninety deacons, and sixty deaconesses—were all supported by funds raised by the Church, the Africans themselves authorizing all payments. A staff of unpaid lay workers, totalling 2,040 in 1938, were responsible, two in each village, for outstation activities. The financial contribution of the missions lay in the fields of education, medical work, industrial training, and promotion of scientific agriculture.[4]

On the Guinea Coast the Anglican mission in Sierra Leone had pioneered in developing an African church organization. With the establishment of the bishopric in 1852 steps were taken to develop self-support and an ecclesiastical system suited to local circumstances in which African pastors were to carry increasing responsibility. The basis was provided in certain " Articles of arrangement " between the Church Missionary Society and the Bishop of Sierra Leone which were drafted by Henry Venn, whose doctrine of the " *euthanasia* of a Mission " was thus being carried

[1] C. L. Crane, "A Growing Church in the Kasai District of the Congo," in *The Growing Church*, Tambaram Madras Series, II (1939), 18–24.
[2] *Ibid.*, 18.
[3] See Vol. III, pp. 125–8.
[4] J. T. Tucker, *Angola, The Land of the Blacksmith Prince* (1933), 138, 141; *The Economic Basis of the Church*, Tambaram Madras Series, V (1939), 477–80.

into effect.[1] To the ensuing Native Pastorate organization, consisting of a Church Council and Church Committee under the bishop, nine parishes in charge of African pastors were transferred.[2] Self-support for pastors, churches, and schools was finally achieved in 1890 when a continuing grant-in-aid from the Church Missionary Society came to an end. The Sierra Leone Church also assumed from 1876 responsibility for certain mission work beyond the boundaries of the Colony, relieving the Society of all its direct obligations in this direction by 1908, though financial aid was still given. However by 1928 the Church itself was raising £2,000 per annum for this work.[3] Valuable as these developments were they did not, under the Anglican ecclesiastical system, result in autonomy. Indeed, Eugene Stock went so far as to say, " The Sierra Leone Church can only be called a ' Church ' by courtesy ", pointing out that " in Church of England Missions all Native congregations and clergy belong to the Church of England temporarily, until a proper Native Church is established, with its own Bishops and Synods and Canons."[4] An important step in that direction was taken in 1937 when the first African assistant bishop was consecrated for service in the diocese.[5]

The Methodist Church of the Gold Coast—until Methodist Union in Great Britain in 1932, the Wesleyan Methodist Church —while enjoying considerable independence in practice, was still subject to the British Conference, the Annual Conference being the sovereign authority in Methodist polity. In the connexional

[1] The Articles were approved by the Archbishop of Canterbury and the Bishop of London. Although dated March, 1853, it was 1860 before they could be acted upon owing to the early death of the first three bishops (see Vol. II., pp. 58–9). The general principle was thus stated : " That the charge and superintendence of the Native Pastors and Christian congregations . . . be placed under the Bishop of Sierra Leone, assisted by a Council and by a Church Committee. And that arrangements be proposed for providing the Native Pastors with a suitable income from local resources, and also for giving them a status assimilated to that of Incumbents at home."—Stock, The History of the Church Missionary Society (1899), II., 416. The Committee was to be concerned with finance, and the Council with administration. Both were in part nominated by the Bishop and the C.M.S. and in part elected by the clergy.

[2] See Vol. II, pp. 217–18.

[3] The Church Overseas, 1 (1928), 59.

[4] Stock, op. cit., II, 422. On the distinction between Church Councils overseas in Anglican and Free Church polity respectively, see Ibid., II, 423 ; N. Goodall, A History of the London Missionary Society, 1895–1945 (1954), 451.

[5] Annual Report of the Church Missionary Society (1939), 72.

system of British Methodism a group of churches form a circuit, the administrative unit to which ministers are appointed. A group of circuits constitute a district with the Synod as its church council, from which delegates are appointed to the annual Conference. The Methodists of the Gold Coast constituted a district with an annual Synod in which African members were in the majority but which did not elect delegates to the British Conference, though finally subject to its authority. In practice, however, local affairs were left to the final decision of the Synod, which was composed of all ordained ministers, European and African, and lay representatives from the circuits. There was one exception to this delegation of authority in practice : the admission of candidates to the ordained ministry, over which the Conference continued to exercise jurisdiction. Complete independence, therefore, could only appear with the grant of conference status. Meanwhile the Missionary Society (more strictly, the Missionary Committee of the Church) acted as the agent of the Conference. In this connexion rules and regulations emanating both from the Committee and the Synod constituted a local polity governing the affairs of the Church. These were codified in 1914 in a handbook of *Local Polity of the Gold Coast District*.[1] By 1938 the Church was served by some fifty ordained African ministers with a supporting force of 400 catechists and a reported total membership in full communion approaching 60,000. European missionaries were largely engaged in educational work. Of the total income received there was raised in the Gold Coast itself some eighty-seven per cent.[2]

The Evangelical Church in Egypt and the Sudan was the fruit of missionary enterprise by the United Presbyterian Church of North America, commenced in 1854. In 1860 missionaries constituted the first presbytery, and a few years later the first congregation was organized in Cairo, four Egyptian elders and three Egyptian deacons being elected—the real starting-point of an indigenous evangelical Church.[3] The training of a ministry was begun, so that by 1897 there were twenty-one ordained Egyptians in the service of the Church. In 1899 an annual synod constituted by the four existing presbyteries was set up.[4] The climax came

---

[1] *Directions of the Missionary Committee and Resolutions adopted by the District Synod for the General Economy and Working of the Circuits in the Gold Coast District* (1914). In a series of 16 brief chapters many matters are handled, ranging from the ordained ministry to the Church's attitude to African custom.

[2] E. W. Thompson, " The Methodist Church of the Gold Coast " in *The Growing Church*, Tambaram Madras Series, II, 6–7.

[3] See Vol. II, pp. 297–9.　　　　　　[4] See Vol. III, pp. 165–6.

when in March 1926 the Synod of the Nile became a self-governing, independent Egyptian Church with full responsibility for all the organized churches and for the theological seminary. It was an extensive commitment: by 1937 a membership exceeding 21,000 was assembled in some 150 organized congregations and 200 other groups extending more than 1,400 miles up the Nile from Alexandria and Port Said on the Mediterranean littoral to Khartoum and Wad Medani in the Sudan. The annual synod of this far-flung Christian community was composed of the ordained ministers from the five presbyteries and elders representing congregations. The moderator was freely elected, resulting in Egyptians being the choice for two successive years and an American for the third in regular rotation, while Egyptians were continuously serving the Synod as secretaries and treasurers, with Arabic the language officially in use. Self-support also moved forward: since 1901 no foreign grants for church buildings had been received, and in due course most of the elementary and primary education had become the responsibility of the Church. But prosperity or lack of it in the country as a whole had naturally been reflected in church affairs, and financial stringency often became acute. The supreme task, however, as of the Church everywhere, has been that of Christian witness, and for the Church in Egypt and the northern Sudan this has meant witness in a hostile Muslim environment—a situation in which, as has happened before in history, the Christian community that has grown large enough to survive as a social entity is tempted to withdraw within itself and remain careless of its non-Christian neighbours. This test threatened to become sterner still with political change.[1]

Enough has been presented here to indicate at once the continuity of purpose with which the Christian missions have in general sought to raise up African Churches as the result of their labours, and the range of ecclesiastical pattern these presented as they were brought into being. On the one hand there were those which faithfully reproduced the ecclesiastical polity of the parent Church even to its terminology, while some on the other, more particularly those in Bantu Africa, incorporated African elements within a framework of western structure—a blending that ranged from the simple use of vernacular terminology (though, even with this slender concession, communicating a real appreciation of function) to the acceptance of a basic African pattern for groupings and assemblies within the Christian community. The satis-.

[1] E. E. Elder, "The Evangelical Church in Egypt: A Study in the Development of a 'Younger Church'", in *I.R.M.*, XXVI (1937), 514–25.

factory functioning of these organizations was facilitated by the very general requirement of literacy in the baptized membership of the churches. A period of two years in the catechumenate had not been uncommon, with a further six months or more under instruction before admission to full communicant membership.

In the matter of African leadership, so vital not only to the successful functioning of church organization but above all to the strength of its inner life and spiritual growth, while the line of advance had been irregular, able and devoted men and women were yet everywhere to be found, even if in numerical strength far below the urgent need. We have already noted the growth in Roman Catholic ordinations to the priesthood. The non-Roman missions were also adding steadily to the number of their ordained ministers though by no means at a rate commensurate with their growing membership. The longer-established missions on the West Coast were naturally in the van, Africans here having for some time reached episcopal status. Thus while in Tanganyika the Berlin Mission in 1934 ordained its first eight African pastors (except one in the war emergency[1]) and in 1935 the Moravians ordained their first four Africans,[2] in West Africa the Methodist Church had in 1936 forty-nine ordained Africans in the Gold Coast and twenty-seven in Nigeria, while two more Africans were raised to the Anglican episcopate in 1937 : one as assistant bishop in Sierra Leone, and the first from the Ibo people to be consecrated as assistant bishop of Lagos.[3]

In regions where churches of a European domiciled community were in existence side by side with mission churches the question of their mutual relationship had naturally arisen. In Kenya a hopeful movement for closer association had emerged in the Kikuyu Conference of 1918, where officials and settlers as well as missionaries were present and took the decision that separate Churches for African and European be abandoned.[4] The movement made steady if somewhat measured headway and from time to time opportunities were taken for African and European Christian co-operation. Thus in 1935 at a conference in Nairobi, attended by both Africans and Europeans and again including officials and settlers, it was agreed that the newly constituted Christian Council on Race Relations should be representative of

---

[1] *Vide supra*, p. 37.
[2] *I.R.M.*, XXIV (1935), 77; XXV (1936), 67.
[3] *The Missionary Prayer Manual, Methodist Missionary Society* (1936), 45, 49, 51; *I.R.M.*, XXVII (1938), 66.
[4] *Vide supra*, p. 131.

both European and African churches.[1] In South Africa the situation varied from the inclusiveness of the Roman Catholic to the separateness of the Dutch Reformed Church. Indeed, it was only the Dutch Reformed Church that on principle required a separate organization for African Christians—the Mission Church, in which they might eventually achieve self-support, self-government, and self-expansion, a Church that by 1936 numbered 154,000 members.[2]

A further question of some importance has been the kind of relationship that should be sought as desirable between these newly planted daughter Churches and the mother Churches overseas. It will have been observed that the familiar trilogy—self-support, self-government, self-propagation—figures largely in these records, with an emphasis on the first two. But along with this a connecting link has often been retained with the wider church fellowship overseas under whose auspices the local Church came into being. It has been steadily realized that an absolute independence is scarcely the Christian ideal, though any persisting bond must be freely accepted by those concerned.[3] But at this point a tension may arise between a desire on the one hand for a larger denominational unit that, while autonomous, retains a close association with the parent body, and on the other an inter-confessional union on a territorial basis issuing in a Christian Church that should supersede all local denominational varieties.[4]

(2) *Christian Discipline*

With the coming of the Church is associated the question of Christian discipline. Every organized community has recognized standards for its members which preserve it as a social organism with a character of its own. In the case of a religious community the nature of the beliefs held will determine the standard of conduct required. The Christian Church, receiving new members on confession of faith, universally makes certain moral demands,

[1] *I.R.M.*, XXV (1936), 65–6.

[2] E. W. Smith, *The Blessed Missionaries, being the Phelps-Stokes Lectures delivered in Cape Town in 1949* (1950), 111–13. This was not always the attitude, as Dr. Smith makes clear; e.g. " The Presbytery and the Synods of 1829 would have no *apartheid* within the walls of the Church ", though not all then agreed with this decision.—*Ibid.*, 112; E. Hellmann (ed.), *Handbook on Race Relations in South Africa* (1949), 572.

[3] Bishop N. S. Booth of the American Methodist Church has commented on the basis of Central African experience: "After dependence we want not independence but interdependence."—*The Africa Christian Advocate*, July 1953.

[4] *Vide infra*, pp. 232–4.

which are broadly described as the Christian way of life, above and beyond the immediate responsibilities that attach to membership of an organized community. The expression of these demands in specific requirements has occasioned much debate in the domain of moral theology. Moreover, while a broad expanse of territory is common to all, the various Christian confessions have nevertheless developed each an emphasis of its own, often expressed in more or less conformity with a national social tradition.

Various problems in this field have confronted those who exercise pastoral care over their African congregations. While there are always shining exceptions, it has generally been experienced that rising to the new moral requirements is a slow process; there may all too easily be somewhat exuberant religious enthusiasm associated with a sadly defective way of life. It may perhaps be remembered in this connexion that the apostle Paul's experience in Corinth was of a similar character.[1]

Derived no doubt in part from such experiences there comes the temptation to legalism which missionaries have by no means always successfully resisted—a temptation against which a more careful study of the Epistle to the Galatians might have guarded them.[2] A peculiar danger among a people accustomed to categories of things permitted and things forbidden, the latter associated with all the phenomena of taboo, is that their Christianity may involve little more than the old outlook on life and the world under a new name, thus surrendering the heart of the Christian gospel with its regenerating, creative power. Where the ideal has been that of the gathered church a stricter discipline has usually been maintained to ensure a clear-cut line between the pagan and

[1] The membership of the church at Corinth was, on Paul's own showing, for the most part of humble origin and not without distressing experiences of moral failure. Yet Clement of Rome, writing to the same church some forty years later, recalls their Christian development: " Who has stayed with you without making proof of the virtue and steadfastness of your faith? Who has not admired the sobriety and Christian gentleness of your piety? "—First Epistle of Clement of Rome, I, 2 (Lake's translation). Again, the frequent exhortations Paul addresses to his converts are significant; he uses a form of the verb meaning " Stop doing " or " Do not (as you are liable to do) ", with the implication that these sins were only imperfectly expelled, leading James Hope Moulton to remark: " The critics who make so much of lapses among Christian converts of the first generation in modern missions might have damned Paul's results with equal reason. Time has shown—time will show."—J. H. Moulton, Prolegomena to New Testament Greek (3rd ed., 1908), 126.

[2] W. T. Balmer produced two booklets for African Christians with this specific danger in mind: The Law of the Friend and The Truth of the Gospel (Atlantis Press, 1923).

Christian communities. Adolphe Mabille of the French mission in Basutoland was a pastor of such standards yet no legalist in religion : "Not a numerous Church but a pure and zealous Church was his ideal." [1] And if at times he was severe, as with a purging of the membership in 1860 when war had wrought much havoc, yet he was a tireless, self-denying shepherd of the flock, as witness his care in 1862 to meet each of the 400 members at Morija in intimate personal interview : " I have not time to talk with more than eight or ten a day, and I have still to call to me over 150 persons. I hear many good things and others which give me no pleasure at all. I fear that for several conversion has not been more than the rejection of certain habits and formulas for taking on other habits and formulas. But at the same time there are many who have a real experience and who feel the need of growing in the grace and knowledge of the Lord." [2] With the setting up of a central council corresponding to the chief's *lekhotla* [3]—a council of sixty over which Mabille presided—disciplinary cases came here for discussion. The point of view of missionary and councillors did not always coincide, and it was clear that sincere Christians often could not understand why certain of their customs had to be discontinued. [4]

This leads to a consideration of what is perhaps the major problem in relation to Christian discipline from the standpoint of the foreign missionary and those African leaders under his immediate influence : what should be the attitude to the African social heritage. Clearly it cannot be accepted just as it stands, for in a pagan community it contains elements that are inconsistent with a Christian way of life, while to ban it entirely has proved neither practicable nor, indeed, desirable on a clearer understanding of what it is. The problem has been where to stand between these two extremes. [5] There would appear to have been two central

[1] E. W. Smith, *The Mabilles of Basutoland* (1939), 123.
[2] *Ibid.*, 123; cf. 124–5. [3] *Vide supra*, p. 200. [4] E. W. Smith, *op. cit.*, 210.
[5] In the *Local Polity of the Gold Coast District* of the Methodist Church successive requirements relating to local customs are codified as follows:
(1) " It will be seen by native Christians that their time-honoured customs are inconsistent with the religion of Christ. We must not be severe with people beyond their light, but must be content to lead them step by step until they see more clearly " (General Letter, 1876).
(2) " Christians who are members of our church may be allowed to be made Captains of Companies or Chiefs of Stools, and that each case of discipline be dealt with on its own merits " (Synod Resolution, 1906).
(3) " Our members shall render all necessary services to the Chiefs providing such services are not inconsistent with the principles of Christianity " (Synod Resolution, 1910).

concerns that together have increasingly guided the African missionary on this issue : first, to distinguish as clearly as possible essential Christianity from the total complex in which it has become embedded for each in his own national social custom; and second, to appreciate the functioning of existing social custom in an African community and so discover what may be usefully retained or adapted, or indeed what for a transition period only may be wisely tolerated. To ignore these two central concerns has in missionary experience all too often led to one of two results : an apparent loyalty to the new demands while the practice of the old has continued in secret, that is, the vice of hypocrisy; or on the other hand, a relapse into the old pagan way of life after a period of futile struggle culminating in acute dissatisfaction, that is, the sin of apostasy. How far then has the African way of life been disowned in response to the demands of a Christian discipline? Two specific cases may illustrate the situation in our period.

Initiation rites for the young at adolescence have been a time-honoured feature of African society. While indigenous education up to this age has been somewhat casual and informal, the rites have stood as a deliberate attempt to prepare the young for their future duties. There has been considerable variation in practice. Both boys and girls may pass through such ceremonies, though separate camps are held. The boys' " schools " have the wider content, those of girls being concerned with preparation for married life.[1] The content (with boys' rites principally in mind) includes some four or five elements. Physical endurance tests are imposed, often so severe that the weaker may not survive.[2] Circumcision as a ritual procedure has usually taken place at this time, and an equivalent operation for girls may be likewise performed. Sex teaching is prominent, the community controls and taboos now being stressed; not that a high moral restraint is inculcated, for stimulation of the sex interest is part of the procedure. But general conduct as husbands and wives has its place.[3] A third

[1] For some standard accounts, see H. A. Junod, *Life of a South African Tribe* (2nd ed., 1927), I, 71–94; Smith and Dale, *The Ila-speaking Peoples of Northern Rhodesia* (1920), II, 18–34; O. F. Raum, *Chaga Childhood* (1940), 314–39; Stayt, *The Bavenda* (1931), 106–10; M. J. Field, *Religion and Medicine of the Ga People* (1937), 185–95; Sibley and Westermann, *Liberia Old and New* (1928), 217–37.

[2] W. Millman writing in 1927 of the rites among the Lokele, a riverine tribe of the Belgian Congo, reported: "At a recent celebration in some thirty centres our teachers assure us that at least twelve boys died of the sufferings imposed."—*I.R.M.*, XVI (1927), 373.

[3] C. M. Doke records some of the things that Lamba girls are taught at this point.—C. M. Doke, *The Lambas of Northern Rhodesia* (1931), 148–58.

element of importance is instruction in social behaviour, supplementing what has been learned during childhood, with a particular emphasis on respect for elders in the community.[1] Boys may now receive instruction in the duties that will henceforth devolve upon them as adult members of the community, such as that of defence.[2] They may also be taught certain handicrafts, as the braying of skins and making of karosses among Bechuana tribes.[3] The social function of such a procedure stands out clearly as the intensive preparation of the young for their future duties as guardians in their turn of the customs and traditions of the community, and as securing its continuity.[4] There are privileges also; only the initiated have full status within the community, and only they are brought into a relationship with the departed ancestors that enables them to share in ritual procedure. The rites deliberately intensify the emotional experience associated with adolescence and then write in the lessons to be learned. Thus deeply engraved, they are never forgotten.

Even so summary an account may have shown that there are at once features of real educational value and elements which by any Christian standard could not remain as they are. Moreover, sometimes the one and sometimes the other will appear to preponderate. It is these facts that have largely accounted for differences in the missionary attitude to the rites. In actual practice there appear to have been four principal positions adopted. There was first the requirement, by missionary fiat, of immediate prohibition. When the initiation procedures had seemed to be on the whole so repugnant to Christian conceptions of human personality and its development that nothing appeared salvable from them, this step has been taken. It has, however, been sooner or later discovered that to prohibit from above is not necessarily to suppress within. Initiation of girls among the Pondos was disallowed to Christians, but an element has survived in the Christian marriage ceremonial which the non-Christians claim is really an essential initiation feature in disguise.[5] It has also happened that, at the call of the

[1] Emile Torday supplies illuminating instances from the rites of the Bushongo of the Congo.—E. Torday, *On the Trail of the Bushongo* (1925), 185–91; Torday et Joyce, *Les Bushongo* (1910), 81–9.

[2] Millman reports that among the Lokele there is teaching about night and river warfare, passwords and secret signs, and treaty making. This element would rather correspond to the conscription period in the West.

[3] W. C. Willoughby, *Race Problems in the New Africa* (1923), 128–38.

[4] There is a background belief here of the cycle of life and death, with reincarnation after a period, but only into the same clan.

[5] M. Hunter, *Reaction to Conquest* (1936), 165–74, 214–15. Cf. C. T.

tribal elders, the prohibition may be ignored and Christian as well as pagan youth be found participating. Thus among the Lokele of the Congo a stand against the rites was taken in 1910, but after a fourteen years' interval the elders arranged an initiation school in 1924 and recruited Christian as well as pagan youths for the ceremonies, while Christian adults who had been initiated were prepared to serve as sponsors.[1] A peculiarly painful experience for the Church occurred in Kenya in 1929–30, when controversy arose over the circumcision of girls, which was of a particularly intensive and harmful character and to be objected to on medical grounds. This did not arise as a simple conflict between pagan practice and Christian demand (African Christian leaders had already expressed themselves as opposed to the rite), but was unhappily complicated by political and racial issues. The Kikuyu Central Association, which had been active in the Closer Union discussions [2] and was anti-Church and anti-European in attitude, made the practice a test of tribal loyalty as against the encroaching white man. The authorities of the Scottish Mission thereupon required from their teachers and other workers a signed declaration against the practice and a refusal to support the Association while anti-mission in its attitude. This the great majority declined to do, many were suspended, village schools were closed, and church membership dropped catastrophically. The Africa Inland Mission and the Gospel Missionary Society were similarly involved. It was urged by critics of this " ecclesiastical thunderbolt " that many Christian Kikuyu would have been found to support a modified form of the rite, but a head-on collision such as took place did but stiffen tribal pride and resistance. The situation was to some extent gradually retrieved.[3]

A second method of dealing with the question may be described as deferred prohibition; that is, the missionary body itself took no

Loram in M. Stauffer (ed.), *Thinking with Africa* (British edition, 1928), 17, for other Pondo experiences.
[1] W. Millman in " Lokele Initiation Ceremonies," *I.R.M.*, XVI (1927), 378–9. " There were many young men, members of the church, who were not initiated and who were quite willing to remain uninitiated if the tribal authorities and the women would permit it. But in the rush of the reaction which set in, hundreds of youths went over, seeking to obtain the privileges belonging to ' men '."—*Loc. cit.* It is not stated how the decision to prohibit the rites to Christians was reached; in the apparent absence of evidence to the contrary it may be presumed the initiative was European.
[2] *Vide supra*, pp. 159–60.
[3] *I.R.M.*, XX (1931), 55–6; XXI (1932), 223–4; J. Huxley, *Africa View* (1931), 193–8; cf. W. McGregor Ross in *The Church Overseas*, IV (1931), 273–4; H. R. A. Philp, *A New Day in Kenya* (1936), 165–6.

direct action at any stage but sought so to educate the Christian community that the decision should in due course spring from their own initiative. W. C. Willoughby, whose extensive knowledge of the Bechuana tribes entitles his verdict to respect, after describing the rites as he had known them with their " frankly sensuous view of sex that runs through the teaching ", argued that the way of reform was not immediate prohibition by superimposed church decree, but that the missionary responsibility should be so to instruct the Church in the Christian moral ideal that the desired reform would arise from within the Christian community as a natural sequel.[1] Lest this should be regarded as admirable in theory but ineffective in practice, there may be cited the experience of the Anglican Diocese on the Niger. The practice of female circumcision has been prohibited by church regulation to all members by African decision voluntarily taken. Several missionaries, in the first instance, gave some teaching on the matter as occasion permitted, and this went on for some fifteen years. Then discussions on the subject sprang up in local committees, and next in District Church Councils which, in succession, passed condemnatory resolutions. Finally a Joint Board, representative of all the Councils, drew up the formal regulation of prohibition, independently of Europeans. G. T. Basden makes the significant comment : " The remarkable feature has been the very few cases calling for disciplinary action since the rule came into operation. This is, without doubt, due to the fact that the people themselves were responsible for it." [2]

A third line of approach, and a noteworthy one, has been the attempt to produce a Christian adaptation of the rites which should omit the unacceptable features and yet be received by the elders as genuine initiation into the tribe. This was undertaken, with some success it was claimed, under the leadership of W. V. Lucas, Bishop of Masasi in southern Tanganyika. The duty of conducting the rites was committed to senior African teachers who were responsible for including elements of Christian instruction, though local chiefs attended at intervals to speak of the manners and customs of the tribe. The policy of adaptation was not intended to make the rites a permanent feature of the Christian community, but had as its purpose the conserving of such social values as the old order contained until the sanctions of the new Christian order should become effective.[3] The Berlin Missionary Society,

[1] *I.R.M.*, XV (1926), 458–60.
[2] G. T. Basden, *Niger Ibes* (1938), 178.
[3] W. V. Lucas, " The Educational Value of Initiatory Rites, " in *I.R.M.*,

also in Tanganyika, took action in the rites for girls in Usaramo, substituting a healthy boarding-school life after only a brief period of seclusion for adolescent girls, and retaining as much of the traditional ceremonies that marked the climax of the period as did not appear incompatible with Christian demands. Beginning with only three girls in 1932 the number had grown to 117 in six years.[1]

Yet another method, while accepting the rites as basic to tribal life, has been the attempt to effect some reformation from within by the admission of some Christian in whom those responsible for the rites have confidence. This has been reported as having taken place in Sierra Leone in connexion with the Sande or initiation school for girls of the Mende tribe.[2] Here the possibility of the venture depends on the relation of confidence already established between the woman missionary concerned and the senior African women in charge, and its success on that missionary's understanding and tact.

In relation to the whole question of the rites, it is of course true that they belong only to the tribal state of society, but even so they have proved remarkably tenacious. The General Missionary Conference of South Africa of 1925 discussed the question and formally requested the Government to investigate the working of the schools but added: " The conference does not suggest the suppression of the schools, which it recognizes are deeply rooted

---

XVI (1927), 192–8; E. R. Morgan (ed.), *Essays Catholic and Missionary* (1928) 138–43; *Central Africa* (U.M.C.A.), XLVIII (1930), 23–6; L. Harries, "Bishop Lucas and the Masasi Experiment," in *I.R.M.*, XXXIV (1945), 389–96. Lyndon Harries comments: " Bishop Lucas never intended the experiment to become a permanent institution . . . The Bishop would have preferred not to have had to make the experiment at all, but it would have been wrong to have denied the good values inherent in tribal life by dissociating ourselves from customs that could be adapted so as to be not unlawful for the African Christian." *Loc. cit.*, 391. Cf. also A. Phillips (ed.), *Survey of African Marriage and Family Life* (1953), 390–1.
[1] G. M. Culwick, " New ways for Old in the Treatment of Adolescent Girls," in *Africa*, XII (1939), 428–32.
[2] Personally communicated. For an account of initiation in the Sande see T. J. Alldridge, *The Sherbro and its Hinterland* (1901), 136–43 ; Sibley and Westermann, *Liberia Old and New* (1928), 231–7 (account by D. Westermann); K. L. Little, *The Mende of Sierra Leone* (1951), 126–30. The Sande leaders have also shown willingness to admit trained medical workers from the Government side.—M. A. S. Margai, " Welfare Work in a Secret Society " in *African Affairs*, XLVII (1948), 227–30; but cf. *African Education*, Cambridge Conference Report (1953), 32. The Sande is also known as the Bundu society.

in Native belief and custom, and which will die eventually through the progress of Christian teaching." [1]

A second case of the problem created by the clash of traditional social custom with ideal Christian demand that may be considered is that of the so-called bride-price as an integral part of the constitution of a marriage. The English term usually employed is unfortunate as suggesting the purchase of a wife, which in traditional African custom has definitely not been the case. Among the Southern Bantu the vernacular *lobola* is now used by most writers —an African term for an African custom is always safe. [2] The practice consists in the transfer of certain articles (the usual form is cattle among pastoral peoples) from the bridegroom's family to the bride's, usually in instalments, the completion of which as a public act corresponds to the sealing of a civil marriage contract in the West. The amount has varied with the status of the girl's family or with the greed of her father (though this is an abuse). The transaction marks the union as a marriage and thus confers on all children of it a status within the society. The conception of purchase in this connexion is as repugnant to the African as to the Western mind. [3] To Africans the practice has served as stabilizing the marriage by giving at once a reasonable guarantee of good treatment of the wife by her husband and of dutiful regard for her husband by the wife. The appearance of a money economy, it is true, has distorted the function of the practice, and governments have latterly even taken a hand in fixing a maximum amount in

[1] *Quarterly Notes, Bulletin of the I.M.C.*, No. 8 (October 1925), v. The General Missionary Conference of Northern Rhodesia several times had the question before it; see *Reports* (1922), 66; (1924), 141–3; (1927), 121–7. Cf. also the *Report* of the Foreign Mission Committee of the Church of Scotland (1950), 40.

[2] No alternative English term, among various proposals made, has proved generally acceptable, such as: indemnity (Radcliffe-Brown), earnest (Torday), bride-wealth (Evans-Pritchard). Cf. *Man*, No. 42 (March 1931), 36–9. Dowry already has other uses, while other suggestions—bride-gift, espousal fee, marriage pledge, marriage insurance—have all had objections lodged.

[3] Cf. Smith and Dale, *op. cit.*, II, 48–51; C. K. Meek, *Northern Nigeria* (1925), II, 97; W. Eiselen in *Africa*, I (1928), 414. For a full account of this mode of marriage among the Ibos, see: C. K. Meek, *Law and Authority in a Nigerian Tribe* (1937), 267–76. Dr. E. W. Smith writes to me: " The main objection to *lobola* is that it binds a wife after her husband's death— she is bound to his heir, but some tribes condition this on the number of her children." On this aspect of the practice among the Ibos, and the reported influence of the Christian mission, see: C. K. Meek, *op. cit.*, (1937), 284. For some of the complexities of the system in operation, see *I.R.M.*, XXXVII (1948), 96–7.

cash terms to be recoverable at law in the event of divorce. In 1954 the Executive Council of the Eastern Region of Nigeria set up a Committee on Bride Price, consisting of four Africans, one a woman, to investigate the social effects of the practice and make recommendations. Their report is a valuable survey of the traditional custom with the variations that changing times have brought.[1] They found the practice deeply rooted : " Everywhere we have been we have made the suggestion that the payment of dowry should be abolished altogether. A few of the educated, both men and women, agreed with the idea. The vast majority received the suggestion with horror!" [2] They found the sums involved would fluctuate with the country's prosperity, and also be usually determined in modern days by the bride's standard of education.[3] Where the sum was high they found a demand for its reduction and some criticism of the creation of a social caste as between the educated and the uneducated.[4] The Committee recommended a maximum of £30 to be fixed throughout the region, irrespective of education, and that all marriages under Native Law and Custom be registered and certificates issued. Strong disapproval of female circumcision was recorded, though it was recognized that sudden abolition would not be acceptable to the people.[5]

Here the alternatives before the Christian mission have been to refuse to recognize the practice in any form, or to accept it as socially valuable during an interim period, with certain conditions to bring it into closer harmony with the Christian outlook on marriage. When the practice was interpreted as the purchase of a wife there was clearly no possible alternative to banning it. This was the general view and consequent practice in early days. There were notable exceptions, among them a remarkable woman of the American Board, Katie Parker, serving among the Zulus, who wrote in the eighteen-sixties of the usually undiscriminating missionary attitude to the African heritage : " We as a Mission have tried too much to make Americans of our Zulus and not enough to make Christians of them. Very many things they give up when they become Christians are merely making them more

---

[1] *Nigeria Eastern Region: Report of the Committee on Bride Price* (Enugu, 1955), *passim*.

[2] *Ibid.*, 8. Dowry has been the current English term in local use for the more usual bride-price.

[3] They found sums as high as £80 to £120 for illiterates, £150 to £160 for semi-literates, £200 for Standard VI, and £250 for Secondary status— but these were exceptional.—*Ibid.*, 26.

[4] *Ibid.*, 8, 20.

[5] *Ibid.*, 46, 48.

like our own nation, not affecting their Christianity in the least." [1]
The refusal to tolerate the custom has but produced social complication, resulting on occasion in a reversal of policy. A case in point is that of the Kgatla tribe of the Bechuanaland Protectorate whose practice is termed *bogadi*. The early missionaries, regarding this as wife-purchase, forbad it to Christians, and when in 1892 the chief Lentswe became a convert, he adopted the change (after lengthy discussion in the *pitso* or tribal assembly) on behalf of the tribe. But when the resulting instability of marriage, over a period of some fifteen years, led to social confusion, he reinstated the practice, leaving it to Christians, however, to please themselves. By 1927 or so the mission authorities had been persuaded to allow the practice of *bogadi* as essentially a registration of the marriage. [2]

The alternative policy of a conditional recognition has been widely though not universally observed by Protestant missions. The two conditions required are, invariably, a pledge of monogamy by the husband, and customarily, a religious service to bless the marriage. [3] The concession may not be allowed to ordained ministers, who are required to be married in church under the Marriage Ordinance of the Government.

These two instances selected from the debatable territory of traditional custom illustrate something of the difficulty of the question of Christian discipline and of the wisdom and tolerance required in not laying upon converts a burden they are unable to bear until a greater maturity has been attained. There are, of course, practices where mission policy is united against recognition as in the case of polygamy, the age-long problem of the Church in

[1] E. W. Smith, *The Life and Times of Daniel Lindley* (1949), 395. She wrote of this particular custom: " I cannot help feeling very decidedly the more I see of the Natives . . . that their marriage custom of paying cattle is to the young Zulu girls the greatest protection they have against the immorality of the nation, while it insures to the *women* good treatment and care they would not otherwise receive . . . I have thought it would be well if white women's fathers had the power to aid them that a Zulu father has."—*Loc. cit.* Italics in original.

[2] I. Schapera in *Africa*, VI (1933), 63; I. Schapera, *Married Life in an African Tribe* (1940), 83–7. Cf. C. T. Loram in M. Stauffer (ed.), *Thinking with Africa* (British edition, 1928), 15–16.

[3] For a survey undertaken in 1934–5, see J. K. Macgregor, " Christian Missions and Marriage Usage in Africa " where the Roman Catholic position is also given.—*I.R.M.*, XXIV (1935), 379–91. For a brief discussion of points at issue, see J. W. Welch, " Can Christian Marriage in Africa be African? " in *I.R.M.*, XXII (1933), 17–32; and for a comprehensive account see Lyndon Harries in *Survey of African Marriage and Family Life* (1953), 360–70, 374–8.

Africa, a question that falls for consideration later [1] ; and also certain matters of strong traditional obligation, such as expiation of a killing by means of the blood feud. The moral heroism required in converts who resist such social demands and brave the charge of cowardice is considerable. Let an experience from the mission of the White Fathers in Ruanda serve to exemplify : " A certain catechumen was under the obligation of avenging the death of a relative. Braving public opinion, he nobly forgave the murderers; but he felt it necessary to show that he had not acted in this way from cowardice or from want of an opportunity to avenge the crime. Accordingly he rose on six successive nights and went round to the dwellings of all the enemies of his family, waking them out of sleep, on one occasion even setting fire to a small hut, in order to prove that he could have killed them all had he wished to do so. Then he went quietly home." [2]

The problem of the moral life of the Christian community was rendered much more acute in cases where, after the sheltered growth of the early years during which missionary control was not seriously offset by contrary influence and example, the young Church was exposed to the seductive attractions of a materialistic age in which money was king and the pursuit of pleasure the supreme aim in life. The pleadings of a Christian conscience, nurtured with much patience through the years, could be easily stifled and a moral crisis arise that imperilled the life of the Church. The experience of the Church in Uganda is illuminating in this connexion. The early record of the devotion of young converts— their faithfulness unto death in the fires of persecution—was a glory to the communions, Protestant and Roman Catholic, to which they belonged, equal to any in the Christian story.[3] There followed an amazing growth as large numbers pressed into both the Protestant and Roman Catholic folds. For a quarter of a century the country was to all intents and purposes sealed off from the advancing tide of secular civilization. But with the opening of the railway from Mombasa to Port Florence (Kisumu) in 1902 the normal three months' caravan journey, with all its expense and vicissitudes, was replaced by one to be reckoned in a matter of hours, the barrier of distance had fallen down, and the waiting tide now

---

[1] *Vide infra*, pp. 344–8. The exception to unity has been willingness in some cases to receive a polygamist as such where he entered upon his obligations before hearing the Christian demand.

[2] J. Bouniol, *The White Fathers and their Missions* (1929), 239.

[3] See Vol. III, pp. 92–3.

began to surge in.[1] At the same time the political status of the
country was determined on the basis of a policy of indirect rule,
replacing a period of military occupation.[2] So the stage was set for
an era of unprecedented economic prosperity. The impact of the
war of 1914–18 was serious, with its dislocation of normal social
life and religious practice. Thus the first two decades of the
twentieth century brought to the life of the Church a new kind
of testing, more sinister and subtle than the old. Contact with
Europeans of no professed religious faith, the overriding concern
for the material benefits of civilization brought in by growing
prosperity, and the relaxation of personal standards with a nominal
rather than a real Christian adherence combined not merely to
threaten but to undermine the moral life of the Christian community.

In 1921 Archdeacon Lloyd offered a frank assessment of the
situation. Speaking of " clouds in the sky " overshadowing the
early sunlit story of the Church in Uganda, and referring to a
discussion of church discipline in the Synod of 1913, he proceeded : " Since that discussion, now eight years ago, there seems
to the casual observer but little improvement in the state of the
Church. The two great evils against which there is constant warfare, drunkenness and immorality, are as flagrant as ever; indeed,
the latter is more open to the world than ever it was. Plurality of
wives and concubinage are everywhere, and the whole Church is
riddled with this sin, while drunkenness follows in its train." [3] He
also deplored the survival of belief in witchcraft and in the power
of spirits of the dead : " That such superstitions should still prevail
among the Christians, and increasingly so, is cause for real appre-
hension." [4] When in these affairs there were leading chiefs involved " example has been followed with a fidelity born of the old
feudal system ".[5] A decade later Dr. A. R. Cook, of Mengo
Hospital fame, passed the situation in review, prompted by the
statement of Rufus M. Jones that the greatest rival to Christianity
was the rapidly encroaching secular way of life.[6] After analysing

[1] Thomas and Scott, *Uganda* (1935), 234. The distance from Mombasa
to Kisumu was 587 miles. Until 1926 the railway was known as " the
Uganda Railway ". The deterioration in Christian morality began to
cause concern in the first decade.—*Proceedings of the C.M.S.* (1904),102–3;
(1909), 64.
[2] Thomas and Scott, *op. cit.*, 39–41.
[3] A. B. Lloyd, *Dayspring in Uganda* (1921), 112.
[4] *Ibid.*, 116.
[5] *Ibid.*, 117.
[6] In a paper " Secular Civilization and the Christian Task", prepared

the many influences that had played upon the country Dr. Cook arraigned the generality of professing Christians in terms reminiscent of the strictures of Archdeacon Lloyd a decade before : " We may say that broadly the danger is that the Christian profession is emasculated by the practice of its adherents. Lying and stealing immorality and drunkenness exist to an almost unbelievable extent among many who profess and call themselves Christian, and they seem almost unaware of the deadly danger of such rank hypocrisy. Nor are these vices confined to the peasant class or the rank and file of church members. While there are many noble exceptions, isolated instances occurring among even the clergy and large chiefs indicate the seriousness of the position. The frequent practice of concubinage or ' marriage without a ring,' and the startling paucity of marriages in church point in the same direction. Church contributions are distressingly low considering the growing wealth of Christian church members, and church services are badly attended." [1]

But it was the eve of spiritual renewal. There were sincere African Christians, both clergy and laity, deeply distressed at the state of affairs and longing for a spiritual regeneration. In 1937 the Diamond Jubilee of the Church Missionary Society in Uganda was to be celebrated and these widespread desires crystallized in the decision to commemorate the event by a mission to the Church as the first step of a general plan of advance.[2] Preparation began as early as 1934. Dr. Warren, in a search for the beginnings of the movement, came to the conclusion there was no clear-cut origin : " We shall be most true to the facts if we recognize that the Holy Spirit was at work in the lives of a number of individuals, each quite unknown to the others." [3] An African noted as a very usual text during this period : " I will restore to you the years that the locust hath eaten " (Joel 2 : 25).[4] A young African deacon expressed his concern on three specific points : " What is the cause of the coldness and deadness of the Church of Uganda? . . . The

for the Jerusalem Meeting of the International Missionary Council in 1928.—*The Christian Message*, Jerusalem Meeting Report, I (1928), 284. Dr. A. R. Cook's paper, " The Church in Uganda To-day " appeared in *I.R.M.*, XX (1931), 254-64.
[1] *I.R.M.*, XX (1931), 261.
[2] The Bishop of Uganda supplied a report to the Tambaram Conference: *Evangelism*, Tambaram Madras Series III (1939), 263-73. An outline of events with an analysis of the total situation is provided in: M. A. C. Warren, *Revival, An Enquiry* (1954), chap. 3, The Revival in East Africa.
[3] M. A. C. Warren, *op. cit.*, 39.
[4] *Ibid.*, 42.

sacred service of meeting at the Lord's Table is being abused by those who are known to be living in sin being allowed to attend and partake.... What must be done to bring Revival to the Church of Uganda? " [1] This concern of sincere African Christians within the Church has been adjudged a vital factor in the uprise of new life in what was felt to be a spiritually barren and impoverished community.

The Mission of 1937 was carried through by teams of missioners, mainly African, carefully selected and prepared; it was not the emotional enthusiasm of the public meeting that was sought : " Most of the real work was done late at night in the people's own houses." [2] Sins that had sapped the life of the Church were openly confessed; the Bishop of Uganda recorded as the more depressing lessons of the revival : " (a) The amount of gross sin in the lives of our church leaders. (b) The power of witchcraft that is still in the country." [3] Positively, for many thousands the Christian faith was now a transforming power, to the extent of their being named *Balokole*.[4] One missionary reported that three things impressed him about them : their overflowing joy, their evident love for one another regardless of class or race, and their deep concern for the Church, " which not without reason they felt was at a dangerously low ebb ", and for their fellow-men.[5] Their fellowship meetings included song, prayer, confession and thanksgiving for forgiveness, and devotional Bible reading which was the longest item.[6] Indeed, as an index of renewed interest in the Bible, the sales of Bibles and New Testaments increased by fifty per cent in a single year.[7]

As always in such movements there were spiritual dangers : the exclusiveness of those who claimed their own experience as the norm for all; the risk of spiritual pride in those who had found deliverance from the grosser sins; and the underrating of the normal worship and service of the Church because the Christian community in the past had been found wanting.[8] But

[1] *Awake! An African Calling* (Anon., 1937), 44–5. Quoted in Warren, *op. cit.*, 43–4.

[2] *Evangelism* (1939), 273.

[3] *Ibid.*, 272.

[4] *Balokole*=saved ones; the name was used of members of the Revival Fellowship.

[5] Warren, *Revival*, 50–1.

[6] A missionary's account of the pattern of the fellowship meeting in the revival is given in Warren, *op. cit.*, Appendix II, 118–21.

[7] From 21,956 in the year ending October 31, 1936, to 34,676 in the following twelve months.—*Evangelism*, 271.

[8] *Ibid.*, 272; Warren. *op. cit.*, 50–4, 81–8.

the positive gains were outstanding; two may be noted. As the revival movement was by sympathy and understanding kept within the Church the renewal became pervasive, and the community was enriched by the experience of cleansing and forgiveness of its members. As one African expressed it in congenial parable : " This pot is about five years old. At first everything cooked in it tasted good. But for some time now, vegetables have not tasted so good. They were sometimes bitter. So last week I took the pot and made a good fire and burnt it again. Now my vegetables taste very good indeed. My life is like that pot. And last week I saw that I must be burnt again in the fire of the Spirit." [1] The second notable gain was the recovery of the urge for evangelism that had characterized the Church in its earliest years. The teams of missioners passed beyond Uganda : in 1937 one visited Kenya, some crossed into Tanganyika and other territories. This impulse to share was in a sense the hall-mark of a Christian faith no longer nominal but real—a faith, as one African put it, secure in " heart-knowledge " and moved to new adventure by Christian love.[2] Thus the spiritual re-birth experienced by many thousands brought the finally effective answer to many a tough, resistant problem of church discipline. A new tenderness of conscience approved the Christian ethic and the grace of the Lord Jesus began to make the ideal actual.

The outstanding demand on a pastoral ministry in connexion with discipline, not less in Africa than elsewhere, is not so much to determine the fault and assess the penalty, almost as it were applying a tariff—a course woefully easy to practise when the pastor is hard-pressed, frustrated, and, it may well be, feeling betrayed by one in whom confidence had been placed—not this summary jurisdiction, but the personal care, direction, and redemption of the wayward which alone are becoming in an under-shepherd. The pattern seen in Paul's treatment of offenders —never " See what regulation you have broken " but rather " Remember Whose you are "—is a personal appeal to a personal relationship, and to this appeal Africans are peculiarly susceptible.

(3) Co-operation and Closer Union

The impulse towards missionary co-operation and the promotion of Christian unity given by the Edinburgh Conference of 1910 had stimulated in a number of territories the drawing together of Protestant missions for mutual counsel.[3] This movement

---

[1] Warren, op. cit., 72–3. [2] Ibid., 52–3.
[3] See Vol. III, pp. 292–3.

had continued to gain some momentum until by 1938 there were Christian or Missionary Councils and Conferences in Sierra Leone, the Gold Coast, Nigeria, Belgian Congo, Angola, Union of South Africa, Southern Rhodesia, Northern Rhodesia, Nyasaland, Portuguese East Africa, Tanganyika, and Kenya. Two only, however, among them—the Congo Protestant Council and the Christian Council of South Africa—qualified as national organizations for affiliation to the International Missionary Council.[1]

The range of Churches and missions co-operating was often remarkable, though abstentions were to be found. The Gold Coast Christian Council, which first appeared in 1929, comprised Anglican, Scottish Presbyterian, British Wesleyan, and American Zionist members.[2] The Christian Council of Nigeria came into being through the necessity of the various missions being able to speak with one voice on important issues involved in co-operation with the Government in education. It included Anglican, Scottish Presbyterian, Wesleyan Methodist, Primitive Methodist, American Baptist, Basel Mission, and Qua Iboe Mission, together with the British and Foreign Bible Society. The Salvation Army acceded in 1934. There were already in existence the Evangelical Union of missions east of the Niger and the Miango Conference in the Northern Provinces. These were merged in the new comprehensive Council.[3] The Government's new education proposals, which were the principal subject for discussion, were likewise of

---

[1] *Quarterly Notes, Bulletin of the I.M.C.*, No. 61 (January 1939), iv–v. Titles varied slightly: thus, Missionary Council (Kenya, Tanganyika), Missionary Conference (S. Rhodesia, N. Rhodesia), Consultative Board of Federated Missions (Nyasaland), Evangelical Alliance (Angola), Evangelical Missionary Association (Portuguese East Africa), Christian Council (Sierra Leone, Gold Coast, Nigeria).

[2] *Ibid.*, No. 26 (April, 1930), iii.

[3] *Ibid.*, No. 27 (July 1930), v; *Report of the Christian Council of Nigeria, March 1930*, 3–4. The Evangelical Union of missions east of the Niger appeared in 1924; the first Conference of Missions in the Northern Provinces, held at Miango in November 1926, was regarded as the sequel to the earlier Lokoja Conferences. The second Miango Conference was held in November 1929. Both the Evangelical Union and the Miango Conference were requested to continue as Regional Conferences within the Christian Council of Nigeria. The Northern Conference was dissolved in 1937.—*Quarterly Notes, Bulletin of I.M.C.*, No. 56 (October 1937), vii. There had been convened in February 1928 a United Conference of Protestant Missionary Societies which met at Port Harcourt with ten missionary bodies represented from Nigeria and Cameroons (British Mandate). It was then proposed that similar conferences be held quinquennially, but the formation of the Christian Council of Nigeria superseded this.

concern to the Roman Catholic Mission, a delegation from which visited the Council on the matter. Protestants and Roman Catholics found themselves in agreement on this issue, and the Roman bishop expressed his hope that the meeting would not be the last of its kind.[1]

A notable event for the Churches in South Africa was the visit of John R. Mott in 1934. He had last been in the country in 1906 and the General Missionary Conference had long sought a renewal of personal contact. While unusual public honours awaited him as a Christian world statesman it was the series of five round-table conferences, held respectively at Cape Town, Fort Hare, Durban, Johannesburg, and Bloemfontein, that were the outstanding events of the visit. Representative leaders of churches and missionary societies in the area, from fifty to a hundred in number, came together in the first four conferences, while the last at Bloemfontein was a general gathering for the Union. Among the subjects discussed two were taken at all centres: evangelization and co-operation. At Bloemfontein eighty-three European and fifteen non-European delegates representing every important Church and Missionary Society in the Union met together in a conference that Dr. Mott described as "a gathering of really great prophetic quality and character". The most significant finding of the conference was that a Christian Council of South Africa should be formed with the object of fostering fellowship in thinking and planning but the function of which should be consultative and advisory only. In September 1935 a formal appeal was addressed to all churches and societies as a result of which the Christian Council of South Africa was inaugurated at Bloemfontein in June 1936 with practically all the non-Roman communions represented. Unhappily this comprehensiveness was not destined to continue, for after five years' experience the Dutch Reformed Church and the Church of the Province of South Africa decided to withdraw.[2]

Meanwhile Dr. Mott had moved into the Rhodesias where conferences took place at Bulawayo and Ndola, evangelism and co-operation again being two topics discussed. A proposal was made for the Missionary Conferences of Southern and Northern

---

[1] *Report of the Christian Council of Nigeria, 1930*, 13–14.
[2] *The South African Outlook*, LXIV (1934), 133–56; LXV (1935), 212–14; LXVI (1936), 9–12; *Quarterly Notes, Bulletin of the I.M.C.*, No. 44 (October 1934), iii; No. 52 (October 1936), vii; No. 71 (July 1941), v. For an account of missionary co-operation based on South African experience, by J. D. Rheinallt Jones, see *The South African Outlook*, LXIV (1934), 70–3. For the later development of the Christian Council, *vide infra*, pp. 250–2.

Rhodesia, either each separately or both together in conjunction with Nyasaland, eventually to seek affiliation to the International Missionary Council, but this did not mature.[1] Dr. Mott proceeded to the Belgian Congo where he held regional conferences, with a final gathering at Leopoldville under the auspices of the Congo Protestant Council. There valuable plans were laid for co-operation in the educational field, and it was on this occasion that the proposal to adopt a common name for all churches connected with Protestant missions in Congo was submitted—*L'Eglise du Christ au Congo*—a name that was agreed to in 1935.[2] The first general conference under the name was held in Leopoldville on the occasion of the Diamond Jubilee celebrations of Protestant missionary work in the territory. The conference was attended by 240 African delegates representing eighteen tribes and from ten co-operating missions.[3]

In Portuguese territory the Protestant missions had their joint organizations for consultation : in Angola the Evangelical Missions Conference, and in Portuguese East Africa the Evangelical Missionary Association. Matters were taken a stage further in Angola in 1934 with the formation of the Evangelical Alliance of Angola whereby greater unity of action could be attained. In the following year Eduardo Moreira, the Secretary of the Portuguese League of Missionary and Educational Action, accepted the invitation of the American, British, and Swiss missions in Portuguese colonies to serve as their liaison officer in Lisbon and arouse interest in the evangelical churches in Portugal.[4]

One feature of this period of growing co-operation was the appointment in Kenya and Nigeria of educational advisers to the Protestant missions : one for Kenya under the Mission Council, the Bishops of Uganda and the Upper Nile requesting an extension of the service to their dioceses; the other under the Christian Council of Nigeria for the Southern Provinces.[5] The co-ordination of mission policy in education thus made possible under expert guidance was a valuable fruit of co-operation. Individual co-operative enterprises were already afoot between Anglican and Wesleyan Methodist at Fourth Bay College, Sierra Leone (since

[1] *The South African Outlook*, LXIV (1934), July 2, August 1; *Quarterly Notes, Bulletin of the I.M.C.*, No. 44 (October 1934), iii.
[2] *Quarterly Notes, Bulletin of I.M.C.*, No. 44, iii–iv; No. 47 (July 1935), v.
[3] *I.R.M.*, XXVIII (1939), 58.
[4] *Quarterly Notes, Bulletin of the I.M.C.*, No. 44 (October 1934), vi; *I.R.M.*, XXV (1936), 74; XXVI (1937), 66.
[5] *Quarterly Notes, Bulletin of I.M.C.*, No. 30 (April 1931), ii; No. 33 (January 1932), ii; *Report of the Christian Council of Nigeria, 1934*, 17–18.

1919), at Igbobi College, Lagos, and in United Colleges for Teacher Training at Ibadan in Western Nigeria and, together with Scottish Presbyterians, at Umuahia in Eastern. An interesting feature of a minor character in Eastern Nigeria was the promotion of a common magazine, *The Eastern Star*, for five training institutions in the area.[1] In East Africa the Alliance High School at Kikuyu in Kenya was an outstandingly successful joint enterprise on rather unusual lines. Named " Alliance " in virtue of its connexion with the Alliance of Protestant Missions,[2] it was controlled by a Board of Governors representative of missions, the Government, elected members of the Legislative Council, and donors. The character of the school as a missionary institution was safeguarded in the constitution. Opening in 1926 with twenty-six pupils and a staff of one, in 1934 there were 120 pupils and a staff of seven, all men " of proved Christian experience ".[3]

A co-operative undertaking of signal importance was the United Missions in the Copperbelt which began in July 1936.[4] Members of the six co-operating missions—Anglican, Baptist, Congregational, Methodist, and Presbyterian, together with the United Society for Christian Literature—worked as a united team under the leadership of A. J. Cross, loaned by the South African Baptist Mission, until his death in 1945. When the work began there were already half a dozen small Christian congregations in existence, thanks to African initiative and some European encouragement. These were gathered into a Union Church of the Copperbelt under a committee of African and European ministers. The Anglican bishop was not able to contemplate participation in such a Union Church, but generously supported the educational and social welfare side of the work. The African members claimed by the four Societies co-operating in the Union Church all belonged to it during their residence at the mines, and returned to their respective Churches on going home again.[5] Other Christian agencies comprised the Roman Catholic Church, whose number of adherents was said at least to equal the combined Protestant totals, and two African Separatist sects whose hold was

[1] These included Anglican, Presbyterian, Methodist and Government institutions. The *Eastern Star* had, unhappily, a short life, with a run of 14 numbers (1934–39).
[2] *Vide supra*, p. 131, and *n*. 1.
[3] H. R. A. Philp, *A New Day in Kenya* (1938), 43–5, 161–4.
[4] *Vide supra*, p. 172.
[5] *United Missions in the Copper Belt, First Annual Report, 1936–37, passim*; *Second Annual Report, 1937–38*, 4–8; *The Economic Basis of the Church*, Tambaram Madras Series, V (1939), 247–9.

on the semi-educated. At two centres of the United Missions Roman priests desired permission for their women members to attend Protestant schools conditionally on their being refused religious instruction.[1] Perhaps the most serious counter-propaganda which the recognized Christian Churches all had to meet in the Copperbelt was that from the Watch Tower' Movement or Jehovah's Witnesses.

This movement, which originated in the United States of America under Charles Taze Russell, was variously known as Russellites, the International Bible Students' Association, Jehovah's Witnesses, and Watch Tower (apparently suggested by Habakkuk 2 : 1). Russell developed his peculiar teachings concerning the millenium through an independent study of the Scriptures. He claimed that Roman Catholic and Protestant communions had been divinely rejected and that social chaos would soon break out which would usher in the resurrection and the last judgment. On Russell's death in 1916 the leadership devolved upon J. F. Rutherford who stressed the imminence of the final celestial conflict, with the corollary that " millions now living will never die ".[2] The movement seems to have reached Northern Rhodesia, where it wrought considerable havoc, from its base in South Africa. The combination of millenarian teaching with announcements of the overthrow of the social order in the interests of the under-privileged proved dangerous propaganda, while the denouncing of the British and American Governments in particular as Satanic organizations and the Roman Catholic and Protestant Churches as Satan's emissaries was scarcely calculated to allay the indiscipline the preachers had induced. Indeed, the Commission appointed to inquire into the disturbances in the Copperbelt in 1935 [3] recorded their conclusion : " The Commission find that the teachings and literature of the Watch Tower bring civil and spiritual authority, especially native authority, into contempt; that it is a dangerously subversive movement; and that it is an important predisposing cause of the recent disturbances." [4]

---

[1] *U.M.C.B.*, *Third Annual Report*, *1938–39*, 6. " We felt, as we encouraged all to worship with us, that the onus should be on them of refusing to let their people come rather than asking us to turn them out." A concise account of the origin of the United Missions in the Copperbelt is given in the *Fifth Annual Report*, *1941*, 3–5.

[2] K. S. Latourette, *A History of the Expansion of Christianity*, IV (1941), 443–4, where relevant bibliography is supplied.

[3] *Vide supra*, p. 173.

[4] *Report of the Commission on Disturbances in the Copperbelt*, Cmd. 5009 (1935), 51. The same *Report* devotes a generous section (pp. 42–51) to the Watch

They added that the circulation of Watch Tower literature in cheap and convenient form had been a principal means of propaganda, and that through the general dearth of literature this had been lapped up by Africans anxious to read English—a significant call to the Christian Churches to develop their literature service.[1]

Passing from the level of missionary co-operation to that of proposals for closer union, two tendencies were here to be seen : on the one hand to gather Churches of different communions in a single territory into one united Church, comparable to the Union then contemplated in the South India proposals (since achieved), and on the other, to group the establishments of a single communion into larger ecclesiastical units embracing several territories. Various unions of Churches in the Western world at this time, while of significance for the Church universal, on the whole scarcely bore on the local African problem, for what had been different denominational enterprises were thereby brought together under a foreign administrative Board rather than into more direct relation with one another. Thus the United Church of Canada, springing from the union in 1923 of Congregational, Methodist, and Presbyterian Churches (with a small residue of " Continuing Presbyterians ") did but change the name for the Canadian Congregational Mission in Angola; the coming together of Scottish Presbyterians in 1929 in the Church of Scotland similarly affected the respective missions of the earlier Church of Scotland and United Free Church—the Livingstonia and Blantyre Missions in Nyasaland had already come together in the Church of Central Africa (Presbyterian);[2] while the Union in 1932 of the Wesleyan Methodist, Primitive Methodist, and United Methodist Churches of Great Britain did the same, as with two exceptions there was no sharing of a common territory.[3] Likewise Methodist

Tower Movement with extracts from their literature poured into Northern Rhodesia, a District Officer's evidence of the effect of their teaching, and a statement to the Commission by an official representative of the movement. See further: K. S. Latourette, op. cit., VII (1945), 232–3; I.R.M., VIII (1919), 457; G. H. Wilson, The History of the Universities' Mission to Central Africa (1936), 208–9, 211, 263; G. Quick, " Some Aspects of the African Watch Tower Movement in Northern Rhodesia " in I.R.M., XXIX (1940), 216–26; I. Cunnison, "A Watchtower Assembly in Central Africa " in I.R.M., XL (1951), 456–69; C. Dundas, African Crossroads (1955), 173–4.

[1] Report, Cmd. 5009, 51.
[2] Vide supra, p. 199.
[3] The exceptions were (1) In Sierra Leone where the United Methodist Church had been invited in 1858 to take charge of an existing group of churches calling themselves the West African Methodists, and had done so;

Unification in the United States in 1939—the merging of the Methodist Episcopal Church, the Methodist Episcopal Church South, and the Methodist Protestant Church—brought into being the Methodist Church, with a resulting unification of Board control but no closer union save in the Belgian Congo.

Two significant proposals for closer union were brought forward during the 'thirties with hope of not too distant realization, one in East Africa and one in West. Kenya had been a lone pioneer with its Nairobi and Kikuyu Conferences of 1909 and 1913 respectively, the latter raising much controversy.[1] The resumption of negotiations in 1918 had produced no advance beyond a federal Alliance. Now the Anglican, Presbyterian, and Methodist Churches, resulting from the work of the Church Missionary Society, the Church of Scotland Mission, and the Methodist Missionary Society, had matured further plans for a united Church, taking as a basis the South India proposals. In 1938 this scheme was awaiting Lambeth approval. It was not, however, found possible to proceed with it.[2]

The corresponding movement in West Africa was in South-Eastern Nigeria where the Evangelical Union had already brought the Anglican, Presbyterian, and Methodist Churches and the Qua Iboe Mission into a regular association. The personal initiative in the matter came from J. T. Dean, one of the pioneer missionaries of the Church of Scotland Calabar Mission, who as Biblical scholar, pioneer theological tutor, and reviser of the Efik New Testament had already made a major contribution to the Church. It was this vision of a united Church, conveyed to others at an intermission gathering in Calabar, that led to the setting up of the Committee on Church Union in South-Eastern Nigeria.[3] A draft basis of Union was prepared which was an adaptation to local

this group proved restive under Methodist Union and eventually seceded (see Vol. II, p. 220); (2) In Northern Rhodesia where Primitive Methodists had pioneered in the early 'nineties (see Vol. III, pp. 149–52). The Primitive Methodist mission in South Africa had been united with the Wesleyan Methodist Church in South Africa in anticipation of the British union and this now became the Methodist Church in South Africa. At the same time the Wesleyan Methodist Missionary Society's work in the Transvaal was transferred to the South African Conference while the Society's interest in Portuguese East Africa was handed over as the mission field of the South African Church.

[1] See Vol. III, p. 294.
[2] *Quarterly Notes, Bulletin of I.M.C.*, No. 38 (April 1933), iv; *The Life of the Church*, Tambaram Madras Series, IV (1939), 432.
[3] Dr. Dean died in retirement in Scotland on April 25, 1947.—*Niger News*, June 1947.

conditions of the 1934 edition of the South India scheme. The presbyterian and episcopal systems were both to be preserved in the government of the Church, a constitutional episcopate being accepted as part of the basis of union. While the United Church was to be autonomous it was the expressed purpose to work towards a wider union of Churches in West Africa.[1] The African churches were reported as enthusiastic for the scheme. It was again a Lambeth decision that was awaited. Again the scheme did not mature.[2]

The question of some form of closer union in Northern Nigeria was discussed at the Miango Conference of 1926, when the hope was expressed that a federation might be achieved with agreement on a common form of ordination of Africans to the ministry, but nothing came of it.[3]

In Tanganyika, where the range of ecclesiastical principles and polity held out little prospect of any closer union, missions of German origin succeeded in reaching agreement on an Evangelical Church of East Africa based on Lutheran principles held in common. The Berlin, Bethel, Leipzig, and Moravian Missions of Germany and the Augustana Synod of the United States together founded in 1937 the Federation of East African Missionary Churches (Ostafrikanische Missionskirchenbund). This brought together some 120,000 African Christians for whom Luther's Catechism was the elementary compendium of faith. At the first assembly in 1938 the concern was to secure some uniformity of practice among the eight churches of the missions concerned, with discussion of existing attitudes to forms of worship, standards of membership, and church discipline. African representatives attended from all areas comprehended by the Federation, and were reported as showing great joy at sharing in a church assembly so widely representative of their country. As one of the German leaders put it : " It was a revelation to realize how even the simpler-minded African Christians understood the implications of this Federation of eight African churches, no members of which, out-

---

[1] *Committee on Church Union in South Eastern Nigeria, Draft Basis of Union* (1935; Revised edition, 1939). African leaders had been interested in union proposals as early as 1931.—*I.R.M.*, XXI (1932), 226. The idea of a federation of churches was first presented by A. W. Wilkie in 1911. See Vol. III, p. 292.

[2] *The Life of the Church*, Tambaram Madras Series, IV (1939), 434.

[3] *Minutes of Conference of Missions, Northern Provinces, Nigeria, held at Miango* (1926), 18–19; *The Life of the Church*, Tambaram Madras Series, IV (1939), 433–4.

side their own church, had they ever seen." This unification was to advance still further.[1]

In the Union of South Africa the question of the Union of Congregational, Methodist, and Presbyterian Churches was explored in 1935. A joint committee meeting at Bloemfontein in March had under consideration both the possibility and the expediency of such a development at that time and remitted its report to the assemblies and conferences concerned. But a long journey lay ahead.[2]

The alternative to such regional unions, namely the inclusion of local units in an inter-territorial denominational organization, was an Anglican objective in East Africa as early as 1920—the proposal to constitute an East African Province, from the dioceses of Uganda (C.M.S.), Upper Nile (C.M.S.), Mombasa (C.M.S.), Zanzibar (U.M.C.A.), Masasi (U.M.C.A.), Nyasaland (U.M.C.A.), and Northern Rhodesia (U.M.C.A). The Uganda and Upper Nile Synods declared themselves unwilling at that time, and the Mombasa Synod proposed an exploratory conference which met in 1927. The reference to the dioceses in 1928 again found Uganda declining the proposal.[3] Meanwhile the new diocese of Central Tanganyika was created with the first bishop coming from Australia, and responsibility for it was thereupon transferred from the Church Missionary Society to the Church in that country.[4] The Anglican policy to make the African Church autonomous by eventually creating a Province with an Archbishop at its head in East and West and thus provide for the consecration of bishops within that Church, valuable as it undoubtedly was, did nevertheless cause the Kenya and Eastern Nigeria pro-

[1] *The Life of the Church*, 433; *I.R.M.*, XXVIII (1939), 62; H. Scholten " The Growth and Expansion of an East African Church ", in *I.R.M.* XXXIX (1950), 270–6.

[2] *Quarterly Notes, Bulletin of I.M.C.*, No. 47 (July 1935), vii; *The South African Outlook*, LXV (1935), 90–1, 255–6. The composition of the non-European membership of the three Churches was interesting: in the Congregational Church, mainly Coloured with Afrikaans as the medium in use (legacy of the pioneer service of the London Mission to Hottentots); in the Methodist Church, principally Bantu of several tribes and vernaculars with some Coloured and Indian membership; in the Presbyterian Church of South Africa only a small Bantu section due to the setting up, in amicable relation with the parent Church, of the Bantu Presbyterian Church which itself participated in the Conference.

[3] *The Church Overseas*, I (1928), 60;' *Report of the C.M.S.* (1928), 5; *I.R.M.* XVIII (1929), 33; XXI (1932), 225.

[4] *Report of the C.M.S.* (1929), 6; *I.R.M.*, XXI (1932), 225.

posals for an inclusive regional union to recede nearer to the horizon.[1]

(4) *World Conference on the Eve*

With these comparatively rapid developments the non-Roman Churches in Africa were now in a better position to be represented at a world conference by their own nationals than ever before. Within a decade of the Jerusalem Meeting of the International Missionary Council the opportunity was offered. In December 1938 there assembled at Tambaram, Madras, delegates to the second enlarged meeting of the Council, which thus became third in the series from Edinburgh 1910.[2] Of the thirty-three delegates appointed by regional bodies in sixteen African territories fifteen or nearly fifty per cent were Africans representative of East and West, South and Central.[3] It was a matter of regret that no African delegate from the Belgian Congo could attend to represent the Church in Congo, chiefly on the ground of language difficulty.[4]

The delegation from Africa met those of other lands in a conference of 471 men and women coming from sixty-nine countries, representative of the Universal Church. And it was a comparatively young conference; most of the delegates were in their forties.[5] The central theme was the Christian Church, its life and witness, and this became doubly significant from the troubled days in world affairs during which it met. The common fellowship in Christ of men and women committed to Him, transcending the barriers of race and nation, was demonstrated more clearly at this conference than ever before, where more than half represented the younger Churches.[6] And the younger Churches played a worthy part. Henry P. Van Dusen declared that the ablest delegation, man for man, was not that from Britain or from America but that from China.[7]

The fifteen Africans at the conference received ineffaceable impressions. They saw the world Christian community in micro-

[1] Anglican Provinces were in due course to be proposed for East, West, and Central Africa.

[2] The original plan was to hold the meeting in China at Hangchow, until the Japanese " incident," developing from 1937, ruled out the possibility.

[3] Tambaram Report, VIII, *Addresses and other Records* (1939), 181–2.

[4] *Quarterly Notes, Bulletin of I.M.C.*, No. 55 (July 1937), ii.

[5] W. Richey Hogg, *Ecumenical Foundations* (1952), 291. An interesting table of the average age region by region is given in *Quarterly Notes, Bulletin of the I.M.C.*, No. 63 (July 1939), ii.

[6] W. Richey Hogg, *op. cit.*, 292.

[7] *World Mission of the Church* (1939), 171.

cosm : not as they knew it for the most part at home—American, European, and African—but with Indian, Chinese, and other Asian peoples bearing a worthy share in the deliberations. Moreover this was the first time African Christians from such a range of territory in their own continent had met together. To do so in such a setting was an inspiring experience of a universal fellowship. The delegates from Africa held a special session of their own to discuss questions affecting their Christian witness in the World Church. It is significant that these related to polygamy, witchcraft, and the growth of the Separatist Churches—major problems for the Church in Africa in respect of social life, the African thought world, and the unity of the Church witnessing in a pagan environment.[1] It was significant, too, of a quickened conscience that these matters were discussed, not at the bidding of European mentors, but as springing from membership in a world Christian community in which the practice of polygamy and belief in witchcraft were universally branded as sub-Christian, and in which separatism was the antithesis of the Christian duty of drawing closer together. This Africa group asked the International Missionary Council in respect of polygamy " to undertake or foster research into this subject and related social customs of the African peoples ".[2]

As illustrating the profound effect of the total experience, reference may be made to the relaying to African audiences by a Nigerian delegate of the impressions he received.[3] They found at the conference, he said, not just black and white, but black and white and brown and yellow; Christianity was not only the white man's religion, it was universal, it was abundantly worth while : " However small our Christian community in our town, let us not forget that we belong to a universal fellowship, a world-wide Church." There were represented, he continued, different missions, different peoples, different colours, but in the Conference they found a unity that should characterize the Christian Church everywhere. He then reported on the special African questions discussed : on polygamy, Africans were shamed before other

[1] *The Life of the Church*, Tambaram Madras Series, IV, 404–7, where the report of the Africa group on these questions is given.

[2] *Ibid.*, 404. The Research Department of the I.M.C. was not able to pursue this at the time, but in 1946 the matter was taken up in association with the International African Institute, the Social Science Research Council of the British Colonial Office, and the Carnegie Corporation of New York. *Vide infra*, p. 300.

[3] Personally communicated by one who attended such a meeting in June 1939, and described the speaker's address as inspired.

peoples by their easy tolerance of it; on witchcraft, they needed a deeper trust in Christ the Light before Whom no powers of darkness stand; on separatism, " Be loyal to the Church in which you have been baptized and do not go away, if you are disciplined take your punishment, win back those who have gone away." Such was his message. To have taken home again such a sense of belonging to the Universal Church and to have thus communicated it to others on his return was a worthy service, on the part of one delegate at least, to the Church of Christ in Africa.

And the Tambaram meeting was only just in time. Three months before the Conference the Munich agreement had purchased a temporary reprieve from advancing totalitarian aggression, and three short months after it, in March 1939, Hitler's entry into Prague finally demolished any hope of continuing peace that might have been entertained. But as the nations were pulling apart the Churches were drawing together. The Oxford and Edinburgh Conferences of 1937, concerning in the main the Churches of the West, had each adopted resolutions pointing forward to a World Council of Churches, while the Tambaram meeting of the International Missionary Council in the following year was ecumenical in a more complete sense than any such gathering had been before. And it met on the eve of tragedy. The Conference closed a decade in which men's hearts, outside the carelessly jubilant totalitarian régimes, grew steadily heavier with foreboding until the storm burst and the fiery trial of all-out war was let loose upon the world.

CHAPTER 6

WORLD WAR ONCE MORE

1939–1945

THE twelve months from the spring of 1939 to the spring of 1940 were twelve months of anxious tension passed by the world in ominous waiting. True, the German army had invaded Poland on September 1, 1939, with Britain and France thereupon declaring a state of war with Germany; but beyond the German manning of the Siegfried Line, with Allied troops facing them west of the Rhine, and the Maginot Line alert at action stations, there was no major military move. German submarines were quickly busy but otherwise the command of the high seas was secure in Allied hands. The war on two fronts had, it seemed, been skilfully avoided by Ribbentrop's deal with Molotov in concluding a non-aggression pact with Soviet Russia who then tried out her military machine in a private campaign against Finland.

But with the spring of 1940 the lightning war flashed out abruptly on the startled consciousness of a now unsuspecting world, and crackled its way through Denmark and Norway, through Holland, Belgium, Luxemburg, and France, until in a matter of weeks the western coast of Europe from the Arctic Circle to the Pyrenees lay in the hand of Hitler. And then, with the fading days of summer, lightning war in the air was unleashed on Britain and the whole world held its breath as the titanic struggle moved to a thrilling climax in the crippling of the German air armada, and British soil was held inviolate at last. Britain, unconquered but sore beleaguered, now waited, without an ally though not bereft of friends, to face the continuing German onslaught. For almost a year and a half this phase of the struggle had lasted when, on December 7, 1941, Japan struck at Pearl Harbour from out of the blue, and the United States forthwith ranged herself, an incomparable ally, with Britain against the totalitarian triumvirate with results that were decisive for the war.

(1) *Africa in World War II*

By contrast to the first world war, Germany in this possessed no territory in Africa. True, in the mandated territories that were formerly German colonies some measure of Nazi infiltration had been attempted, but the mandatory Powers were on their guard and no local *blitzkrieg* could develop. In two respects, however, African soil soon became involved. With the collapse of France and the setting up of the Vichy régime under Pétain, the French colonial empire in Africa was divided : North Africa and French West Africa fell under Vichy control, while French Equatorial Africa aligned itself by the side of de Gaulle standing for Free France.

The second case was that of Italy. When Mussolini judged it opportune he entered the war on the German side and thereby risked the considerable Italian Empire in North and East Africa as a hostage to fortune. And in the end he lost. While in the desert war the armoured columns of Italy, Germany, and Britain swept to and fro across the Libyan sands until the final duel between Montgomery and Rommel, in the East the Italians were steadily dispossessed until Abyssinia was free once more with Haile Selassie on his throne again, and even Eritrea was occupied by British troops.

The Belgian Congo, with the mandated territory of Ruanda-Urundi, suffered as did French Equatorial Africa by being cut off from Europe for the period of the war. It meant much for the Belgian Congo that French territory to the north, under the Negro Governor-General Eboué, stood with de Gaulle. Professor Denis Saurat, visiting Brazzaville at the request of de Gaulle, saw the Congo and reported on his contact : " The fall of France has filled Africa with awe. De Gaulle has filled Africa with hope. The friendly Belgians said to me. ' With a German commission at Brazzaville what could we do ? On the other side of us is ex-German South-West Africa. Rhodesia and the Cape were in danger. We were lost. . . . Watch over the Chad, the first fort of defence for Cape Town '." [1]

A dramatic development came with American participation in the conflict, when airfields were laid out on the Guinea Coast and beyond to provide a trans-African ferry service to what the military began to call the Middle East. With American troops thus on the ground, a new feature appeared in the West African scene.

It will be observed that it was Africa north of the equator that was more directly involved in World War II, either by actual invasion or by threat of it. Yet South Africa did not remain aloof : General Smuts returned to power and armed forces were

[1] D. Saurat, *Watch over Africa* (1941), 37.

despatched to North Africa. Moreover, as the Mediterranean was no longer an easy thoroughfare for Allied transport, the Cape route came into use again with considerable consequent activity at South African ports.

(2) *The Second German Elimination*

The German Missionary Societies, returning to their fields in the first post-war decade, had mastered their many difficulties with remarkable success. It was reported in 1930 from a recent survey that the number of their missionaries had then reached seventy-five per cent of the total in 1914, while the number of African helpers had grown to be one hundred more than at that date. The Christian community also showed an increase of thirty-three per cent. Perhaps most surprising of all, in view of domestic difficulties in the German economy, the income of the Societies had in 1930 reached eighty-three per cent of the pre-war figure.[1] The German missions were well on the way to resume the honoured position they had held in the missionary enterprise in pre-war days. But the development was not to proceed unhindered. The first setback appeared in 1933 when the Nazi régime instituted a plan for winter relief of the unemployed to which the charitable diverted some of their gifts on the ground of this being a prior claim.[2] But worse was to follow. Within a year the severe restrictions imposed by the German exchange policy had cut down at a stroke the funds that could be transmitted overseas to a limited amount for the personal maintenance only of German missionaries. Thus all the usual grants for institutions, salaries of African workers, and general maintenance of mission activities remained locked in Germany. In response to an appeal by German missionary leaders in October 1934 an emergency fund was opened in their behalf to which generous contributions were made by American, British, and Scandinavian Societies.[3]

Then came the war. As the French and Belgian authorities had never allowed the return of German missionaries to mandated territory they controlled after the first war, the German Societies were now to be found only in British territory: colonies, British mandates, and the Union of South Africa; together with Abyssinia under Italian rule where missionaries of the Hermannsburg Society were acceptable to the authorities. With the outbreak of war the missionary world was better prepared than in 1914, with

[1] *Quarterly Notes, Bulletin of I.M.C.*, No. 26 (April 1930), vii.
[2] *Ibid.*, No. 41 (January 1934), ii.
[3] *Ibid.*, No. 45 (January 1935), ii–iii; No. 46 (April 1935), vi–vii.

the experience of the first war behind it and the organization of the International Missionary Council and its affiliated national conferences, to take action for safeguarding missionary interests. Arrangements were made to assist German missionaries not interned but cut off from their Societies, and the policy of the Versailles Treaty—that mission property should be preserved for mission purposes—was accepted and observed by the British Government. Further, the British Colonial Office, in a letter of October 1939, expressed its appreciation of the importance of the Societies' work and declared its intention to allow missionaries of enemy nationality to continue as far as possible, that is, after inquiry into their relation to the Nazi régime.[1]

In the Gold Coast and the adjoining British mandate of Togo German missionaries of the Basel and Bremen missions were interned; the women were soon repatriated, the men (after transfer to England) not until the end of the war. Happily the Basel and Scottish missions shared in the Presbyterian Church of the Gold Coast, and the Swiss members of the former mission were able to continue at their posts. In the case of the neighbouring Ewe Presbyterian Church Scottish missionaries came to the rescue when the Bremen workers left.[2]

German missionaries of two Societies—the Basel and the German Baptists—were serving in the British Mandate of Cameroons. They were removed in 1940 and the majority kept in internment in Jamaica. Swiss members of the Basel Mission were then responsible for the field, and American Baptists cared for the German Baptist work.[3]

In Tanganyika Territory, where some 100 men missionaries were in the service of five German societies, terms of parole were offered when the missionaries were interned at the outset of the war.[4] A number continued their work under these conditions but later withdrew their undertaking on the ground that they must stand with their fellow-countrymen. There were pressures from Germany in this situation as well as personal reconsideration, and declining to give parole was therefore no evidence of revolutionary

[1] *I.R.M.*, XXIX (1940), 110; *The International Missionary Council and Continental Missions in the War of 1939–1945*, (n.d.), 3–4.
[2] *The I.M.C. and Continental Missions in the War of 1939–1945*, 8.
[3] *Ibid.*, 8.
[4] The terms were as follows: " I declare upon my honour that I am not in possession of any kind of weapons, that I will not participate in any way in military enterprises, that I will refrain from revolutionary propaganda, and that I will immediately carry out the directions given me from time to time by the Government."—*I.R.M.*, XXX (1941), 104.

intention. Thus by the summer of 1940, with one or two special cases excepted, all had been interned. Some were repatriated but the greater number remained in internment camps in South and East Africa throughout the war.[1] Their orphaned missions soon received oversight and financial help from foster parents. The extensive work of the Berlin, Bethel, and Leipzig Societies was cared for by fellow Lutherans—the Augustana Lutheran Mission of the United States. The Church of Sweden Mission and the Swedish Evangelical National Missionary Society also gave valuable help by loaning members of their staffs. The Moravian Mission from Herrnhut was supervised by the English Province of their Church, and the Neukirchen Mission by the Anglican Bishop of Central Tanganyika. British grants as well as liberal American funds kept all the work in being.[2]

In South-West Africa the Rhenish Mission had only five missionaries interned. Collaboration with the Dutch Reformed Church of South Africa, which began after the first war, together with some American help, served to maintain the Mission.[3] In South Africa German Missions continued without interruption, receiving local support and grants from Lutheran sources.[3] In Kenya the small Tana River field of the Neukirchen Mission was cared for, though indirectly, by the Kenya Missionary Council.[4]

Abyssinia was rather a different case. During the Italian régime the Hermannsburg missionaries, who had been allowed to return to the country, continued without hindrance, but on its fall the German missionaries were interned. Some were still in Uganda at the end of the war.[5]

Thus for a second time within a generation German missions, with little exception, were eliminated from colonial territory. And this time their absence was to last longer.[6] It was a grievous loss to the Christian cause.

---

[1] *I.R.M.*, XXX (1941), 105–6; XXXIII (1944), 58; *The I.M.C. and Continental Missions in the War of 1939–1945*, 9; W. Richey Hogg, *Ecumenical Foundations*, 306.

[2] *The I.M.C. and Continental Missions*, 9.

[3] *Ibid.*, 9.

[4] *Ibid.*, 9–10. The Methodist Missionary Society, and to a limited extent the Church Missionary Society, gave help to the mission. The work was finally taken over by the M.M.S. in 1956.

[5] *Ibid.*, 10.

[6] When German missionary leaders, at a meeting with British representatives at Hermannsburg in November, 1945, asked when they might expect to return, one authoritative spokesman replied that if it was five years after the first war it was more likely to be not less than ten after the second—a forecast that has been fulfilled. (Personally communicated.)

(3) *The Plight of Other Continental Missions*

With the overrunning of countries on the western seaboard of Europe by the German armies in the spring of 1940 other Continental missions besides the German were cut off from their base.

Finland, though not occupied by Germany, was effectively isolated. The Finnish Missionary Society's African field lay in the north of South-West Africa among the Ovambo; the mission was now supported from Lutheran sources in addition to receiving help from South Africa, Sweden, London, and New York. Finnish missionaries pioneering among the Ovambo in Angola were eventually taken into the service of the Swiss Philafrican Mission.[1]

Norwegian Missions were at work in South Africa, Southern Rhodesia, the Belgian Congo (north and east), and the French Mandate of Cameroons. The Norwegian Missionary Society took the lead, others being Baptist and Pentecostal missions in the Congo and two Pentecostal groups in South Africa, while Norwegian Methodists co-operated with the American Methodist mission in Algeria and Southern Rhodesia.[2] These received help from the Royal Norwegian Government (then in exile in London), from the funds of the International Missionary Council, the fund of the Congo Protestant Council, and (in the case of the Norwegian Missionary Society) from Lutheran sources also.[3]

Danish missions were represented at two points: the Sudan United Mission in Northern Nigeria had a Danish branch and this was helped by Lutheran and I.M.C. funds. In the Belgian Congo the Danish Baptist Mission was assisted by Danish Baptist friends in the United States.[4]

Belgium had but one Protestant mission which had entered Ruanda after the first world war. The Congo Government allowed it support and the Congo Protestant Council fund also helped.[4]

The Paris Missionary Society was hard hit. With work in French West Africa, in French Equatorial Africa, and Cameroons, and also in two British areas—Basutoland and Northern Rhodesia—they were hard pressed to keep afloat. In addition to financial stringency their manpower was seriously reduced by conscription.[5]

[1] *The I.M.C. and Continental Missions*, 9. The Mission Philafricaine entered Angola, its only field, in 1897. It was inter-denominational in control.—Beach and Fahs, *World Missionary Atlas* (1925), 53.
[2] S. Solberg, *Norsk Misjonsatlas* (1944), 18–21.
[3] *The I.M.C. and Continental Missions*, 8, 9.
[4] *Ibid.*, 8, 9.
[5] Fifty of the ninety-eight missionaries, together with the Society's Secretary, were conscripted.—W. Richey Hogg, *op. cit.*, 307.

Until the Allied landings in North Africa the Paris Mission was able to keep in touch with French West Africa while that region adhered to Vichy, and to be of help to English and American missions there. Although from the end of 1942 to 1944 contact with Metropolitan France was interrupted, there were nevertheless French missionaries serving the area after the transfer of Senegal's allegiance to the Allied cause.[1] In French Equatorial Africa and Cameroons the severance from Paris was complete, thanks to the Free French régime of General de Gaulle. Here the International Missionary Council's New York fund came to the rescue, and American Presbyterians in Cameroons were also able to give assistance. The appearance of a Federation of Evangelical Missions of the Cameroons and Equatorial Africa was evidence of their vitality despite their isolation.[2] The Basuto and Barotse missions received financial aid from a far-flung constituency : Canada, Britain, Switzerland, and South Africa.[3]

That the plight into which these missions were so suddenly plunged did not lead to such damage to their work as would not readily be repaired was due in the main to the activity of the officers of the International Missionary Council, together with Lutheran World Action which accepted responsibility for all Lutheran missions. Not all that was desired was raised; local budgets had to be cut down and various development projects abandoned, but the fact remains that no Protestant orphaned mission ceased to exist.[4] It was an achievement in keeping with the Christian unity expressed at Tambaram.

With the end of hostilities a normal procedure, save for German Societies, was hoped for, but the Basel and Paris Missions in particular were still in financial straits (the former had lost its once powerful German partner, and the latter was hard hit by the devaluation of the franc), and it was clear that help must be continued. Further, the German missions, Lutheran and non-Lutheran, still surviving (mainly in Asia) were virtually derelict without outside support and must have help; so the funds went on.[5]

[1] The I.M.C. and Continental Missions, 8. In particular there may be mentioned the loan during this period of Georges Mabille, of the distinguished Basutoland family, to the Christian and Missionary Alliance in the French Sudan. See: G. Mabille, L'Appel du Soudanais (n.d.), passim; I.R.M., XXXIII (1944), 53.

[2] The I.M.C. and Continental Missions, 8; I.R.M., XXXI (1942), 57.

[3] The I.M.C. and Continental Missions, 9.

[4] W. Richey Hogg, op. cit., 308–11, 317.

[5] Ibid., 315; B. D. Gibson, "Am I my Brother's Keeper?" in I.R.M., XXXVIII (1949), 193–6.

(4) *Progress Despite Privation*

The inevitable embarrassments which most missions experienced throughout six years of war—reduction of missionary staff through conscription and loss by enemy action, severe limitation in securing further recruits, African enrolment in military units, depletion of foreign funds, restriction of local resources—all did far less than might have been expected to slow down the momentum the Christian mission had now gained. Such statistics as became available showed a continuing increase in full membership and in the catechumenate, while African leaders were drawn into new positions of responsibility in the emergency and acquitted themselves with a devotion and an efficiency for which their missionary mentors often enough were scarcely prepared. The momentum acquired in the inter-bellum period, despite the mounting difficulties of the time, may be illustrated in the progress reported between 1925 and 1938. Protestant communicants increased from 996,000 to 2,131,000; while Roman Catholics also made rapid strides, rising from 2,294,000 to 4,613,000.[1] Protestant missionaries grew during the same period from 5,556 to 7,514, while Roman Catholic foreign workers were returned as 7,006 and 10,384 respectively.[2] The enrolment in Protestant elementary schools rose from 882,000 to 1,452,000 and in secondary from 14,000 to 17,000.[3] And the progress did not slacken appreciably during the years of war. K. S. Latourette offers some " glimpses which presumably, were fairly typical " in the case of Roman Catholic missions. In the Belgian Congo and Ruanda-Urundi their number grew in a single year (June 1941–June 1942) by 249,899 or some thirteen per cent.[4] The White Fathers, with their far-flung African missions, reported the number of Christians in their charge as mounting from 1,587,558 to 1,827,518 between June 30, 1939 and June 30, 1941, while catechumens rose from 400,917 to 590,491.[5] Even the number of priests had grown from 910 to 985, but lay brothers and sisters showed a decline.[5] African staff under their direction showed an increase all along the line : priests from 171 to 221; lay brothers from 91 to 154; sisters from 546 to 689.[5] During the war Roman

---

[1] M. Searle Bates, *Data on the Distribution of the Missionary Enterprise* (1943), 5.
[2] *Ibid.*, 6.
[3] *Ibid.*, 10.
[4] K. S. Latourette, *A History of the Expansion of Christianity*, VII (1945), 223–4.
[5] *Ibid.*, 224.

Catholic territorial advances also took place both east and west. In Uganda the Mill Hill Fathers had by 1940 set up six new stations and opened a new college since the war began, while in Nigeria the White Fathers entered the Oyo Province.[1]

New religious communities also appeared : in Nigeria the first African girls took their vows as novices of the Handmaids of the Holy Child in 1940, while in the same year the Congregation of our Lady of Sorrows (affiliated to the Holy Cross Sisters) was founded for Coloured women in South Africa.[2] In Basutoland the Oblates of Mary Immaculate, whose seminary for African candidates for the priesthood was at Roma their earliest station,[3] had the enterprise to launch in 1940 the *Roma College Review* for their South African constituency.[4]

The war years brought no relaxation of the pressure for education. Colonial Governments were more sensitive than usual to African opinion and more concerned than ever to have a literate constituency that need not be at the mercy of irresponsible propaganda. The missions, already deeply committed to the cause of education, therefore continued to play their part in increasing measure. Nigeria was a case in point. Here the Southern Provinces experienced a growth of primary education in the decade 1937–47 in respect of voluntary assisted schools (almost entirely a mission category) from 339 to 473 with an enrolment of 69,464 in 1937 and of 153,759 in 1946. The growth of institutions under mission auspices for training teachers was even more spectacular : from nineteen voluntary assisted centres in 1937 to fifty-three in 1947, the student enrolment being respectively 752 and 2,730.[5]

Coupled with this development came the increasing demand for Christian literature. In the nature of the case the missions were more dependent upon their local resources during the war years, and while these could well have been larger, they were by no means negligible. Thus in 1943 alone the Morija Press of the Paris Mission on Basutoland printed no fewer than 370,000 books in twenty languages distributed over Africa south of the Sahara; in addition two periodicals were regularly issued. This was the achievement of a European staff of two with forty-two African helpers, while it was reported : " Most of the presses are ' ageing ',

---

[1] *I.R.M.*, XXXIII (1944), 85, 86.
[2] *I.R.M.*, XXX (1941), 128.
[3] See Vol. II, p. 272.
[4] *I.R.M.*, XXX (1941), 129.
[5] *African Education: A Study of Educational Policy and Practice in British Tropical Africa* (1953), 47–8.

and there is an epic struggle for paper." [1] Meanwhile the International Committee on Christian Literature for Africa, under the direction of its secretary Margaret Wrong, gave outstanding service, while the United Society for Christian Literature (heir of the former Religious Tract Society and others) was able to subsidize publications for Africa required by missions as well as maintain its own agent for literature in the Copperbelt. [2] A notable enterprise of the Society was carried out in Johannesburg in 1939–41 with such success that municipal support was given to maintain it, and the Society invited to further co-operation with the Department of Native Affairs. [3]

The movement among Protestant missions for joint counsel, fuller co-operation, and where feasible the promotion of facilities for a united African Church, was already well under way before 1939, and continued without intermission—indeed, continued with a growing sense of urgency in view of the unmistakable signs of the times that Christian missions were reaching the end of an era. In French territory the founding in 1941 of the Federation of Evangelical Missions of Cameroons and Equatorial Africa was a gain to Protestant missionary co-operation in a region where Roman Catholic membership was reported as well above the half-million mark in 1939. [4] In 1942 Nyasaland missions took a step forward with the formation of a Christian Council. The Consultative Board of Federated Missions was not altogether replaced as some missions it brought together did not then feel able to join the Council. The Dutch Reformed mission which was one of these took the decision to adhere however in the following year. [5]

In 1943 the Christian event of the year in Kenya was the constitution of the Christian Council of Kenya of which churches and missions were invited to become members, though the Kenya Missionary Council continued for the time being. In 1945 the Christian Council began the issue of an Occasional Bulletin, reporting matters discussed at meetings of the Council and its interim activities, ranging from fundamental theological presuppositions involved in working in a multi-racial society to such

---

[1] *The British Committee for the Paris Missionary Society, Report for the Year 1944,* 7.

[2] *Books for Africa, Quarterly Bulletin of I.C.C.L.A., XII* (1942), 39–40.

[3] *I.R.M., XXXI* (1942), 67.

[4] *I.R.M., XXXI* (1942), 57; *Quarterly Notes, Bulletin of the I.M.C.,* No. 77 (January 1943), iii. The Roman Catholic membership claimed in 1939 was: French Cameroons 355,542; French Equatorial Africa 213,752.—*International Fides Service,* October 1, 1949.

[5] *I.R.M., XXXII* (1943), 48; *XXXIII* (1944), 59.

immediate practical concerns as the demobilization of the African soldier, the future of education, and African marriage problems.[1] Also in 1943 the Congo Protestant Council with a membership of thirty missions, having set up a Church Polity Commission, undertook an exploratory inquiry among all those missions which had adopted the name L'Eglise du Christ au Congo, to discover what further steps towards establishing one strong African Church were desirable, and meanwhile to encourage common standards of church discipline and the training of African pastors.[2] The year 1944 saw four more Councils appear: in Egypt a Council of Churches was formed with the Coptic Patriarch of Alexandria as its President; while in Ethiopia (as Abyssinia was now usually known) an Inter-Mission Council represented a first step towards closer co-operation in which it was hoped the Church of Ethiopia would participate.[3] In Northern Rhodesia an African Christian Conference had been officially constituted to represent Africans of all societies and churches co-operating in the General Conference; it met first in 1939 and proved a very active body.[4] At its meeting in July 1944 the General Missionary Conference formally constituted the Christian Council of Northern Rhodesia which was to replace the General Conference. Provision was made in the constitution for regular attendance of representatives from the African Christian Conference.[5] Finally, also in 1944, the evangelical missions of Portuguese East Africa moved forward from the Evangelical Missionary Association to the adoption of a constitution for the Christian Council of Mozambique.[6] This doubling of the number of territorial Councils in the continent was no small achievement while under the stress of war.

That there were restrictions to be found over and above those imposed by war was not altogether surprising. In Egypt various draft laws relating to the schools were brought forward but eventually withdrawn, leaving the situation in somewhat disturbing uncertainty, while the setting of an age limit below which no change

[1] The Christian Council of Kenya, Occasional Bulletin, No. 1, February 1945; No. 2, June 1945.

[2] I.R.M., XXXIII (1944), 54; XXXIV (1945), 46.

[3] I.R.M., XXXIV (1945), 37, 39. The earlier Egypt Inter-Mission Council had served missions only; the new Council, by including representatives of Churches, was fully comprehensive of the non-Roman Christian movement.

[4] I.R.M., XXX (1941), 70.

[5] The General Missionary Conference of Northern Rhodesia, Report of Proceedings of Ninth Conference (1944), 10, 13–15.

[6] I.R.M., XXXIV (1945), 47.

of religion was permissible was primarily designed to circumvent conversion in mission schools, but this measure also was postponed.[1] With the return of Haile Selassie to the throne of Ethiopia the discriminatory action of the Italian authorities against Protestant missions automatically ceased, but the welcome now offered to their return was not as unqualified as had been hoped. All who were concerned with educational, medical, or social service were warmly received but the evangelistic missionary was regarded as somewhat of an intruder in a country with its own ancient Christian tradition. The Ethiopian Government was prepared, however, to permit full missionary activity among non-Christian sections of the population with two main provisos : that a right of entry was retained for authorized religious teachers of the Church of Ethiopia, should parents desire this teaching for their children; and that Amharic as the language common to the country as a whole should be promoted. Even so, difficulty was experienced in securing permits for new workers, especially if these were neither teachers nor medicals, but by 1945 most missions, to some extent at least, had resumed their work.[2] In Portuguese colonies, where restrictions in the matter of language have already been noted,[3] evangelical missions were led to fear yet further embarrassment from the Concordat between Portugal and the Vatican, ratified in 1940; a Missionary Agreement accompanied the Concordat. By these instruments a highly privileged position was accorded the Roman Catholic Church, with liberal subsidizing of its activities and exemption from taxation. It was stated that the Concordat and Missionary Agreement were not designed to affect directly the non-Roman missions in Portuguese colonies, but past experience of intimidating pressures, more particularly in Portuguese East Africa, led Protestant missionaries to accept all such assurances with caution. Moreover, even when the missionaries might be relatively undisturbed, discrimination against Protestant Africans might seriously curtail their work.[4] It was, therefore, with some relief that the Swiss Mission in Mozambique received in 1944 official government recognition of the youth movement,

---

[1] *I.R.M.*, XXIX (1940), 64–5; XXX (1941), 56–7; XXXI (1942), 45–6; XXXII (1943), 33–4; XXXIII (1944), 45; XXXIV (1945), 37; M. Searle Bates, *Religious Liberty: An Inquiry* (1945), 11–12. Cf. H. C. M. Davis, *Some Aspects of Religious Liberty of Nationals in the Near East* (1938) 26–7, 33–4.

[2] *I.R.M.*, XXXI (1942), 47–9; XXXII (1943), 35; XXXIII (1944), 46; XXXIV (1945), 39; M. Searle Bates, *op. cit.*, 117–19.

[3] *Vide supra*, p. 184.

[4] M. Searle Bates, *op. cit.*, 96–101.

based upon the church, which it had organized and which was a vital instrument in developing in the young a sense of Christian responsibility.[1]

Despite the handicaps there were also some encouragements elsewhere in Portuguese lands. The 1940 census in Angola had disclosed, it was claimed, the dominance of the Ovimbundu, the high proportion of Christians among them being largely the fruit of the work of the American Board with Canadian collaboration.[2] Again, in 1939 the Worldwide Evangelization Crusade was granted by the Portuguese Government permission to enter Portuguese Guinea. Within two years the right had been exercised and work commenced in Bolama the capital.[3]

It was during the war years that the Christian Council of South Africa successfully surmounted a crisis in its fortunes and embarked on a bold policy of constructive Christian action. After its inception in 1936 [4] the support of the Dutch Reformed Churches had been limited: of the seven Churches in the Union [5] only the Church of the Transvaal and its Mission Church adhered to the Council. It was an uneasy partnership on more grounds than one: the agreed equality of Afrikaans with English as a medium proved fictitious rather than real, the Dutch Reformed members, despite generous allowance of representation, naturally found themselves in a minority out of relation to their position in the country,[6] and most serious of all, the cleavage in outlook on racial affairs—what were to be regarded as acceptable relations between European and African—was fundamental. The withdrawal of the Dutch Reformed Church of the Transvaal and its Mission Church took place in 1941. There followed in due course the formation of the Federal Mission Council of the Dutch Reformed Churches where it was felt the views and policies of the Dutch Reformed Church could be more satisfactorily expressed.[7]

[1] *I.R.M.*, XXXIV (1945), 47.

[2] *I.R.M.*, XXXIII (1944), 55–6. *Vide supra*, p. 205. Out of an African population of 3,670,000 there were 741,000 returned as Roman Catholics and 286,000 as Protestants.

[3] *I.R.M.*, XXIX (1940), 71; XXXI (1942), 58–9.

[4] *Vide supra*, p. 227.

[5] The Dutch Reformed Church in South Africa (Cape Province), the Dutch Reformed Church in Natal, the Dutch Reformed Church in the Orange Free State, and the Dutch Reformed Church in South Africa—Church of the Transvaal, together with three Mission Churches (Cape, O.F.S., and Transvaal).

[6] An overall majority of the European population adhered to the Dutch Reformed Churches.

[7] R. H. W. Shepherd and E. W. Grant, " The Christian Council of

Despite this acknowledged setback, the Christian Council set out upon a career of educating its constituency in the Christian outlook on the social and racial problems confronting the peoples of South Africa, publicizing its findings, and presenting the Government with its considered views on proposed enactments coming within its purview. In this course of action it was eminently successful and gathered strength from its achievements. It began to issue its own periodical, the *Christian Council Quarterly*, by way of keeping both its own constituency and the public informed of its concerns.[1] It organized conferences on social, economic, and racial affairs in the attempt to educate the Christian conscience. As early as May 1940 a conference was held at Pretoria on African family life which, while voicing the general concern expressed at Tambaram, was specifically addressed to the South African situation.[2] Of outstanding importance, however, was the Conference on Christian Reconstruction held at Fort Hare in July 1942. Not only was it fully interracial but delegates had all been prepared, as members of study groups for some months in advance, to discuss the main themes of the Conference. In the light of the nature of the Christian revelation in its bearing on human personality and social obligation there were reviewed questions of health, housing, family life, education, and a wide range of economic and social issues in which the community as a whole, of all racial complexions, was involved. The Conference was not an isolated episode but provided both stimulus and programme for much subsequent thought and action. An appraisal two years later stated : " More than any other single event, the conference has given the Council its rightful place as a co-ordinating agency of the Christian forces of the country." [3] The Council, its right thus established to represent its extensive constituency, was now able to speak with some measure of authority and to offer its considered views which were received with respect at the highest level. Thus when in 1942 a National Health Service Commission was appointed to survey the whole health situation and to make recom-

South Africa," in *I.R.M.*, XXXIII (1944), 258–66; cf. XXXI (1942), 63–4. It was further suggested from the Dutch side that the four German Societies—Moravian, Rhenish, Berlin, Hermannsburg—might adhere to the Federal Council since " they have gone furthest in the Afrikaans-izing of their labours as far as both language and policy are concerned." *I.R.M.*, XXXIII (1944), 262.

[1] *Quarterly Notes, Bulletin of the I.M.C., No. 79* (July 1943), ii. The first issue of the *Quarterly* appeared in October 1942.

[2] *I.R.M.*, XXX (1941), 74.

[3] *I.R.M.*, XXXII (1943), 50–1; XXXIII (1944), 264–6.

mendations, the Council, in view of the large commitment of Christian missions to medical work, was able to submit a memorandum, " The Future of Mission Hospitals in relation to a National Health Service for South Africa ", which was endorsed not only by the member churches and missions but also by the Roman Catholic Church in South Africa. The Memorandum gave support to the proposal of a State medical service but argued for the retention of mission hospitals as an integral part of such a service.[1] This resuscitation of so considerable an organ as the Christian Council of South Africa not only had importance for the years of war but was to be significant in the political turmoil of the post-war years of Nationalist ascendancy. While the Council's activities were the most notable expression of Christian opinion in South Africa during the war years, there were of course a number of collateral Christian pronouncements and discussions. Thus in 1941 the Synod of the Anglican Diocese of Johannesburg set up a Commission which was instructed to define " what it believed to be the mind of Christ for this land ". Its Report was accepted by the Synod in 1943 and issued under the title " The Church and the Nation ".[2] In Southern Rhodesia similar concerns concurrently found expression. In 1944 the Federation of African Welfare Societies, to which a missionary had been seconded as organizing secretary, promoted a conference on African welfare based on a survey of African urban life by the secretary.[3] Anglican Synod resolutions also in 1944 expressed concern, in the light of official policy on immigration, about the availability of land and housing facilities for Africans.[4]

Also in the war years there occurred an event that demonstrated the increasing attention Africa was now securing overseas—the first general conference on African affairs to be held in North America. The initiative sprang from the Africa Committee of the

[1] N. Macvicar, " The Christian Council of South Africa and the National Health Services Commission," in *I.R.M.*, XXXIII (1944), 407–14, where selected passages from the memorandum are presented.

[2] After a statement of Christian principles it reviewed the relation of the Church to the State, to economics and industry, to racial segregation, and to effective Christian teaching. It condemned " enforced segregation arising out of racial discrimination ", whether occupational, educational, territorial, social, or political.—(Clause E.5).

[3] *I.R.M.*, XXXIV (1945), 55. The missionary seconded, Percy Ibbotson, was elected a member of the first Federal Parliament of Rhodesia and Nyasaland in 1953 representing African interests. In 1954 he was appointed Chairman of the African Affairs Board of the Federal Government but had little time to exercise his influence. He died in April, 1955.

[4] *I.R.M.*, XXXIV (1945), 56.

Foreign Missions Conference whereby 199 delegates representing some forty-eight organizations with African interests met in conference at Westerville, Ohio, in June 1942. Missionaries from seventeen African territories and Africans from four were included in the delegations. The indigenous church, education and literature, and the African rural economy were matters of particular concern.[1] Among the comprehensive recommendations adopted was one requesting the setting up of a study group by the Africa Committee of the Foreign Missions Conference, to be charged among other things " to consider how the total resources of African Churches and Missions may be utilized to better advantage ".[2] This resulted in due course in a survey being undertaken in West Africa in 1944–45, financed from the United States. Despite the limitations imposed by a state of war it was found possible to visit seven territories : three British (Sierra Leone, Gold Coast, Nigeria), two French (Cameroons and French Equatorial Africa), the Belgian Congo, and the Republic of Liberia. The objectives were limited : the central concern was with rural life, considered in its various aspects of agriculture, education, health, and social welfare, together with relevant colonial policies.[3] The report was a survey by competent observers of the changing situation towards the end of the war period, in the light of which they concluded : " The real task in Africa is to educate and develop the African, through self-discipline and responsibility, for self-government." [4]

(5) Africans in World War II

If the first world war brought Africans willy nilly into the turmoil of European conflict, the second did no less. But there was a difference : they were now more awake to the world beyond Africa, and many had some idea of the treatment they might themselves expect from a victorious dictator; Abyssinia had already taught them that.

[1] *Christian Action in Africa, Report of the Church Conference on African Affairs held at Otterbein College, Westerville, Ohio, June 19–25, 1942* (1942), *passim*.
[2] *Ibid.*, 168.
[3] J. Davis, T. M. Campbell and M. Wrong, *Africa Advancing, A Study of Rural Education and Agriculture in West Africa and the Belgian Congo* (1945), *passim*. Jackson Davis, with a wide experience of Negro schools in the Southern States, was an officer of the General Education Board, a Rockefeller Foundation; Thomas M. Campbell was an American Negro eminent in agricultural affairs, and field agent for seven States under the Extension Service of the United States Department of Agriculture; Margaret Wrong was secretary of the International Committee on Christian Literature for Africa.
[4] *Ibid.*, 88.

Africans were involved in many ways, but not altogether in the manner of the generation before. They joined the established African regiments where they served in many capacities often involving special skills. As a case in point the King's African Rifles, into which some 30,000 Africans had been recruited during the first world war, had its strength raised to 150,000 in the second, with its men in most branches of army service. It is estimated that altogether some 300,000 Africans from East Africa were employed in the second world war.[1] These men, from British territories across the continent, saw service, as in the first world war, both in regions of Africa other than their own and in territories overseas. From West Africa they went to East Africa, Abyssinia, India, and Burma. Men from Nyasaland, Northern Rhodesia, Tanganyika Territory, Kenya, and Uganda not only saw each other's countries but included in their travels Abyssinia, Somaliland, and North Africa; while Madagascar, Mauritius, Palestine, Aden, India, Ceylon, and Burma also saw their service. As their fathers had done in their day, they gathered many impressions. One chaplain reported receiving a letter from an old scholar in Ceylon with the request : " When I come home I want you to help me to build a temple in my village." The chaplain comments : " He was a Christian and probably meant a church but behind the request was the ferment of new ideas." The remark of an able African from Nyasaland, a Christian leader in the forces, was significant of a growing sense of racial solidarity : " Men of many tribes have lived and worked together happily—Bemba, Tumbuka, Angoni, Kikuyu, Achewa, and others. In the future we must still help one another." A number returned with the desire to build better dwellings with the money they had earned.[2]

The African contribution from the Union of South Africa gave distinguished service. In 1940 the Cape Corps (Coloured) and the Native Military Guards, later the Native Military Corps (Bantu), were constituted and saw active service in non-combatant capacities in various fields but notably in the grim struggle of the North African desert, also sharing in the invasion of Italy.[3] They were a non-European army of 125,000 men (including the Indian and

[1] C. Dundas, *African Crossroads* (1955), 227–8.

[2] J. R. Shaw, " The Men of Northern Rhodesia and the War (1939–1945) "—unpublished MS. Major the Rev. J. R. Shaw, through whose courtesy I have been able to make use of his MS, already had twenty-five years' service in Northern Rhodesia to his credit when he became Army Chaplain to African troops during 1941–1946.

[3] E. Hellmann (ed.), *Handbook on Race Relations in South Africa* (1949) 538–45.

Malay Corps), and won high tribute for their gallant service. Thus: " The Cape Corps drivers drove their lorries from Cape Town to Cairo in rains, across slippery roads and rivers, rounding Lake Victoria through the valleys of Uganda into Abyssinia and Somaliland, into the terrible heat and fine dust storms of the Sudan, and then through the desert and the cultivated fields of Egypt; thence forward to the front lines, with supplies and ammunition to assist the British, Indian, Polish, New Zealand, and other Allied forces in Egypt, Libya, Tunisia, Algeria, Morocco, and Italy." [1] Members of the Native Military Corps, attached to European formations, "took part and were engaged in every battle in which Springbok troops participated ".[2] From this comradeship in arms there sprang an interracial welfare group in peace. The Springbok Legion of Ex-Servicemen was founded " to carry over into peace-time the co-operation which existed between the races during the war ", membership with all its privileges being open equally to both European and non-European. A second organization, the National War Memorial Health Foundation, also without a colour bar and with non-Europeans on its national council, " grew out of the desire of European soldiers when in Italy that means to better health should be provided for the non-European peoples of South Africa ".[3] Thus white and black from the Union, when in mutual dependence away from South Africa, discovered a new understanding of each other which it was desired to perpetuate at home.

The men were well cared for; if there was army discipline and dangerous duty, there was also good food, medical care, often special training, and good pay. It was a higher standard of life than they had known. Indeed, one man said to a chaplain from Nyasaland : " It seems a good thing to have a war, bwana. People are better fed, better clothed and better paid than ever before." [4] The Army Education Corps carried out a large-scale service for African soldiers, raising the literacy level and giving instruction which was an asset of permanent value. The Army Medical Corps in its own department trained Africans for hospital and field service, again with results beneficial to community health in peace-time. Thus the training which many Africans had received while on active service had prepared them for a better type of employment

[1] *Ibid.*, 540.
[2] *Ibid.*, 543.
[3] *Ibid.*, 662.
[4] A. B. Doig, " The Christian Church and Demobilization in Africa," in *I.R.M.*, XXXV (1946), 174–82.

in civil life, for which, however, the way was not always immediately open. Thus among the men returning to the Gold Coast on demobilization were 5,475 lorry drivers, a number higher than the total number of lorries in the territory before the war.[1]

But such positive results of military service did not stand alone. There were aspects of army experience, in that relaxation of normal moral standards incidental to the social dislocation produced in time of war, that cast their dark shadow over many lives. True, those with some personal conviction and standards of their own found their moral fibre toughened and their spiritual tone improved, but the unguarded fell an easy prey to the enticements of the hour. Nor did the example of white men they met always serve as that restraint upon their conduct which contact with government official and Christian missionary in village life at home had led them to expect.[2]

By contrast to the first war, many more in the African ranks were at least nominally Christian—indeed, some sixty per cent has been estimated.[3] Of units that went to Madagascar it was reported: " There were no pagans and it did not matter to what branch of the Church men belonged. We were one company of men in a far country but we knew that we needed the help of God and that He was near us." The witness of committed Christians was seen in this continuing confidence although far from home. As one returning soldier put it: " The pagans in the battalion made no offerings to their *mizhimo* (clan ancestors) in the far countries. They thought they were lost if they died far from home. The Christians had faith that they were in the hands of God everywhere." More than one African reported that a number had become Christian while on active service.[4]

Most areas of the continent felt the impact of the struggle in one way or another. The proximity to Kenya of the East African theatre of war produced a mass migration of some 50,000 Somali

[1] *African Affairs*, XLV (1946), 2.

[2] These issues were discussed in a session on " Demobilization and Post-war Problems " at the General Missionary Conference of Northern Rhodesia in 1944 on the basis of reports by J. R. Shaw and J. C. C. Pauw, who commented *inter alia:* " Now they have seen many a drunken man and heard more than a little bad language . . . There were women . . . who were eager and ready to receive our soldiers for the money they would pay " (J. R. Shaw); " War does this (hard drinking and sexual laxity) for many men, and the African soldier has been no exception. In the villages his behaviour is proverbial " (J. C. C. Pauw).—*Report of Proceedings of Ninth Conference* (1944), 55–63.

[3] A. B. Doig, *loc. cit.*

[4] J. R. Shaw, *loc. cit.*

from the northern frontier district.[1] A considerable industrial development also took place in the Colony, such as canning factories and manufacture of sisal products, which drew large numbers of Africans into the industrial labour force, at the same time posing welfare problems on an unprecedented scale.[2]

The mines in the Copperbelt were naturally geared to the highest production possible as the winners of a metal essential for war purposes. In March 1940 there was a strike of European miners for increased rates of pay; these were secured, in various categories, whereupon a movement began among African workers to do likewise. Serious disturbances resulted, to inquire into which a Commission was appointed by the Governor. The Commission found that the European strike had prompted that of the Africans " but for which it is unlikely that any African strike would have taken place ". Increased rates of pay, in categories similar to those of the Europeans to avoid suspicion of differential treatment in this regard, were recommended, as well as more attention to general welfare for Africans : housing, rations, education, and so forth.[3] A settlement having been reached the work went ahead once more, with increase of population as the mines advanced to full production; at the end of 1943 the European workers numbered 7,700 and the African 7,600.[4] The recruiting of African workers brought in Christians from the areas served by the Brethren, who were a distinct language group and for whose welfare several Brethren missionaries came to the Copperbelt. Their association with the Union Church presented difficulties, but the principle of co-operation was at least preserved.[5] Education went ahead during these years, and by the end of 1943 the United Missions were responsible for eight schools with a total enrolment of over 6,000.[6]

In West Africa from Sierra Leone to Nigeria the improving of a " highway " for the transport of equipment and munitions of war from America and Britain, to the Middle East so-called,

---

[1] *I.R.M.*, XXX (1941), 69.

[2] *I.R.M.*, XXXI (1942), 62.

[3] *Report of the Commission appointed to inquire into the Disturbances in the Copperbelt, Northern Rhodesia* (Lusaka, July 1940), 50–3. See also *Statement by the Government of Northern Rhodesia on the Recommendations of the Copperbelt Commission, 1940* (Lusaka, February 1941); *Memorandum by the Anti-Slavery and Aborigines Protection Society on the Report of the Commission*, etc. (September 1941).

[4] *United Missions in the Copperbelt, Sixth Annual Report, 1942–44*, 3. The labour force eventually rose to 60 per cent over the 1939 level.—*Seventh Annual Report, 1945–6*, 5.

[5] *Sixth Report*, 6.

[6] *Ibid.*, 7.

brought in considerable establishments of military with all the consequent disturbance, economic and moral, incidental to such an invasion.

That the African peoples as a whole, who were intelligent enough for the most part to realize the issues at stake in meeting the challenge of the dictators, were joyfully relieved at the success of Allied arms there can be no doubt. But all the same they were not prepared to return to the *status quo ante bellum*. The world was in ferment and they shared in it. The Atlantic Charter had laid down principles, over the authoritative signatures of Franklin D. Roosevelt and Winston S. Churchill, that they were eager to see applied in full measure to their own countries. It opened up a new outlook on world affairs and the educated among them were aware of it.[1] The eight points of the Charter—no imperial aggrandizement, consultation of people concerned before territorial change, form of government to be popularly approved, equal access for all to raw materials, economic collaboration and safeguarding of the labour force, freedom from fear and want, freedom of the seas, provision of a permanent system of security—these all were received, so to speak, with acclamation. Africa, granted the honourable application of these principles, would reach her true stature at last. It was at least a shaft of light penetrating the pervading gloom of world conflict.

The net effect of their wartime experience was to increase expectations of life in the post-war world and at the same time to reduce patience in waiting for their fulfilment.

[1] See *The Atlantic Charter and Africa from an American Standpoint* (New York, 1942), *passim*.

CHAPTER 7

POST-WAR SURVEY
1945–1954

W ITH the tide of war at last receding the Christian scene
in Africa could be once more surveyed. Despite the six
years of conflict, with man-power both European and
African reduced and depletion of foreign funds, every mission had
survived, orphans among them being assigned to foster-parents,
and the African Churches had conspicuously proved their vitality.

Any prospect, however, of speedily overtaking the arrears of
mission development soon vanished with steeply mounting costs
which affected all Societies, while the attempt quickly to replenish
the missions and churches with workers from overseas was largely
baffled by the acute shortage of transport, thanks to heavy destruction of shipping by both submarine and bomber. Indeed, the enterprising spirit of Scandinavian missions led them to set up their own
aeroplane service for Sweden, Norway, and Denmark in conjunction, to bring home workers long overdue and take out the relief
force that had been preparing at home.

But resumption of the work was by no means at the point or in
the atmosphere of 1939. The world had suffered severe shock in
the interval and a somewhat drastic re-assignment of familiar rôles
was in progress. Asia, it is true, experienced this change more
directly than Africa, with Russia and the United States now the
two leading first-class Powers in world affairs, and India, Burma,
and Ceylon on the very threshold of political independence. But
Africa shared in the new movement, though there was here far
more leeway to make up.

If it was a testing time for the growing Church in Africa, it was
also a new day of opportunity—rather more grimly framed than
at the dawn of the century, but a day of opportunity none the less.

(1) The Prevailing Climate

It was soon clear that Christian work in Africa in the post-war
period would have to be carried on in a new climate. The whole
continent was agog as it had never been before, and the ensuing
decade was to disclose a rapidity of change that had not been

experienced even in Africa on its express journey from a tribal economy and medieval quiescence into the glare and tear of the twentieth century. Political pressures increased sharply with some irregularity in the line of African advance, but advance for the most part it was, whether wrung from a somewhat reluctant over-lord or conceded with reasonable generosity as in line with, if not at the speed of, official policy.

Moreover, African welfare was everywhere accepted as a government responsibility, with missions invited in consequence to share in development programmes (though the expansion might well be beyond their capacity in personnel), or alternatively being displaced as their voluntary activities became State services.

There was thus considerable readjustment facing the Christian mission in its new environment, while at the same time it was called upon to give even greater attention than hitherto to the growing Church and its needs. Indeed, there were those who saw in the relief from the burden of what have been termed its " second-line activities " [1] in services which the State was now assuming, an opportunity to concentrate more effectively upon its primary task of direct evangelism and the building up of the Christian Church.

On the political stage the setting up of the United Nations Organization in 1946 brought with it a Trusteeship Council to replace the Mandates Commission of the League of Nations, which had ceased to function in 1939, since when no reports from mandated territories had been received.[2] The British, French, and Belgian Governments facilitated the transfer from mandate to trust territory,[3] but the Union of South Africa declined to co-operate in respect of South-West Africa, proceeding instead to give it electoral status within the Union as in effect a fifth province.[4] The new régime was a change in more than name. Asian countries with newly-won independence and Arab states with a growing

[1] G. E. Phillips, *The Gospel in the World* (1947 ed.), 117-22.

[2] *African Affairs* (Journal of the Royal African Society), XLV (1946), 169-70; XLVI (1947), 62.

[3] E.g., *Ruanda-Urundi, Text of Trusteeship Agreement as approved by the General Assembly of the United Nations*, New York, 13th December 1946, Treaty Series No. 64 (1947), Cmd. 7196 (1947); *The Cameroons under French Administration, Text of Trusteeship Agreement*, etc., New York, 14th December 1946, Treaty Series No. 66 (1947), Cmd. 7198 (1947); *Togoland under French Administration, Text of Trusteeship Agreement*, etc., New York, 13th December 1946, Treaty Series No. 67 (1947), Cmd. 7199 (1947).

[4] South-West Africa Affairs Amendment Act, 1949 (No. 23 of 1949); *African Affairs*, XLIX (1950), 271, for deliverance of the International Court of Justice at the Hague on July 11, 1950.

sense of political influence, not to mention the Soviet Union and
its satellite following, kept a sharp eye upon the colonial behaviour
of the fast waning imperial powers. Indeed, the intervention of
the new mentors was often resented as officious and ill-founded.
But it was in keeping with the new day.

Political change in Africa itself was speeded up throughout
British territories. It was on the West Coast that the most spectacular developments took place, with the Gold Coast in the van.
The immediate impulse was given by serious disturbances in the
Gold Coast in February and March 1948, where good relations
between Government and people had long been taken for granted.
A commission of inquiry was speedily at work and among underlying causes of discontent reported : " The large number of African
soldiers returning from service with the Forces, where they had
lived under different and better conditions, made for a general
communicable state of unrest. Such Africans by reason of their
contacts with other peoples including Europeans had developed a
political and national consciousness. The fact that they were disappointed at conditions on their return, either from specious
promises made before demobilisation or a general expectancy of a
golden age for heroes, made them the natural focal point for any
general movement against authority." [1] Combined with this were
a feeling of frustration politically among educated Africans, the
influence of the achievement of self-government by India, Burma,
and Ceylon, and a collateral suspicion of the Government as unwilling to move with the times in a more rapid liberalization of
policy. The economic causes were also far from negligible.[2] The
Commission found that the 1946 Constitution, which conceded an
African majority in the Legislature and little more, was totally
inadequate to meet the post-war situation. They indicated the
broad pattern of Government they regarded as essential, leaving
to others the drafting of a Constitution.[3] Steps were taken without
delay to appoint a Committee on Constitutional Reform under an
African chairman, Mr. Justice J. H. Coussey, with a membership
entirely African. The Committee reported in August 1949
and within two months the general acceptance of its proposals was
announced by the Secretary of State for the Colonies.[4] With this

[1] *Report of the Commission of Enquiry into Disturbances in the Gold Coast,
1948*, Colonial No. 231 (1948), 7.
[2] *Ibid.*, 7–8, 20–3, 36–47.
[3] *Ibid.*, 24–9. For the reaction of the Home Government, see *Statement
by His Majesty's Government on the Report of the Commission of Enquiry into
Disturbances in the Gold Coast, 1948*, Colonial No. 232 (1948).
[4] *Report to His Excellency the Governor by the Committee on Constitutional*

unprecedented acceleration of constitutional change the Gold Coast was soon far ahead on the road to self-government with in due course an African Cabinet and Prime Minister responsible under the British Government for conducting the affairs of the country.[1] The last step but one towards the assumption of full responsibility for its own affairs within the Commonwealth had been taken in 1954, but at the vital stage of constitution making differences arose within the country between the elected majority of the Convention People's Party who were for a unitary structure (covering the Gold Coast Colony, Ashanti, the Northern Territories, and the British Trust Territory of Togoland, the last pending United Nations' approval), while the important Ashanti section and to some extent the North, fearing overlordship by the Fanti politicians in power, stood for a federal form. With differences still unresolved, despite Conferences on the subject in the country, the British Government in 1956 gave the promise of full independence following a general election if a motion for it was then passed in the newly elected Legislature by a reasonable majority.[2] The election was held in July 1956 and the Convention People's Party with Dr. Kwame Nkrumah at its head was returned to power with almost a two-thirds majority.[3] The motion for independence was duly passed by seventy-two votes to nil, the Opposition led by Dr. K. A. Busia still standing out for a federal constitution and boycotting the debate.[4] With the British Government's condition thus fulfilled the stage was so far set for full independence in 1957 under the name of Ghana.[5] Differences between the parties were sufficiently composed to enable the transfer of power to be completed on March 6, 1957. Ghana was thereupon admitted to the British Commonwealth with full dominion status, and as a sovereign state was granted membership of the United Nations.[6]

Nigeria was a good second in the advance to self-government,

Reform, Colonial No. 248 (1949) ; Statement by His Majesty's Government on the Report of the Committee on Constitutional Reform, Colonial No. 250 (1949).

[1] African Affairs, L (1951), 98–9; LI (1952), 189; LII (1953), 277.

[2] African Affairs, LV (1956), 166–9.

[3] The C.P.P. won 71 seats out of 104: all 44 seats in the Colony, 8 out of 21 in Ashanti, 8 out of 13 in Trans-Volta Togoland, and 11 out of 26 in the Northern Territories. Ibid., LV (1956), 253.

[4] Ibid., LV (1956), 253–4.

[5] See Vol. I, pp. 93–5, 124, n. 3.   The Proposed Constitution of Ghana, Cmnd. 71 (February, 1957).

[6] African Affairs, LVI (1957), 95–6.   It is of interest to note that the special commemorative postage stamps on the occasion figured Aggrey's eagle.—Vide supra, p. 81.

though here the size of the territory with a population of some 31,000,000 [1] and three well-marked regions of different type presented a more difficult problem to solve with satisfaction to those concerned. Here the post-war situation developed on lines similar to though not identical with those of the Gold Coast. Proposals for constitutional reform which were laid before the British Parliament in March 1945 envisaged a gradual development towards responsible government, the immediate steps being to give the already established Native Authorities a place in the legislative procedure and to grant unofficial majorities on the Regional Councils and the Legislative Council.[2] In 1948 a general constitutional review was set in motion, but before the proposals could finally mature unfortunate disorders broke out in the Eastern Provinces. An industrial dispute at the Enugu colliery, a Government-owned enterprise, which unhappily developed into a conflict with fatal casualties, was exploited by leaders of extremist views and touched off serious political disturbances.[3] The Commission of Enquiry, in a review of political trends in the country, gave it as their view that the Government must offer " a political programme that can be accepted by a progressive African people ", and enunciated as the recognized objective : " It is to grant them as soon and as completely as possible the government of their own affairs." [4] Against such a background the constitutional review was carried to completion and the resulting recommendations approved in 1950 by a General Conference called for the purpose, fifty of the fifty-three members being Nigerians. In 1951 the new constitution came into force; it was characterized by increased regional autonomy, more representative legislatures, and a ministerial system.[5] Within two years the constitution was reluctantly redrawn to meet criticisms of the division of functions between the Centre and the Regions in the Federal Government.[6] The question of self-government by 1956 was considered and a compromise reached for the time

[1] 1952–53 Census returns.
[2] *Proposals for the Revision of the Constitution of Nigeria*, Cmd. 6599 (1945). This is sometimes referred to as the " Richards Constitution " from the Governor responsible for it.
[3] *Report of the Commission of Inquiry into the Disorders in the Eastern Province of Nigeria, November 1949*, Colonial No. 256 (1950); *Report of the Commission of Enquiry—Exchange of Despatches*, Colonial No. 257 (1950).
[4] Colonial No. 256, 12.
[5] *The Story of the New Constitution* (Public Relations Department, Nigeria, 1951), 4–10.
[6] *Report by the Conference on the Nigerian Constitution*, Cmd. 8934 (1953); *Report by the Resumed Conference on the Nigerian Constitution*, Cmd. 9059 (1954); *African Affairs*, LIII (1954), 188.

being.[1] Thus by 1954 all seemed set for a not distant transfer of power.[2] Here again the rapidity of development was beyond all expectation and startling evidence of the post-war climate in political affairs. Sierra Leone, the oldest colony, was soon following suit, here the characteristic problem being the coaxing into double harness of the limited colony, self-conscious and sophisticated, with the extensive protectorate of able and rapidly advancing tribal peoples.[3]

Colonial liquidation was therefore in rapid progress in the West, with independent Negro States coming to the birth whose leaders agreed in aspiring to an honourable place in the British Commonwealth of Nations. The new political leadership was for the most part western-educated but by no means necessarily Christian; though individual African Christians played their part with honour.

If such was the making of new history in the West, the story was far other in the South. Here General Smuts had won an unparalleled election triumph in July 1943 as the head of a Coalition Government pledged to see the war through to a finish—in a house of 153 members no less than 110 were his supporters.[4] Hertzog's political eclipse had begun in 1939 with the split between himself and Smuts on the war issue, and was complete when in 1940 his most important followers transferred their allegiance to Daniel François Malan, " the dour, unbending Dr. Malan, leader of the Purifieds ".[5] Malan had suffered heavy defeat in 1943, but he bided his time. In May 1948 the Nationalists were returned to power with D. F. Malan as Prime Minister of the Union.[6] His policy of *apartheid* on the racial issue was well

---

[1] Cmd. 8934, 10–11. At the Resumed Conference the right of secession from the Federation was considered.—Cmd. 9059, 16.

[2] While a Federal form had been agreed, giving substantial powers to Regional Governments in the West, East, and North, a further constitutional Conference, anticipated to take place in London in September 1956, was postponed in July through a dispute in the Eastern Region over the alleged self-interest of Dr. Azikiwe, the Premier of the Region, in his relations with the African Continental Bank, which involved the appointment of a commission of inquiry.—*African Affairs*, LV (1956), 247–9. The postponed Conference met in London in May, 1957.—*Ibid.*, LVI (1957), 103.

[3] *African Affairs*, XLIX (1950), 280; LI (1952), 102; LIII (1954), 62–3.

[4] *The Round Table*, XXXIII (1943), 383–4.

[5] J. C. Smuts, *Jan Christian Smuts* (1952), 386.

[6] *Ibid.*, 510–11. The victory is said to have taken the Nationalists themselves by surprise, Malan characterizing it as a " miracle." Their majority in the House was only five, but it put them in power.

enough known—he had never made any bones about it—and now came the opportunity to put it into practice.[1] On December 3, 1948 came the heaviest blow to those who sought, by contrast to *apartheid*, a progressively liberal policy in race relations : Jan Hendrik Hofmeyr, brilliant lieutenant to General Smuts, passed away. Hofmeyr was not only the ablest of Smuts' supporters, he was a deeply Christian man who preferred principle to expediency whatever the immediate political disadvantage. Malan now had one opponent the less, and that his ablest. Hofmeyr had had the courage to say that South Africans must re-examine their prejudices. That was not a popular appeal in South Africa.[2] There followed in the policy of the Malan Government a more rigid control of the non-European population, with attempts to modify the provisions of the Act of Union by a mere Parliamentary majority, but this was declared, on appeal to the Courts, to be *ultra vires*.[3] This determined stand on the policy of *apartheid*, by the Nationalist Government, which was confirmed in office at the general election in 1953, was at the same time accompanied by a paternally benevolent expenditure on African services and genuine efforts to secure Bantu welfare within the terms of the policy.[4] When the controversial issue of the transfer of the High Commission Territories therefore was raised once more,[5] the sacrifice of liberty threatening Africans who might be transferred to the Union was not only clear, but the continent-wide repercussions of such action in the existing circumstances were seen to be serious. The African attitude was reported to be as definite as ever. Dr. E. W. Smith declared in Cape Town in 1949: "If the Bechuana dread one thing more than another it is incorporation into the Union. One old headman whom I questioned replied

---

[1] *Ibid.*, 500, 508.

[2] *Ibid.*, 515–16. See also, for Hofmeyr's leadership as opposed to rigid Nationalist policy: " Colour Policy in South Africa: Race Privilege and World Opinion " in *The Round Table*, XXXVII (1947), 29–34. The writer concludes with insight: " South Africa has a unique opportunity of contributing to world order by demonstrating practically how different races can live peacefully in the same country without resorting to force and to racial laws. But the opportunity is slipping by. We are losing not only world goodwill; we are forfeiting African goodwill at an alarming rate. And without that we shall labour in vain." The article was written in South Africa in October 1946. Cf. J. H. Hofmeyr's Hoernlé Lecture, *Christian Principles and Race Problems* (1945).

[3] *The Times*, August 30, 1952.

[4] *The Times*, April 17, 1953.

[5] *Vide supra*, pp. 155–7.

with the utmost gravity: 'Sir, that is a subject not to be mentioned!' " [1] In 1949 the British Council of Churches jointly with the Conference of British Missionary Societies registered their views, and in 1951 the British Council of Churches issued a further statement.[2] Dr. Malan's request was not complied with.

In East and Central Africa new policies also appeared, not on the lines of West Africa, for here multi-racial societies were concerned, yet not on the lines of the uncompromising Nationalist policy of the South. In East Africa three contrasting territories call for brief notice. Kenya had been in the limelight for a quarter of a century, though latterly less the centre of stormy controversy than in the 'twenties.[3] African resentment at wrongs long brooded upon, even where reparation had been genuinely attempted,[4] finally blazed out among the Kikuyu in a cruel and murderous reversion to barbarism—the Mau Mau rising.[5] All Europeans were a target but so were loyal Africans declining to compromise themselves with the Mau Mau oath, and these were by far the heaviest sufferers. As one well-advised report summarized it : " It must be remembered that the Mau Mau promoters, though a small minority, are utterly ruthless; that those who are resolute enough to oppose them openly are an even smaller minority, and that the great mass of the tribe . . . desires peace almost at any price. . . . It may be asked why the leaders, knowing their resources to be so limited, should have risked everything on a coup de force. . . . They attempted a coup because they had energy, drive, and ambition; and because their principles were opportunist and their judgment warped." [6] A Parliamentary delegation to Kenya in 1954 stigmatized Mau Mau as " a conspiracy designed to dominate first the Kikuyu tribe and then all other Africans and finally to exterminate or drive out all other races and seize power in

[1] E. W. Smith, *The Blessed Missionaries, Being the Phelps-Stokes Lectures delivered in Cape Town in 1949* (1950), 102.

[2] L. B. Greaves, *The High Commission Territories* (1954), 17–19, for the text of the statements. That of 1949 urged fuller economic development of the Territories " lest Africans should be forced for economic reasons to sacrifice that liberty which the Government is pledged to protect."

[3] *Vide supra*, p. 93.

[4] As in the accepted findings and recommendations of the Morris Carter Commission.—*Sup.* 161. The pressure of an ever-increasing population was making the best use of the available land an urgent matter. Cf. Negley Farson, *Last Chance in Africa* (1949), 104–12.

[5] See L. S. B. Leakey, *Mau Mau and the Kikuyu* (1952); *Defeating Mau Mau* (1954); *I.R.M.*, XLIV (1955), 205–11.

[6] *Mau Mau and the Church* (The Church of Scotland Foreign Mission Committee, February 1953), 6–7.

Kenya. It is a political and social conspiracy, a secret society, which uses terrorism to secure obedience where it cannot command willing support or compliance. Mau Mau has progressed from the political oath with which it began, through successive oaths each one more violent than its predecessor. . . . Mau Mau intentionally and deliberately seeks to lead the Africans of Kenya back to the bush and savagery, not forward into progress ".[1] While the campaign to control the elusive movement was still proceeding, constitutional changes were introduced, with Africans and Indians sharing with elected Europeans in the responsibility of Government at ministerial level.[2] The case of Tanganyika by contrast was that of peaceful development by agreement. Here the European, Asian, and African communities accepted a new constitution assigning each an equal number of seats on the Legislative Council, thus placing Europeans in the minority to the chagrin of their neighbours in Kenya.[3] Uganda seemed peaceably disposed, though eager for industrial development and not too happy about Indian penetration, until an unfortunate reference to a possible East African Federation—date unspecified—by a British Minister touched off a train that led to the deposition of the Kabaka by the British Government.[4] There was a constitutional issue behind the disagreement, related to the place of the kingdom of Buganda as one unit in the larger Uganda Protectorate under changes incidental to democratic development. Eventually a new Buganda Agreement was drawn which made more precise the constitutional position. Mutesa II returned from exile in 1955 to the joy of his subjects, and publicly stated his acceptance of the new situation prescribed by the Agreement.[5] If, therefore, East Africa was not as rapid in advance as West, at least the situation was no longer static.

In Central Africa the issue of the closer union of Southern Rhodesia, Northern Rhodesia, and Nyasaland, inquired into by the Bledisloe Royal Commission, was revived.[6] Contrary to the recommendation of that Commission, a policy of federation was

---

[1] *Report to the Secretary of State for the Colonies by the Parliamentary Delegation to Kenya, January 1954*, Cmd. 9081 (1954), 4.

[2] *African Affairs*, LIII (1954), 198; *Kenya, Proposals for a Reconstruction of the Government*, Cmd. 9103 (1954).

[3] *Tanganyika, Report of the Committee on Constitutional Development, March 1951* (1951); *African Affairs*, LI (1952), 283–4.

[4] *Withdrawal of Recognition from Kabaka Mutesa II of Buganda*, Cmd. 9028 (1953).

[5] *African Affairs*, LIII (1954), 202–3; LV (1956), 3–4.

[6] *Vide supra*, p. 164.

taken up and pursued, despite African reluctance to endorse it, until in 1954 a new territory of British Central Africa, though now a larger unit than in the 'nineties, once more appeared upon the map as the Federation of Rhodesia and Nyasaland.[1] Safeguards for existing African rights in the territories concerned were given statutory authority, and the ideal of racial partnership declared to be that of the Federation. The economic and other advantages of the union none would dispute; African unwillingness to accept the scheme was due, not to the proposals in themselves, so much as to lack of confidence in European promises. Past experience in Kenya and current developments in South Africa demonstrated how pledges once given were not necessarily honoured. The Christian Churches had wished for delay that would have given opportunity to win African consent, but, once the die was cast, it was recognized that the task was to see that promises were kept and a genuine partnership put into practice.[2] Resolutions in the Northern Rhodesia Legislature sought to safeguard this position.[3]

Meanwhile, farther to the north, the Anglo-Egyptian Sudan

[1] Official documents recording the progress of negotiations are as follows: *Central African Territories: Report of Conference on Closer Association, London, March 1951*, Cmd. 8233 (1951); *Central African Territories: Geographical, Historical and Economic Survey*, Cmd. 8234 (1951); *Central African Territories: Comparative Survey of Native Policy*, Cmd. 8235 (1951); *Southern Rhodesia, Northern Rhodesia and Nyasaland: Draft Federal Scheme*, Cmd. 8573 (1952); *Draft Federal Scheme, Report of the Judicial Commission*, Cmd. 8671 (1952); *Draft Federal Scheme, Report of the Fiscal Commission*, Cmd. 8672 (1952); *Draft Federal Scheme, Report of the Civil Service Preparatory Commission*, Cmd. 8673 (1952); *Report by the Conference on Federation, London 1953*, Cmd. 8753 (1953); *The Federal Scheme prepared by Conference in London, 1953* Cmd. 8754 (1953).

[2] *I.R.M.*, XLII (1953), 43; XLIII (1954), 45.

[3] In the Legislative Council of Northern Rhodesia the two European members for African interests, J. S. Moffat and E. G. Nightingale, had voted with the two African members against the motion approving of federation in 1953. On July 29, 1954 J. S. Moffat submitted four resolutions, on the basis of the expressed official policy of partnership and commended them in a notable speech on the occasion. The first of the four repudiated political domination by either race; the second recognized that in a transition period special arrangements for representation were necessary to avoid such domination; the third endorsed the statement of the British Government that on contentious issues it was the duty of that Government to see that the balance was fairly held; the fourth, " by far the most important " as J. S. Moffat claimed, ran as follows: " Every lawful inhabitant of Northern Rhodesia has the right to progress according to his character, qualifications, training, ability and industry, without distinction of race, colour or creed." The resolutions were passed with only one dissentient.— *The Moffat Resolutions, The text of the Resolutions and the Speech of Mr. J. S. Moffat* (Lusaka, 1954).

was leaping forward to self-government, with an interested Egypt, herself soon to be in revolution, seeking to draw the country within her orbit. Here the problem of Muslim, Christian, and pagan sharing in a form of representative government appeared as it had done in Nigeria though with the Muslim population far in the lead. A prelude to Sudanese self-determination was a statute designed to introduce internal self-government which was passed by the Sudanese Legislative Assembly and approved by the British Government in October 1952.[1] The policy of Egypt, to have the Sudanese handed over to the Egyptian Crown with or without their consent, was reversed when the monarchy was liquidated and General Neguib came to power. He conceded the right of the Sudanese to self-government, and the subsequent Anglo-Egyptian agreement of February 12, 1953, made it possible to move in this direction, though Egyptian promises of non-interference were not taken by them too seriously.[2] By the agreement the future of the Sudan—independence or a union with Egypt were the alternatives—was to be decided by a constituent assembly elected for the purpose which would then draw up a constitution. But relations with Egypt were only one side of the problem; the Sudan itself was divided: politically by the pro-independence and pro-union with Egypt parties; and regionally between the Muslim north and the pagan south with its Christian missions—a division only bridged by the British Administration. The first elections in November 1953 put the National Unionist party, supported by Egypt, in power in both the House of Representatives and the Senate.[3] Once in power the party proved more wary of Egyptian blandishments than had been foreseen. On the acute issue of the sharing of the Nile waters Egypt failed to have her way, and talks were broken off in April 1955.[4] The Sudanese Government meanwhile declared its preference for independence, an issue to be decided by future elections or plebiscite. The internal problem of the restiveness of the south against northern control flared up in a mutiny of troops there. Although the Government in Khartoum claimed that the eruption had been pacified (temporarily at least), many thousands of southern Sudanese crossed the border into neighbouring territories : Uganda, the Belgian Congo,

[1] *The Times*, October 23, 1952.
[2] J. Robertson, "The Sudan in Transition", in *African Affairs*, LII (1953), 317–25.
[3] The N.U.P. won 50 seats in the House against 28 for Umma and 24 for Independents and others; while in the Senate they secured 21 out of 30.—*African Affairs*, LIII (1954), 231–2.
[4] *African Affairs*, LIV (1955), 177.

and French Equatorial Africa. The end of the journey was abruptly reached when in December 1955 the Premier, flouting Egyptian desires and ignoring the provisions of the 1953 Agreement, declared an independent Republic of the Sudan. On January 1, 1956, the two Houses of the Sudanese Parliament in joint session received from Britain and Egypt the recognition of their independence. There followed application for membership of the United Nations, approval of which made the Republic of the Sudan the seventy-seventh member.[1]

North Africa also was in post-war ferment with Tunisia and Morocco straining at the leash of French control while in Algeria, especially esteemed by the French as an integral part of metropolitan France, there came fierce contesting of the claim to independence. When terrorism had flared up in Tunisia the Premier, M. Mendés-France, boldly seized the initiative and in July 1954 announced to the Bey the grant of home rule, save that finance, public works, and education were reserved to French directors. The reform was pacifying, not least because the 180,000 French settlers had not secured political control for themselves. M. Mendés-France had a clear North African policy, as he declared to the French National Assembly : " There are only two possible policies in North Africa : co-operation and reform, or repression and force. . . . The Government has chosen the first." He was not, however, confirmed in power to carry through his proposed reforms by stages in Morocco, though it was said there were moderate Muslims prepared to negotiate with him. His successors eventually had no option. With the restoration in 1955 of a Sultan two years in exile and a declared French policy " to lead Morocco to the status of a modern State, free and sovereign ", albeit linked to France by free consent, the Moroccan question appeared on the way to solution, with at least an interim understanding between the parties. In Algeria, however, the French stubbornly resisted the demand for home rule. They had been established for a century and a quarter in the country which was rated not as a protectorate, as in the case of Morocco, but as part of France herself. The refusal was costly, as terrorism took its toll and the French military forces were stepped up to considerable strength. With extremists on both the French and Muslim sides the conflict was kept ablaze where, it was reported, moderates on both sides would have willingly come to terms.[2] Against this background of

[1] *African Affairs*, LIV (1955), 253–4; LV (1956), 2–3, 90–1.
[2] *African Affairs*, LIII (1954), 277–8; LIV (1955), 86; LV (1956), 12–14, 93–5.

political disturbance the Roman Catholic Church steadily continued its ministrations, with some encouraging developments in Morocco and Tunisia. Particularly cheering in Morocco, Tunisia, and Algeria was the report of some activity in the lay apostolate : a recognition of the layman's responsibility in evangelism, though the approach was rather to the European than the Muslim, the latter being largely regarded as the province of the White Fathers.[1]

The determination of the future of the ex-Italian colonies lay with the United Nations Organization. Its Political Committee, after running the gauntlet of much complicated negotiation among interested parties,[2] finally decided in November 1949 that a unified Libya (constituted by the adjoining provinces of Tripolitania and Cyrenaica) should achieve independence by 1952, and that Italy should be granted a ten-year trusteeship over Somalia in the eastern horn of Africa, with U.N.O. representatives as assessors. The fate of Eritrea was still in abeyance, but the autonomous federal area was finally assigned to Ethiopia, administrative powers being assumed by the Emperor in September 1952.[3]

In the Belgian Congo African political aspirations were much slower in appearing. The fragmentation of tribal society into thousands of petty chiefdoms—there were 6,095 after World War I, and some so small as to have only some 50 to 150 adult males—was not conducive to the rise of political claims. The economic development of the country was regarded as a first charge on the administration, though by re-erecting traditional units that had become divided they had succeeded in twenty years (1919–39) in reducing the number of chieftainships from 6,095 to 1,500. Moreover, although by 1955 there were some 86,000 Europeans among the twelve million Africans, they as well as the Africans did not have the franchise. Africanization of the public services had proceeded to a limited degree and socially the policy of assimilation had been pursued. The drift to urban centres helped to create a new situation in which educated and skilled Africans from many tribes found themselves in one community. Thus the African population of Leopoldville rose from 30,000 before World War II to 260,000 after it. There had been reported some restlessness among the European population as early as 1940 at still being denied the franchise, while ten years after the war an awakening nationalism among Africans in the towns was apparent, and as

[1] I.R.M., XLIII (1954), 73–4; XLV (1956), 82–3.
[2] A. Sillery, " Libyan Aspirations," in African Affairs, XLVI (1947), 13–21.
[3] African Affairs, XLIX (1950), 2–3; LI (1952), 122; 304.

these were in personal touch with many tribes scattered over a wide area their ideas would readily filter through. And the towns themselves were still growing : by 1956 Leopoldville was reported to have a population of 300,000. Furthermore, the expressed African desire was not for a racial *élite* assimilated to European civilization but was rather opposition to it in favour of racial solidarity and an African national ideal.[1]

Political development in French Africa followed a revised pattern in the post-war years. The Constitution of the French Republic of October 27, 1946 had, in Article VIII, concerned the oversea territories. It declared the French Union to consist of three organs : the Presidency, the High Council (with delegates from the French Government and representatives from Associated States), and the Assembly the members of which were to be from metropolitan France and France overseas in equal numbers. The rôle of the Assembly was to be consultative only. The French Legislature had direct representation from tropical Africa : thirty-three deputies in the National Assembly (with Africans in the majority), and thirty-three Senators in the Council of the Republic. In Africa each territory had its local assembly while the two Federations of French West and French Equatorial Africa had each a Grand Council to which territorial assemblies nominated members. By an electoral law of May 23, 1951 the electorate in French West Africa was increased to some 3,000,000. This was a generous extension of the franchise designed to prepare the way for fuller African participation by recognized stages in administrative affairs.[2]

There was thus arising the third major situation, in respect of political power, which the Christian mission had had to face in tropical Africa. On first arrival missionaries had found African tribal authorities in full control, though largely in local isolation; with the partition of the continent among European powers the African authorities were subordinated to their European overlords, with western influences steadily streaming into the country. Now the third stage was being achieved, with developing African peoples asserting their independence, no longer in isolation, but as active participants in world affairs. It was a matter for thankful-

---

[1] A. F. G. Marzorati, " The Political Organisation and the Evolution of African Society in the Belgian Congo," in *African Affairs*, LIII (1954), 104–12; *African World Annual, 1955*, 27; *The Times*, December 5, 1956.
[2] T. Monod, " French Tropical Africa: The Current Situation ", in *Africa is Here, Report of the North American Assembly on African Affairs*, (1952), 53–5.

ness that in this time of national resurgence young churches were already in existence in many territories.

(2) *African Welfare Development*

Lying behind these political changes in British territory, which made the post-war period one of eager expectancy among alert Africans, were developments which ran farther back into the war period and before it, but which were essential factors in any well-based political advance. The first of these was the development of Native Administration, a vital part of the training in responsibility, at local level, of peoples destined for eventual self-government. In this connexion Africans destined for local government duties were, in the stepping-up process of training in the post-war years, brought to Britain for further study of the functions of government at this level.[1]

Indeed, these were but a fraction of the considerable body of African students in Britain, those from West Africa predominating, pursuing varied courses of study, no longer restricted to the one-time favourite faculties of law and medicine but covering a wide range of scientific and technical training. North America and the Continent of Europe also had their own liberal quota of these eager aspirants. The considerable influence these students were likely to exert in their own country on their return could tell either for or against the Christian mission, according to the conclusions they had reached in their impressionable student days in the world of the West during the troubled post-war years.

The whole question of African labour also began to engage the attention of colonial authorities, beyond the urgent case of migrant labour, which had already called for study and official oversight. In 1938 a comprehensive investigation of labour conditions was undertaken by the Government of Northern Rhodesia,[2] while during the progress of the war the Colonial Office appointed its Labour Adviser to undertake a similar survey of labour conditions in Nigeria, the Gold Coast, Sierra Leone, and the Gambia. His observations related to such questions as housing, wages, employment of women and children, juvenile delinquency, trade unions,

---

[1] An early study of one territory was by M. Perham, *Native Administration in Nigeria* (1936). The authoritative post-war survey is: Hailey, *Native Administration in the British African Territories*, Part I, East Africa (1950); Part II, Central Africa (1950); Part III, West Africa (1951); Part IV, General Survey (1951); Part V, The High Commission Territories (1953).

[2] G. St. J. Orde Browne, *Labour Conditions in Northern Rhodesia*, Colonial No. 150 (1938), *passim*.

and Government labour officers.[1] One result of the Labour
Adviser's territorial inquiries was to lead him to regard the problem of African efficiency as the dominant labour question in East
Africa, and to suggest that the Colonial Social Science Research
Council might consider this among other projects for research. At
the same time the General Manager of the Kenya and Uganda
Railway, with a concern for the efficiency of his African labour
force of some 25,000 in respect of food, housing, and social environment, made a similar proposal. The result was an inquiry undertaken by a team of research workers in 1947 into a limited group
of 6,000 Africans located in Nairobi, the capital of Kenya. Their
report was made available in 1949.[2] Their general conclusion was
that " an increasing standard of technical efficiency can be expected of East Africans if the handicaps from which they suffer are
removed on European initiative and under European guidance ".
They found the most serious handicap to be the meagre provision
of education, both primary and technical, while the physical
handicap arising from malnutrition was also rated as grave. On
this latter point they quoted Dr. H. C. Trowell as advancing the
hypothesis that " the malnutrition recognised in childhood pro-
duces chronic lesions in liver and pancreas and, less positively, the
kidneys; that these in turn affect the normal working of body and
mind in the case of those who survive, and that the listless,
apathetic, and ineffective Africans of farm and field, of *shamba*
and street corner, bear upon them the brand of malignant malnutrition ". A further handicap of importance, though in the nature
of the case less obvious to appreciate, they recorded as " European
ignorance of African attitudes and of the motives which lie behind
their actions ". They also recorded their impression that " African
confidence in the European is slipping ".[3] If only a pilot survey,
it nevertheless exposed fundamental factors in the complex problem of African labour.

A further measure of considerable significance for Africa was
the passage of the Colonial Development and Welfare Act in July
1940 by the British Parliament, authorizing a Colonial Development and Welfare Fund with an annual maximum expenditure of

[1] G. St. J. Orde Browne, *Labour Conditions in West Africa*, Cmd. 6277
(1941), *passim*; *I.R.M.*, XXXI (1942), 53; XXXII (1943), 38. For post-
war developments see *Labour Administration in the Colonial Territories, 1944–
1950*, Colonial No. 275 (1951).
[2] C. H. Northcott (ed.), *African Labour Efficiency Survey*, Colonial Research
Publications No. 3 (1949).
[3] *Ibid.*, 118–20.

274

£5,000,000.[1] It was indeed a gesture of goodwill to colonial peoples that in a summer which saw the invasion of Denmark and Norway, the overrunning of the Low Countries, and the collapse of France, this far-sighted policy should have been adopted. Measures thus facilitated covered a wide range of welfare projects: agricultural development, locust control, malaria control, training of African medical staff, and educational enterprises.[2] With the end of hostilities the activity gathered momentum and generous development plans were produced by territories in both East and West Africa.[3]

Already by March 1945 over 500 schemes had received approval. When in 1945 Parliament extended the operation of the Act of 1940 from five years to ten the total grant to the Fund was raised to £120m.[4]

In East Africa a major inquiry of regional dimensions and with the high authority of a Royal Commission was undertaken in the 'fifties into the fundamental yet complex problem of land, population, and economic development. The initiative had been taken by Sir Philip Mitchell, Governor of Kenya, in a dispatch to the Secretary of State for the Colonies in November 1951. In this he directed attention to the interlocked questions of growth of population, availability of land, the failure of tribal agriculture to meet increasing needs, and the necessity to develop on an adequate scale the total resources of the territories, coupled with concern for health and nutrition of the African people. He stressed the necessity of seeing the whole as a human problem of vast dimensions.[5] The Royal Commission on East Africa, finally constituted in January 1953, reported its findings in 1955.[6]

[1] This replaced the Colonial Development Fund whose annual expenditure had been limited to £1,000,000.

[2] *Colonial Development and Welfare Act, 1940, Report on the Operation of the Act to the 31st October, 1942*, Cmd. 6422 (1943).

[3] E.g., *Nigeria; Ten Year Educational Plan* (1944); *Nyasaland Protectorate: Report of the Post-war Development Committee* (1946); *A Development Plan for Uganda* by E. G. Worthington (1947); *Ten-Year Development Plan for Northern Rhodesia* (1947); *Gold Coast: The Development Plan, 1951* (1951).

[4] E. W. Smith, *Plans and—People! A Dynamic Science of Man in the Service of Africa* (1948), 26–8.

[5] *Land and Population in East Africa*, Exchange of Correspondence between the Secretary of State for the Colonies and the Government of Kenya on the Appointment of the Royal Commission, Colonial No. 290 (1952). The Governors of Tanganyika and Uganda supported the proposal. In further exposition Sir Philip Mitchell wrote two articles on the subject: "East African Inquiry: I—Need for a New Social Structure; II—An Industrial and Social Revolution."—*The Times*, September 24 and 25, 1952.

[6] *East Africa Royal Commission, 1953–1955, Report*, Cmd. 9475 (1955).

s 2

The Report was described as possessing "an intellectual incisiveness and doctrinal clarity characteristic of some of the great commissions of the past ".[1] If its diagnosis was clear, the treatment proposed was equally so. In respect of land the Commission's proposals were revolutionary : nothing less than eliminating the idea of security as bound up with a policy of reservations and basing it instead upon what they regarded as the solid foundation of individual ownership. Condemnation of the policy of allocation of land to tribes and races as such led equally to criticism of European reserved areas. As a specific implementation of a free labour policy they recommended that the Government should acquire sites for villages in the White Highlands where African farm workers could then have their homes and so be free to offer their labour where they would. Many aspects of the economic and social problems of the territories received their attention. The fight against poverty in East Africa, they contended, not only demanded a free economy but also a unitary development throughout the region, though they recognized that the existing political and racial interests made this impossible of immediate realization. The courage and candour of the Report, combined with its masterly analysis, its firmly based conclusions, and its long-term proposals made a deep impression, though by no means commanding universal assent where so many vested interests were at stake. But its publication was a landmark in the troubled history of East Africa and as such it has demanded chronicling here.

In yet another direction the initiative was taken during the war period—that of adult literacy. As early as 1941 the Colonial Office took the matter up and issued its statement of policy two years later.[2] The urgency of the education of the whole community was underlined, and definite proposals for a campaign of mass education set forth. These inevitably envisaged a considerable force of eager voluntary workers, and here a point of weakness was revealed. The voluntary workers were not forthcoming in the numbers required, due in part perhaps to the experience of wartime work which was generally well paid for, while the educated who were intent on political power also felt that such resources as

---

The Report was published on June 10. A summary of its findings was given in *The Times*, June 10, 1955. Cf. *African Affairs*, LIV (1955), 256–8; *I.R.M.*, XLV (1956), 50.

[1] *The Times*, June 10, 1955.

[2] *Mass Education in African Society*, Colonial No. 186 (1943). A further step, in preparation for further political responsibility, was taken in *Education for Citizenship*, Colonial, No. 216.

were available should rather be directed to the higher development of the few than diverted for the elevation of the many.

Yet higher education was by no means neglected. Commissions appointed in 1943 reported just before the war was over in 1945.[1] Institutions of University College rank were set up in the Gold Coast and in Nigeria, while Makerere in Uganda was of the same status for the service of East African territories.[2] An Inter-University Council for Higher Education in the Colonies was appointed to safeguard academic standards and promote the development of these institutions towards full university status.[3] Fourah Bay College, Sierra Leone, which in earlier days had given distinguished service to all the British West African territories, now became in practice largely restricted to Sierra Leone students and thus had a more limited rôle to play. Up to 1950, in virtue of its affiliation to Durham University, 296 students of the college had received Durham degrees, 242 of which were awarded since 1900.[4] With the inauguration of the Federation of Rhodesia and Nyasaland in 1953 came the decision to establish at Salisbury in Southern Rhodesia a multi-racial university to serve the three constituent territories. In the first instance it was of University College rank under the aegis of the University of London, its degrees being those of that University. An early endowment was that of a Chair of Race Relations. This venture in higher education was offered as a first instalment in implementation of the ideal of racial partnership which had been declared basic to the Federation.[5]

[1] *Report of the Commission on Higher Education in the Colonies*, Cmd. 6647 (1945); *Report of the Commission on Higher Education in West Africa*, Cmd. 6655 (1945).
[2] The University College of the Gold Coast is at Accra, that of Nigeria at Ibadan. In the three East Africa territories of Uganda, Kenya and Tanganyika there was a growing desire for each to have its own University College; in this connexion an inquiry into higher education in the region, led by Sir Alexander Carr-Saunders, was undertaken in 1955. Enrolment in the three University Colleges in 1954–55 was as follows : Gold Coast, 349 ; Nigeria, 527; East Africa, 448.—J. McLeod Campbell, *African History in the Making* (1956), 104.
[3] *Inter-University Council for Higher Education in the Colonies, Third Report 1949–50*, Colonial No. 273 (1951).
[4] P. E. H. Hair, " An Analysis of the Register of Fourah Bay College, 1827–1950 ", in *Sierra Leone Studies*, New Series No. 7 (1956), 155–60.
[5] *African Affairs*, LII (1953), 289; LIV (1955), 25; *I.R.M.*, XLV (1956), 51–2. The foundation stone was laid on July 3, 1953, by the Queen Mother, and within three years the first students were being received. A capital grant of £1·25 m. was made from Colonial Development and Welfare Funds.

An event of outstanding importance for education policy in British Tropical Africa in the post-war years was a survey of British West and East Africa respectively by two small study groups, more particularly in the field of primary and secondary education. A Conference to consider their reports, convened at Cambridge in September 1952, was representative of the many interests concerned : the Colonial Office and Advisory Committee on Education, Education Departments and training colleges in the territories, Protestant and Roman Catholic missions. Approximately one third of the ninety-two members from Africa were Africans. Subjects discussed ranged from such time-honoured themes as organization and curricula to the immediately pressing problems of expansion of the school system, and administrative control. The Conference was not in any sense empowered to issue directives on these matters, but its carefully reached conclusions could not fail to influence, in the direction of a uniform policy, the many executive officers, African and European, who took part in framing them.[1]

While occupied France and Belgium were prohibited from initiating at metropolitan headquarters any such programmes during the period of the war, they nevertheless became active in the years that followed. In French West and French Equatorial Africa there were development programmes in health, education, social and economic affairs, though all were handicapped by limited resources in money and men. By 1951 the health services could report for French West Africa and French Equatorial Africa respectively eight and nine principal hospitals, 192 and 196 auxiliary medical centres, 402 and 212 dispensaries, 100 and 154 special centres (maternity, leprosy, sleeping sickness, etc.), with 68 and 13 mobile health units.[2] In education there was still much leeway to make up with 129,089 primary pupils out of a

---

[1] The inquiry was sponsored jointly by the Nuffield Foundation and the Colonial Office. The reports of the two teams, named after their respective chairmen, were the Jeffery Report of the West Africa Study Group and the Binns Report of the East and Central Africa Study Group. These, together with the proceedings of the fortnight's Conference at Cambridge, were issued as: African Education, A Study of Educational Policy and Practice in British Tropical Africa (1953). See also L. B. Greaves, "African Education: A Commentary on the Cambridge Conference," in I.R.M., XLII (1953), 318–31; J. McLeod Campbell, African History in the Making (1956), which presents a valuable exposition of the Conference discussions in a historical perspective.

[2] T. Monod, Director, Institut Français d'Afrique Noire, Dakar, to North American Assembly on African Affairs.—Africa is Here, Report of the Assembly (1952), 55.

school-age population estimated at 2,115,000 in 1951 in French West Africa, while in French Equatorial Africa the corresponding figures were 88,810 and 700,000. In the same respective regions the secondary school pupils were 4,206 and 1,201, and those in trade schools 2,202 and 2,934, while an Institute for Higher Studies at Dakar offering courses in medicine, law, science, and letters had 135 students. A programme for the mass education of adults was also in being but still only in an experimental stage in 1952.[1] In illustration of the Administration's concern for social welfare there may be mentioned the legislation on African marriage passed in 1952, by which the bride-price so-called was made illegal in the case of a woman who had reached the age of twenty-one, at which age she would be free to marry as she pleased.[2] Sociological research into urban and industrial problems was also proceeding.[3]

In the Belgian Congo much progress was to be registered, due in considerable measure to a Belgian Welfare Agency set up in 1947, Fonds du Bien-Etre Indigène, in grateful recognition to the Congo for help given during World War II. From this foundation came funds in 1949 to promote African co-operatives in an effort to make village life more attractive; while in 1950 nearly half its budget went to the control of epidemics and insect plagues, the supplying of fresh water schemes for child and maternity welfare, and the promotion of research in medicine and sociology. It later supplied booklets on both hygiene and child care, and provided funds for publications based on the Laubach methods in aid of adult literacy.[4] A further post-war development of importance was the setting up, by Royal Decree of May 11, 1946, of a labour and social welfare organization—Service du Travail et de la Prévoyance Sociale—supplementing the Government Service of Native Affairs and Labour already established.[5]

But these enterprises by the individual metropolitan authorities were by no means the total activity in the interests of African welfare in the post-war years. An extensive series of international conferences occurred, twenty-one in number in the first six years,

[1] *Ibid.*, 56.
[2] *I.R.M.*, XLII (1953), 38. There was of course the risk that unscrupulous parents might urge marriage at a younger age for the sake of the bride-price.
[3] *African Affairs*, LIII (1954), 37.
[4] *I.R.M.*, XXXIX (1950), 44; XL (1951), 44; XLI (1952), 301; XLIII (1954), 425, 427.
[5] *Abundant Life in Changing Africa, Report of the West Central Africa Regional Conference* (1946), 99.

covering various aspects of African life as follows : labour, rinder-pest, soils, trypanosomiasis (1948); nutrition, rural economy (1949); education, labour, malaria (1950); education, medical co-operation and training, forestry, statistics (1951); nutrition, child welfare (1952); labour, housing, rural welfare, treatment of offenders, sociology, and protection of fauna and flora (1953). Their value lay in the pooling of knowledge and their fostering of co-operation on a regional basis. A Commission for Technical Co-operation south of the Sahara eventually grew out of earlier bilateral and mutual co-operation and technical conferences and was organized in 1950.[1]

With such political, economic, educational, and social welfare movements afoot the colonial scene in the post-war years was one of such rapid change as to make the rate of progress achieved in the decades between the wars seem slow of pace indeed.

(3) Facets of the Christian Movement

The many and varied developments thus taking place were in the nature of the case by no means unwelcome to the Christian mission. Its own pioneering enterprise had always had in view the growth of the African peoples to a full maturity among the more developed races of the world, as equally children of the One Father, though this had been envisaged as an achievement in the somewhat distant future. Fundamentally welcome therefore though the changes were, they nevertheless brought with them certain embarrassments for the Christian mission, largely due to the insistent demand from the African side for high-speed political action with corresponding progress in other fields. As already noted, all territories were not equally clamant, but all were on the move at an accelerated pace. Emerging from this situation were not only organizational problems, assessment of priorities, and redeployment of resources, but also sharpened moral and spiritual issues, since those eagerly claiming extensive privileges were for the most part not equally sensitive to the collateral responsibilities. The effect on the Christian mission, therefore, of the general political ferment and the almost feverish activity in matters of economic and social welfare was bound to be profound. The developments of the 'twenties and 'thirties which had seemed impressive at the time against an earlier more leisured background,

[1] P. M. Henry, "A Functional Approach to Regional Co-operation ", in African Affairs, LII (1953), 308–16. For a summary of the agenda of the international conferences held from 1948 to 1953, see African Affairs, LIII (1954), 113–18.

were appraised as but modest instalments in a programme now urgent of fulfilment. Time was seen to be fast running out, with much more demanding to be done than available resources would easily permit. Coupled with the paramount claims of the growing Church, to be more fully prepared for its life and witness in a new era, were attractive invitations from a harassed secular authority to extended commitments in education and in welfare activities generally, failing which the State would perforce proceed alone. Hard choices these, and complex situations demanding the highest Christian statesmanship.

It was in respect of education that some of the sternest decisions had to be made. The pioneering of missions in this field, together with an impressive extension through generous grants-in-aid in British Tropical Africa at least, had resulted in mission control of some eighty to ninety per cent of the schools and had created what was tantamount to a considerable vested interest. Denominational rivalry, with consequent failure to make the most effective use of available resources for the community as a whole, could and did become a serious liability in the total account. The appointment of educational advisers to the non-Roman Catholic missions in East and West Africa had indeed fostered happier relations and progressively enabled the missions to discover a common policy and pursue it in some measure of co-operation.[1] With the development in British territories of a Local Government system Local Authorities began to appear with education coming within their purview.

These Local Authorities, as the earlier Native Administration units, with their own revenues at disposal could and did open their schools on popular demand where necessary, as well as continue grants-in-aid to mission schools as they might deem desirable. But in such instances it was now the decision of an African authority rather than that of the central Government that was to become progressively operative. This had introduced a new factor into the local situation. While those who thus controlled the purse-strings as State and Local Authorities might well seem to possess an overall advantage, yet one inescapable problem at least beset them all—whether Government or Local Authority, Church or mission—in any plan to expand the school system : the acute shortage of qualified teachers. At this very point a further embarrassment confronted the missions through the rather widespread restiveness of African teachers in their employ, in some

---

[1] *Vide supra*, p. 228; L. B. Greaves, " The Educational Advisership in East Africa ", in *I.R.M.*, XXXVI (1947), 329-37.

cases on grounds of mission discipline but often through a nationalism that aspired to a State system of secular education freed from the trammels of mission control with its seeming implication of overseas interference.[1] In West Africa, where political enthusiasms were keenest, these attitudes were most apparent, but they were not absent elsewhere as the Binns' Report on East and Central Africa found them : " We cannot conceal from ourselves or others that many representatives of African bodies who gave evidence to us showed strong anti-missionary feeling and told us that in their opinion the connexion of the Churches and missions with education should come to a speedy end." [2] And again, as a further tacit agreement with such critics : " In giving evidence to us, representatives of African bodies have quite often referred to ' their ' schools and ' our ' schools as defining the difference between the mission schools and the schools provided by African local authorities." [3] The Cambridge Conference, it is true, strongly deprecated such a distinction, regarding the partnership between the Government and Christian Churches as a vital one.[4] But if the partnership were to be effective it was clear that the churches and missions must have regard to the community as a whole and be prepared to sink their denominational preferences in the interests of an efficient educational system—an attitude that would involve surrender of the claim to maintain a self-contained

[1] S. G. Williamson, " Missions and Education in the Gold Coast ", in *I.R.M.*, XLI (1952), 364–73.

[2] *African Education*, Cambridge Conference Report (1953), 64. The Report proceeds: " We have taken a lot of trouble in trying to analyse the causes for this feeling, which we deplore. To some extent no doubt it springs from a desire for the emancipation of Africans from European control, but this is by no means the only reason for its existence. The autocratic control of schools is usually another cause." A similar restiveness under mission control, with a desire for an entirely state system, was reported among mission teachers in South Africa by the Inter-departmental Committee on Native Education, 1935–1936: " One of the reasons for the attitude taken up by the teachers advocating sole Government control is that their aims tend to be educational rather than religious. They are becoming restive under the paternal form of control exercised by the missionary and look for emancipation to some other system similar to that which prevails for the local control of European education."—*Report*, 69.

[3] *African Education*, Cambridge Conference Report (1953), 68.

[4] " Three African speakers emphasized that although they meant the effective control of education to be in the hands of the properly constituted representatives of the African people, they had no desire to exclude the voluntary agencies, including the Christian Churches, from effective partnership. They were grateful for what the missionaries and other voluntary workers had done for African education, and needed them as partners in the work of development ".—*Ibid.*, 150.

school system of their own at State expense and that would sooner or later demand relinquishment of parts of their work to the Local Education Authority. In so far as such action was in the public interest the transfer could be made without vain regrets, certainly without concealed resentment at a fancied lowering of mission prestige. If this might prove in some instances to be the negative aspect of the partnership, there was also a positive side of supreme importance : that in the training of teachers the churches and missions had still a vital part to play.[1] And further : it was a widespread Christian concern that Christian schools should not only continue to have some place in the total system, but that with its expansion the opportunity of Christian teaching should be available to other schools as well. The Christian Council of Nigeria in 1953 declared itself on this issue, while the Christian Council of the Gold Coast sponsored an agreed syllabus of religious instruction in 1952 for which in the following year a teachers' handbook was prepared which was offered " for use in all non-Roman Catholic schools and in Government. and Local Authority Schools ".[2] In East Africa a corresponding opportunity was presented. In the Beecher Report, *African Education in Kenya*, accepted by the Legislative Council of the Colony in 1950, the services of the Christian teacher in Government as well as mission schools were seen as bound up with the moral basis of the educational system. In Uganda the acceptance by the Church Missionary Society in 1951 of the task of supervising primary schools, and in Tanganyika the pressure on missions to expand their school systems as well as the opportunity for Christian instruction in Government schools were openings of the same order.[3]

The staffing of Christian schools and training colleges in British territories, whether these were controlled directly by missionary societies or were under independent boards of governors, was greatly assisted by the recruitment of qualified teachers who were

[1] Thus it was reported in 1950 from Northern Rhodesia: " With the control of education passing gradually to the local African authorities, missionary policy tends toward a concentration on a smaller number of schools and on teacher-training, to ensure the staffing of government schools with as many Christian teachers as possible."—*I.R.M.*, XL (1951), 49-50.

[2] *I.R.M.*, XLII (1953), 36; XLIII (1954), 40; A. W. Banks, *Teaching Religion: Teachers' Handbook for use with an Agreed Syllabus of Religious Instruction* (1954). The Committee of the Christian Council which approved this manual was representative of the Anglican, Scottish Presbyterian, British Methodist, and American M.E. Zion Churches and the Salvation Army.

[3] *I.R.M.*, XL (1951), 48; XLI (1952), 45.

engaged, not upon the usual missionary conditions of service, but on terms approximating to those of Government schools. It began in Uganda in 1940 when the societies agreed to recruit on this plan rather than leave their schools inadequately supplied, the plan being made possible by the grants-in-aid received. In due course representatives of missionary societies and of the Colonial Office constituted the interviewing panels, and these sought to ensure that the applicants selected were convinced and practising Christians. This scheme was organized through the Institute of Christian Education in London. In this connexion it may also be noted that at the Willingen Conference of the International Missionary Council in 1952 the Swiss Missionary Council raised the question of the witnessing Christian layman overseas: the many engaged in secular occupations who, though confessed Christians at home, went abroad without any understanding of the younger churches or concern for their own Christian witness among them.[1] In 1953 Oversea Service was set up by the Joint Committee of the British Council of Churches and the Conference of British Missionary Societies, to provide training courses introductory to living abroad in the post-war world. Similar enterprises were in due course afoot on the Continent.

The educational situation in the Belgian Congo was of a somewhat different kind, though here also new openings for missions brought new pressures to bear on mission resources. The favoured position accorded to Roman Catholic missions had been based ostensibly on national rather than on religious grounds. Christian missions were officially classified as " national " and " foreign ", the former being eligible for subsidy for their schools. By decree of July 19, 1926, the principal condition of recognition as " national " was that two-thirds of the administering authority must be Belgian; that meant, in practice, missions with headquarters in Belgium. This naturally excluded all Protestant missions but the Belgian, though on the other hand " the British Roman Catholic missions seem to have encountered less difficulty "[2]

Early in the post-war period a revolutionary change in this situation was announced: in September 1948 the Protestant missions

---

[1] *The Missionary Obligation of the Church, Willingen, Germany, July 5–17, 1952* (1952), 16–17, 18; *Report of the Commission set up by the Methodist Conference 1953 to consider the Missionary Obligation of the Church* (1955), 71–2.

[2] Hailey, *An African Survey* (1938), 1270; M. Searle Bates, *Religious Liberty: An Inquiry* (1945), 102–3. In 1935 pupils in " foreign " schools numbered 253,841 while 213,463 were in schools of " national " missions, the former schools being maintained almost entirely from private sources.— Hailey, *op. cit.*, 1270.

were offered equality with the Roman Catholic in their educational work, being eligible for the same subsidies subject to meeting the required standards.[1] All non-Belgian missionaries thus electing to work with State co-operation would be required to spend a minimum period of twelve months in Belgium during which prescribed studies would be taken. The deadline for compliance by the Protestant schools with the necessary conditions was first fixed as December 31, 1952, but in that year the period of grace was extended to 1957. The missions eagerly responded to this new opportunity for co-operation with the State in a vital section of their work and to secure for graduates from their schools the invaluable advantage of recognized diplomas. They responded, despite the obligation to allocate qualified workers who were needed elsewhere, and in some instances to increase their outlay on the schools to comply with recognition standards.[2] In October 1954 the first State primary schools were opened, and their first secondary schools in the following year.[3] The first university in the Congo emerged after a generation, thanks to Roman Catholic nurture from the Centre Universitaire Lovanium established at Kisantu in the 'twenties by the University of Louvain. In 1955 it was inaugurated as Lovanium, the University of Leopoldville, retaining a direct link with the mother University.[4]

In the Union of South Africa the Churches and missions were confronted with a quite different situation in respect of their schools. In 1936 the Inter-departmental Committee on Native Education had reported in favour of two major administrative changes : that control should be transferred from the Provinces to the Union Government, and that African education should not be associated with the Native Affairs Department but placed under the Union Education Department. These recommendations were not carried out, though the Committee's strong endorsement of

[1] It was reported in 1947 by Robert Godding: " On my initiative the Belgian Government decided in February 1946 that a different policy should be followed and that, given equal guarantees as to efficiency of teachers and curricula, all Christian missions should be put on the same footing, subject to Government inspection."—R. Godding, " Development in Administration of the Belgian Congo ", in *Colonial Administration by European Powers* (1947), quoted by O. J. Davis in " Educational Development in the Belgian Congo ", in *I.R.M.*, XLIII (1954), 422.

[2] *I.R.M.*, XXVIII (1949), 44; XXXIX (1950), 44–5; XLII (1953), 38–9; O. J. Davis, " Educational Development in the Belgian Congo ", in *I.R.M.*, XLIII (1954), 421–8.

[3] *I.R.M.*, XLV (1956), 47.

[4] *International Fides Service*, February 26, 1949; February 18, 1950; *I.R.M.*, XLIII (1954), 74; XLIV (1955), 44.

the retention of mission schools in the system was tacitly accepted.[1] Now under the Bantu Education Act of 1953 control was indeed transferred from the Provinces to the Union Government but placed with the Native Affairs Department in a new Division of Bantu Education, thus running counter to the recommendation of the 1936 Report on that point.[2] And the reason was clear : African education was to be shaped to conform to the Nationalist policy of *apartheid*. The Bantu Education Act. came into force on January 1, 1954.[3] By the Bantu Education Amendment Act of the same year the Minister of Native Affairs was authorized to set up local bodies for the management of schools or alternatively to entrust control to a Bantu Authority or Native Council.[4]

In August 1954 the Secretary for Native Affairs addressed a letter to all managers of State-aided Bantu schools, setting forth the Department's policy and stating the conditions on which the transfer of control would take place, in the course of which the central purpose was clearly stated : " It should be emphasized that the transfer of control from the missions to Bantu communities is part of a wider scheme of social development, designed to assist in the progress of the Native people in the form of self-sufficient and responsible communities in all directions. The purpose is not therefore the removal of religious influence from the life of the Bantu—an influence which the Department realizes has been and will continue to be a most valuable contribution to Bantu development—but the enlistment of the energies of the Bantu in the development of a healthy social and economic life of their own." [5] Managers were requested to inform the Department by the end of the year which of two courses they proposed to follow : (a) to retain control of State-aided schools and hostels as private unaided institutions, or as aided institutions with reduced subsidy at the discretion of the Minister; (b) to relinquish control to Bantu community organizations, the transfer normally to occur after April 1, 1955; school buildings when taken over would be leased rather than purchased. An assurance was included that religious instruc-

---

[1] *Vide supra*, pp. 183–4.

[2] The Report had stated, regarding administration by the Native Affairs Department: " This view, however, finds little support amongst educationists or the Native people."—*Report of the Inter-departmental Committee on Native Education, 1935–1936* (1936), 58.

[3] For a summary of its contents see M. Horrell, *A Survey of Race Relations in South Africa, 1952–1953* (1953), 66.

[4] M. Horrell, *A Survey of Race Relations in South Africa, 1953–1954* (1954), 93–6.

[5] *The South African Outlook*, LXXXIV (1954), 133.

tion would be provided in all schools, with right of entry if the mother tongue was used, and with an undertaking that church interests would be represented on the Bantu Authorities.[1] A second letter of the same date covered the case of teacher training schools where the options were : (a) to transfer both schools and hostels; (b) to transfer school and retain hostels on an agreed subsidy; (c) to close the training school. This complete denial to the Churches of the opportunity to train teachers—an opportunity which elsewhere in Africa was being accepted as a responsible contribution to Christian education as the schools progressively came under public authority [2]—was the most objectionable feature of the Bantu Education Act. The Secretary added: " The Department is desirous that Christian influences should be strongly felt in Departmental training schools and calls upon the churches to assist . . . " [3] As these decisions related only to institutions in receipt of a State subsidy it was still open for them to continue as private ventures but entirely at their own charges, though in that case State registration was compulsory, and permission to open a new school at any time would have to be granted by the Department.[4]

This assumption by the State of full control of Bantu education was not, in itself, an exceptional step. In many parts of Africa control of the schools was steadily passing from the missions to the rising Local Authorities. It was the motive behind the Act that was deplored by many, and which, it was feared, would reduce to a vocational level on *apartheid* lines such education as was given, thus depriving the Bantu of the right to enjoy an education as rich in content and as stimulating to personality as that provided for the European.[5]

---

[1] *Ibid.*, 133–4.

[2] *Vide supra*, p. 283.

[3] *Ibid.*, 134, 137. Both letters are given in full in the *Outlook* as above, pp. 133–7; cf. M. Horrell, *A Survey of Race Relations in South Africa, 1953–1954* (1954), 96–100.

[4] This was admitted to be a reasonable requirement if not unfairly or oppressively used. But cf. *The South African Outlook*, LXXXVI (1956), 50, for such an instance. The Christian Council of South Africa, convinced that there was still a place for private schools in Bantu education, presented its case to the Minister on March 27, 1956. He made clear the conditions on which existing schools might continue but declared that no new private schools in competition with Bantu community schools would be permitted.— *The South African Outlook*, LXXXVI (1956), 69–70.

[5] Nevertheless an editorial comment on the first syllabus ran: " The fact remains that the first syllabus has much to commend it and that it is clearly the work of educationists and not of politicians ".—*The South African Outlook*, LXXXV (1955), 18.

The reaction of the Christian Churches was by no means uniform. At one extreme stood the Dutch Reformed Churches, approving of the doctrine behind the policy of *apartheid*—a doctrine it claimed as Biblical—and, while standing for a segregation so complete, with a self-contained " Bantustan ", that the Nationalist Government itself had rejected that form of *apartheid* out of hand, yet honestly seeking for the African peoples as full a development, though on separate lines, as they were capable of achieving. The Dutch Reformed Churches therefore naturally approved of the new Act.[1] At the other extreme stood the Roman Catholic Church in South Africa. The bishops resolved to retain and to operate at their own expense all schools under their auspices (681 State-aided and 130 private schools for Africans), but were prepared to lease their five teacher training colleges to the Department provided a measure of control on the academic side was allowed them. To maintain the schools a Catholic Missions Schools Fund was launched with a target of £400,000, the amount achieved by the end of 1955 being reported as well in excess of half a million.[2] Between these two extremes stood the Church of the Province of South Africa (Anglican), the Presbyterian Church of South Africa, the Methodist Church of South Africa, and the Congregational Union. While the object behind the policy of the Bantu Education Act was universally deplored, it was felt that, in the interests of the African people, the lesser of two evils was to lease school buildings to the Department, the alternative being to close the schools and thus deprive the Bantu of the facilities already existing.

The Episcopal Synod of the Church of the Province referred to " a grievous choice of evils ", and one diocese, that of Johannesburg, took individual action and closed its schools rather than transfer them.[3] The General Assembly of the Presbyterian

[1] Their point of view was set out in a booklet, *Bantu Education, Oppression or Opportunity?* issued by SABRA (South African Bureau of Racial Affairs), an organization set up by the Dutch Reformed Churches to promote their ultimate ideal of separate racial development. Cf. M. Horrell, *A Survey of Race Relations in South Africa, 1954–1955* (1955), 8. For a review of the booklet against the background of the Act see: L. B. Greaves, " Bantu Education ", in *I.R.M.*, XLIV (1955), 339–43.

[2] M. Horrell, *A Survey of Race Relations in South Africa, 1953–1954* (1954), 102–3; *Survey, 1954–1955* (1955), 175. For the text of the pronouncement by the Bishops' Conference see *The South African Outlook*, LXXXIV (1954), 164.

[3] *The South African Outlook*, LXXXIV (1954), 181; M. Horrell, *A Survey of Race Relations in South Africa, 1954–1955* (1955), 176.

Church of South Africa, while not opposed to State education
per se, stated its convictions that education was ever to be regarded
as a means of grace and not merely " to fit man for a precon-
ceived place in society "; but, while in opposition to the theory
underlying the Act, they authorized the individual Presbyteries to
lease, but not to sell, school premises as they saw fit.[1] The Bantu
Presbyterian Church, which had its own schools, also took the
hard decision to lease them all to the Department.[2] The Conference of the Methodist Church of South Africa in the same
dilemma, after similar protest took similar action : " Nevertheless,
in order to provide for the immediate educational needs of the
African people, the Church feels compelled to relinquish control
of its schools to the State." The same decision applied to the leasing
of the training colleges not required for other purposes, but hostels
were to be retained.[3] The Annual Assembly of the Congregational
Union of South Africa, having the resolutions of the Presbyterian
Assembly before it, felt these so adequately represented its own
views that it affirmed its attitude in similar terms.[4] Other Churches
followed suit. Thus the Minister of Native Affairs was able to state
in February 1955 that altogether forty Protestant Churches in
control of 5,000 schools had agreed to their transfer to the Department.[5] On the one hand inability to maintain the schools without
State subsidy, and on the other unwillingness to penalize the
Bantu by closing the schools, had led to the reluctant decision.
Leaders of the African National Congress discussed a boycott of
the schools from April 1, 1955, when the new system was to come
into operation, but decided on postponement until alternative
schooling appeared possible. Younger Congress members however
proceeded to organize the boycott, in particular on the eastern
Witwatersrand. The ultimate effect was only to deprive some
7,000 children of any schooling at all, since schools boycotted were
then closed and teachers transferred—the very penalty, falling

[1] *The South African Outlook*, LXXXIV (1954), 145; M. Horrell, *A Survey
of Race Relations in South Africa, 1953-1954* (1954), 103-4.
[2] *The Church of Scotland, Report of the Foreign Mission Committee for 1954*
(1955), 23-4.
[3] *The South African Outlook*, LXXXIV (1954), 164-5; M. Horrell,
A Survey of Race Relations in South Africa, 1953-1954 (1954), 103.
[4] *The South African Outlook*, LXXXIV (1954), 165-6; M. Horrell,
A Survey of Race Relations in South Africa, 1953-1954 (1954), 104. For the
reservations of the American Board Mission in South Africa, see *Outlook*
(1954), 182.
[5] M. Horrell, *A Survey of Race Relations in South Africa, 1954-1955* (1955),
176-7.

on Bantu children, the Churches had happily determined to avert.[1]

If the general situation was a severe one for the Churches and missions that had a long record of devoted service in South African schools, there were inevitable pangs of separation in the transfer of specific institutions, hailing from the pioneering days, which had long stood to the Bantu as gateways into the larger life of European civilization and world culture where no barriers restrained the aspiring student. It is no invidious distinction to name here two outstanding institutions that had each completed a century of service to the Bantu of the south. Under the auspices of the American Board of Commissioners for Foreign Missions, who pioneered among the Zulus in the eighteen-thirties,[2] a school was founded in 1853 which developed into an institution of college rank bearing the name of Dr. Newton Adams of the early days. It was the oldest educational institution in Natal. In 1940 the American Board had handed over the college as a matter of policy to a Board of Governors for yet wider service, the Christian character of the institution being suitably safeguarded. Prohibited in 1954 from continuing their Teachers Training College, they at least hoped to maintain the High and Industrial Schools intact. But, with the refusal of the Minister of Native Affairs to register Adams College as a private institution, it ceased to be at the end of 1956. It was a tragic end to a high adventure. In the Cape Province the famous Lovedale Institution had preceded Adams by a dozen years. Established under Scottish Presbyterian auspices it had yet served all the Churches and drawn its students from within the whole orbit of Southern Africa. It had entered upon its second century in 1941,[3] but now in respect of all its schools and hostels passed under Nationalist Government control. Well might the Foreign Mission Committee of the Church of Scotland speak in this connexion of " the end of an era ".[4]

Closely linked with the expansion of the school system and an extensive series of adult literacy campaigns [5] was the growing demand throughout Africa for reading matter. In meeting this demand it fell to the Churches to play a leading part.

[1] M. Horrell, *A Survey of Race Relations in South Africa, 1954–1955* (1955), 184–5.
[2] See Vol. I, pp. 263–5.
[3] See Vol. II, pp. 135–6.
[4] *The South African Outlook*, LXXXV (1955), 132–4; *The Church of Scotland, Report of the Foreign Mission Committee for 1955* (1956), 16. Such services as the Bible School and the Lovedale Press remained as mission activities.
[5] Thus in 1947–48 Dr. F. C. Laubach conducted literacy campaigns in

It was essentially a task to be undertaken in co-operation, as price was a vital factor and this was determined, apart from subsidy, by the extent of the reading public. Co-operation in this field was at two levels: between missions and State or other agencies for the supply of material for schools, and for adults relating to health, agriculture, and welfare generally; and among the missions themselves for the production of specifically Christian literature. At the first level a Conference sponsored by the International Committee on Christian Literature for Africa and the Institute of Education in the Colonial Department of London University was held in 1947, at which questions of literacy development, the preparation of literature in African languages, and its effective distribution were discussed by university teachers, government officers, and missionaries.[1] Colonial Governments also took action. In Northern Nigeria the Government in 1945 converted its Translation Bureau at Zaria into a grant-aided Literature Bureau with a programme which included a Hausa newspaper and literature for both Muslim and Christian sections of the population, while a Christian missionary was appointed to the staff.[2] In Central Africa there were also developments: Northern Rhodesia and Nyasaland joined forces in a Publications Bureau with headquarters at Lusaka, which rendered valuable service to both territories. In East Africa the Governments of Kenya, Uganda, Tanganyika, and Zanzibar set up a joint organization in the East Africa Literature Bureau with headquarters in Nairobi, charged with stimulating the production of reading material for the African populations of the four territories. Periodicals and general literature as well as school text-books were to be on its production list, and the development of a library system was included in the proposals.[3] Helpful relations were maintained between the Bureau and the local mission organizations. Co-operation of another kind took place in the Belgian Congo where the Belgian welfare agency set up in 1947, Fonds du Bien-Etre Indigène, in addition to supplying health booklets, made a grant to La Libraire Evangélique au Congo, a literature enter-

Sierra Leone, Liberia, Gold Coast, Nigeria, Cameroons, Belgian Congo, N. and S. Rhodesia, and Transvaal.—*African Newsletter Series* (New York, 1947–48).

[1] L. J. Lewis and M. Wrong, *Towards a Literate Africa* (1948), contains the Report of the Conference.

[2] Davis, Campbell, and Wrong, *Africa Advancing* (1945), 189–90; L. J. Lewis and M. Wrong, *op. cit.*, 17–23.

[3] Lewis and Wrong, *op. cit.*, 75–7; *I.R.M.*, XXXVIII (1949), 47–8.

prise of the Congo Protestant Council, for the production of adult literacy material.[1]

At the second level of co-operation it naturally lay with the Christian Councils to take the initiative, and this would be most happily done in the wake of an adult literacy campaign. Thus, following such a campaign among the Mendes of Sierra Leone, the Protectorate Literature Bureau was established at Bo by the United Christian Council, and with it was associated the Bunumbu Press. In 1956 at the end of its first decade it could report ninety-four titles published in five vernaculars (Mende preponderating with seventy-two), with a total production of 344,000 copies and a sales total of 274,661 [2]—this in a population of some one and three-quarter million. In the vastly larger territory of the Belgian Congo notable co-operation among missions in the production of Christian literature also took place in the post-war period. The restrictions of the war years gave the impulse to missions to make larger use as a central agency of a book depot set up in 1935 jointly by the British and Foreign Bible Society and the Congo Protestant Council. At the end of the war in 1945, with an ever-increasing demand for locally produced books in French [3] and in African vernaculars, a decision had to be made : either to enlarge local mission presses, of which a score or so maintained a somewhat precarious existence; or to concentrate resources in a strong central printing, publishing, and distributing centre for all the Protestant missions.

The second alternative was wisely chosen, and there emerged La Libraire Evangélique au Congo (known as Leco), situated at Leopoldville, with capital provided by the Congo Protestant Council, twelve Protestant missions, and two Bible Societies. In the first five years of its activity there were printed seventy million pages of books and periodicals in some twenty languages, though French and two African languages of the western Congo, Kikongo and Lingala, were easy priorities. In addition to its own series of publications with a more than local appeal—some dozen new titles a year—printing was undertaken for individual mission needs.[4] These two solvent and successful enterprises in

[1] *I.R.M.*, XLIII (1954), 425.

[2] *The Protectorate Literature Bureau and the Bunumbu Press, Report for 1955* (1956), 11–12.

[3] Not only because French and Flemish were the official languages of the Belgian Congo, with French the recognized customary medium, but because, unlike English, books in French were not produced in Europe for general African use.

[4] G. W. Carpenter, " Co-operation in Christian Literature Production in Belgian Congo ", in *I.R.M.*, XLIII (1954), 414–20.

Sierra Leone and Belgian Congo, thanks to mission co-operation, while indicating the field open to such joint action, yet admittedly fell far short in each case of their desirable output, largely through limitation of capital. By contrast the flood of secular literature available for African consumption reached impressive dimensions. Yet a further instance of Christian co-operation in this field was the holding in Johannesburg of a Conference on Christian Literature for the Bantu of Southern Africa. It met under the auspices of the International Committee on Christian Literature for Africa with the happy co-operation of both the Christian Council and the Dutch Reformed Churches of South Africa. This was largely an exploratory conference to survey the field, tabulate the major problems, and attempt a preliminary assessment of priorities. The matters of more vital importance that emerged were referred to a newly established Commission for Christian Literature for the Bantu for examination and report. An outstanding question was the urgent need for co-operation in this field among the Christian agencies; it was said, for example, that from twenty to thirty independent Protestant mission presses were in active production.[1]

One particular aspect of Christian publication stressed in the post-war period was the need for Christian periodicals. This was emphasized more particularly for urban centres, where a flood of secular periodicals, with selling capacity as the usually accepted standard of production, catered for the newly literate African. Occasionally a Government had attempted to meet the need; thus as early as 1936 the Government of Northern Rhodesia issued a monthly news magazine, using English and four African languages in each issue.[2] Within ten years it was reported to have a circulation of 20,000.[3] Despite the financial obligations involved there was some successful mission entry in this field. Thus in the Belgian Congo the Congo Protestant Council published *L'Evangile en Afrique*, while in French Cameroons a weekly newspaper, *Vie Nouvelle*, was launched in 1949.[4] In one respect more notable than either was the enterprise of the Dondi Press, of the American Board and the United Church of Canada in Angola, in securing official permission to produce a newspaper in the vernacular, the first concession in this direction since 1922 when by Decree 77 African

[1] *The South African Outlook*, LXXXVI (1956), 132-4. The Conference sat August 7-10, 1956.

[2] *Mutende*, The African Newspaper of Northern Rhodesia, in English, Bemba, Lozi, Nyanja and Tonga. Each issue of twenty pages was well though not lavishly illustrated and cost twopence.

[3] *Colonial Annual Report, Northern Rhodesia, 1946* (1948), 46.

[4] *I.R.M.*, XV (1951), 44. This church paper was published at Duala.

languages were forbidden in print save with Portuguese in bilingual editions.[1] In this field of publication, with keen secular competition, attractive appearance was significant for success. That a Christian magazine with plentiful illustration, articles on topics of current interest and pleasing format would be eagerly bought and read was shown by the Sudan Interior Mission's publication in Nigeria, *African Challenge*, which secured a circulation exceeding 100,000.[2] A major problem for mission publishers was that of distribution; to rely on mission stations might up to a point serve rural areas, but urban centres needed a more specialized system. In this respect the United Society for Christian Literature served well the Christian cause in Northern Rhodesia with a literature headquarters in Lusaka the capital from which the territory could be effectively reached, while a bookroom at Mindolo in the Copperbelt aimed at covering the needs of that large industrial region. Book displays at gatherings of Native Authorities throughout the territory and arrangements to meet African passengers by bus and train with a selection of books were methods of distribution based on the motto: take the books to the people.[3] Meanwhile the International Committee on Christian Literature for Africa, whose first secretary, Margaret Wrong, had largely shown the way in co-operation among missions and between missions and Government Departments, continued to promote the interests of Christian literature at all levels from the territorial conference, as in the Union of South Africa, to the individual missionary through the Bulletin *Books for Africa*. It would be superseded when its central concern—to see that the cause of Christian literature should be adequately maintained—had become in due course the firm concern of the African Churches themselves.[4]

Among the varied activities for African welfare in which the Christian mission had engaged as the authentic endorsement of its religious message, the ministry of healing held a foremost place. Many distinguished names and others barely known adorn an illustrious roll of honour of those dedicated to the service of suffering—men and women who took to Africans in their need the best that the science of their day could give together with that Christian compassion that transformed their service into a ministry of the

---

[1] *I.R.M.*, XXXIX (1950), 46. *Vide supra*, p. 120.
[2] *I.R.M.*, XLIII (1954), 440.
[3] *On the Frontiers, United Society for Christian Literature 154th Annual Report, 1952–1953* (1953), 25–6.
[4] *I.R.M.*, XLIII (1954), 436–42. Margaret Wrong died in Uganda in April 1948 when on tour in the course of her duties.

gospel. If a name or two be here admitted it is but as representative of the company to which they have belonged. To Uganda
in 1896 came Dr. Albert R. Cook to give more than forty years'
service, with Mengo hospital which he founded in 1897 attaining
a well-nigh world-wide repute; while he and Dr. J. H. Cook his
brother were the first to identify sleeping sickness in Uganda in
1901. He retired as Sir Albert Cook.[1] In South Africa Dr. Neil
Macvicar, after a brief period at Blantyre in Nyasaland, came to
Lovedale where he not only gave thirty-five years' service as
Medical Superintendent of the Victoria Hospital but devoted
himself unsparingly to causes affecting Bantu welfare. He was
mainly responsible for arousing the Government's concern in
tuberculosis, for the introduction of health subjects in schools, for
opening the way to the training of African girls as nurses, and was
deeply concerned at the effect on family life of the steady migration of the men to industrial centres. While maintaining the highest
professional standards he yet touched to beneficent effect many
sides of the African community he served.[2] It is sufficient but to
name the distinguished Dr. Albert Schweitzer—musician, philosopher, theologian, physician—who first came to serve sick
Africans on the edge of the primeval forest in Gabon in 1913.[3]
Secure in his world-wide fame he had the highest awards bestowed: the Nobel Peace Prize for 1952, and honorary membership of the Order of Merit in 1955. The Nobel Prize for 1952 was
reputed to be worth some £11,800 which Dr. Schweitzer proposed
to devote to his medical work in equatorial Africa.[4] But the day
of pioneering leadership of such men was fast fading as qualified
African doctors were multiplying and Governments were more

[1] E. Stock, *History of the Church Missionary Society* (1899), III, 737;
H. B. Thomas and R. Scott, *Uganda* (1935), 299; A. R. Cook, *Uganda
Memories* (1945), *passim*. The identification of sleeping sickness led to action
by Manson, and local research by Castellani (1902), Bruce (1903), and
Koch (1906) elucidated the ætiology of the disease. Rational treatment
of African victims was now possible and preventive measures could be
taken to eliminate the scourge.

[2] R. H. W. Shepherd, *The Life of Neil Macvicar, M.D., D.P.H., LL.D.*
(1952), *passim*. He died in December 1949.

[3] *Vide supra*, p. 47.

[4] The award of the Nobel Prize was announced in 1953.—*The Times*.
October 31, 1953. *The Times* citation stated: " He has repeatedly advocated
a return to fundamental Christian principles as the only remedy for what
he regards as the decline of civilization ". The British Order of Merit,
established in 1902 as a special distinction for eminent men and women,
is limited in membership to 24 but foreign honorary members may be
added. The only other honorary member was General (later President)
Eisenhower in 1945.

and more assuming responsibility for the health programmes of their territories and collaborating in inter-territorial consultation.[1]

The medical work of missions however was supplemented rather than displaced in the immediate post-war period, while two developments, in addition to a considerable expansion of leprosy service, were noteworthy: medical training centres were being fostered, and African doctors were being given responsibility as they became available. Medical students still studied in Europe and America to qualify, with the exception of the early years of training provided by the university colleges, but African medical assistants, nurses and midwives were trained at home, and here the mission contribution was significant as providing Christian students with a sense of vocation. Thus in the Belgian Congo in 1953 a new Institut Médical Evangélique in which five missions co-operated was opened at Kimpese where such training schools were associated with an important hospital centre.[2] As indicating the assumption of responsibility in mission institutions by African doctors there may be named Sir Francis A. Ibiam of the Church of Scotland in Eastern Nigeria, who held medical appointments in the mission hospitals, and became a valued member of the Legislative Council of the Eastern Region.[3] If therefore the old order was passing, the new revealed trends of hope in a growing African maturity.

An aspect of African welfare already noticed became yet more acutely disturbing in the post-war years: the social problems of urban areas. These were in the nature of the case largely characteristic of industrial regions, and among these the Copperbelt in Northern Rhodesia was notable. It was inevitable that Christian missions should be peculiarly sensitive to the human problems of such areas, seeking to diagnose the social ills and to offer such rational treatment as might appear indicated. The United Missions in the Copperbelt were naturally alert at this point, and on behalf of the Christian Council of Northern Rhodesia organized a conference on the social adjustment and economic adaptation

[1] Thus in November 1949 there assembled in Cameroons a conference concerned with food and nutrition in Africa, with representatives from Belgium, France, Great Britain, Portugal, and the Union of South Africa. In 1950 an international conference on malaria took place in Uganda.—*I.R.M.*, XL (1951), 38.

[2] *I.R.M.*, XLIII (1954), 43.

[3] Dr. F. A. Ibiam held medical appointments under the mission from 1936. He received the British decoration of K.B.E. in the New Year's Honours List of 1951.—*The Church of Scotland, Report of the Foreign Mission Committee for 1950* (1951), 40.

required of the African who passed from village to town, and the needs of young children and adolescent youth in the new environment.[1] Such social demands on the Christian mission were steadily increasing. Here again while the pressures were great the resources were strictly limited.

Yet a further interest in the expanding welfare programme was that of rural life and the provision of more specific training for the improvement of rural resources. This again was not a new concern but was pursued in the post-war years with a renewed vigour.[2] The Church Missionary Society in the diocese on the Niger had made the decision in 1938 to adopt a rural programme but the incidence of the war seriously retarded its operation. A beginning however was made in the endeavour to present rural life as a worth-while sphere for those with an elementary or higher education who would normally regard themselves as " emancipated " from the " drudgery " of tilling the soil. By contacts with students at the diocesan training college and with church leaders at district councils and the diocesan synod the point of view of rural activity as a worthy Christian career was expounded and was well received. A system of education based on rural science, now introduced by the Government, gave a further impulse in the same direction. With the post-war years came a major development : the co-operation of the Church of Scotland and the Methodist Missionary Society with the Church Missionary Society in setting up at Asaba on the Niger an Inter-mission Agricultural Training Centre where courses in elementary agriculture and forestry and relevant trades were offered to boys who had completed an elementary school course, while for girls of the same standard domestic training with appropriate gardening and poultry-keeping with improved strains were provided. For adults a model village was prepared where selected families in rotation could be encouraged in maintaining an improved home standard and guided in all activities from farm to market.[3] While the direct contribution to an improved life and livelihood for rural people

[1] *The Christian Council of Northern Rhodesia, Report of the Fourth Meeting, Lusaka, July 1951*, 11–12; B. Coppens, " Social Work in Urban Areas, with special reference to Family Life ", in *I.R.M.*, XLI (1952), 464–70.

[2] *Vide supra*, p. 176.

[3] K. H. Prior, "An African Diocese Adapts a Rural Programme ", in *I.R.M.*, XXXVI (1947), 370–8; XL (1951), 43; *The Church of Scotland, Report of the Foreign Mission Committee for 1948* (1949), 30. Dr. Kenneth H. Prior, a missionary of the United Church of Canada, seconded in the first instance to the C.M.S. in direction of their rural programme, had already pioneered in rural enterprises in Angola with marked success.

through such programmes was no small alleviation of human need, yet the deeper significance lay in breaking down the prevalent idea that education was to prepare for life in the towns. The association of Christian teaching with such a programme therefore pointed to a fully satisfying life in rural tasks which could be accepted as a divine vocation.

There is little need to stress the bewildering range of welfare activities in post-war Africa in which the Christian mission was now invited to engage. There was as always the hidden danger that the missionary should become so enveloped in a maze of uplift schemes and welfare dreams that the central missionary purpose should be lost in a welter of fascinating humanitarian activities largely pursued for their own sake. That there was a danger could not be denied, but awareness of it at the highest executive level tended to keep in balance the total missionary service, while the rapidly expanding programmes of colonial administrations promised a steady transfer to the broad shoulders of Government, determined by the rate at which qualified workers could be recruited. This inevitable development began to throw into yet sharper relief a basic need of the newly emerging African nations : the need for men and women of integrity to serve in posts of responsibility, from Local Government officers to cabinet ministers, from doctors and welfare officers to agricultural engineers.

The traditional background of African life was scarcely propitious. If a chief of the old order had amassed resources at the expense of others, he not only increased his own magnificence but won, certainly within liberal limits, the plaudits of his admiring subjects. If his modern counterpart should, in a position of high administrative responsibility, feather his own nest, who would say him nay? For most would do the very same, given the opportunity. The public opinion which in countries of a different tradition had served as a powerful sanction to curb the wayward when subject to temptation had here still to be created. All the more vital therefore was the need for leaders of unimpeachable integrity in the early days of independent nationhood when precedents were being set. The churches by their own democratic processes had already provided some experience in self-government through church courts and associated agencies, including the stewardship of funds, which had proved a useful preparatory discipline for public service. But in addition there had been specific efforts to educate a Christian conscience. In 1936, under much less exacting political conditions, a campaign against bribery as a corrupting influence in public life had been launched in Eastern Nigeria, and it was reported that among its supporters were constables, customs officers, interpreters, postmasters, prison contractors, tax collectors, teachers, traders, and others. The Synod of the Anglican Diocese on the Niger in May 1936 pledged unanimously its 300 clerical and lay members to act vigorously in the campaign.[1] Twenty years later, with the political situation completely transformed, the Christian Council of Nigeria found it advisable to issue a statement on " Christians and Political Development ", reminding the members of the churches of their obligations under political independence.[2] Here therefore an obligation second to none in the field of national well-being confronted the Christian churches : to nurture men and women of character who, as leaders of their people, would ever recognize their moral obligations and remain humble before God in the exercise of power. If direct participation on the educational and welfare front was now steadily receding as a missionary activity, there was coming into full focus the high obligation to prepare the people who were now to lead—an ample compensation for surrendering the levers of control.

(4) The Growing Church

The raison d'être of the Christian mission is to win converts to the Christian faith and way of life and to foster their growth to Christian maturity in the fellowship of believers, however imperfect it may appear, which is the visible Church. This is the heart of the matter. In the process many problems of communication and adaptation have had to be faced, while the national variety and ecclesiastical tradition of the sending countries have been duly

[1] The Eastern Star, No. 6 (June 1936), 42–3. Vide supra, p. 229.
[2] I.R.M., XLV (1956), 45. A penetrating comment by a student of African affairs assessed the situation on the eve of self-government: " The austerity underlying British ideals, derived from that Puritan spirit which is an enduring element in British life, strikes but a feeble spark from the African soul. Puritanism, self-denial, austerity, atonement—these are not at home under hot skies. An East African, asked what he thought would happen if the Europeans left, replied with a smile: " We should revert to more human standards! "—The South African Outlook, LXXXVI (1956), 91, quoting The Round Table. For the writer's fuller reflections on self-government and its perils in African territories, see ibid., 75–7, 88–91.
The Methodist Church of the Gold Coast issued for its constituency a booklet on the subject, The Church and the State (Cape Coast, 1949).

reflected in the faith and order of the younger churches, entailing their own problems.

Two comprehensive inquiries, closely affecting the life of the Church in Africa, were undertaken in the post-war years. Both had been proposed by the Tambaram Conference of the International Missionary Council in 1938, but the outbreak of war prevented earlier action. It was a general recommendation of the Conference, on a proposal of the African delegates, " that studies be undertaken with a view to securing co-operation in church discipline, in regard both to the treatment of individual Christians who are under.discipline, to marriage and to other customs which are inherent in the social structure of the people ".[1] In 1946 the proposal was revived, and from discussions with other interested bodies there emerged the plan for a joint inquiry under the auspices of the International Missionary Council and the International African Institute with the generous support of the Carnegie Corporation of New York and the Social Science Research Council of the British Colonial Office. Associated with these bodies on the executive committee were the Conférence Romaine des Missions Catholiques, the Association of Social Anthropology, and the Royal Anthropological Institute. The first phase of the inquiry so notably sponsored was concerned with an exhaustive study of documentary sources, and three reports on these constituting a comprehensive and fully authoritative survey—African Marriage and Social Change, Marriage Laws in Africa, and Christian Marriage in African Society—were issued in 1953.[2]

Apart from the requirement of monogamy there was little uniformity to be found in the approach of the Christian Churches to the many problems involved. The survey however now made available accurate knowledge in an ordered form on intricate questions of social behaviour that was of service in two respects : in illuminating many cases calling for Christian discipline so that the African angle, and not a merely transferred European slant on the situation, could be appreciated, and thus action taken with more justice to the Africans involved; and also in presenting clearly the fundamental aspects of social practice so that joint discussion, as in Christian Councils, could start from certain accepted data and thus enter the sooner upon profitable interchange of views.[3]

[1] *The Life of the Church*, Tambaram Madras Series IV (1939), 403.
[2] A. Phillips (ed.), *Survey of African Marriage and Family Life* (1953). A brief summary of the survey is provided in *African Marriage*, by Thomas Price (I.M.C. Research Pamphlets, No. 1, 1954).
[3] The subject was before the Christian Council of Nyasaland in 1955,

Meanwhile two colonial governments, in territories where Roman Catholic missions wielded considerable influence—Portuguese Angola and the Belgian Congo—legislated on polygamy. In Angola a decree was issued in 1949 prohibiting polygamy to Africans domiciled in urban centres but continuing to countenance the practice in rural areas.[1] In April 1950 the Government of the Belgian Congo followed suit by a decree rendering invalid before the law all future polygamous unions and reserving certain areas for monogamists alone. It is of interest that the Council of Government in Leopoldville had desired to take this action in 1948 but the Metropolitan Government, whose consent was necessary, had not then been prepared to approve.[2] Especially noteworthy was the attitude of educated Africans of the younger generation as expressed in an editorial of their paper, La Voix Congolese : " I am certain that the educated, the builders of the Congolese world of to-morrow, agree that polygamy should be abolished. It is the duty of the government, our protector, to suppress—for the good of its protégés—as soon as possible a custom which does not fit into the civilization that it brings us. Would that this antiquated polygamy disappear to give place everywhere to civilizing monogamy. Every progressive évolué should help to bring this about." [3]

Among the human factors in the development of the churches to maturity none had greater significance than the growth of an indigenous Christian ministry, sufficient in numbers and adequate in quality. It was therefore natural, in view of the importance of the matter, that a comprehensive inquiry should also be proposed on this subject by the Tambaram Conference. They recorded their conviction that " the present condition of theological education is one of the greatest weaknesses in the whole Christian enterprise ".[4] They proceeded to instruct the Committee of the International Missionary Council to arrange for a survey of the situation by means of detailed studies, including visits to centres of

with a paper by Ernest Gray, " Some Present-day Problems for African Christian Marriage."—*I.R.M.*, XLV (1956), 267–77.
[1] *International Fides Service*, April 9, 1949; *I.R.M.*, XXXIX (1950), 46. *Fides* (*loc. cit.*) stated: " The decree manifests the goodwill of the civil authority of Angola toward the Catholic missions."
[2] The Colonial Council was reported in 1946 to be already " working out a decree to protect monogamy "—statement by G. H. Sands, Chief of Government Service of Native Affairs, Belgian Congo, to Leopoldville Conference.—*Abundant Life in Changing Africa, Report of the West Central Africa Regional Conference* (1947), 99.
[3] *International Fides Service*, June 24, 1950; *I.R.M.*, XL (1951), 45.
[4] *The Life of the Church*, Tambaram Madras Series IV (1939), 211.

theological training, and " to work out a policy and programme for the training of the ministry in the younger churches ".[1] Once again the incidence of war prevented immediate action, though in India the programme was carried through.[2] The African theological survey for the continent south of the Sahara was undertaken in three stages as required by so vast a field.[3] The first, covering British East and West Africa, was carried out in 1950.[4] The second covered Belgian, French, and Portuguese territories together with Liberia and was done by an international survey team in 1953.[5] The third related to the Union of South Africa and the Federation of Rhodesia and Nyasaland and was also completed in 1953.[6] So comprehensive a survey had never before been available.[7] It stressed the training of the ministry as an unquestioned priority for the nurture of the churches in critical days. Bishop Neill found the key to seizing the unexampled opportunity presented to the Church in tropical Africa to be the Christian minister: " The African minister is at the very centre of the picture. If he fails to rise to the height of the opportunity, the harm that can be wrought is illimitable. For good or ill on him almost everything depends." [8] The second commission regarded one-fourth of missionary personnel as the minimum that should be assigned to the training of ordained and lay workers in the

[1] *Ibid.*, 212.

[2] C. W. Ranson, *The Christian Minister in India; His Vocation and His Training*, A Study based on a Survey of Theological Education conducted by the National Christian Council (Madras, 1945).

[3] Stephen Neill, "African Theological Survey", in *I.R.M.*, XXXIX (1950), 207–11.

[4] *Survey of the Training of the Ministry in Africa*, Part I (1950), by Stephen Neill. Bishop Stephen Neill had served as chairman of the Theological Education Committee of the N.C.C. of India, and at the time of the Africa survey was an Associate Secretary of the World Council of Churches.

[5] *Survey of the Training of the Ministry in Africa*, Part II (1954), by M. Searle Bates, C. G. Baëta, F. Michaeli, and B. G. M. Sundkler. The members of the team came respectively from the United States, Gold Coast, France, and Sweden. See further: M. Searle Bates, " The Training of Christian Ministers in non-British Africa ", in *I.R.M.*, XLIII (1954), 294–300.

[6] *Survey of the Training of the Ministry in Africa*, Part III (1954), by Norman Goodall and E. W. Nielsen.

[7] For a study of the African pastor at his task, see B. G. M. Sundkler, *They Serve the Church in Africa*. Although Madagascar does not come within our purview (see Preface to Vol. I), it may perhaps be mentioned here that a fourth stage of the Survey concerned that island and was undertaken in 1956, again by an international team: C. W. Ranson (I.M.C.), Birkeli (Lutheran World Federation), F. Michaeli (France), and A. Rasendrahasina (Madagascar).

[8] *Survey*, Part I, 59.

churches.[1] The third estimated the gravity of the situation in these terms : " There are many signs that during the next twenty years or so the Churches in Africa will be passing through a period comparable to the first three or four centuries of the Christian era in the radical nature of the spiritual and intellectual issues at stake. In this setting it is impossible to exaggerate the importance of the work of those who teach theology and train ministers of the African Churches." [2]

Among the many issues raised by an inquiry so fundamental to the life of the Church two were projected as claiming prior attention : the type of minister required and its bearing on training; and the obligation to co-operation in training. On the first point it was agreed that while a reasonable academic standard should be maintained, bearing in mind the rise in educational level in the membership of the churches and the subtle challenges of the time confronting the Christian religion, yet academic attainment was not of itself sufficient for the discharge of a pastoral ministry, but that a deep spiritual understanding of the faith and the flock was essential. The apparent unevenness in demand between urban and rural congregations was to some extent offset by the fundamental spiritual needs they had in common. Nevertheless there should be opportunity for training of recruits at all academic levels from the secondary school candidate to the university graduate, to serve the varied needs of the Christian community in the swirling life of modern Africa.[3]

The need for inter-confessional training centres was posed partly by the waste of effort and the inefficiency inseparable from a number of small denominational units, but principally by the urgent necessity of full Protestant co-operation for which nothing could be so effective as a joint training of the ministry. Indeed, one commission went so far as to declare : " The judgment of the succeeding generation may well be that the fateful issue of our own time for the advance or the decline of Protestant Christianity in Africa was the achievement or refusal of Christian co-operation;

[1] *Survey*, Part II, 94. This estimate stimulated some vital thinking as to re-deployment of resources.

[2] *Survey*, Part III, 61.

[3] The Church of Scotland in its reflections on the subject suggested that there might be a case for each Christian community of limited resources having as its local minister an elder ordained to lead worship and administer the sacraments but not requiring support as a full-time servant of the Church.—*Report of the Foreign Mission Committee for 1951* (1952), 24.

and that the issue was basically determined in the type, spirit, and quality of the schools for pastors." [1] Experiments in joint theological training had already appeared in the post-war years in East and West Africa. At Limuru in Kenya St. Paul's College, which Bishop Neill found the scene of a tentative phase of co-operation between Anglicans and Presbyterians, had after a five-year experimental period become a United Divinity School under its own board of governors, with the Anglican, Presbyterian, and Methodist Churches by unanimous decision training their ordinands together. [2] In West Africa two united theological colleges had appeared. In the Gold Coast Methodists and Presbyterians co-operated in Trinity College at Kumasi, of which Bishop Neill reported : " This remarkable institution had more of the feel of a college than any other that I visited in Africa." [3] Later in time came Trinity College at Umuahia in Eastern Nigeria in which Anglicans, Methodists, and Presbyterians came together for ministerial training. [4] The possibility of setting up three church colleges adjacent respectively to the University Colleges of the Gold Coast at Accra, of Nigeria at Ibadan, and of East Africa at Kampala, while a central recommendation of the first survey report, was regarded as too ambitious a project to undertake at the time. [5]

Another major problem, steadily becoming more insistent of solution in the post-war crisis of African affairs, was that of the relations between the various Christian bodies who proclaimed a common message and shared a common faith. As in the sending lands of the West the difficulties of closer union were found to lie in traditional order rather than in the faith of believers. The fundamental breach within the Christian mission between the Roman Catholic Church and the non-Roman Churches in view of exclusive claims by Rome had perforce to be accepted without prospect of healing. [6] But there remained a generous field within which the non-Roman Churches were able to contemplate their mutual

[1] *Survey*, Part II, 95.

[2] *Survey*, Part I, 34–5; *The Church of Scotland, Report of the Foreign Mission Committee for 1953* (1954), 12; *I.R.M.*, XLIV (1955), 48; XLV (1956), 50–1.

[3] *Survey*, Part I, 51.

[4] *The Church of Scotland, Report of the Foreign Mission Committee for 1953* (1954), 12.

[5] *Survey*, Part I, 60; *Report of the Foreign Mission Committee for 1951* (1952), 23–4. The University College of the Gold Coast possessed a full Faculty of Theology, while the University College of Nigeria had a Department of Theology.

[6] See Vol. II, pp. 246–7.

relations. And here the tendency was unmistakably for the extension of confessional organizations rather than for the fostering of inter-confessional unions. That the Roman Catholic Church should develop an exclusive organization with the growth of its work goes without saying. In 1950 the time was deemed propitious for the erection of the episcopal hierarchy in British West Africa : in the Gold Coast and Nigeria with the adjoining British trust territories of Togo and Cameroons. Three ecclesiastical provinces were constituted : one in Eastern Nigeria and Cameroons consisting of the Archiepiscopal Metropolitan Church of Onitsha with the three suffragan dioceses of Owerri, Calabar, and Buea; a second in Western Nigeria, the Archiepiscopal Metropolitan Church of Lagos with the two suffragan dioceses of Ondo and Benin City; the third situated in the Gold Coast, consisting of the Archiepiscopal Metropolitan Church of Cape Coast with the four suffragan dioceses of Accra, Kumasi, Tamale, and Keta. In Sierra Leone the Diocese of Freetown and Bo was simultaneously erected but declared directly subject to the Holy See. Meanwhile the same missionary societies and congregations continued as in the now superseded vicariates apostolic.[1] There followed in January 1951 the establishment of the South African hierarchy which included, in addition to the Union of South Africa, the four territories of South-West Africa, Basutoland (where the Church had developed considerable strength), Southern Rhodesia, and Northern Rhodesia, thus reaching on the north the confines of the Belgian Congo.[2] Meanwhile in the same year the hierarchy in Ethiopia underwent reconstruction with an Ethiopian consecrated as titular Bishop of Suzusa and appointed as Apostolic Administrator for Catholics of the Ethiopian rite in that country.[3]

In the organization of the Anglican communion the setting up of a Province under an archbishop as Metropolitan removed the dioceses constituting it from the direct oversight of Canterbury, though the various Provinces were themselves associated under the leadership of Canterbury, the relationship finding expression in the decennial Lambeth Conferences. The Church of the Province of South Africa had appeared as early as 1873 though it was nearly the end of the century before the Metropolitan assumed the title of archbishop.[4] In the post-war years two new Provinces

[1] *International Fides Service*, June 3, 1950.
[2] *I.R.M.*, XLI (1952), 74.
[3] *I.R.M.*, XLI (1952), 72.
[4] Lewis and Edwards, *Historical Records of the Church of the Province of South Africa* (1934), 115–16, 134.

came to birth in Africa. The Church of the Province of West Africa was set up in 1951, comprehending the five dioceses of the Gambia, Sierra Leone, Accra, Lagos, and the Niger.[1] The diocese of Northern Nigeria, formerly a missionary diocese of Lagos, was inaugurated at Kano on January 31, 1954, by the Archbishop of the Province and thus became a full diocese in its own right and the sixth in the Province.[2] In 1955 the Church of the Province of Central Africa was established, comprehending the dioceses of Nyasaland, Northern Rhodesia, Matebeleland, and Mashonaland.[3] The inauguration, originally expected to take place at an earlier date, had been postponed until the Federation of Rhodesia and Nyasaland (covering the same area) had been set up, in order to avoid any suspicion on the part of Africans that there was collusion with the Government in the affair. A projected Province for East Africa was still delayed pending agreement by the Synods concerned. Meanwhile the three Anglican Provinces covered a generous portion of British Africa, and as autonomous Churches were all eligible for direct affiliation to the World Council of Churches.

The Lutheran missions, to be found in South, East, and West Africa, had also come together in closer association on a confessional basis. The co-operation of Lutheran missions in Natal reached back to 1912. The Berlin Missionary Society, the Norwegian Missionary Society, and the Church of Sweden Mission were the original co-operating units. They were joined in 1928 by the mission of the Norwegian Lutheran Church of America, while ten years later the Hermannsburg mission adhered in part. The Co-operating Lutheran Missions, as they were known in association, established a united theological school, a joint teacher training institution, and a publishing house. The next step of federation, with an Evangelical Lutheran Church of South Africa as the outcome, was a more distant objective.[4] In Tanganyika German and American Lutherans had come together in 1937 to found the Federation of East African Missionary Churches in

[1] The dioceses in the Gambia and Rio Pongas and in the Gold Coast had been served by S.P.G., those in Sierra Leone and Nigeria by C.M.S.

[2] *Northern Nigeria News Sheet*, No. 111 (June 1954).

[3] *I.R.M.*, XLV (1956), 51. The dioceses of Nyasaland and Northern Rhodesia were in the care of U.M.C.A.; those of Southern Rhodesia, of S.P.G.

[4] O. G. Myklebust in *Det norske misjonsselskaps historie i hundre år*, III (1949), 145–8; H. Schlyter, *The History of the Co-operating Lutheran Missions in Natal* (1953); A. Burgess, *Unkulunkulu in Zululand* (1934), 216–19; *I.R.M.*, XLIII (1954), 478.

which eight African Churches were associated. The first assembly of the Federation was held in 1938.[1] After the war African Lutherans were brought together on a wider scale with an All-Africa Lutheran Conference in 1955, when there assembled at Marangu in Tanganyika one hundred African leaders and fifty Europeans from across the continent. "Two factors", said a European reporter, "were uniting them: Faith in Jesus Christ and Luther's *Small Catechism*," but it would appear that the Europeans were rather more emphatic than the Africans about the Lutheran colour of their faith.[2] Nevertheless such a gathering on a confessional basis of African church leaders from Liberia, Nigeria, Cameroons, Tanganyika, Southern Rhodesia, South Africa, South-West Africa, Ethiopia, and Madagascar to discuss the four main subjects laid before them was deeply impressive.[3]

The same policy of confessional consolidation was pursued by the British Methodist Church where its constituency was strongest. Of the total Christian community of 411,505 claimed in Africa in 1955 (not including the autonomous Methodist Church of South Africa), 358,314 or eighty-seven per cent were in the six West African Districts.[4] Inter-District conferences, with the African delegates in the majority, had been held in the post-war years, thus bringing together the regional African leaders of the Methodist community in mutual understanding and fellowship. There eventually emerged the proposal, laid before the British Conference of 1955, for the setting up of an independent West African Conference. The proposal was favourably received and direction given for a constitution for such a Church to be prepared.[5]

If in the matter of closer union the trend thus lay rather in the direction of a wider denominational consolidation than the encouragement of a more local United African Church on an inter-confessional basis, there was none the less growing consulta-

---

[1] *Vide supra*, p. 233.

[2] When, for example, the African delegates met in separate session it was reported that, in their discussion on the necessity for higher theological training, the emphasis was placed on the fact that the desired institution should be of high standard rather than that it should be Lutheran.

[3] P. D. Fueter, " The All-Africa Lutheran Conference, Marangu 1955 ", in *I.R.M.*, XLV (1956), 289–96. The four subjects were: Faith and Confession, The Growing Church, The Serving Church, and The Church and its Environment. While complete agreement on fundamentals was reported, there was found to be wide diversity in practice.

[4] *The Changing Church, 1955, The Annual Report of the Methodist Missionary Society* (1956), 47.

[5] *Ibid.*, 20.

U 2

tion and collaboration in territorial Christian Councils and inter-territorial conferences in all of which African leaders were increas-ingly playing their part. By 1955 fourteen African territories had Christian Councils in existence, though only three of these—those of the Belgian Congo, Sierra Leone, and South Africa—were affiliated to the International Missionary Council.[1] A Council not infrequently owed its inception to the necessity of some common policy for missions *vis-à-vis* the Government in education. The consequent risk that absorption in these affairs might easily de-flect attention from the weightier concern of a united Christian witness was no imaginary one, a risk that the sheer pressure of administration with expanding education programmes made the more acute. But apart from such an emphasis the Councils were by no means of equal vigour, and the infusion of more vitality into the weak was an urgent priority of the post-war period.

The decision to appoint a full-time secretary was a mark of expanding usefulness, as in the case of the Aliança Evangélica de Angola, set up in 1934,[2] when J. T. Tucker of the United Church of Canada received such an appointment in 1946.[3] An aspect of the Councils of considerable importance was the opportunity afforded African leaders to share in interdenominational conference at terri-torial level. Characteristically the Christian Council of the Gold Coast had advanced farthest with an African secretary, while in Southern and Northern Rhodesia, as befitted their endorsement of racial partnership under the Federation, separate European and African Conferences were merged in Christian Councils to which African members might be sent direct from their churches in the normal way. In 1954 the Southern Rhodesia Missionary Con-ference and the Southern Rhodesia African Missionary Con-ference were thus combined in the Christian Conference of Southern Rhodesia.[4] In Northern Rhodesia, where delegates nominated from the African Christian Conference had for some years attended sessions of the Christian Council, the Council con-stitution was amended in 1955 to enable African delegates to be sent from their churches direct instead of through the African Conference, which thereupon decided to disband.[5] A further effect of political federation was the proposal in 1954 to establish

[1] *I.R.M.*, XLV (1956), 134–5.
[2] *Vide supra*, p. 228.
[3] *I.R.M.*, XXXVI (1947), 45. Dr. Tucker was later Director of the Liga Evangélica de Acção Missionária e Educacional in Lisbon. *Vide supra*, p. 205n.
[4] *I.R.M.*, XLIV (1955), 51.
[5] *I.R.M.*, XLV (1956), 51.

an inter-territorial Council covering the two Rhodesias and Nyasaland, as a step towards which a Consultative Board representative of the three territories came into being.[1]

A form of consultation less intimate and regular but serving its own special purposes was that of the regional conference. The first regional missionary conference to be held in Africa, or indeed anywhere, after World War II was the West Central Africa Conference which met at Leopoldville in the Belgian Congo in July 1946. The 200 delegates, of whom thirty-five were Africans, represented no fewer than seventy-three missionary organizations, the region covered comprising Angola, the Belgian Congo, French Equatorial Africa, and Cameroons, where the Protestant missions at work hailed mainly from North America and the Continent of Europe. The Conference was principally concerned with the new responsibilities devolving upon church and mission in the light of the rapidly changing conditions in the Belgian, French, and Portuguese territories concerned.[2] More limited regional conferences were held in due course in the Belgian Congo in which the African and European membership was in inverse ratio to that at Leopoldville. In 1950 at Blukwa in the north-east seventy-two African Christian leaders coming from twenty-one different tribes and fourteen Europeans met for discussion of problems of the growing African Church.[3] A second conference for the north-west Ubangi region in 1952 with a similar purpose was attended by sixty-four Africans and fourteen missionaries.[4] These proved to be valuable experiences for Christian leaders in Congo who had farther to go in preparation for the larger responsibilities awaiting them than those in African Churches with a longer history behind them.

The varied pattern of integration of local Christian groups, which were separate because distinct in origin, may be indicated by the policy pursued by the Church of Scotland for fostering the growth of the African Church in three contrasting regions. In Northern Rhodesia the African congregations, Presbyterian and Congregationalist in origin as deriving from the Church of Scotland and London Missions, had united in the Church of Central Africa in Rhodesia with an autonomous Presbytery. It was this Church to which Protestant African Christians in the Copperbelt

---

[1] *I.R.M.*, XLIV (1955), 51.
[2] *Abundant Life in Changing Africa, Report of the West Central Africa Regional Conference* (1946), *passim.*
[3] *I.R.M.*, XL (1951), 45; *Ecumenical Press Service* (Geneva), January 6, 1950.
[4] *I.R.M.*, XLII (1953), 39.

belonged, if hailing from the labours of the United Missions team in which the Methodist Missionary Society also shared.[1] This African Church was said in 1951 to be " something more than a lusty infant ".[2] In 1955 the United Missions in the Copperbelt ceased to be, its work being entrusted to a new Copperbelt Christian Service Council. In deference to Anglican desires church affairs had never come within the purview of the United Missions though the three Free Churches had pursued them in company. They were still together though now in a Liaison Committee representative of European and African congregations in the Copperbelt, while discussions proceeded with a view to ultimate union.[3] In Nigeria, with the European group limited to the missionary body, the situation was different. Here, in pursuance of the basic principle of the integration of church and mission, authority was given by the General Assembly of the Church of Scotland for the dissolution of the presbytery of Calabar, after nearly a century of existence,[4] with the consequent transfer of the ordained missionaries to the Presbyterian Church of Eastern Nigeria at its invitation. The African Church was thus encouraged " to assume full missionary responsibility in partnership with the men and women from the Western Churches who come to help them ".[5] In Kenya the situation was characteristic of an area with a multi-racial society. Congregations of African Christians in the care of the Presbyterian mission had been gathered into an African Church while European members had their spiritual home in St. Andrew's Church, Nairobi, officially included in the Overseas Presbytery of Kenya to which the missionaries belonged. The merging of both in a United Church as authorized by the General Assembly of the Church of Scotland, took place with the inauguration on February 11, 1956, of the Presbyterian Church of East Africa.[6] This expression of inter-racial unity in Christ came as a cheering ray of light in a much troubled land.

[1] *The Growing Church, 1954. The Annual Report of the Methodist Missionary Society* (1955), 28. The Church of Barotseland, arising from the work of the Paris Missionary Society and still in association with it, also enjoyed cordial relations with the Church of Central Africa in Rhodesia.—*The Church of Scotland, Report of the Foreign Mission Committee for 1956* (1957), 28.

[2] *United Missions in the Copperbelt, Tenth Report, 1950–51,* 4.

[3] *The Church of Scotland, Report of the Foreign Mission Committee for 1955* (1956), 28–9.

[4] See Vol. II, p. 40.

[5] *The Church of Scotland, Report of the Foreign Mission Committee for 1954* (1955), 31–2.

[6] *Ibid., Report for 1951* (1952), 25; *Report for 1954* (1955), 31; *Report for 1955* (1956), 66.

One feature of the growing Church in Africa that caused considerable concern was the not infrequent indifference to evangelism. The Church in Africa was not unique in this. The Tambaram meeting of 1938 underlined the centrality of this obligation, vital to the life of the Church, and sadly recorded that " a very small part of the potential strength of the Church is now engaged in the task ".[1] Beyond the individual obligation of Christian believers and of denominational activity they urged : " That henceforth Churches and missions view their total evangelistic task as a joint responsibility of all and expend a far larger proportion of their evangelistic effort in interdenominational co-operation." [2] At the Enlarged Meeting of the Committee of the International Missionary Council which met at Willingen, Germany, in 1952, with the Missionary Obligation of the Church as its theme, the delegates of the younger churches presented a statement of their own to the Conference in the course of which they said : " We know that in some places we have lost the Gospel; we have to that extent lost the initiative. . . . The secret of achieving recovery is that every Christian in the younger churches should be a witnessing Christian. . . . We believe that responsibility for the initiative should rest on the baptized community of Christians in every local area." [3] This was a call not less to the Church in Africa than elsewhere. J. S. Trimingham, in his survey of Islam in West Africa, found the local churches for the most part so concerned with their own affairs as to fail to evangelize their neighbours.[4] Churches in Sierra Leone and Yorubaland, with over a century of history, had been content to leave their neighbours pagan; indeed, he went so far as to assert : " Africans in general have shown little impulse to carry their acquired religion beyond their immediate family and village circle. Sometimes they have reacted against missionary work amongst other peoples by refusal to co-operate." [5] It is a serious charge. Whether the cause was to be found in a merely nominal faith for respectability's sake so that there was no sense of a gospel to be shared, or in such preoccupation with an ecclesi-

---

[1] *Evangelism*, Tambaram Madras Series, III (1939), 436.

[2] *Ibid.*, 436.

[3] *The Missionary Obligation of the Church, Willingen 1952* (1952), 39–40.

[4] " Missionaries in partnership with African Christians have to subordinate their aims to those of the Churches which, with some exceptions, are concerned with internal organization and not with evangelism among non-Christians. So absorbed are most missionaries in institutional work that they can do little to arouse the Church to the need for wider witness ".— J. S. Trimingham, *The Christian Church and Islam in West Africa* (1955), 28.

[5] *Ibid.*, 29.

astical organization on the Western model that committees took precedence of campaigns, the failure was the same.

But there were indications here and there of an African awakening to the Christian obligation. Thus from Cameroons came news in 1950 of students in the theological school at Ndunge undertaking evangelistic tours; while teams of local Christians, with a European leader, had carried through evangelism weeks in towns and in plantation camps.[1] In the Gold Coast both Church of Scotland and Basel missions reported in 1950 that African Christians were coming to regard the backward Northern Territories[2] as their special responsibilty for evangelism.[3] Indeed, within five years the Church of Scotland was able to record that the Church of the Gold Coast had committed itself to a mission field in the Northern Territories and had already sent its evangelists into the area.[4] In 1955 the Methodist Church in the Gold Coast also launched its own mission to the North.[5] The most spontaneous action, however, took place in East Africa. As a sequel to the revival in the Church in Uganda in the mid-'thirties[6] missionary teams of Africans first visited centres in Uganda, then districts farther afield in adjacent territories. Their message was God's call for revival. In 1937 one team visited Kenya with effects little foreseen for the Church in that country. A Revival Fellowship in due course appeared, and its members proved to be the steadfast core of Christian believers in the dark days of the Mau Mau rising when the merely nominal Christians slipped away like a landslide.[7] This was the most spectacular issue, for as Dr. Warren writes of a cruelly battered area : " When the real days of testing came, with blood and flame and sword, it was the men and women of the Revival Fellowship who saved the Church. That is literally true and needs no allowance for exaggeration." [8] And the Revival Fellowship sprang out of African evangelism.

[1] *I.R.M.*, XL (1951), 44.
[2] See R. S. Rattray, *The Tribes of the Ashanti Hinterland* (1932), *passim.*
[3] *I.R.M.*, XL (1951), 41.
[4] *The Church under the Cross, Church of Scotland Report of the Foreign Mission Committee for 1955* (1956), 24.
[5] *The Changing Church, 1955, Annual Report of the Methodist Missionary Society* (1956), 26.
[6] *Vide supra*, p. 225.
[7] Dr. M. A. C. Warren records the facts: " Some of those who have been giving outstandingly courageous witness in the Mau Mau terror were deeply influenced by this visit of the team from Uganda in 1937 ".— M. A. C. Warren, *Revival, An Enquiry* (1954), 52.
[8] *Ibid.*, 57.

This continuing progress was made during a period of increasing instability in world affairs, despite the fact that the white man's prestige, with which the Christian mission had been so long associated, no longer remained what it was, and that the powerful position missions had occupied as the major purveyors of education was of necessity being steadily relinquished. But, if such contingent attractions were on the wane, there was at least genuine satisfaction to be found in the fact that those now responding were more likely to find the appeal in the Christian message itself and in the realization of a fuller life within the Christian fellowship.

In reviewing Christian developments during this post-war decade against the background of surging life throughout the continent, we have inevitably been more concerned with high-level policy and planning than directly with the missions and churches through whose steady activity at ground level the rooting of Christianity was taking place. Before concluding this post-war survey, therefore, it will be well to take some account however brief, of this unspectacular service which remains, none the less, the very life-blood of the Christian mission. Some reference to the territory of French Equatorial Africa, with its estimated population of four and a half million, will sufficiently serve the purpose.

Less accessible than most, this extensive region remained for long comparatively neglected. Roman Catholic pioneers were first on the scene, making their initial contact at Brazzaville in the 'eighties, and by 1910 were becoming established in the new prefecture apostolic of Ubangi-Chari, claiming at that date some 3,500 Catholics and 2,500 catechumens.[1] In the same year the Edinburgh Missionary Conference called attention to this great stretch of territory untouched by Protestant missions whose nearest stations were barely 250 miles inland from the west coast. One estimate named 360 missionaries as needed for effective Protestant advance.[2]

By the mid-twentieth century there was a different story to be told. The number of Roman Catholics had increased tenfold in little more than a quarter of a century—from 31,908 in 1921 to 310,812 in 1948[3]—while the ranks of the priesthood had swelled from 78 to 207 in the same period.[4] Meanwhile Protestant missions were at last beginning to enter the interior by the nineteen-twenties.

[1] See Vol. III, p. 227 ; *Cath. Ency.*, XV (1912) 115.
[2] See Vol. III, p. 282; *World Missionary Conference Report* (1910), 223-4.
[3] *Agence Internationale Fides, Supplément*, October 1, 1949.
[4] *Ibid.*, October 8, 1949. Of the 78 priests of 1921, 8 were African and 28 of the 207 of 1948.

A representative enterprise was that of the Brethren Church of the United States.

The pioneer party of Brethren missionaries—a party of four, but reinforced within a year—reached Brazzaville, the Federation capital, in 1918, but it was 1921 before official permission to enter Ubangi-Chari, the largest constituent territory of the Federation, was received. In 1922 the first station was located at Bassai among the Karre people, some 275 miles from Bangui the provincial capital which remained the point of entry. In the twelve years 1922–34 three stations were in operation, each placed to serve a different language area, with fifteen missionaries engaged in itineration, translation, and medical work. Catechetical schools, not subject to control by the French authorities, were favoured as in line with the objectives of the mission. During the next dozen years, 1934–46, despite the incidence of World War II, the American missionary staff was more than doubled and further stations were begun. The post-war decade, 1947–56, saw yet more stations opened, bringing the number to fourteen with fifty-eight missionaries in active service. The area now served by the Brethren mission, by delimitation agreement with Protestant missionary neighbours, was an ample one the size of the State of Illinois: some 60,000 square miles with an estimated population of 400,000. Meanwhile the African churches scattered over the countryside were being developed to accept responsibility for their own affairs under trained elders and to be active in evangelism among their neighbours. This Christian community of some 20,000, representing five per cent of the population in the mission's area, the fruit of one generation's work, was thus being prepared to play its part in the Africa of the future.[1]

Lutheran, Reformed, and Baptist Churches, and others, variously estimated to number some 10,000 members or more each, also made their own contribution to the Protestant Community.[2] Meanwhile the traditional Protestant activity of translation of the Scriptures had gone steadily forward: no fewer than seventeen new languages of French Equatorial Africa were added to the list of Bible translations from 1927, of which five were done in the decade 1945–54.[3]

While public attention was naturally directed to the newly emerging African States, these less politically advanced territories, with their Christian communities steadily growing through much self-denying missionary service at ground level, remained none the less vital to the planting of Christianity in Africa.

[1] O. D. Jobson, *Conquering Oubangui-Chari for Christ* (1957), *passim*.
[2] *Missionary Research Library Occasional Bulletin*, VIII, No. 7 (1957), 26–7.
[3] See Appendix.

CHAPTER 8

PROBLEMATIC OUTLOOK

WE have attempted to trace the fortunes of the Christian enterprise in Africa through the twenty centuries of the Christian era, and have noted the three opportunities for entry that have been presented, of which the third is so far the briefest. The question naturally presents itself : What prospect is there that this third phase of the total movement will eventually survive the cataclysms of history better than its predecessors ? This is but one aspect of the larger question : How far is the future course of events predictable? Clearly a realistic reply can do no more than offer an analysis of the factors in the situation in so far as it is currently perceived, and indicate what appear to be the elements essential to survival. Beyond that it is scarcely permissible to go. It is of course to be remembered that we are concerned with more than the historian as a rule is prepared to contemplate. As Professor Butterfield has reminded us : " Even serious students, like our great Cambridge historian, Lord Acton, have been greatly interested in church history while regarding it as a form of politico-ecclesiastical history, and they have tended to overlook that more intimate thing, the inner spiritual life of the Church." [1] While the temptation is to be pre-occupied with the human-activity side of the picture, there is, as the Christian sees it, the aspect of super-human intervention in affairs that finds direct expression through committed human lives. The Christian Church is not man's erection, but God's creation : " I have planted ", said Paul, " Apollos watered, but God gave the increase." [2] The inner spiritual life of the Church is in the end the factor decisive for survival.

(1) Favouring Conditions

There are outstanding characteristics of the modern Christian movement in Africa not shared with either of the preceding periods of activity. Perhaps the most obvious, though none the less signifi-

[1] H. Butterfield, *Christianity and History* (1949), 131.
[2] I Corinthians 3: 6.

315

cant for that, is that the whole continent now lies open for the first time in history, and that Christian forces have already largely occupied it. The end of the geographical feat has indeed proved to be the beginning of the missionary enterprise in an Africa hitherto unevangelized because so largely unknown. But the period of an open Africa has been astoundingly brief in the life of a continent: scarcely a century since the interior was penetrated, with evangelization of large areas barely begun fifty years ago.

Related to this opening up of the continent has been the bringing of Africa into more intimate contact with the rest of the world. For weal or woe the links of Africa with lands overseas have become closer than ever before. Communications by land and sea and air have so improved that the time factor normally imposed by distance has almost been eliminated, while the radio enables Africans to share news and events simultaneously with the rest of the world—communications which only a major disaster could now disrupt. Africa will not readily be isolated again.

The remarkable spread of formal education among the peoples of Africa, with which the Christian mission has been so closely associated, is another feature characteristic of the modern situation. There had always been an indigenous education, the value and quality of which were at first often overlooked.[1] But the lure of literacy was irresistible, and young Africa crowded to school, drawn by the magnet of the book and avid for the new learning.[2] With government support in many territories missions often became the purveyors of some eighty to ninety per cent of the education of a territory.[3] They thus exerted an extensive influence on the community through the network of their schools. True, this could not be expected to remain a permanent feature of their work in view of the State's acceptance of the provision of education as eventually its own direct service. Even while it lasted it was not undiluted advantage. The question has arisen whether the Christian mission's large preoccupation with education had not often led Africans to regard this as its major object, so that when the same provision was available elsewhere their interest in the mission might easily come to an end. Be that as it may, the transfer

[1] E. W. Smith, " Indigenous Education in Africa ", in *Essays Presented to C. G. Seligman* (1934), 319–34; O. F. Raun, " Some Aspects of Indigenous Education among the Chaga ", in *Journal of the Royal Anthropological Institute*, LXVIII (1938), 209–21.

[2] A. V. Murray, *The School in the Bush* (1929), 80.

[3] French colonies were an exception.—W. B. Mumford and G. St. J. Orde Browne, *Africans Learn to be French* (n.d.), 39.

of direct responsibility was by no means all loss to the Christian mission. With the ever-expanding educational demand the administrative burden lying on missionary shoulders had grown to be a heavy one, even though generous financial support had been given by the State.[1] The hard-pressed managers of schools might now find more opportunity to devote attention to the nurture of the church, and indeed through its agency help to produce those men and women of moral integrity and Christian outlook who are the key to any system of education deserving the name of Christian.[2]

Again, Christianity as the religion of a book has become more firmly planted in Africa than in any earlier period. Whereas the Church in North Africa was limited to the Latin Bible for its members, and even in Abyssinia with its surviving national Church the scriptures had been enshrined in the classical Ethiopic rather than the vernacular Amharic of later centuries, the Bible or some part of it is now to be found in some four-fifths of the 500 or more languages and major dialects of the continent. And a number of these versions also serve a larger area than is strictly their own, if linguistic relation is close and the size of the smaller constituency has scarcely justified separate translation. The list of versions already provided is eloquent testimony of the extent to which the peoples of Africa have been provided with the Book in the mother tongue.[3] The significance of the achievement is to be estimated by the fact that, whatever the education, the mother tongue always remains the language of religious devotion. J. E. K. Aggrey once confessed that, despite his twenty years in the United States away from his homeland, when after a weary day he knelt down to pray, it was in the language his mother taught him.[4] What it means to have the Word of God thus put into the mother tongue was admirably expressed by the translators of the Authorized Version of the English Bible : " Translation it is that openeth the window, to let in the light; that breaketh the shell, that we may eat the kernel;

---

[1] The danger of undue absorption in such administration was pointed out by A. J. Haile in a communication to the Tambaram Conference: " We estimate that at least one-third of our time is given up in South Africa to tasks which might be described as those of unpaid clerks of the Education Department ".—*The Life of the Church*, Tambaram Madras Series IV, 141; cf. 145.

[2] Sir Philip Mitchell when Governor of Kenya stated his Administration's policy to be that of providing a Christian education for Africans in this sense.

[3] See Appendix for list of Scripture translations into African languages.

[4] Personally communicated.

that putteth aside the curtaine that we may looke into the most Holy place; that removeth the cover of the well, that wee may come by the water, even as Jacob rolled away the stone from the mouth of the well, by which meanes the flockes of Laban were watered. Indeede without translation into the vulgar tongue, the unlearned are but like children at Jacob's well (which was deepe) without a bucket or some thing to draw with; or as that person mentioned by Essy, to whom when a sealed booke was delivered, with this motion, Reade this, I pray thee, hee was faine to make this answere, I cannot, for it is sealed." [1] The incomparable boon to the life of the Church in Africa conferred by Bible translation cannot be overrated.

With growing literacy the vital necessity of the provision of an adequate range of Christian literature has received increasing attention. The activities of the International Committee on Christian Literature for Africa for a quarter of a century have already been recorded, while the United Society for Christian Literature (inheritor of the goodwill of the Religious Tract Society that sprang into being for the same purpose at the time of the missionary awakening) has effectively collaborated in meeting African needs. The use of the printed page in addition to the spoken word has greatly increased the range of missionary penetration and at the same time provided the message in a form to which there can be return again and again. [2]

Another method of spreading the Christian message was to reach the vastly greater listening public by means of radio where a local broadcasting system was available. Thus in Nigeria the N.B.S. [3] set up in 1952 a Christian Religious Broadcasting Department with support from the principal Christian bodies in the

[1] "The Translators to the Reader", Authorized Version of the English Bible, First edition, 1611. An old Papuan testified in his own way to the effectiveness of the mother tongue : "There is no language like it anywhere. It gets right into you—into your body—you feel it—you see it with your eyes. Other languages you breathe and they die. With our speech it is different. You feel it right through you."—*Each in His Own Language* (1950), 1. On the missionary's mastering of hitherto unknown, unwritten languages and the subsequent task of translation, see E. W. Smith, *The Shrine of a People's Soul* (1929), *passim*.

[2] For a detailed survey of the provision of Christian literature in Africa by 1938, see *The Life of the Church*, Tambaram Madras Series, IV (1939), 359–71. Library provision was a recent development, and in this the Carnegie Corporation of New York took an active interest.—*I.R.M.*, XXX (1941), 64; XXXI (1942), 54.

[3] N.B.S. = Nigerian Broadcasting System. It had three regional stations at Ibadan (West), Enugu (East), and Kaduna (North) respectively.

country; thus its morning " Family Prayers " proved acceptable to Roman Catholics, Anglicans, Baptists, Methodists, and the Salvation Army. From 1954 an African Christian was in charge of the programmes. A notable by-product of the service of this Department was the use of vernacular hymns set to African tunes which did no violence to the tonal languages in which they were sung. This was a contribution of no mean order in bringing the Christian religion nearer to the hearts of the common people.[1]

A trained and disciplined leadership, securely grounded in the faith, is a vital need for a religious community that is to survive through the centuries. Such a ministry brings young converts to maturity and helps to carry the fellowship as a whole through the oscillations of human experience and the constant changes of un-folding history. The growing extent and strength of African leadership within the Church, though still far short of what was needed, has nevertheless been a positive feature of the modern situation that also brings encouragement. The Roman Catholic Church has been far-sighted in this respect and has long encouraged Africans with a vocation to the secular priesthood to enter upon their seven-year course of training and accept the responsibility of leadership, as well as fostering those with a voca-tion to the religious orders. From small beginnings numbers have grown considerably in recent years. Thus in 1939 the number of African priests in the continent was reported as 388; by 1949 the number was 1,097 and in 1951 it had grown to 1,248.[2] It was in Central Africa, with the Belgian Trust Territory of Ruanda-Urundi as the highlight, that the most striking progress was recorded, so that as one report put it : " In the centre of the conti-nent, where conversions are numerous there is a corresponding flowering of mission institutes of all kinds and in looking at the figures for the clergy one might say that the centre of Africa is a desert in full bloom." [3] The Ruanda mission began in 1900; in 1920 the first five African priests were ordained; by 1925 there were twenty-five, and by 1950 one hundred Africans had been ordained to the priesthood of whom ninety-one survived to that

[1] This was not an altogether new development, but it was now pursued on an unprecedented scale. From 1890 Christian lyrics in Yoruba began to be produced, until S.P.C.K. was able to issue a collection of 57 with music as an Appendix to the Yoruba Hymn Book. Four specimen lyrics are given in: S. S. Farrow, *Faith, Fancies and Fetich* (1926), Appendix C.

[2] *International Fides Service* (Rome), May 6, 1950; S. Paventi, " Survey of the Church in Africa ", in *World Mission*, III (1952), 200. The number of major seminarians in the decade 1939–1949 had risen from 844 to 1,246.

[3] *Fides*, May 6, 1950.

date. The result was that in the jubilee year of the mission, of the forty mission posts in Ruanda nineteen were under the direction of African priests.[1] But African leadership has not been limited to the priesthood at parish level. The first vicariate to be wholly entrusted to the secular African clergy was that of Masaka in Uganda, with Bishop Kiwanuka, consecrated by Pope Pius XII in 1939, as the vicar apostolic. A second was added with the consecration of Bishop Rugambwa in 1952 to be the vicar apostolic of the territory of the Lower Kagera in Tanganyika. On June 9 in the same year Bishop Bigirumwami of Ruanda-Urundi was consecrated at Leopoldville in the Belgian Congo; and in 1955 Bishop Etoga was raised to the episcopate and appointed auxiliary to the vicar apostolic of Yaunde in Cameroons.[2]

The Anglican Church had long before taken the initiative in the consecration as bishop of Samuel Adjai Crowther in 1864.[3] The development of African leadership was everywhere encouraged, with African clergy in every field and as many as ten African bishops by 1952. And still the number grew. In 1955, on the occasion of the visit of the Archbishop of Canterbury to Central Africa to inaugurate the new Province, he also consecrated in Namirembe Cathedral, Uganda, four more Africans as assistant bishops—two for the diocese of Mombasa, and one each for the Sudan and Central Tanganyika.[4] The missions of the non-episcopal Churches pursued the same policy, Africans serving in growing numbers in the pastoral ministry and reaching positions of authority and oversight comparable to that of the episcopate. Thus, to take a limited group in a limited field, the British Free Church missions operating in British tropical Africa could claim in 1952 some 390 ordained Africans as against some ninety ordained European missionaries.[5]

It is interesting in this connexion to note the activity of the Coptic Church in appointing higher clergy to territories outside

---

[1] *Fides*, September 30, 1950. Of the 100 priests ordained in Ruanda 47 were born of Christian parents.

[2] *Fides*, June 10, 1950; Archbishop Mathew, Apostolic Delegate in Africa, " Catholic Missions in Africa ", in *The Times Review of the British Colonies* (Spring 1952); *Race Relations News*, XIV (1952), 95; *I.R.M.*, XLV (1956), 84.

[3] See Vol. II, p. 236.

[4] Bishop Stephen Neill, " Christianity in Africa: Steady Progress in the Work of Anglican Missions ", in *The Times Review of the British Colonies* (Autumn 1952); *I.R.M.*, XLV (1956), 51.

[5] " Christian Missions in British Tropical Africa: The Free Churches ", in *The Times Review of the British Colonies* (Spring 1953).

Egypt. In 1950 the Coptic bishops of Khartoum and Omdurman in the Sudan were elevated to the archiepiscopate, while a bishop of South Africa and Nigeria, Bishop Anba Morqos, was consecrated in St. Mark's Cathedral in Cairo.[1] In the following year the first Ethiopian, Archbishop Basilios, was enthroned in Cairo as *abuna* of the Ethiopian Church. This offered a significant opportunity for progressive reforms in line with the current policy of the Emperor.[2] These unmistakable tendencies in all confessions pointed to a steady growth·in African leadership with increasing release from direct European tutelage. The survey of the subject in relation to non-Roman missions, under the auspices of the International Missionary Council, held the promise of a policy that would direct and economize much disconnected local effort, to the upraising of a worthy African leadership in the Church of the future.[3]

It is a corollary of what has already been said that the Christian Church in Africa is now linked up with world Christianity more intimately than ever before. The Roman Catholic Church through the office of the Propaganda gathers its African missions under the ultimate direction of the Holy See, save where the hierarchy has been erected. For Protestants the International Missionary Council is the world organization that serves the Christian Councils of the territories as well as the national councils of the parent missionary societies; while the World Council of Churches, holding its first Assembly at Amsterdam in 1948 and its second at Evanston, Illinois, in 1954, has brought together in ecumenical conference the autonomous Churches of the non-Roman Catholic world.[4] African leaders in both ecclesiastical streams have begun to play their part at this level of international interchange. Thus, Bishop Kiwanuka, Vicar Apostolic of Masaka, in Uganda, on April 16, 1950, celebrated pontifical high mass in St. Patrick's Cathedral in New York, Cardinal Spellman of New York assisting at the throne of the mass and the President of the Republic of Chile doing so in the sanctuary. On the same visit Bishop Kiwanuka was introduced to a joint gathering of American Protestants and Roman Catholics, and spoke of the common interest

---

[1] *Ecumenical Press Service* (Geneva), September 22, 1950. The Coptic Orthodox Church claimed some 300,000 members in South Africa, descendants of emigrants from Egypt and Ethiopia.

[2] *I.R.M.*, XLI (1952), 33.

[3] *Vide supra*, pp. 301–4.

[4] W. Richey Hogg, *Ecumenical Foundations* (1952), 334, 342, 347–50; R. Rouse and S. C. Neill, *A History of the Ecumenical Movement* (1954), 697–731.

in education which both communions shared in Uganda.[1] Correspondingly, the Rev. C. G. Baëta of the Gold Coast not only served on the international team visiting Latin Africa for the survey of the training of the ministry, but also as a Vice-President of the International Missionary Council he has represented his people at the highest level of missionary consultation. In another direction and at a different level a link between India and East Africa appeared with the appointment by the United Church of North India of their own missionary to Kenya to work among Indians there. He arrived at Nairobi, his station, in 1955.[2]

A further aspect of the modern period may be noted. The Christian Church in Africa, in its various forms, is fast becoming in many respects a part of the world Christian community not only organizationally but also in respect of the pressure of common human problems of the modern age. In Africa, as in Asia and the West, the fundamental human needs are recognized as essentially the same, and even the very setting produced by industrial development, urbanization, and engrossment with the material side of life is increasingly held in common. This situation has made both feasible and valuable the interchange of Christian leaders between Africa and the West, yet another link in the ecumenical chain.[3] But valuable as these ecumenical contacts at a high ecclesiastical level may be they only have meaning in so far as an active Christian life and witness pulsate at the level of the local churches.

The matter of numbers cannot be overlooked, and yet requires to be handled with caution. The size of the Christian constituency has significance as an indication of the extent to which the Christian name at least has been adopted, by contrast to rival

[1] *International Fides Service*, April 29, 1950; *Ecumenical Press Service*, February 17, 1950.

[2] Communicated by Dr. C. E. Abraham of Serampore. For an earlier proposal, *vide supra*, p. 187. For earlier influences by Indian Christianity on the Church in Africa see N. C. Sargant, *The Dispersion of the Tamil Church* (1940), 56–68.

[3] It may perhaps be mentioned here that, thanks to the wisdom and foresight of the late Dr. Edward Cadbury, there was established in 1944 at Selly Oak the William Paton Lectureship to enable leaders of the younger churches to join the Central Faculty for a session with full equality of status, thus sharing in the preparation of missionaries in the sending country. Similar provision was made for women leaders in the founding of the Dorothy Cadbury Fellowship. Africans have several times held each of these appointments and have done so with distinction. There followed a similar foundation in the United States, the Henry Luce Visiting Professorship at Union Theological Seminary, New York, where Africans also held the appointment in their turn.

faiths. Comprehensive totals, because of the varying standards of enumeration that lie concealed, are far more dubious than numbers at confessional or territorial level where some homogeneity in calculation may be presumed. In particular, comparative figures by the same authority, showing rate of increase or decrease over a given period, are of value as indications, by one measuring rod, of the vitality of the Christian movement among the population. The Roman Catholic Church, according to figures made available in 1951, claimed a growth in numbers throughout the continent in the last half-century from 1,197,000 in 1900 to 14,095,000 in 1949, or an increase twelve times that at the dawn of the century. The comparative advance claimed in specific regions is of interest : in North Africa (Tunis to the Atlantic) from 670,000 to 2,230,000; in North-East Africa (Libya to Somaliland) from 107,000 to 452,000; in West Africa (Senegal to British Cameroons) from 51,000 to 1,506,000; in Central Africa (coast to coast north of the Zambesi) from 122,000 to 7,887,000; and in South Africa (south of the Zambesi) from 44,000 to 906,000. The increase in West Africa—twenty-nine times that of 1900—is startling, but the sixty-five times growth in fifty years in Central Africa is staggering. Indeed, in the Belgian Congo and Ruanda-Urundi alone twenty-four per cent of the population were claimed as Catholics.[1]

In two territories, where the Christian Councils had prepared statistics of the Protestant missions and where Roman Catholic figures were also available, the total Christian community could be seen as a percentage of the population. In Tanganyika the Christian Council in 1952 put the total number of non-Roman Christians at 462,000, the Roman Catholics claiming 750,000. The total of 1,212,000 Christians in a population of 7,499,000 was then sixteen per cent.[2] In the Belgian Congo the Conseil Protestant du Congo in 1953 worked out the Protestant population at some 1,600,000. With the 3,511,000 claimed as Roman Catholics the Christians of the Congo would then number some 5,111,000 in a population of 12,026,000 at the 1952 census with a further 4,071,000 (1953 census) in the Trust Territory of Ruanda-Urundi. The Christian portion of this total population of 16,097,000 under Belgian rule could therefore be computed as some thirty-one per cent.[3] The compilation of grand totals for the continent is much more speculative but has been attempted,

---

[1] *Agence International Fides.*—Supplément statistiques, 1951.
[2] *I.R.M.*, XLI (1952), 73; XLII (1953), 42.
[3] *I.R.M.*, XLIII (1954), 43; *Fides*, supp. statistiques, 1951.

x 2

though with the usual caution as to use of the figures.[1] The totals emerging from careful calculation territory by territory have been offered as follows: Roman Catholic community, 12,043,732; Protestant community, 8,806,786; Orthodox and Coptic communities, 4,602,986; Separatist Sects (South Africa), 1,089,479; yielding a grand total of 26,542,983.[2] This includes, of course, the considerable European populations of North and South Africa. It should further be remembered that, however approximately correct the figures may be at the time of computation, each succeeding generation has to be won afresh; unless the losses by death are replaced by recruits from the younger generation growing up within the fellowship, fresh accessions from outside cannot well be credited as an increase, a fact that may become painfully evident with the passage of time.[3] Indeed, it is also a regrettable fact that those who are easily won may be easily lost, a form of wastage of even greater concern. As one acute observer of West African affairs wrote of the Church as he had seen it: " In West Africa it seems easy to ' fall in ' and disastrously easy to ' fall out ' of the Christian company. If the adults, baptized in such large numbers for many years past, had stood fast, the community should be much larger than is generally reported to-day; there must be a heavy loss by backsliding." [4] Statistics then, as a form of comfort, must be used with circumspection.

The various circumstances we have enumerated would seem, as far as they alone are concerned, to afford some reasonably solid ground for confidence in the survival and the growth of the Christian Church in Africa from this modern planting. There are, however, considerations of a different order that must also be taken into account.

(2) Counterbalancing Considerations

Christianity in Africa has its rivals, of which the most powerful historically has been Islam. In its advance from the seventh century onwards it became deeply rooted in North-East and North

---

[1] Not only do they have to be compiled from various sources, but these sources are themselves usually .of different dates, thus rendering totals only approximately correct at the best.

[2] *Missionary Research Library, New York, Occasional Bulletin*, Vol. V, No. 14, December 30, 1954.

[3] It was alleged by those concerned with the prohibition movement in the United States that, when the cause seemed won in the early nineteen-twenties, temperance education ceased and the young were lost to the movement, which then suffered serious reverse.

[4] *The Growing Church*, Tambaram Madras Series, II (1939), 6.

Africa, with much of the Western, Central, and Eastern Sudan coming under its sway, as well as the littoral of East Africa from which there was penetration to the Great Lakes and beyond.[1]

The question of the continuing spread of Islam in Africa is one not easy to determine. Communities of travelling traders, such as the Hausa, might set up establishments beyond their home territory and gather a few pagan neighbours around, but whether these would remain Muslim when the traders departed is another matter. At the West Central Africa Regional Conference at Leopoldville in 1946 H. Endresen of the Norwegian mission posed the question : Does the danger of the Muslim advance in Africa still exist or is it eliminated by the Christian front we have established ? He replied : " We must confess that this front is still weak and the Moslem advance is far from being arrested." He found chiefs of pagan villages readily capitulating to Islam, and Hausa merchants effective in making converts. Hausa settlements were to be seen as far south as Elisabethville.[2] A trained observer, G. Parrinder of Ibadan in Nigeria, has reported his local investigations. He would estimate some 40,000 to 50,000, or a sixth of the total population, as attending the 190 mosques of the town for worship, though he would hazard that as many as half the inhabitants were occasional participants at the great festivals, " but the 80 per cent claimed by enthusiastic supporters is too much exaggerated ".[3] Nevertheless Islam, he reports, is on the advance. By contrast the 1950 census of Lagos, the capital of Nigeria, with a population of 230,000, gave the number of Christians as 122,000 or rather more than fifty per cent, most of the rest being Muslim. Christianity was said to be strongest among young people under twenty-five years of age; of those over forty-three years of age more than half were Muslims. The census report regarded the facts disclosed as confirming that Christianity had been gaining ground in Lagos and the neighbouring Western Provinces.[4]

Another aspect of Muslim advance has appeared in the Sudan —the one time Anglo-Egyptian condominium—with the introduction of self-government leading to the final achievement of independence. Before World War II the Muslim north and the pagan south had largely minded their own affairs, going their

---

[1] See Vol. I, chapters 5–6; Vol. II, pp. 62, 72–3, 75–8, 92–5, 213–14, 317–18; Vol. III, pp. 129–34, 161, 168, 170–2, 254–65.

[2] *Abundant Life in Changing Africa, Report of the West Central Africa Regional Conference, 1946* (1947), 122.

[3] G. Parrinder, *Religion in an African City* (1953), 84.

[4] *Ecumenical Press Service* (Geneva), January 12, 1951.

separate ways under the benevolent guidance of the central Government. The circumstances of the war years, however, drew the south out of its isolation. In missionary affairs there were also developments; in the Anglican Church of the south, for example, when European staff was reduced, there occurred an encouraging emergence of African leadership, apparently unsuspected hitherto. Steady growth in the post-war period brought the number of baptized members of the Anglican communion to 20,000 with another 20,000 under instruction, while 1,000 confirmations were taking place each year.[1] The characteristic emphasis in the mission had been on evangelization through education. Then in 1946 a Missionary Council for the south had been formed on the initiative of the Church Missionary Society (British), the United Presbyterian Mission (American), and the Sudan United Mission (International).[2] " The primary aim of Missions," it was reported in 1949, " is to build up a stable self-expanding Church which will be able to hold its own against Islamic penetration under changing political conditions." [3] In seven years the changed political conditions had come, with a Sudanese Government predominantly Muslim in control. The first move was pressure for the teaching of Arabic in the schools of the south, ostensibly to facilitate unity with the Arabic-speaking people of the north, but interpreted by Christian leaders as springing from a programme of Muslim penetration of the south.[4] The rapid expansion of a government school system in the south—a programme in which missions had been invited to co-operate in 1945—seemed destined, on the completion of the five-year plan, to place these schools in a dominating position in areas that had hitherto been virtually a mission preserve.[5]

Here was provided an instrument, innocently enough, through which a Sudanese Government of Muslim complexion might later assert its influence. Meanwhile the agreed constitution of the Sudan guaranteed freedom of conscience and the right of all freely to profess their religion. But all the same, pressure on the south was continued by such activities as a Muslim mission sent by the Council of the Al Azhar University in Cairo. The teaching of Islam was also made compulsory in all intermediate schools, and a required subject in the final government examinations.[6] Finally,

[1] J. S. Trimingham, *The Christian Church in Post-War Sudan* (1949), 20–1.
[2] *I.R.M.*, XXXVI (1947), 35.
[3] J. S. Trimingham, *op. cit.*, 21.
[4] *I.R.M.*, XXXIX (1950), 37.
[5] *I.R.M.*, XLII (1953), 33; J. S. Trimingham, *op. cit.*, 22.
[6] *I.R.M.*, XLIII (1954), 36–7.

some months after the declaration of independence, came the announcement on May 28, 1956, of the Government policy of unifying the education system which would entail the taking over of all mission schools by the Government. The reason advanced was the necessity of raising a generation in the south with full allegiance to the Sudanese State. Nevertheless the local Arabic press was reported to welcome the policy as a first step in eliminating Christian mission influence.[1]

An inquiry concerning the Guinea Coast and hinterland was undertaken in 1952 by J. S. Trimingham.[2] His investigations ranged from the Gambia to Nigeria and reached inland to such regions as Haute Volta in French West Africa and Sokoto in Northern Nigeria. His findings, outside such established Muslim areas as Hausaland, present a varied picture of stagnation and advance. In the Gambia and French Guinea, with a reported Muslim percentage of ninety in the one and sixty-five in the other, the unremitting pressure of Islam was regarded as now leaving little chance of establishing a Christian community among the indigenous tribes. In the central regions of the Guinea Coast—Ivory Coast, Gold Coast, and Dahomey—Islam was found to be a comparatively feeble streak in the religious pattern and to all intents and purposes a stagnant element, ranging from seventeen per cent for the Ivory Coast and fifteen per cent for Dahomey to a mere two per cent for the Gold Coast.[3] In two areas where the Church had long been established—Sierra Leone, and Yorubaland in south-west Nigeria—Islam was found to be advancing steadily in competition with Christianity. Indeed, in 1950 there was held the first annual Muslim Congress of Nigeria, which was also attended by delegates from beyond Nigeria.[4] While it is admitted that in the first instance adoption of Islam is superficial, with the retention of much pagan outlook and practice, yet it is affirmed that simple adherence usually proves permanent, with a steadily progressing incorporation into the new religious com-

[1] *The Times*, May 29, 1956.
[2] J. S. Trimingham, who had been a missionary of the C.M.S. in north-east Africa from 1937, spent one year on this West African survey at the instance of the C.M.S. and M.M.S. conjointly. His experience in Egypt and the Eastern Sudan and his study of Islam in those lands as well as in Abyssinia gave him unusual qualifications for the task. His report to the Societies in 1953 was the basis of his I.M.C. Research Pamphlet: *The Christian Church and Islam in West Africa* (1955).
[3] All percentages quoted are from census returns.—Trimingham, *op. cit.*, 54. Trimingham was inclined to five per cent. for the Gold Coast.
[4] G. Parrinder, *op. cit.*, 82–3.

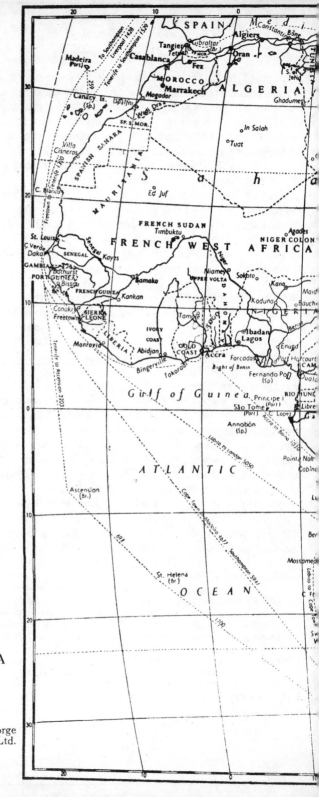

AFRICA
in
1954

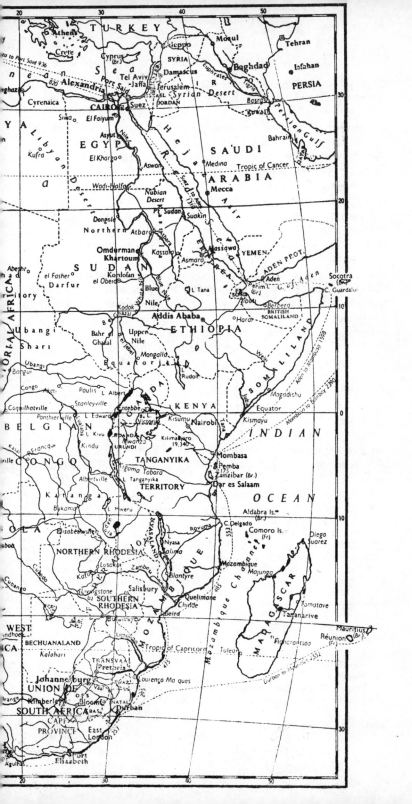

munity.[1] Adoption of Islam, even if it be a thin veneer, cannot therefore be viewed with complacence. This outpacing of Christianity in areas where it has been established for well over a century has thus posed urgent questions about the evident failure of the African Church to win its pagan neighbours.[2] It has been the concern of the Western missions and not that of the African churches for example, that has initiated and maintained an encouraging Christian penetration of the Mende, Temne, and other peoples of the Protectorate of Sierra Leone.[3]

Lyndon Harries, who has surveyed the situation in East Africa, estimates the number of Muslims there as two million or more.[4] Both Arab-Swahili and Indian communities were represented at a conference of East African Islamic Associations which met at Nairobi in 1953. Of the 200 delegates nearly half were African, though Indians for the most part held the platform. Indian solicitude for African welfare was judged to have a political rather than a religious motive.[5] The fact that Islam is not now identified with political power in East Africa is likely to make it a more formidable rival to Christianity: " There is always the possibility that the pendulum may swing once again towards Islam." [6]

The net result of these reports is not comforting to the Christian evangelist who thus finds himself in competition with an active and attractive rival in seeking the suffrages of pagan Africa. The Christian advance in east and west has hitherto been made among pagan peoples and little if any impression has been made on the Muslim communities, for work among whom specific preparation of a high order is indispensable.[7] The method of the crusade, transferred from arms to arguments, in the approach to the Muslim has been steadily abandoned in favour of an attempt at fuller mutual understanding in a spirit of Christian love. A generation

---

[1] Trimingham, *op. cit.*, 23.

[2] " Christianity has settled down within tribal or political boundaries within which its existence is confined. The political boundary limit may be seen in the Yoruba, divided between the western and northern regions. The Yoruba churches have shown no desire to evangelize among their fellows in the Ilorin region."—*Ibid.*, 29. Tribalism within the Church is also a peril to its unity. For experiences in West Africa and South, see *The Church under the Cross, Church of Scotland Report of the Foreign Mission Committee for 1955* (1956), 10–11.

[3] *Ibid.*, 29.

[4] L. P. Harries, *Islam in East Africa* (1954), 11 *n*.

[5] *Ibid.*, 15–16.

[6] *Ibid.*, 30–2.

[7] French Protestants attempted such work on the hard soil of North Africa during the Second World War.—*I.R.M.*, XXX (1941), 61.

ago Professor Lootfy Levonian showed the long accepted polemical method of presenting the Christian faith to be bankrupt and pleaded for an approach more consonant with the heart of the gospel [1]; while more recently such authorities as J. W. Sweetman and J. S. Trimingham have in the same spirit urged the method of the dialogue, with the fullest respect for the other's convictions, and carried on in understanding friendship, as the only way of meeting the Muslim when the Christian disciple seeks, from personal experience, to present the claims of his Master.[2] Meanwhile this somewhat grim background of a rival faith, already long-established in the continent, sternly resistant to any attempt at conversion, and itself still seeking the adherence of the African peoples on terms that can readily win assent, must not be allowed to slip out of the picture.

Communism as a competitor with Christianity in Africa has been regarded by some observers as a sinister intruder. Roman Catholic missionaries reported in the early post-war years the activities of the Rassemblement Démocratique Africain in French territories. In French Equatorial Africa a paper, *A. E. F. Nouvelle*, appeared in August 1948 with advanced and communistic tendencies, the organ of the R.D.A. It was said to have acquired a good circulation and to be calling for opposition to missionaries.[3] In French West Africa the Ivory Coast seems to have been the first objective for propaganda of the R.D.A., which for some time maintained an equivocal position, but at its conference at Abidjan welcomed delegates from the French Communist party, and proclaimed its aim " to establish a democratic and anti-colonial government ". A new party of socialist persuasion was soon found in rivalry, the Parti Progressiste, which contested the claims of the R.D.A.[4] While these reports are evidence of Communist propaganda they do not indicate the African response. Indeed, an estimate of African reaction must be based on something more than scattered episodes, or the fact that Africans coming to Europe have often found Communist party members waiting to welcome them while the not unfriendly ordinary citizen has often enough appeared indifferent. The strongest bid for African support was made by the Communist Party of South Africa. As early as 1928

[1] L. Levonian, *Moslem Mentality, A Discussion of the Presentation of Christianity to Moslems* (1928).

[2] J. S. Trimingham, *The Christian Approach to Islam in the Sudan* (1948); E. F. F. Bishop, " Desideranda Islamica et Christiana ", in *I.R.M.*, XLIV (1955), 161–9.

[3] *International Fides Service*, January 8, 1949.

[4] *Fides*, March 12, 1949.

it floated its own Bantu newspaper which, after bearing different names, became *Inkululeko* (Freedom), and by 1949 was stated to be "the most militant of all Bantu newspapers, putting forward the Stalinist case" and principally concerned "to fight for the abolition of all discriminatory legislation hampering the advance of all Non-European peoples, more particularly that of the Africans, to the status of full citizenship on an equal footing with the Europeans ".[1] The South African Communist party was the only political party in the Union which admitted non-Europeans on a basis of full equality with Europeans and consequently attracted a certain number of politically conscious Africans.[2] In 1950 the Government took action and passed the Suppression of Communism Act which authorized the winding up of the affairs of the party. To complete its purpose the Suppression of Communism Amendment Act was passed in the following year, by which the definition of a communist received a generous extension to cover any person who at any time "professed to be a communist; whether within or outside the Union, encouraged in any way the achievement of any of the objects of communism; or had at any time been a member or active supporter of any organization which in any way furthered any of the objects of communism ".[3]

There were in the Union many European critics, not of the professed object in view, but of the unhappy means, in violation of democratic principles, by which it was proposed to achieve it. The South African Institute of Race Relations declared its conviction that the Amendment Bill (as it then was) "destroys the very basis on which the established rights of the individual rest ".[4] Indeed, the more sinister interpretation came to be that under cover of the legislation the Government could deal more effectively with any opposition to its racial policies.[5] But it was held by Africans that the Government had greatly magnified the Communist bogey : "Communism is not the important factor in South Africa which the government makes it out to be. The African is concerned

[1] E. Hellmann (ed.), *Handbook of Race Relations in South Africa* (1949), 486, 492. The paper was issued twice monthly in English, Xhosa, Zulu, Tswana, and Sotho.
[2] *Ibid.*, 533.
[3] *A Survey of Race Relations in South Africa, 1950–1951*, The Twenty-second Annual Report of the South African Institute of Race Relations (1951), 9–10.
[4] *Ibid.*, 10–11.
[5] The arrests for alleged high treason at a later date were seen as confirming this.—*The Times*, December 6 and 7, 1956; *The South African Outlook*, LXXXVII (1957), 1, 17–18.

with achieving emancipation. He regards communism only as a complicating factor in the life and death struggle he is waging against the tyranny of race."[1] South Africa was certainly the tenderest spot for communist exploitation of African grievances. Elsewhere its appeal was usually judged unimportant. This was confirmed by African speakers in the discussion on Communism in Africa at the North American Assembly on African Affairs in 1952.[2] A fundamental feature sometimes overlooked is that the African already enjoys a communal society, unless pulled out into the individualist society of the West, and normally is not at such a bare subsistence level as continually to risk becoming submerged. An imported Communism therefore scarcely makes the same appeal as to certain Asian peoples. But meanwhile it is a good stick to beat the white man with when he is particularly overbearing.

A disconcerting aspect of the modern situation is the preference occasionally expressed by the educated for their ancestral faith. This rejection of Christianity in favour of the traditional belief in a Supreme Being, benevolent but remote, between whom and the living the departed ancestors are mediators, raises a serious issue, for it is on the alleged merits of the two that the choice is made. This may appear strange to those unfamiliar with the warm human quality to be found in the relationship of the living to the departed elders—a relationship that seems to be more correctly described as reverence for ancestors than as ancestor-worship. They have moved up in status but are still regarded as within the one community of the living and the dead; and moreover they are not deified, but rank as mediators with the Supreme Being upon whom they too are dependent.[3] As illustrating the relationship

[1] J. K. Ngubane, " The Hardening Temper of the African ", in *Race Relations Journal*, XXIII (1956), Nos. 2 and 3 (October), 20.

[2] *Africa is Here, Report of the North America Assembly on African Affairs*, Springfield, Ohio, 1952 (1953), 135–7.

[3] C. P. Groves, *Jesus Christ and Primitive Need* (1934), 159–60; E. W. Smith (ed.), *African Ideas of God, A Symposium* (1950), 39, 60, 137, 164, 243–4. As one Christian African student of his people has expressed it: " If the West African believes in the protecting influence of ancestral spirits, near and yet roving, with whom he must maintain harmonious relations; and if his conscience is subject to the approval of the all-inclusive community of the dead and the living, then to understand the place of ancestors in the religious life of West Africa one must associate the living with the dead in one continuous life, indeed in one social group who are subject to the guiding and protecting influence of a *paterfamilias* of long ago. One section of a single society does not worship another; it shows reverence. West Africans show reverence to elders, departed and alive ".—F. L. Bartels in *I.R.M.*, XL (1951), 116–17.

between the living and the ancestors the verdict of a pioneer missionary in Central Africa may serve : " From one point of view we may define their attitude by the word *shoma* (=trust). The meaning of the word is clear. On the first occasion we heard it we were standing on the top rung of a rickety ladder, papering a room in our house, and were just reaching up to place the paper in position when we heard a boy below saying, ' If I were the master I would not *shoma* this ladder, he will fall and break his neck.' The word means to put reliance upon, have confidence in, to trust." [1] That the attitude may at the same time be modified by a certain fear of the elders, as it was in life, is not to be wondered at, for their characters have not changed, but they still have the welfare of their descendants at heart. That they have become intermediaries with the Supreme Being is a widespread element of African belief.[2] An educated African trained in mission institutions, a man of about forty-five years of age who had risen to an outstanding position in government service in Nyasaland, adhered once more to the ancestral faith, and wrote of it : " Just as others do, we Bantu people believe in a Supreme Being whom we recognize as the Creator of all things. Our regard for the spirits of our ancestors does not make them gods; they are merely media between us and the God-spirit, and they can exercise that authority which was given them during this earthly life towards relatives who are still alive, and under Him they can punish as do our Resident or Governor under King George. The punishment comes from the God-spirit but to reach us it can only pass through and be known to the ancestral spirit. . . . As in social organizations, messages from the Supreme Being come through ancestral spirits to the living." At the time of the dire influenza epidemic of 1919 [3] his father besought the ancestral spirits for protection, and the writer concludes : " In the mind of my father, which I share, it showed great faith and his appeal was effective." Although influenza had already broken out in the village and the father been attacked, there was no death from the disease.[4]

[1] Dr. E. W. Smith, in Smith and Dale, *The Ila-speaking Peoples of Northern Rhodesia* (1920), II, 167.
[2] See Vol. I, 26; E. W. Smith (ed.), *African Ideas of God*, 26, 60, 67, 100–1, 137, 141–2, 152, 281–2.
[3] *Vide supra*, p. 72.
[4] " The Religion of My Fathers ", in *I.R.M.*, XIX (1930), 362–76. T. Cullen Young wrote in an introductory note: " Unless Jesus is ' lived ' before those whose own faith stands upon laws of action and reaction between mankind and the spirit-world which are visibly acted upon by their fathers, the Christian mission may be crowned with success only in

A Gold Coast student of the religious beliefs of his people, highly trained in philosophical and legal studies, has likewise found deep satisfaction in his African religious inheritance. " Even though the African ", he writes, " had not Moses and the prophets, he was able to discover for himself all the God that there was or could be." And in reference to the moral ideal he declares : " The Akan says, ' Better death than disgrace ', and a higher moral ideal than this in any epoch or people it will be hard to find." He believes that : " The surest way to goodness, and to God is education." True, he interprets the religious conceptions of his people somewhat liberally, presumably under the influence of his western philosophical studies, but his desire to present these conceptions as worthy and satisfying evidently springs from his own contentment with them.[1]

Such defences of the traditional view of God and the world, where they occur, raise a serious issue for Christian evangelists as to the effectiveness of their presentation of the Christian faith and the adequacy of their hearers' apparent response to it. It may well be that in these instances the approach was on too exclusively intellectual a plane, leaving the deep springs of emotion untouched —springs which leapt to life, nevertheless, at " the call of the blood " through family association and clan loyalty.[2] Attention has also been called to the " two-level mind " which western education has often enough produced in the African student, " one aspect of his life orientated towards western civilization and culture, the other still rooted in what remains of the traditional life ".[3] For some the state of tension is then resolved by rejecting

externals ". One is reminded of the Gnostic heresies in this respect of ancestor function, with their characteristic belief in the interposition of a hierarchy of spiritual powers between man and the Supreme.

[1] J. B. Danquah, *The Akan Doctrine of God* (1944), 17, 94, 125.

[2] Dr. D. J. Fleming has called attention to the western missionary's inclination to expect reason to perform more than it can in a religious situation heavily charged with emotion.—D. J. Fleming, "Limitations of an Intellectual Approach in Missions", in *Missionary Research Library Occasional Bulletin*, VIII, No. 1 (New York, 1957). Thus, missionary experience shows that the story of the Cross is unmatched by any other appeal in reaching the human heart. Cf. Luke, *Pioneering in Mary Slessor's Country* (1929), 76 ; Crantz, *History of Greenland* (2nd ed., 1820), II, 43–4, quoted in Raoul Allier, *La Psychologie de la Conversion chez les Peuples Non-civilisés* (1925), I, 43 ; Burckhardt et Grundemann, *Les Missions évangéliques, Amérique*, 179–80, quoted in Allier, *op. cit.*, I, 47.

[3] *I.R.M.*, XLI (1952), 370. A similar zoning of ideas, in this instance as associated with language, may appear among African ministers whose theological training has been (e.g.) in English: the mother tongue is the natural language of devotion, but English (or other European language)

the new religion, which has never been really appropriated, as not having meaning for their life, while the educational equipment still seems to serve them well.

An insidious enemy, second to no other rival of the Christian faith in Africa, is the prevailing secularist temper of the West. African students, the leaders-to-be, studying at schools and universities in America and Europe, where the cult of scientific humanism gains prestige from the intellectual eminence of many who profess it, readily fall under its influence. The educated man, they may think they discover, has no need for religion. It is not an accident that political leaders of ability in territories receiving responsible government or with independence recently achieved, are by no means necessarily Christian because first trained in mission schools. And on a lower level than that of intellectual self-sufficiency the material values of the West have all too often made money the new god of the people, while white men who preach by their lives civilization without religion also make their own disciples. The Church thus faces a new problem among the products of its schools. The meeting of the International Missionary Council at Whitby, Ontario, in July 1947 had this question before it. In the Congo the *évolué* was said either to turn his back completely on the African past, or to seek a synthesis between it and the civilization of the West, but either way he had his problems.[1] In the Gold Coast it was reported to be a general experience that illiterate members showed a deeper loyalty to the Church than their more privileged literate brethren.[2] A voice from the heart of Africa has declared the secular way of life to be a growing challenge to the Church : " The time of the Church's advantage is rapidly passing. There are clear signs all over the continent that secularization, with the breakdown of tribal life, the emphasis on materialism, the mad search for pleasure, is going forward much more rapidly than the christianization of the people." [3] The warning sounded at the Jerusalem Meeting of 1928 on the advance of secularism was never more relevant than to-day.[4] Materialism has been rated as the ultimate enemy of mankind. An authority in his field of the study

proves easiest for the sermon. For the implications for theological training, see S. C. Neill, *Survey of the Training of the Ministry in Africa*, Part I (1950), 21–3.

[1] *I.R.M.*, XXXVII (1948), 19.

[2] *I.R.M.*, XLI (1952), 370.

[3] Bishop Newell S. Booth of the American Methodist Church, in *I.R.M.*, XXXVII (1948), 95.

[4] *The Christian Message*, Jerusalem Meeting Report, I (1928), 284–338, 373–5, 402–14.

of religion, in a forecast of the situation in A.D. 3000, stated at the end of his argument : " I suggest that by A.D. 3000 there will still remain a doughty opponent of Christianity, to which I give the name of Materialism. If you like to define the word ' religion ' somewhat broadly, you may call Christianity and Materialism the two religions which will remain significant in A.D. 3000." [1] And in the mid-twentieth century the doughty opponent was already making a bid for Africa's soul.

A serious entry on the *per contra* side of the total account is that of race relations, with the situation in South Africa more particularly in view. The actions of the Nationalist Government in the post-war years in marshalling its powers to carry through the declared policy of *apartheid,* even to the point of modifying constitutional and legal procedures to enable the entrenched clauses in the Union Act, safeguarding African franchise rights, to be rescinded, deeply wounded the African population in the loss of a much-prized (even if limited) political status. The official policy stood in African eyes for the entrenchment of white privilege and civilization at any cost, even of human brotherhood as involving some self-denial to provide equality of opportunity for another. This was underlined once more by the Government's rejection of a number of the main, admittedly costly, proposals of the Tomlinson Commission for the effective development of the Bantu areas with the consequent implications for the future of South Africa.[2] The Tomlinson Report itself was anything but acceptable to the Bantu, based as it was upon the *apartheid* conception of two communities. They considered the Report in October 1956 in a three-day national conference at Bloemfontein which the Interdenominational African Ministers' Federation had taken the initiative in calling. After a careful examination of its principles and policies they recorded their " total rejection of the report as a comprehensive plan for the implementation of apartheid in South Africa ", stating in some detail the grounds of their fundamental objection to the whole policy on which the Report was based.[3]

Under such repeated hammer-blows the African temper was

[1] L. E. Browne, " The Religion of the World in A.D. 3000 ", in *I.R.M.,* XXXVIII (1949), 463–8.

[2] *Summary of the Report of the Commission for the Socio-Economic Development of the Bantu Areas within the Union of South Africa* (U.G. 61/.1955), 194–211. The Commission submitted its Report in October, 1954. It was too lengthy for complete publication, but a Summary was not available until April, 1956. The unacceptability of a number of the main recommendations was suggested as the reason for the Government's delay in publication.

[3] *Africa South,* I, No. 2 (January 1957), 22–6.

steadily hardening and the situation of racial tension had consequently become so much the more dangerous. As one African
spokesman saw the position : " A lot depends on what White
South Africa does. If wise counsels prevail and generous political
and economic concessions are made in time, the concept of partnership still has a very powerful attraction for the bulk of the
African people. But if apartheid continues to have its way one or
both of two courses will be open to the African : either to accept
the concept of a common destiny for the man of colour in the
world and see salvation for himself in identifying himself with the
peoples of Asia, or to embrace African irredentism and work for
the ideal of ' Africa for the Africans '. Either ideology will be a
rejection of the partnership concept and will lead to the ultimate
expulsion of the White man from this part of the world, for it must
be understood that there is not enough room for the African and
the apartheider in Africa." [1]

Such a situation in race relations could not exist without a
Christian Church at all worthy of the name feeling deeply involved. And in South Africa the Churches have been alert to the
issues for the country and for themselves, and have not remained
silent. Thus the Bishops of the Church of the Province of South
Africa on October 16, 1953, issued an important statement,
making clear their attitude to racial discrimination in the Union,
in which they declared : " We believe that the only national policy
which is morally defensible must be that which gives the fullest
opportunity of development to the members of all racial groups,"
and after indicating some of its implications, stated its simple
Christian basis : " What we have said arises out of the Christian
doctrine of man, as made known to us through the teaching and
practice of our Lord." [2] An acute embarrassment for the Christian
cause was the general support of the Dutch Reformed Churches
on Biblical and theological grounds for the policy of *apartheid*,
though indeed a more thorough-going form of it than the
Nationalist Government under Dr. Malan had been prepared to
contemplate. The attitude was sincerely taken and maintained
with that stability which is a feature of the Afrikaner character.

The gravity of the whole question led the Federal Mission Council of the Dutch Reformed Churches to take the initiative in calling
an interchurch conference which met at Pretoria in November
1953, to be followed in December 1954 by an inter-racial confer-

[1] J. K. Ngubane, in *Race Relations Journal*, XXIII (1956), Nos. 2 and 3
(October), 19-20.
[2] *The Times*, October 27, 1953.

ence of church leaders at Johannesburg.[1] Of the 160 delegates, who included representatives from the World Council of Churches and the International Missionary Council, some sixty were Africans. The official subject provided scope for frank discussion on current issues from the Christian angle : " The extension of the Kingdom of God in multi-racial South Africa." A three-day conference could scarcely be expected to produce results of a dramatic order on such a searching theme, but its inter-racial membership, holding serious divergences of view, did meet on the basis of the Christian faith to discuss them, and decided to continue to do so through an effective instrument of co-operation which it set up.[2]

These conferences disclosed a difference of opinion within the Dutch Reformed Churches themselves, Professor B. B. Keet, of Stellenbosch, a senior theologian, being a notable spokesman for a re-examination of the alleged scriptural basis for the Church's attitude on race relations. His book, *Suid-Afrika—Waarheen ?* published in 1956, courageously challenged the prevailing view, criticized the way in which scriptural evidence was handled, asserted that total *apartheid* (as advocated by SABRA[3]) was a mere dream-solution, and made the forthright declaration : " The Gospel does not separate us in any respect from our neighbours, but binds us together in every field of life. *Apartheid* in all its forms is a flight from our Christian vocation, which obliges us not only to live with our equals in sentiment and development, but also and particularly to stand up for the under-privileged, to bear their burdens and to help them to achieve a standard of living worthy of human beings." [4] Also in 1956 there was published the

---

[1] *I.R.M.*, XLIII (1954), 49; XLIV (1955), 54–5. The Pretoria Conference had been preceded in December 1952 by a conference with Bantu church leaders under D.R.C. auspices. At the Pretoria Conference the Lutherans concluded that they were called to serve as a liaison group between the Dutch Reformed and the other European Churches.

[2] N. Goodall, "The Inter-racial Conference of Church Leaders, Witwatersrand, December 1954 ", in *I.R.M.*, XLIV (1955), 193–7; *The South African Outlook*, LXXXV (1955), 21 (for resolutions of the Conference); *ibid.*, 22–5, 39–41, 72–3 (for some of the papers presented).

[3] *Vide supra*, p. 228 *n.*

[4] *The South African Outlook*, LXXXVI (1956), 36–7. Comments from the official standpoint were offered by Dr. G. B. A. Gerdener, chairman of SABRA.—*Ibid.*, 52–5; cf. *The Church Under the Cross, Report of the Foreign Mission Committee of the Church of Scotland for 1955* (1956), 14–15. Exchanges followed between the editor of *Die Kerkbode*, the official organ of the D.R.C. Churches, and Professor Keet. For a summary of these, see *The South African Outlook*, LXXXVI (1956), 145–6, 174.

Professor Keet's book also appeared in an English translation by Mrs. Leo Marquard, *Whither South Africa?* (1956).

Y 2

Report of a Commission on Race Relations, appointed by the Federal Council of Dutch Reformed Churches in South Africa in June 1955. It was a notable document, offering a historic outline from 1652 of the relation of the races in the Church, a critical review of the founding of separate Churches, and stating the doctrinal approach ·with a declaration of policy and principles.[1] The fact that Professor B. B. Keet was among the twenty-two signatories to a unanimous report indicates that he felt it allowed for his contention as to scriptural teaching, as in its statement : " A spirit of superiority dare not arise which seeks to get rid of the less privileged fellow-believers in Christ on the grounds of race and colour by establishing and furthering such independent Churches. . . . We regret to observe that some among us are inclined this way. As a Church we disapprove of it as a total contradiction of the unity in Christ. . . . It is our outspoken conviction that by virtue of this deeper unity in Christ all believers—irrespective of race or colour—are called to acknowledge, respect and love one another as ' fellow-citizens with the saints and of the household of God' (Eph. 2 : 19)." While they deplored certain racial conditions in South Africa they added : " We yet feel equally strongly that the enforced practice of our unity in Christ will not improve matters ", though for progress in the practical expression of it they must seek guidance from the Word of God.[2] The fact that adherents of the Dutch Reformed Churches together constitute 53·8 per cent of the total European population of the Union [3] indicates the great significance to be attached to an official declaration such as this, which becomes the basis for the education of its constituency.

Such processes, however, are slow, and whatever gratitude there may be for the promise of a closer understanding between the Christian Churches on this racial issue, it cannot be overlooked that the situation does not remain static for the reformers to overtake it at their leisure. Time presses, with contemporary developments elsewhere in Africa and the revolutionary changes among Asian peoples stimulating into perilous hostility the deep South African discontents. The successes of the Church in an earlier day among the uneducated are not to be repeated in a new more sophisticated generation, while the African intellectual sees the Christian teaching of the Churches in the context of current race

[1] *The South African Outlook*, LXXXVI (1956), 136–9, 150–2, 171–3.
[2] *Ibid.*, 172, 173.
[3] *Summary of the Report* (Tomlinson Commission on the Bantu Areas), (1955), 21.

relations which denies it. And which denies it within the Churches as well as outside them, for their practice at parish level in the Union has by no means lived up to the public pronouncements of their leaders, despite notable and worthy exceptions.[1] The Church with the cleanest record in relation to the colour bar within it is the Roman Catholic, and this has been attributed to the authoritarian rule of its clergy : " Its laity having no control in Church affairs, the hierarchy has been able to disregard ordinary South African lay prejudices, and insist on unity and community within the Church." [2] The other Churches "face the difficulty that authority is circumscribed by the primacy of the individual Christian conscience ".[3] True, there were not lacking particular instances of Christian fellowship across the colour line, the community established at Wilgespruit, a site of seventy-two acres in the Transvaal near Johannesburg, being especially notable. This Christian Fellowship Centre—inter-denominational and inter-racial— entered upon its beneficent activity under a resident warden in April 1955.[4] Excellent as such enterprises were, the mass of white South Africans remained nevertheless unresponsive to the desperate need for a radical change of heart—a change of heart which would allow that perfect love that casts out fear to rule its life and determine its treatment of its neighbour. Meanwhile the dwindling hope of African intellectuals in a fair deal from the white man had almost reached vanishing-point. As one of their spokesmen has put it : " I believe that to most intellectuals white leadership or Christian trusteeship has become a chimera. We regard it as dishonest because it seems to us that it has become the very expression of the dishonesty of the West. The Church in South Africa has been on the retreat for many years. . . . We have become disillusioned in missionary teaching, because while we were being evangelized and taught to tolerate our oppressors, very little if any similar evangelizing was being done among the whites. Missionary teaching may have been good for its own sake, but it has become inadequate in a South African context because, as it seems to many of us, it adopts an outworn, orthodox, and even

[1] See a forthright and factual article: C. W. M. Gell, " Colour and the South African Church ", in *Africa South*, I, No. 2 (January 1957), 64–76.

[2] *Ibid.*, 70. Despite this clear stand on the colour bar within its borders, the Roman Catholic Church is reported to have been limited in the lead it has given on relevant public issues when these have not concerned its own ecclesiastical interests.—*Ibid.*, 71–2.

[3] *Ibid.*, 71.

[4] *The South African Outlook*, LXXXVI (1956), 153–5.

reactionary approach to intricate political problems. The African intellectual ... wants justice : a universal justice." [1]

There is little need to underline a forecast from an authoritative source : " The church's bitterest struggle of the future will be waged on the plane of race relations." [2]

Such are some of the conditions favourable to the deeper rooting of Christianity in Africa, and some of the counterbalancing considerations that make that conclusion somewhat uncertain at the least. Nevertheless, that Christianity in some form will now widely survive, there can be little doubt. Elements in its environment which appear inimical to the growth of the Church and as restricting its opportunities are not the ultimate peril. A hostile environment is no new experience for the Church in the course of its stormy history and has not been responsible for periods of decline so much as a failing life within. Granting therefore the reasonable expectation of survival, the question remains: What kind of a Christianity will survive ?

(3) *The Decisive Factor*

In the last resort Christian survival, not in name only but in deed and in truth, is not so much a matter of organization or intellectual equipment, valuable as these are in their place, as of personal loyalty to the living Lord expressed in a life consistent with the faith. And such lives are the self-authenticating witness that wins the world to Christ. Edwyn Bevan has written words on the Church in general that directly apply to the Church in Africa to-day : " If the Christian Church is going to further its cause in the days to come, it will be by exhibiting a certain type of life realized in practice. An essential part of its case rests . . . upon judgments of value, where only individual perception, and not argument or scientific demonstration, can decide. The utmost that we can do to prove the value of a work of art to any other man is to call his attention to it. And if the Christian Church wants to convince the world of the supreme value of its ideal of love, it can only do so by steadily confronting the world with the actual thing. The real attraction to a society consists in what we call its special atmosphere. Supposing that the love which shines in certain individual lives became general in the Christian Society

[1] E. Mphahlele, " The African Intellectual ", in *The Listener*, August 23, 1956.
[2] E. Hellmann (ed.), *Handbook on Race Relations in South Africa*, (1949), 571.

—a quickening of emotion and will which could be called love, not in any pale metaphorical sense, but in literal truth, a force shaping all conduct and social organization, heightening all life with an inexhaustible interest and energy—there would perhaps not be much need for books of Christian evidences." [1]

It may be urged that we must remember to be patient with a young church that has by no means attained maturity; that we must not expect too much too soon. Granted, there must be great patience with spiritual growth not less than with any other. The pioneers were well aware of it. John Mackenzie relates a conversation he had with an English trader one Sunday morning as he was standing at the church door after service :

" I'm afraid this is slow work, Mr. Mackenzie."

" Well, in one sense you are quite right. The history of our own native land leads us to expect that."

" Well, sir, you are very sanguine."

" God is merciful, and the ages are long." [2]

If, however, the pagan observes Christians still behaving as they did before taking the name, he will naturally conclude that Christianity makes little contribution to the security and joy of human life. A recent study of the Mende in Sierra Leone disclosed such a situation : " Most chiefs who are professing Christians also have an ancestral shrine in their compounds. . . . A number of other individuals who are nominally Christians continue the ancestral practices at the same time. . . . Many of them turn instead to magic. They rely quite often on special talismans. Others are regular clients of medicine men whose help they seek in love affairs and to further personal careers." [3] It is equally disconcerting to find an African sociologist, with intimate knowledge of the people of whom he writes, able to assert : " It is a commonplace to describe Christianity in Ashanti and the Gold Coast generally as a thin veneer. The description is not inaccurate or superficial if it means that the people have not taken over the concept of the universe and of the nature of man within which Christianity finds its fullest meaning. . . . To most Ashanti people the world is ruled from afar by a Supreme Being . . . nearest of all are the ancestors of whom he is reminded daily by speech and action." [4] That there has often been a survival of the pre-Christian background among churches

---

[1] Edwyn Bevan, *Hellenism and Christianity* (1921), 273–4.
[2] J. Mackenzie, *Ten Years North of the Orange River* (1871), 82–3.
[3] K. Little, " The Mende in Sierra Leone ", in *African Worlds: Studies in the Cosmological Ideas and Social Values of African Peoples* (1954), 136 and n.
[4] K. A. Busia, " The Ashanti of the Gold Coast", in *African Worlds*, 208.

around the world cannot, unhappily, be denied. But we are not now concerned as to whether the Church in Africa is better or worse than other growing churches have been, but whether its own inner life and loyalty are such as to enable it to withstand the unremitting pressures of an unfriendly world in the evil day, and having done all, to stand. Three aspects of its life that cause concern may be considered in relation to its high vocation, which affect practice in social life, the surviving view of God and the world, and the slippery slope of separatism when it offers a bridge back to the twilight of pagan ritual and belief.

In respect of social life there is the inherited practice of polygamy in the form of polygyny, which has been aptly defined as a series of families with the husband as the common factor.[1] Though the practice could never be universal, partly through natural limitation imposed by the existing balance of the sexes and partly through the economic limitation of the necessity of bride-price, yet it has been a socially desirable objective in African society, conferring prestige and encouraging the prospect of offspring, this latter a dominating desire through belief in the interdependence of ancestors and descendants.[2] But there have been severely practical considerations as well. With the woman as traditionally the food-preparer, the chief found himself almost inevitably a polygamist in discharging his duty of hospitality. Again, such prac-

[1] W. H. R. Rivers, *Social Organization* (1924), 12.
Cf. B. Malinowski, Art. " Marriage ", in *Ency. Brit.* (14th ed.), par. 28. The superior status normally accorded the first wife appears to suggest that she is the one wife while successive partners are more strictly concubines. The first wife's privileged position is also reflected in the standing of her children. Emil Torday has offered representative evidence on the subject for the Bantu, in *Africa*, II (1929), 263–9. Thus, among the Chagga, the first wife's consent was required for all subsequent unions; among the Basuto a man was only counted a widower when he had lost his first wife; and so forth.—*Loc. cit.*
[2] The strength of this desire as influencing outlook on life may be illustrated by the case of the Nigerian preacher who argued from the practice of Abraham, as a good man of faith, that if a first marriage proved childless over a period of years, then and only then might a Christian be allowed a second wife for the sake of offspring.—Personally communicated. For evidence from the Belgian Congo of Christians reverting to polygamy when monogamous marriage had not proved fertile, see: *CEPSI, (Centre d'étude des problèmes sociaux indigènes*, Elisabethville), Numéro 13 (1950), 71. Cf. the remark of a Myao of Nyasaland : " If the rule were one wife only, I might die without a child! "—M. Perham (ed.), *Ten Africans* (1936), 156–7.

tices as levirate marriage [1] and late weaning were also responsible for a multiplicity of wives.

A custom so firmly set in the social fabric is not easily surrendered and the Christian Church has found this its greatest obstacle in the social sphere. Donald Fraser of Nyasaland once reported : " One day an evangelist sat by the kraal gate and talked with a group of men. He told them of the way of the Gospel. And when he had finished, one old man said, ' Ah, if God would only say to us men, " Keep your plurality of wives and drink your beer ", there's not a man of us but would follow Him '." [2] This question became so insistent in the West African fields of the Church Missionary Society that in 1856 Henry Venn, at the instance of the Committee, drew up a comprehensive minute upon the whole subject, including the specific question of the baptism of polygamists, in which he set forth the Society's views.[3] A contemporary statement from the Scottish Presbyterian side came from the Calabar mission.[4] In 1888 the Conference of Anglican bishops at Lambeth made its pronouncement that polygamy was inconsistent with the law of Christ respecting marriage and that the usage of the early Church offered no precedent for its recognition. Baptism of polygamists was therefore to be withheld, though they might remain under instruction in the catechumenate " until such time as they shall be in a position to accept the law of Christ ". Meanwhile the baptism of the wives of a polygamist was permissive " in some cases ". This position was reaffirmed by the Lambeth Conference of 1908.[5] Nevertheless the reluctance of African Christians to abandon the practice continued, the argument being that monogamy was a European tradition rather than a Christian requirement. Thus in 1912 Christians in Yorubaland, Nigeria, argued for the recognition of polygamy in the African Church, and in 1916 the Christians of Kavirondo in East Africa followed suit.[6] The International Conference on Africa at Le Zoute in

[1] Cf. Deuteronomy 25: 5–6.
[2] Donald Fraser, *The New Africa* (1927), 88.
[3] *Proceedings of the C.M.S.* (1857), 48–9. The Minute was published as an Appendix to the Report.—*Ibid.*, 207–12. The subject was frequently appearing in Reports; cf. *Proceedings* (1878), 23, 25; (1882), 18; (1888), 25, 37–8; (1897), 89.
[4] This was a personal statement by H. M. Waddell, the founder of the mission.—H. M. Waddell, *Twenty-Nine Years in the West Indies and Central Africa, 1829–1858* (1863), 486–92, 667–72.
[5] *The Church in the Mission Field*, World Missionary Conference, 1910, II, 321–3. The Lambeth Conference of 1920 (Resolution 67) again affirmed monogamy as the only Christian form of marriage.
[6] *Proceedings of the C.M.S.* (1912), 36; (1916), 65.

345

1926 once more affirmed the Christian ideal : " This Conference is convinced that Christian society must be built on Christian family life and that the ideal of the Christian family life can only be realized in monogamy." [1] But Africans still remained largely unconvinced. In 1938 at the Conference of the International Missionary Council at Tambaram this question was a major concern of the African Section. At the instance of Gold Coast churches a statement was issued which opened with a recognition of the precarious position of many on this issue : " In most parts of Africa polygamy has been the custom, and insistence on monogamy is one of the great bars preventing the entrance of men into the Christian Church. Even within the Church there is grave danger of serious hypocrisy in that men professedly monogamists are secretly carrying on illicit connections. In some areas men brought up in a Christian atmosphere are reverting to polygamy and other social customs, and declare that these bring to them no sense of guilt, no pricking of conscience. The question is raised as to whether monogamy is essential to Christianity or is merely a factor in European civilization—whether in the practice of polygamy there is something radically incompatible with a vital faith in Christ, and living of a true life in fellowship with Him." [2]

The plea for a more adequate recognition of the African social heritage has never gone so far as to include an unqualified recognition of the practice. That eminent missionary and *doyen* among early students of African society, Henri A. Junod, was able to assert : " All missionaries who have lived amongst the Bantus and know something of Native life, agree on one point. Polygamy is incompatible with the high moral ideal and the ideal of the family life which Christianity brought into the world." [3] The point on which some compromise has been sought, though here by a minority only, has been the baptism of polygamists who had entered upon their obligations before being apprised of the Christian standard. Bishop Colenso, for example, held the view that their baptism on confession of faith should be unconditional. [4] The Moravian attitude, as expressed in 1879 and again in 1926,

[1] E. W. Smith, *The Christian Mission in Africa* (1926), 51.
[2] *The Life of the Church*, Tambaram Madras Series, IV (1939), 405. The statement, which was for circulation to Christian Councils in Africa, proceeded to indicate the implications for the Christian Church of monogamous marriage.—*Ibid.*, 405–7. Cf. *I.R.M.*, XLIV (1955), 299. More than three-quarters of the Africa section's report at Tambaram was devoted to this one question.
[3] H. A. Junod, *The Life of a South African Tribe* (2nd ed., 1927), I, 532.
[4] See Vol. II, p. 262.

was that in exceptional cases polygamists might be admitted to baptism.[1] And some others have held the same position.[2] Indeed, H. A. Junod distinguished four points of view on this question.[3] But with the progress of time such cases inevitably dwindle to vanishing point, and the problem has rather become that of the polygamist who is content to remain in the catechumenate while his wives are accepted for Christian baptism as being themselves bound to one partner only. The resulting excess of women members in the church, now apparent for some decades, has raised the issue of the acceptability of even this concession.[4]

The Christian demand for monogamous marriage is no arbitrary fiat of ecclesiastical courts but is rooted in the Divine purpose as taught by the Master Himself.[5] It thus became symbolic of the intimate union between Christ and the Church as His bride, so that St. Paul can pass with ease from the one to the other : " There is more here than appears on the surface; there is an inner meaning of high importance : I speak it of Christ and the Church." [6] A high argument indeed, and one from which there is no appeal for the Christian believer. The peril for the Church in Africa lies not so much in the open endorsement of polygamy, as may indeed happen among some separatist sects, but the nominal acceptance of Christian marriage with a tacit condonation of concubinage. The fact that this has been known elsewhere in earlier centuries is no disproof of the deadly injury which hypocrisy ever inflicts on the life of the Church and of the family itself. The hope for the future in this respect is in the nucleus of committed Christians who honourably exemplify the Christian way. As Lyndon Harries has put it in concluding his survey : " In emphasizing the weak-

---

[1] *The Church in the Mission Field*, World Missionary Conference, 1910, II, 324–5; E. W. Smith, *The Christian Mission in Africa* (1926), 52.
[2] The Presbyterian Church of the United States (Southern Presbyterians) in their Belgian Congo Mission.—*The Missionary Review of the World* XVI (1903), 594–6; E. W. Smith, *The Golden Stool* (1926), 278–9; *Abundant Life in Changing Africa* (1946), 48.
[3] H. A. Junod, *op. cit.*, I, 532–5.
[4] E.g. In 1915 the church of the Paris Missionary Society at Ogowe in Gabon reported 2,300 communicants only one-fifth of whom were men, " the striking disproportion being accounted for by the opposition of the church to polygamy and drink ".—*I.R.M.*, V (1916), 63 and *n.* 7. An admirable review of missionary practice in the conflict with polygamy has been provided by Lyndon Harries in: A. Phillips (ed.), *Survey of African Marriage and Family Life* (1953), 335–59.
[5] Mark 10: 7–9.
[6] Ephesians 4: 31–2. Cf. J. Armitage Robinson, *St. Paul's Epistle to the Ephesians* (2nd ed., 1907), 126–7.

nesses of mission discipline and the difficulties involved in promoting the Christian ideal of marriage, we should not lose sight of the growing numbers of sincere African Christians who voluntarily maintain the highest standards of Christian family life. . . . The conviction is religious, rather than intellectual, and the missions consider that upon such a religious conviction depends the future welfare of the Christian family in Africa." [1]

The second aspect of weakness demanding attention is that of the fear of sorcery and witchcraft—a fear long surviving even among the sophisticated. Father Placide Tempels has brilliantly expounded the fundamental notion of the Bantu view of the world as the conception of vital energy, streaming from the Supreme Being as Creator, mediated through the ancestors, found at its highest in man in the visible world (with gradations in chiefs, elders, and juniors), and yet not confined to him. This vital power can be enhanced or diminished—man as a person may become more or less effective. This dynamic view of man is anything but humanist, since the Creator is *fons et origo*, upon whom all are ultimately dependent.[2] But there is a dark side to it all, for influences hostile to life are also in the picture. Here enter sorcery and witchcraft.

The two terms are now distinguished by modern students, largely on the initiative of Evans-Pritchard whose researches among the Azande have provided the classical account of the subject.[3] Sorcery or black magic (i.e. magic employed with an antisocial purpose) is defined as characterized by the use of a material medium, the rite, and the spell or words addressed to the " medicine ". The sorcerer is guilty of anti-social acts, but if he desists all is well. Witchcraft, on the other hand, is the destructive act of a personality with inherently evil power in the sense that it is the automatic action, as by psychic influence or emanation, of one organically so conditioned.[4] Among the Azande this power was regarded as having its seat in a material substance (*mangu*) which could, it was claimed, be discovered at death by a post-mortem

---

[1] A. Phillips (ed.), *Survey of African Marriage and Family Life*, 456.
[2] Placide Tempels, *La Philosophie Bantoue* (1949 ed.), *passim*.
[3] E. E. Evans-Pritchard, *Witchcraft, Oracles and Magic among the Azande* (1937). Zandeland is located in the south-west of the Anglo-Egyptian Sudan with some extension of influence into the Belgian Congo and French Equatorial Africa.
[4] E. E. Evans-Pritchard, *op. cit.*, 21; *Africa*, IV (1931), 26–7.

examination.[1] Meanwhile there was recourse to the poison oracle to diagnose the presence of *mangu* in an accused person.[2] Distinct vernacular terms, when ascertained, have revealed how widespread is this distinction in thought between the inherent evil influence of the witch and the otherwise normal citizen who may relapse into the practice of sorcery. Thus among the Efiks of South-East Nigeria the one guilty of witchcraft is again characterized by a physical trait (*if ot*) which a man is said to acquire, it may be quite unwittingly, from one already having it. Again, the specific activity of a witch (using the term to cover both sexes) is that of a vampire, save that it is the living who are the victims. These will eventually fade away as their vital energy has become sapped by this malign influence. The poison ordeal is the detective agency, the *esere* bean being regarded as antipathetic to *if ot*.[3]

The European denial of the existence of witchcraft is quite unconvincing to the African mind; to him it functions as a theory of causation in cases of personal misfortune and disaster where the European can do no more than murmur, " Coincidence ".[4] The European is regarded as incapable of feeling the evil. And the verb is appropriate, for emotion and not mere intellect is the dominating element. It has often seemed strange that when witchcraft is suspected the accused should be looked for among near relatives or neighbours—never, apparently, among strangers. That is, it is among those with whom one is in continual personal

---

[1] E. E. Evans-Pritchard, *op. cit.*, 9, 40–9. Evidence of the practice of a post-mortem examination to identify one accused of witchcraft is widespread. The Negro John Kizell reported it to Governor Columbine of Sierra Leone from the River Sherbro in 1810.—*Sixth Report of the African Institution* (1812), 129. On the belief among the Kono of Sierra Leone, see E. W. Smith (ed.), *African Ideas of God* (1950), 275. A. C. Good of the American Presbyterian Mission in Gabon reported an experience among the Bulu: " Late in the evening the *post-mortem* examination came on, and they found, true enough, a witch . . .", which discovery he identified as " a small, oval fleshy tumour, about an inch long, lying just inside the spinal column." —E. C. Parsons, *A Life for Africa* (1898), 272.

[2] E. E. Evans-Pritchard, *op. cit.*, 258–61, 299–302. Among the Azande *mangu* is regarded as a hereditary physical trait, but there are two qualifications: it can only be transmitted by the same sex, and it may remain inoperative, or " cool " as the Azande say, so that the question put to the oracle is not, " Is so-and-so a witch? " but, " Is so-and-so bewitching me?"— *Ibid.*, 23–6.

[3] C. P. Groves, *Jesus Christ and Primitive Need* (*1934*), 125–7. Cf. Vol. II, 38, 238. For various papers on the subject, see: *Africa*, VIII (1935), 417– 560. Also on the legal aspect, F. Melland and Cullen Young, *African Dilemma* (1937), 126–64.

[4] E. E. Evans-Pritchard, *op. cit.*, 63–83.

relationship that the evil lies. This would seem to provide the clue to the basis of the belief: envy, jealousy, hate, are elemental human passions, and the harbourers of such evil and destructive attitudes of mind and heart find pleasure, secret or overt, in the misfortunes of those who are their object. What then more reasonable than to relate the evil will to destructive execution? " A witch attacks a man," says Evans-Pritchard, " when motivated by hatred, envy, jealousy, and greed. . . . Therefore a Zande in misfortune at once considers who is likely to hate him." [1] The tenacity of the belief in witchcraft, then, is as great as the persistence of such attitudes. Dr. S. T. Pruen, a medical man with experience of East Africa in the eighteen-eighties, wrote with unusual insight : " Another difficulty which besets the African convert . . . is his belief in witchcraft. But witchcraft is not so much an obstacle to the reception of Christianity as it is to the living of a consistent Christian life. . . . Where witchcraft is, there is bitter hatred, envy, jealousy, revenge, and therefore no possibility of brotherly love, or of the charity which thinketh no evil; no possibility of the unity, the oneness which Christ came to bring, and which is the very evidence of Christianity to the outside world." [2]

Emancipation of the Christian convert is often far slower than is realized, for silence on the subject is no proof of deliverance from the fear of it. J. D. Viccars, who found the identical belief in Belgian Congo after forty years of the Protestant mission's work, has reported the question of a respected elder of the Church at a church meeting : " Is it wrong to accuse a friend of *boloki*? If we hear such accusations made by church members should we remain silent? We all know that this matter still perplexes everyone now here. We believed the early missionaries when they told us that witchcraft was impossible, but the evidence of its working is always before our eyes." [3] Viccars concludes : " The belief is so widespread, and so firmly held, that it may be described as the greatest ' unheard palaver ' and problem confronting them and us at the present time." [4]

[1] *Ibid.*, 100–2. Likewise Placide Tempels, *op. cit.*, 71; cf. 84–5. The Christian answer is to proclaim the cleansing of the heart of the evils that infect it.—Mark 7: 21–3; Galatians 5: 19–26.

[2] S. T. Pruen, *The Arab and the African* (1891), 273. Cf. 274–5. Here is the identical emphasis laid by Edwyn Bevan on the nature of effective Christian witness.—*Vide, supra*, p. 342.

[3] J. D. Viccars, " Witchcraft in Bolobo, Belgian Congo ", in *Africa* XIX (1949), 220–9. *Boloki* is given as the gerund of the verb *loko* (= to bewitch) and is used to describe the activity of an infected personality, one with " an evil-infected intestine ".   [4] *Ibid.*, 221.

Dark as is this persistent shadow over Africa, unhappily it does not stand alone. The practice of magic, whether as by the sorcerer for personal ends condemned as anti-social and illegal or as protective " medicine " and therefore socially approved, likewise enlarges the area of fear in life on the one hand, and encourages the search for personal security by the attempt to tap still more powerful " medicines " on the other. How far this may go and how sturdily persist where Christian teaching has long been known has been demonstrated in the so-called " Medicine Murders " in Basutoland in 1947–48 and later.[1] Belief in the " medicinal " power of human flesh, which was found to be the proximate cause of the murders, was not limited to pagans. Both Protestant and Roman Catholic communions are found in the country, the former having a history of a century and a quarter and the latter having only made an outstanding drive in the last generation. The fact that most of the important chiefs involved were Roman Catholic and that no Protestant chief was implicated, was rejected by the official investigator as conveying any implication unfavourable to the Catholics. He concluded : " The fact that Basuto Christians can engage in *diretlo* murders indicates all too clearly that the Church in Basutoland as elsewhere has failed to get the average Christian to apply the ethics of his religion to his everyday life. He has no difficulty in keeping his Christian ideals in one compartment of his mind, and his worldly values in another; protective medicines come in the latter category; they are things appertaining to Cæsar, not to God." [2]

Whether this diagnosis be accepted or not, the warning against complacency in these matters is clear to read. So long as belief in witchcraft has not been expelled from the African Christian's view of the world, and so long as he has a lurking faith in magic as a means of closing for him the circle of personal security, so long he has not experienced that final irrefutable faith : " For I am persuaded, that neither death, nor life, nor angels, nor principalities, nor things present, nor things to come, nor powers, nor height, nor

[1] *Basutoland Medicine Murder. A Report on the Recent Outbreak of " Diretlo " Murders in Basutoland*, Cmd. 8209 (1951).

[2] *Ibid.*, 27–9. Nevertheless, the fact that the Protestant mission, which had trained its people in the Christian way for well over a century, had no chief implicated, was of some significance. A Sotho minister reported the view current among his people: " It is believed in Basutoland that in districts where the chiefs are Protestants, ritual murders are rare."— E. Mphatsoe, " Ritual Murders in Basutoland ", in *Basutoland Witness*, VI (1952), 82–5.

depth, nor any other created thing, shall be able to separate us from the love of God which is in Christ Jesus our Lord." [1]

The third aspect of the life of the Church that must occasion disquiet is the rapid growth of separatist sects, partly on the ground of the further splintering of the Christian witness, partly through the implicit reflexion on the established churches, and also because an advancing syncretism may, all unwittingly, provide a bridge-head leading back to paganism. Thus a sect, while congenial to its adherents through its admission of features familiar in pagan cults, may easily find itself on the slippery slope not merely of a diluted but of a contaminated version of Christianity.

There is nevertheless a wide range in the type of sect, from those that adopt most of the teaching and practice of the western-established churches to the movements with faith healing as a central feature and more pagan than Christian behaviour evident in their ritual. That the more reputable among them have arisen under sincere leaders pursuing, as they believed it, a divine vocation, cannot be denied. They have often met Africans in their need at a level not condescended to by the established churches and so have commended themselves as relevant to a situation that was otherwise neglected. Two enterprising movements, in the Gold Coast and Nigeria respectively, will illustrate the type of appeal successfully made among these able African peoples on the verge of nationhood.

The Apostolic Revelation Society in the Gold Coast sprang from the prophetic witness of one man in 1939. C. K. N. Wovenu, after serving in succession as police recruit, prison warder, diamond miner, and labourer, in that year yielded to the now irresistible urge, as it was reported, to bear public witness to the claim of God on human life and the blessing of yielding Him full obedience. Wovenu's evident sincerity, the healing of the sick by faith and prayer, and his preaching from the Bible combined to establish him as a prophet of the Lord. Commencing at Tadzevu in the Keta district the Society grew until in eighteen years they claimed some 150 congregations cared for by fifty-two pastors, and an active membership exceeding 60,000. An efficient organization maintained a hospital with a bus service for the sick (for healing by medicine or operation was not rejected), a chain of primary schools, a Middle School, and a training centre for pastors. A

[1] Romans 8: 38–9. Cf. O. F. Raum, " Magic and a Christian Policy," in *I.R.M.*, XXIV (1935), 358–65.

visitor to the headquarters reported : " One cannot fail to be impressed by the calm religious atmosphere of Tadzevu. The Society, a 100 per cent African enterprise, is built on simplicity and the fear of the Lord." [1]

In the Western Region of Nigeria the sect of the Cherubim and Seraphim dates from the mid-'twenties. Apparently Yoruba in origin, its founder, Moses Orimolade Tunolase, an Anglican by church attachment, hailed from Ikarre in Ondo. After suffering from a disease that paralysed his legs for ten years (poliomyelitis would seem indicated) he claimed to have been healed through his own prayers. Then began his mission : he walked through the countryside teaching and gathering for prayer those who came to him. At first he encouraged those already connected with Christian churches to remain with them and to " worship God in spirit and in truth, depending on God alone and having faith in Jesus Christ ". As, however, some of his activities were frowned upon by these churches, his prayer meetings were developed into full religious services to meet the needs of his followers as an independent sect. It gained considerable accessions in Lagos, it is alleged, from among the influx of rural folk from the hinterland who soon found themselves socially adrift under urban conditions. In the Society's warm, human fellowship amidst congenial surroundings they felt their needs were catered for rather than in the formalized worship of the fashionable churches whose inclination to a self-conscious respectability, perhaps, was a little chilling. In doctrine they proclaimed " salvation through Christ alone ", holding the Bible (in the Revised Version) to be the ground of faith, though current prophecy might supplement it. They practised baptism by immersion and observed the sacrament of Holy Communion, though prayer remained their central activity. The organization was in due course developed with the selection of seventy *Aladura* or prayer-men (both men and women), the head being *Baba Aladura*. From these, twelve apostles were appointed with lower ranks of deacon, evangelist, and prophet. But the movement failed to maintain its unity. When the founder died in 1932 secessions had already taken place and more were to follow until in Lagos alone about ten sub-sects were to be found. An attempt in 1948 to reconstitute a central authority, prompted by alleged " evil practices " creeping into the divided groups, did not succeed. Despite the failure to achieve unity by agreement upon an acceptable *Baba Aladura*, there were developments in establishing schools, carrying on maternity homes, and, in the case of one group, starting a three-

[1] *The African World* (July, 1957), 24.

year training course for priests with Bible study as a central concern. It is eloquent of the popular appeal of the movement that it claimed to have won some half a million members in thirty years, gathered from among Christians of western-established churches, Muslims, and pagans. While the various sub-divisions of the Society were in amicable association with one another in the sense that none excluded others as heretical, yet the admitted danger of sub-Christian practices seeping in began to loom larger in such a fragmented Society than in one whose cohesion could permit of firm discipline by a central authority.[1]

In Dr. Bengt Sundkler's intensive study of the separatist church movement among the Zulu people, he was able to follow in certain cases the later stages of development, and has called attention to what he has termed an emerging Bantu syncretism. He notes that in proportion as a separatist organization loses effective contact with the Christian traditions and teaching of the Church, the more marked does " the Zulu nativistic trend become ", and proceeds : *" The syncretistic sect becomes the bridge over which Africans are brought back to heathenism*— a viewpoint which stresses the seriousness of the whole situation. It can be shown how individuals and groups have passed step by step from a Mission church to an Ethiopian church, and from the Ethiopians to the Zionists, and how at last via the bridge of nativistic Zionism they have returned to the African animism from where they once started." [2] It is a grave peril that besets any separatist sect pursuing its own way in isolation from its Christian neighbours—a peril that means nothing less than the devitalizing of its Christianity, leaving little but the name. To avert such a fatal regression as far as may be possible must be a concern of all the Churches.[3]

---

[1] *Nigeria*, Number 53 (Lagos (1957), 119–34.

[2] B. G. M. Sundkler, *Bantu Prophets in South Africa* (1948), 297. Italics in original.

[3] It was a request of the Africa group at Tambaram that the International Missionary Council should institute, " in those areas where a survey has not been undertaken, a full enquiry into the reasons for the separatist movement in Africa and to suggest remedies ".—*The Life of the Church*, Tambaram Madras Series, IV (1939), 407. The United Missions in the Copperbelt organised such a survey covering nineteen churches and groups, which was reported to the Christian Council of Northern Rhodesia by Dr. D. Lehmann in 1951.—*Report of the Fourth Meeting of the Council, Lusaka, July, 1951* (1951), 15–16. A revised edition of Dr. Sundkler's study is about to be undertaken at the time of writing. A positive step of value was that of the late Dr. J. M. Nhlapo, editor of the *Bantu World*, in organising joint Bible study for pastors of various sects.—Personally communicated.

It is the Christian claim that human need everywhere can be met in Jesus Christ. When Christian converts once experience their new allegiance as fundamentally satisfying in their daily living, the risk of a resurgence of pagan thought and practice steadily recedes, since the situations of strain and stress in which the traditional religion was accustomed to function no longer require it. The growing experience of a new resilience in facing minor frustrations and of a steady endurance in accepting major trial and adversity, through faith in God the Father, as revealed in Jesus Christ, from whose love nothing can separate, establishes the heart securely in its new affection.

The African heart, which is little moved by abstract duty or the claims of an institution, beats warmly in response to personal interest and trust. Booker T. Washington could proudly claim : " I do not know how many have noticed it, but I think that it will be found to be true that there are few instances either in slavery or freedom, in which a member of my race has been known to betray a specific trust." [1] Devotion to a master, as Livingstone's faithfuls showed, can surmount all obstacles. And when that acknowledged Master is Jesus Christ, to whom life is committed as to a personal Saviour, within the fellowship of the Church, the resurgence of pagan thought and practice is so much the less to be feared as there is no remnant of unsatisfied desire left alive to welcome it. That there are those within all branches of the Church in Africa for whom this is a growing personal experience is the all-sufficient ground for hope persistent.

The shining example of this loyalty in recent days has come from Kenya where revival has renewed the Church.[2] " Revival as it has come to East Africa," says one who has known it at first hand, " is really a return to the simplicity of apostolic faith in a time of apostasy. . . . What has really happened is that accepted doctrine has become alive ".[3] In face of the Mau Mau terror the ultimate loyalty was proved beyond all question : " Amid issues so confused and threats so terrible that the majority of professing Christians gave way, the remnant that stands faithful unto death is largely composed of those who in this fellowship and witness of revival have come to know Christ as so infinitely precious that nothing else of this world counts. . . . Once again the Church is

[1] B. T. Washington, *Up from Slavery* (Nelson ed.), 25. See also Vol. I, p. 152.

[2] *Vide supra*, p. 312.

[3] N. Langford-Smith, "Revival in East Africa ", in *I.R M* , XLIII (1954), 77–81.

z 2

privileged to see something at which the world wonders—those who gladly, by deliberate choice, are ready to die with Christ rather than to deny Him."

The Church in Africa will survive, and survive in purity and power, as she forgets herself in utter loyalty to her Lord, for the Master's word to the individual disciple is also the word for His Church :

" For whosoever would save his life shall lose it; and whosoever shall lose his life for my sake and the gospel's shall save it."
—Mark 8 : 35. (R. V.).

NOW TO HIM THAT IS ABLE TO STABLISH YOU ACCORDING TO MY GOSPEL AND THE PREACHING OF JESUS CHRIST, ACCORDING TO THE REVELATION OF THE MYSTERY WHICH HATH BEEN KEPT IN SILENCE THROUGH TIMES ETERNAL, BUT NOW IS MANIFESTED, AND BY THE SCRIPTURES OF THE PROPHETS, ACCORDING TO THE COMMANDMENT OF THE ETERNAL GOD, IS MADE KNOWN UNTO ALL THE NATIONS UNTO OBEDIENCE OF FAITH; TO THE ONLY WISE GOD, THROUGH JESUS CHRIST, BE THE GLORY FOR EVER. AMEN.

—St. Paul to the Romans, 16 : 25–7 (R.V.)

LIST OF BIBLE TRANSLATIONS IN AFRICAN LANGUAGES

(1) *Ancient Versions*
(2) *Printed Versions*
(3) *Summary Tables*
(4) *Bibliography*

(1) *Ancient Versions*

Versions were made in the days of the early Church in both Egypt and Abyssinia.

(a) Egypt

Five versions into which Biblical translations were made are now recognized, with suggested approximate dating as follows :—

Sahidic .	.	Early third century (possibly late second).
Achmimic	.	Second half third century or early fourth ;
Sub-Achmimic		eventually superseded by Sahidic in early
Fayyumic	.	fifth century.
Bohairic .	.	Late fourth century or early fifth century.

By the sixth century Sahidic was the official dialect of the Church in Egypt, but by the tenth century it had been displaced by Bohairic, this version then becoming the accepted version of the Egyptian Church.[1]

(b) Abyssinia

Ethiopic .	.	Approximately sixth century.[2]

[1] I am indebted for this information on the Egyptian Versions to Professor J. Martin Plumley of the Chair of Egyptology in the University of Cambridge. The above section supersedes the relevant paragraphs in Vol. I, pp. 39–40. On the relationship between Sahidic and Bohairic Mr. Plumley comments: " It is clear that the relationship between Sahidic and Bohairic is much closer than has hitherto been thought. The old idea that Sahidic and Bohairic represented the extremes of geographical distance is no longer tenable. What does seem more probable is that they represent the extremes in historical sequence both for the translation of the Bible and the compilation of the Liturgy."

[2] Cf. Vol. I, p. 53. E. Ullendorff, in *The Semitic Languages of Ethiopia* (1955), speaks of " the period of Bible translations between the fifth and seventh centuries " (p. 13). I owe this reference to Professor W. D. McHardy.

(2) *Printed Versions*

N.B. (1) The chronological periods taken, after the first, are those adopted in the present history.

(2) In the case of Bantu languages a prefix in brackets completes the local name, and is given in cases where this name has come into more general use.

(3) A name in brackets following that of the language indicates the dialect.

(4) Where the older form of a name is preserved the modern ethnologist's spelling follows in italics.

(5) The territorial names are those of political units current in 1954.

(6) Abbreviations used are as follows : Mt. = Gospel of Matthew ; Mk. = Gospel of Mark ; Lk. = Gospel of Luke ; Jn. = Gospel of John ; Goss. = Gospels ; I Jn. = First Epistle of John ; Pent. = Pentateuch ; Ru. = Ruth ; Jon. = Jonah ; Sel. = Selections (i.e. no complete book at that date) ; Cat. = Catechism (where e.g. the Ten Commandments and other Scripture passages quoted); Ps. = Psalms.

No.	Language	Territory	First Book	Date	N.T.	Bible
	I. To 1804 (foundation of B.F.B.S.)					
1	Ethiopic . . .	Abyssinia . .	Ps.	1513	1549[1]	1919
2	Arabic . . .	Egypt & N. Africa	Ps.	1516	1616	1645
3	Coptic (Bohairic) .	Egypt . .	Sel.	1663	1716	
4	Fanti . . .	Gold Coast .	Sel.	1764	1896	1948
5	Coptic (Sahidic) .	Egypt . .	Sel.	1786		
	II. 1805–1840					
6	Ga	Gold Coast. .	Sel.	1805	1859	1866
7	Coptic (Fayyumic) .	Egypt . .	Sel.	1811		
8	Bullom . . .	Sierra Leone .	Sel.	1814		
9	Susu . . .	French Guinea .	Sel.	1816	1884	
10	Amharic . . .	Abyssinia . .	Goss.	1824	1829	1840
11	(Se-)Chuana (*Tswana*)	Bechuanaland .	Sel.	1826	1840	1857
12	Nama . . .	S.W. Africa .	Goss.	1831	1866	

[1] The first N.T. *printed* in an African language.

No.	Language	Territory	First Book	Date	N.T.	Bible
13	Kabyle (Lesser) . .	Algeria . .	Sel.	1833		
14	Xhosa . . .	South Africa .	Lk.	1833	1846	1859
15	Mandingo . .	Sierra Leone .	Mt.	1837		
16	Grebo . . .	Liberia . .	Mt.	1838		
17	Galla (S. Shoa) .	Abyssinia . .	Sel.	1839		
18	(Se-)Suto (*Sotho*) .	Basutoland .	Mk.	1839	1855	1878[1]
	III. 1841–1858					
19	Bassa (Liberia) . .	Liberia . .	Mt.	1844		
20	Nyika (Rabai) . .	Kenya . .	Lk.	1844		
21	Isubu . . .	Cameroons .	Mt.	1846		
22	Zulu . . .	South Africa .	Sel.	1846	1865	1883
23	(Ki-)Swahili (Mombasa)	Kenya .	Sel.	1847	1909	1914
24	Duala . . .	Cameroons .	Mt.	1848	1861	1872
25	Bubi . . .	Fernando Po .	Sel.	1848		
26	Yoruba . . .	S. Nigeria . .	Sel.	1848	1862	1884
27	(Otji-)Herero .	S.W. Africa .	Sel.	1849	1879	
28	Kamba . . .	Kenya . .	Mk.	1850	1920	
29	Mpongwe (Omyene) .	Gabon . .	Mt.	1850	1893	
30	Hausa . . .	N. Nigeria . .	Sel.	1853	1880	1932
31	Kanuri or Bornu .	N. Nigeria . .	Sel.	1853		
32	Temne . . .	Sierra Leone .	Sel.	1854	1868	
33	Benga . . .	Spanish Guinea .	Mt.	1858	1872	
34	Ewe . . .	Togoland . .	Jn.	1858	1877	1914
35	Efik . . .	S. Nigeria . .	Jn.	1858	1862	1868
	IV. 1859–1878					
36	Fula (Adamawa) .	Cameroons .	Sel.	1859		
37	Twi . . .	Gold Coast .	Goss.	1859	1864	1871
38	Ibo (Isuama) . .	S. Nigeria . .	Mt.	1860		
39	Nubian (Fiadidja) .	Sudan . .	Mk.	1860		
40	Nupe . . .	N. Nigeria . .	Sel.	1860	1915	1952
41	Arabic (Algerian) .	Algeria . .	Sel.	1862		
42	Tigrinya . . .	Eritrea & Abyssinia	Goss.	1866	1909	

[1] Date of last portion completing O.T. Complete Bible issued in 1881.

No.	Language	Territory	First Book	Date	N.T.	Bible
43	Dinka or Jieng (Kyec)	Sudan	Lk.	1866		
44	Mende . . .	Sierra Leone	Mt.	1867	1955	
45	(Ki-)Swahili (Zanzibar)	East Africa	Ru.	1868	1879[1]	1891
46	Kabyle (Greater)	Algeria	Sel.	1869	1902	
47	Galla . . .	Abyssinia	Lk.	1870	1876	
48	(Se-)Chuana (Rolong)	Bechuanaland	Cat.	1870	1894	
49	Afrikaans . . .	South Africa	Sel.	1873		1933
50	Wolof or Jolof (Senegal)	Senegal	Mt.	1873		
51	Galla (Bararetta)	Abyssinia	Jon.	1878		
52	Nyika (Ribe) .	Kenya	Jon.	1878		
53	(Oshi-)Ndonga .	S.W. Africa	Sel.	1878	1903	1954
	V. 1879–1896					
54	(A- or Di-)Kele (Gabon)	French Congo	Jn.	1879		
55	(Chi-)Nyanja (Chewa)	Tanganyika & Port. E. Africa	Mk.	1880	1886	
56	Yao . . .	Nyasaland & Port. E. Africa	Mt.	1880	1898	1920
57	Makua . . .	Port. E. Africa	Sel.	1881		
58	Bogos . . .	Abyssinia	Mk.	1882		
59	Bondei . . .	Tanganyika	Sel.	1882		
60	Jolof or Wolof (Gambia)	Gambia	Mt.	1882		
61	(Ki-)Kongo (Cataract)	Belgian Congo	Sel.	1882		
62	Thonga or Shangaan .	Port. E. Africa	Sel.	1883	1894	1907
63	(Sin-)Tebele . .	S. Rhodesia	Mt.	1884	1884	
64	Falasha (Kara) .	Abyssinia	Mk.	1885		
65	Kaguru . . .	Tanganyika	Lk.	1885		
66	(Ki-)Kongo (Buende) .	Belgian Congo	Jn.	1885	1891	1905
67	Shilha (Northern) or Rifi	Morocco	Sel.	1885		
68	Galla (Ittu) . .	Abyssinia	Mt.	1886		
69	(Lu-)Ganda . .	Uganda	Sel.	1886	1893	1896

[1] Date of Revelation completing N.T. Complete N.T. issued in 1883.

No.	Language	Territory	First Book	Date	N.T.	Bible
70	Gogo . . .	Tanganyika .	Mt.	1886	1899	
71	Gu (Alada) . .	Dahomey . .	Mt.	1886	1892	1923
72	Ijo (Nimbi) . .	S. Nigeria . .	Jn.	1886	1927	
73	(Ki-)Kongo (San ·Salvador)	Belgian Congo .	Mk.	1888	1893	1916
74	(Ki-)Mbundu (Loanda)	Angola . .	Jn.	1888	1922	
75	Tonga (Inhambane) .	Port. E. Africa .	Mt.	1888	1890	
76	Tswa (Sheetswa) .	Port. E. Africa .	Sel.	1888	1903	1910
77	(U-)Mbundu (Benguella)	Angola . .	Mk.	1889	1897	
78	Mwamba . . .	Nyasaland . .	Sel.	1889		
79	Teke . . .	Belgian Congo .	Jn.	1889		
80	Tigré . . .	Eritrea . .	Mk.	1889	1902	
81	Ngoni . . .	Nyasaland . .	Sel.	1890		
82	Pedi . . .	South Africa .	N.T.	1890	1890	1904
83	(Chi-)Tonga (Nyasa)	Nyasaland . .	Mk.	1890	1921	
84	Igbira . . .	N. Nigeria . .	Mt.	1891		
85	(Chi-)Nyanja (Eastern)	Tanganyika .	Mk.	1891		1912
86	(Ki-)Chaga or Mochi	Tanganyika .	Mt.	1892	1939	
87	(Ki-)Giryama . .	Kenya . .	Lk.	1892		1908
88	Ibo (Bonny) . .	S. Nigeria . .	Jn.	1892		
89	(Chi-)Nyanja (Southern)	Nyasaland . .	Mt.	1892		
90	(Ki-)Taita (Sagalla) .	Kenya . .	Mk.	1892	1906	
91	(Ki-)Taveta . .	Tanganyika .	Mk.	1892	1906	
92	Bobangi . . .	Belgian Congo .	Mt.	1893	1912	
93	Galla (Northern) .	Abyssinia . .	N.T.	1893	1893	1899
94	Ibo (Onitsha) . .	S. Nigeria . .	Goss.	1893	1900	1906
95	(Ki-)Mambwe . .	N. Rhodesia .	Mk.	1893	1901	
96	Mongo or Lolo . .	Belgian Congo .	Sel.	1893	1908	
97	Mongo (Nkundu) .	Belgian Congo .	Jn.	1893		
98	Akunakuna . .	S. Nigeria . .	Lk.	1894		
99	Fang . . .	Gabon . .	Mt.	1894		
100	(Oshi-)Kuanyama .	S.W. Africa .	Lk.	1894	1927	
101	(Ki-)Pokomo . .	Kenya . .	Mk.	1894	1901	
102	(Ki-)Shambla a .	Tanganyika .	Sel.	1894	1908	

No.	Language	Territory	First Book	Date	N.T.	Bible
103	(Chi-)Kunda . .	Port. E. Africa .	Sel.	1895		
104	Konde or Ngonde .	Nyasaland . .	Lk.	1895	1908	
105	Ngala or Bangala .	Belgian Congo .	Mt.	1895		
106	(Ki-)Sukuma . .	Tanganyika .	Mt.	1895	1925	
107	Umon . . .	S. Nigeria . .	Mk.	1895		
108	Bulu . . .	Cameroons .	Goss.	1896	1926	1940
109	Ntumba . . .	Belgian Congo .	Sel.	1896		
110	(Shi-)Ronga .	Port. E. Africa .	Jn.	1896	1903	1923
111	(Lu-)Soga . .	Uganda . .	Mk.	1896		
	VI. 1897–1913					
112	Arabic (Judaeo-Tunisian)	Tunisia . .	Lk.	1897		
113	Fon . . .	Dahomey . .	Sel.	1897		
114	(Ki-)Nyamwezi .	Tanganyika .	Mk.	1897	1909	
115	(Chi-)Sena . .	Port. E. Africa .	Mk.	1897		
116	Nyungwi . . .	Port. E. Africa .	Goss.	1897		
117	Poto or Lifoto .	Belgian Congo .	Lk.	1898		
118	(Chi- or Se-)Shona	S. Rhodesia .	Mk.	1898	1907	
119	(Chi- or Se-)Shona (Swina) or Chi-Manyika	S. Rhodesia .	Sel.	1898	1908	
120	Ibo (Ungwana) .	S. Nigeria . .	Mk.	1899		
121	Kuranko . . .	French Guinea .	Lk.	1899		
122	Kele . . .	Belgian Congo .	Sel.	1900	1918	
123	(Lu-)Nyoro .	Uganda . .	Mt.	1900	1905	1912
124	Yalunka . . .	Sierra Leone .	Sel.	1901		
125	Arabic (Mogrebi) .	Morocco . .	Lk.	1902	1932	
126	Chopi . . .	Port. E. Africa .	Sel.	1902		
127	Fang (Ogowe) or Pahouin	Gabon . .	Mt.	1902	1927	1950
128	Lwena or Lovale .	Angola . .	Jn.	1902	1928	1955
129	Eleku . . .	Belgian Congo .	Sel.	1903		
130	(Ge-)Kikuyu . .	Kenya . .	Jn.	1903	1926	1951
131	Luba (Sanga) .	Belgian Congo .	Mt.	1903	1923	1928
132	Luba (Lulua) . .	Belgian Congo ,	Sel.	1903	1920	1927

No.	Language	Territory	First Book	Date	N.T.	Bible
133	(Chi-)Namwanga .	Nyasaland . .	Lk.	1903	1933	
134	(Chi-)Ndau . .	S. Rhodesia .	Sel.	1903	1919	
135	Ngombe . . .	Belgian Congo .	Mt.	1903	1915	
136	Omyene (Galwa) .	Gabon . .	Pent.	1903	1907	
137	(Chi-)Bemba or Wemba	N. Rhodesia .	Jn.	1904	1916	1956
138	(Lu-)Gisu or Masaba .	Kenya . .	Goss.	1904		
139	(Se-)Kalanya . .	S. Rhodesia .	Mt.	1904		
140	(Tshi-)Karanga .	S. Rhodesia .	Mt.	1904	1919	
141	(Shi-)Nyika (Nyasa) .	Tanganyika .	Mt.	1904	1913	
142	Puthsu . . .	Port. E. Africa .	Sel.	1904		
143	(Ki-)Taita (Dabida) .	Kenya . .	Mk.	1904	1922	
144	Tumbuka . .	Nyasaland . .	Mk.	1904	1911	1957
145	Arabic (Egyptian) .	Egypt . .	Lk.	1905	1932	
146	Gang or Acholi .	Uganda . .	Mk.	1905	1933	
147	Kuba (Inkongo) .	Belgian Congo .	Mt.	1905	1911	1927
148	Masai . . .	Kenya & Tanganyika	Mk.	1905	1923	
149	(Ki-)Swahili (Western)	Belgian Congo .	Sel.	1905	1954	
150	(Ch-)Ila . . .	N. Rhodesia .	Sel.	1906	1915	
151	Kunama . . .	Eritrea . .	Mk.	1906	1927	
152	Shilha (Southern) .	Morocco . .	Jn.	1906		
153	(Ki-)Zigula . .	Tanganyika .	Mt.	1906		
154	Senji . . .	Port. E. Africa .	Lk.	1906		
155	Heso . . .	Belgian Congo .	Sel.	1907	1920	
156	(Lunya-)Nkole .	Uganda . .	Mt.	1907		
157	Ngala or Lingala (Lingua Franca)	Belgian Congo .	Lk.	1908	1944	
158	Ora . . .	S. Nigeria . .	Mt.	1908		
159	Chekiri . . .	S. Nigeria . .	Sel.	1909		
160	Wiza or Bisa . .	N. Rhodesia .	Mk.	1909		
161	(Ch-)Asu . . .	Tanganyika .	Mt.	1910	1922	
162	Kele (Ongom) . .	Gabon . .	Mt.	1910		
163	(A-)Teso . . .	Uganda . .	Mk.	1910	1930	
164	Yaunde . . .	Cameroons .	Sel.	1910		
165	Vai	Liberia . .	Sel.	1910		

No.	Language	Territory	First Book	Date	N.T.	Bible
166	Arabic (Tunisian) .	Tunisia . .	Lk.	1911		
167	Digo . . .	Tanganyika .	Sel.	1911		
168	Limba . . .	Sierra Leone .	Lk.	1911		
169	(Dho-)Luo . .	Kenya . .	Mk.	1911	1926	1952
170	Shilluk . . .	Sudan . .	Jn.	1911		
171	(Lu-)Ragoli . .	Kenya . .	Mk.	1911	1928	1951
172	Tonga (Zambezi) .	N. Rhodesia .	Mk.	1911		
173	Ijo (Batani) . .	S. Nigeria . .	Mk.	1912		
174	Kipsigis . . .	Kenya . .	Mk.	1912	1952	
175	Manda . . .	Tanganyika .	Sel.	1912	1937	
176	Nubian (Kunuzi) .	Sudan . .	Goss.	1912		
177	Wiza or Bisa (Lala) .	N. Rhodesia .	Goss.	1912	1949	
178	Gbari (Gayegi) . .	N. Nigeria . .	Sel.	1913	1954	
179	Gbari (Gyengyen) .	N. Nigeria . .	Mk.	1913		
180	(Lu-)Haya . .	Tanganyika .	Goss.	1913	1930	
181	(Chi-)Mpoto . .	Tanganyika .	Ps.	1913		
182	Ngumba . . .	Cameroons .	Sel.	1913		
183	Sura . . .	N. Nigeria . .	Sel.	1913		
	VII. 1914–1918					
184	Addo or Edo .	S. Nigeria . .	Mt.	1914		
185	(Lu-)Hanga . .	Kenya . .	Mt.	1914	1939	
186	Jukun (Wukari) .	N. Nigeria . .	Mk.	1914		
187	(Lu-)Konjo . .	Belgian Congo .	Mk.	1914		
188	Lamba . . .	N. Rhodesia .	Sel.	1914	1921	
189	Lunda (Kalunda) .	Angola . .	Mk.	1914	1918	
190	Lunda (Kambove) .	Belgian Congo .	Mk.	1914	1933	
191	(Urunya-)Ruanda .	Ruanda-Urundi .	Goss.	1914	1931	1954
192	Tivi or Munchi .	N. Nigeria . .	Sel.	1914	1936	
193	Bachama . . .	N. Nigeria . .	Mk.	1915		
194	Dinka or Jieng (Bor) .	Sudan . .	Lk.	1915	1941	
195	Jukun (Donga) . .	N. Nigeria . .	Sel.	1915		
196	Mpama . . .	Belgian Congo .	Sel.	1915		
197	(Olu-)Nyore . .	Kenya . .	Sel.	1915	1936	
198	Sengele . . .	Belgian Congo .	Mk.	1915		
199	Somali (Ogaden-Harti)	Somaliland . .	Mk.	1915		

No.	Language	Territory	First Book	Date	N.T.	Bible
200	(O-)Tetela . .	Belgian Congo .	Sel.	1915	1937	
201	Yergum . . .	N. Nigeria . .	Sel.	1915		
202	Angas . . .	N. Nigeria . .	Mk.	1916		
203	Burum . . .	N. Nigeria . .	Mk.	1916		
204	Chokwe . . .	Angola . .	Jn.	1916	1927	
205	Dinka or Jieng (Chich)	Sudan . .	Mk.	1916		
206	Ngala (Uele) . .	Belgian Congo .	Mk.	1916	1928	1952
207	(Chi-)Nsenga .	N. Rhodesia .	Sel.	1916	1923	
208	Lomwe . . .	Port. E. Africa .	Mk.	1917	1930	
209	Mashi . . .	Belgian Congo .	Jn.	1917		
210	(Pa-)Zande . .	Sudan . .	Mk.	1918	1938	
	VIII. 1919–1928					
211	Arago . . .	N. Nigeria . .	Sel.	1919		
212	Kono . . .	Sierra Leone .	Mt.	1919		
213	Mbunda . . .	N. Rhodesia .	Jn.	1919		
214	Shilha (Central) .	Morocco . .	Lk.	1919		
215	(Chi-)Bena .	Tanganyika .	N.T.	1920	1920	
216	Igabo (Isoko) .	S. Nigeria . .	Mk.	1920		
217	Mukuni or Lenje .	N. Rhodesia .	Sel.	1920		
218	Luba (Songi) .	Belgian Congo .	Lk.	1920	1952	
219	Ngandu . . .	Belgian Congo .	Mk.	1920	1941	
220	Popo . . .	Dahomey . .	Mk.	1920		
221	Rundi . .	Ruanda-Urundi .	Lk.	1920	1951	
222	Tangale . . .	N. Nigeria . .	Lk.	1920	1932	
223	(Se-)Venda .	South Africa .	Goss.	1920	1923	1936
224	Jaba . . .	N. Nigeria . .	Mk.	1921		
225	Kru . . .	Liberia . .	Lk.	1921		
226	Luba (Katanga) .	Belgian Congo .	Goss.	1921	1923	1950
227	Lur . . .	Belgian Congo .	Jn.	1921		
228	Meru . . .	Kenya . .	Mk.	1921	1952	
229	Sobo (Urhobo) .	S. Nigeria . .	Sel.	1921	1952	
230	Swahili (Ituri) .	Belgian Congo .	Mt.	1921	1937	
231	Bassa (Cameroons) .	Cameroons .	Mt.	1922	1939	
232	Kpelle . . .	Liberia . .	Mk.	1922		
233	Lozi or Kololo .	N. Rhodesia .	Mt.	1922	1925	1952

No.	Language	Territory	First Book	Date	N.T.	Bible
234	Lugbara . . .	Belgian Congo .	Mk.	1922	1936	
235	(A- or Doa-)Lur .	Belgian Congo .	Jn.	1922	1933	1936
236	Bambara . . .	French Sudan .	Lk.	1923	1937	
237	Chawi . . .	N. Nigeria . .	Jn.	1923		
238	Iregwe . . .	N. Nigeria . .	Mk.	1923		
239	Kisii or Gusii .	Kenya . .	Sel.	1923	1948	
240	Luba (Kaonde) .	Belgian Congo .	Mk.	1923		
241	Agni . . .	Ivory Coast .	Sel.	1924		
242	Bura . . .	N. Nigeria . .	Sel.	1924	1939	
243	Igala . . .	N. Nigeria . .	Jn.	1924	1935	
244	Logo . . .	Belgian Congo .	Mk.	1924		
245	Rukuba . . .	N. Nigeria . .	Mk.	1924		
246	Waja . . .	N. Nigeria . .	Sel.	1924		
247	Wurkum . . .	N. Nigeria . .	Sel.	1924		
248	Bamum . . .	S. Nigeria . .	Mk.	1925		
249	Nubian (Heiban) .	Sudan . .	Sel.	1925		
250	Adjukru . .	Ivory Coast .	Cat.	1926		
251	Dinka or Jieng (Padang)	Sudan . .	Lk.	1926	1952	
252	Gbari (Paiko) .	N. Nigeria . .	Jn.	1926		
253	Hungana . . .	Belgian Congo .	Jn.	1926		
254	Lendu (Batha) .	Belgian Congo .	Mk.	1926	1936	
255	Mbuti or Efe or Ifi .	Belgian Congo .	Sel.	1926		
256	Nandi . . .	Kenya . .	Jn.	1926	1933	1939
257	Nkoya . . .	N. Rhodesia .	Sel.	1926		
258	Pende . . .	Belgian Congo .	Lk.	1926	1935	
259	Tera . . .	N. Nigeria . .	Sel.	1926		
260	Arabic (Sudan) .	Sudan . .	Mk.	1927		
261	Bari . . .	Sudan . .	Mk.	1927	1952	
262	Idoma . . .	N. Nigeria . .	Mk.	1927		
263	Jukun (Kona) .	N. Nigeria . .	Mk.	1927		
264	Nyemba . . .	Angola . .	Sel.	1927		
265	Sango . . .	French Equatorial Africa	Jn.	1927	1935	
266	Songoi . . .	French W. Africa	Goss.	1927	1936	
267	Avikam . . .	Ivory Coast .	Sel.	1928		

No.	Language	Territory	First Book	Date	N.T.	Bible
268	Moru . . .	Sudan . .	Mk.	1928	1950	
269	Tamachek (of Air) .	French Sahara .	Sel.	1928		
	IX. 1929–1938					
270	Bali . . .	Cameroons .	Mk.	1929	1933	
271	Ebrié . . .	Ivory Coast .	Sel.	1929		
272	Fula (Futa-Jalon) .	French Guinea .	Mt.	1929		
273	Fuliro . . .	Belgian Congo .	Mk.	1929		
274	Hunde . . .	Belgian Congo .	Sel.	1929		
275	Kwese . . .	Belgian Congo .	Jn.	1929		
276	Tula . . .	N. Nigeria . .	Jn.	1929		
277	Bari (Kakua) .	Sudan . .	Lk.	1930		
278	Bira . . .	Belgian Congo .	Jn.	1930		
279	Bungili . . .	French Equatorial Africa	Mt.	1930		
280	Dida . . .	Ivory Coast .	Mk.	1930		
281	Kakwa (Congo) .	Belgian Congo .	Mk.	1930		
282	Karamojong .	Uganda . .	Sel.	1930		
283	More . . .	French W. Africa	Mk.	1930	1939	
284	Ogoni . . .	S. Nigeria .	Mk.	1930		
285	Suk (Sebei) .	Uganda . .	Sel.	1930		
286	Zinza or Sinja .	Tanganyika .	Mt.	1930		
287	Atche . . .	Ivory Coast .	Mk.	1931		
288	Dakkarkari .	N. Nigeria . .	Mk.	1931		
289	Eggon or Mada .	N. Nigeria . .	Sel.	1931		
290	Karré . . .	French Equatorial Africa	Jn.	1931	1947	
291	Meninka or Malinke .	Senegal . .	Mk.	1931	1942	
292	Mamvu . . .	Belgian Congo .	Mk.	1931		
293	Shamba . . .	Uganda . .	Mk.	1931		
294	Banu . . .	French Equatorial Africa	Mk.	1932		
295	Chaga (Machame) .	Tanganyika .	Goss.	1932		
296	Fula (Macina) . .	French Sudan .	Jn.	1932		
297	Kasene . . .	French Sudan .	Cat.	1932		

No.	Language	Territory	First Book	Date	N.T.	Bible
298	Mbai . . .	French Equatorial Africa	Lk.	1932	1942	
299	Ndandi . . .	Belgian Congo .	Jn.	1932		
300	Baya (Mbere) . .	French Equatorial Africa	Mk.	1933	1950	
301	Bobo (Red) . .	French Sudan .	Sel.	1933	1954	
302	Gurunsi . . .	French Sudan .	Cat.	1933		
303	Habbe . . .	French Sudan .	Jn.	1933		
304	Kamberri . .	N. Nigeria . .	Mk.	1933		
305	Lumbu . . .	French Equatorial Africa	Mk.	1933		
306	Mundang . .	Cameroons .	Mk.	1933	1948	
307	Sidamo . . .	Abyssinia . .	Mk.	1933		
308	Tsamba . . .	N. Nigeria . .	Mk.	1933		
309	Yaka . . .	French Equatorial Africa	Lk.	1933		
310	Baya (Gbea) . .	French Equatorial Africa	Mk.	1934		
311	Boran . . .	Kenya . .	Lk.	1934		
312	Dyerma . . .	Niger Colony, F.W.A.	Jn.	1934	1954	
313	Gofa . . .	Abyssinia . .	Mk.	1934		
314	(Ki-)Jita . . :	Tanganyika .	Lk.	1934	1943	
315	Kituba . . .	Belgian Congo .	Jn.	1934	1946	
316	Krongo . . .	Sudan . .	Mk.	1934		
317	Lega . . .	Belgian Congo .	Mk.	1934		
318	Masana . . .	Cameroons .	Mk.	1934	1954	
319	Tamachek (Tamahaq of Hoggar)	French Sahara .	Ru.	1934		
320	Tharaka . . .	Kenya . .	Jn.	1934		
321	Dagbane . . .	Gold Coast .	Mt.	1935		
322	Gimbunda . .	Belgian Congo .	Jn.	1935		
323	Gudeila . . .	Abyssinia . .	Mt.	1935		
324	Jatsi . . .	Belgian Congo .	Sel.	1935		
325	Kissi . . .	Sierra Leone .	I Jn.	1935		
326	Luchazi . . .	Angola . .	N.T.	1935	1935	

No.	Language	Territory	First Book	Date	N.T.	Bible
327	Luimbi . . .	Angola . .	Mk.	1935		
328	Madi . . .	Sudan . .	Mk.	1935		
329	Mongwande . .	Belgian Congo .	Mk.	1935		
330	Nuer (Nyuong) .	Sudan . .	Lk.	1935		
331	Shanga . . .	Port. E. Africa .	Jn.	1935	1949	
332	Somali . . .	British Somaliland	Goss.	1935		
333	Bembe . . .	Belgian Congo .	Mk.	1936		
334	Bolia . . .	Belgian Congo .	Lk.	1936		
335	Mbum . . .	Cameroons .	Lk.	1936		
336	Ngambai . . .	French Equatorial Africa	Mk.	1936	1954	
337	Ngbaka or Bwaka .	Fr. Eq. Africa & Belgian Congo	Jn.	1936		
338	Pero . . .	N. Nigeria . .	Lk.	1936		
339	Songo . . .	Angola . .	Mk.	1936		
340	Suk	Kenya . .	Mk.	1936		
341	Aladian . . .	Ivory Coast .	Mk.	1937		
342	Bua or Libua .	Belgian Congo .	Sel.	1937		
343	Dioula . . .	Ivory Coast .	Sel.	1937		
344	Egede . . .	N. Nigeria . .	Mk.	1937		
345	Kanakuru . .	N. Nigeria . .	Mk.	1937		
346	Lualaba (Ngwana) .	Belgian Congo .	Goss.	1937	1939	
347	Luba (Kalebwe) .	Belgian Congo .	Sel.	1937	1952	
348	(Ki-)Mbundu (Uige) .	Angola . .	Sel.	1937		
349	Nkutu or Bankutu .	Belgian Congo .	Mk.	1937		
350	Nuba (Nirere) .	Sudan . .	Mk.	1937		
351	Sakata . . .	Belgian Congo .	Jn.	1937		
352	Baya (Kalla) .	Cameroons . .	Jn.	1938		
353	Hangaza . .	Tanganyika .	Mk.	1938		
354	Ikota . . .	Gabon . .	Mk.	1938		
355	Mumuye . .	N. Nigeria . .	Mk.	1938		
356	Nuer (Jikany) .	Sudan . .	Jn.	1938		
357	Pere . . .	Belgian Congo .	Jn.	1938		
358	Salampasu . .	Belgian Congo .	Mk.	1938		
359	Wongo . . .	Belgian Congo .	Lk.	1938		

No.	Language	Territory	First Book	Date	N.T.	Bible
	X. 1939–1945					
360	Ilamba . . .	Tanganyika .	Mk.	1939		
361	Kiyaka . . .	Belgian Congo .	Jn.	1939		
362	Yipounon . .	Gabon . .	Lk.	1939		
363	Bandi . . .	Liberia . .	Mt.	1940		
364	Ganawuri . .	N. Nigeria . .	Mk.	1940		
365	Jarawa . . .	N. Nigeria . .	Mk.	1940		
366	Lobi . . .	Ivory Coast .	Jn.	1940		
367	(Se-)Chuana (Central)	Bechuanaland .	Mt.	1941		
368	Okela . . .	Belgian Congo .	Mk.	1941		
369	Gio	Liberia . .	Lk.	1943		
370	Walamo . . .	Abyssinia . .	Jn.	1943		
371	Kim . . .	French Equatorial Africa	Mt.	1944	1954	
	XI. 1946–1954					
372	Baouli . . .	Ivory Coast .	Mt.	1946	1952	
373	Bassa (Nigeria) . .	N. Nigeria . .	Mk.	1946		
374	Maban . . .	Sudan . .	Mk.	1946		
375	Mano . . .	Liberia . .	Lk.	1946		
376	Margi . . .	N. Nigeria . .	Mt.	1946		
377	Gourma . . .	French Sudan .	Jn.	1947		
378	Nanjeri . . .	French Equatorial Africa	Mk.	1947		
379	Bamileke . . .	Cameroons. . .	Mk.	1948		
380	Kasem . . .	French W. Africa	Mk.	1948		
381	Luba (Kalanga) .	Belgian Congo .	Mk.	1948		
382	Sara (Kabba-Laka) .	French Equatorial Africa	Mk.	1948		
383	Zanaki . . .	Tanganyika .	Mt.	1948		
384	Loma	Liberia . .	Mk.	1949		
385	Sara (Madjingai) .	French Equatorial Africa	Jn.	1950		
386	Agatu . . .	N. Nigeria . .	Jn.	1951		
387	Gouro . . .	Ivory Coast .	Mk.	1951		
388	Kimbala . . .	Belgian Congo .	Jn.	1951		

No.	Language	Territory	First Book	Date	N.T.	Bible
389	Nuba (Moro) . .	Sudan . .	Mk.	1951		
390	Nyimang . . .	Sudan . .	Mk.	1951		
391	Bano'o . . .	Cameroons. .	Goss.	1953		
392	Bariba . . .	Dahomey . .	Jn.	1953		
393	Gbeapo . . .	Liberia . .	Lk.	1953		
394	Pana . . .	French Equatorial Africa	Jn.	1953		
395	Tamachek (Timbuktu)	French Sahara .	Mt.	1953		
396	Tchien . . .	Liberia . .	Mk.	1953		
397	Goulei . . .	French Equatorial Africa	Jn.	1954		
398	Nyemba . . .	Angola . .	Jn.	1954		
399	Pila . . .	Dahomey . .	Mk.	1954		

Union Versions

In several areas where neighbouring dialects show sufficient affinity for the purpose so-called union versions have been introduced, which become readily intelligible to speakers of the dialects concerned. These union versions are listed separately as they are not new languages ; indeed, if successful they reduce the total number of translations in circulation.

(1) Union Nyanja . .	E., S., and W. of Lake Nyasa.	N.T., 1906; Bible, 1922.
(2) Union Ibo . . .	S.E. Nigeria . .	N.T., 1909; Bible, 1913.
(3) Union Omyene . .	Gabon . . .	N.T., 1919; Bible, 1927.
(4) Union Mongo-Nkundu.	N.W. Belgian Congo.	N.T., 1921; Bible, 1930.
(5) Union Mambwe-Lungu	S. of Lake Tanganyika	N.T., 1922.
(6) Union Ngala . .	N. Belgian Congo .	Mk. 1934.

(3) *Summary Tables*

(a) New languages by periods

I.	To 1804 . .	5
II.	1805–1840 . .	13
III.	1841–1858 . .	17
IV.	1859–1878 . .	18
V.	1879–1896 . .	58
VI.	1897–1913 . .	72

(b) New languages by decades and half-centuries

To 1804 . .	5	
1805–1814 . .	3	
1815–1824 . .	2	
1825–1834 . .	4	
1835–1844 . .	6	
1845–1854 . .	12	32

(a) New languages by periods

VII.	1914–1918	.	. 27	
VIII.	1919–1928	.	. 59	
IX.	1929–1938	.	. 90	
X.	1939–1945	.	. 12	
XI.	1946–1954	.	. 28	399

(b) New languages by decades and half-centuries

1855–1864	.	. 9	
1865–1874	.	. 9	
1875–1884	.	. 13	
1885–1894	.	. 39	
1895–1904	.	. 42	112
1905–1914	.	. 48	
1915–1924	.	. 55	
1925–1934	.	. 73	
1935–1944	.	. 51	
1945–1954	.	. 28	255

399

(c) Analysis of First Translations

Portion	To 1854	1855–1904	1905–1954	Totals
Mk. . . .	2	21	98	121
Sel. . . .	18	28	45	91
Mt. . . .	6	25	24	55
Jn. . . .	—	13	41	54
Lk. . . .	2	12	28	42
Goss. . . .	2	6	11	19
N.T. . . .	—	2	2	4
Cat. . . .	—	1	3	4
Ps. . . .	2	—	1	3
Ru. . . .	—	1	1	2
Jon. . . .	—	2	—	2
Pent. . . .	—	1	—	1
I Jn. . . .	—	—	1	1
Totals . .	32	112	255	399

(4) *Bibliography*

Historical Catalogue of Printed Bibles. By T. H. Darlow and H. F. Moule. British and Foreign Bible Society. 1911.

Out of print. The standard record for its period. While based upon books in the Bible House Library it includes others, so far as known, printed by any organization. Dr. Kilgour comments: " The accuracy and scholarship of this work become increasingly impressive the more one uses it."

The Gospel in Many Years: A Chronological List of the Dates of the First Publication of Any Portion of God's Word in 835 Languages. By R. Kilgour. British and Foreign Bible Society. 1925. 2nd edition 1929.

Includes dates of successive portions after the first.

The Bible Throughout the World: A Survey of Scripture Translations. By R. Kilgour. World Dominion Press. 1939.

Chapter III, " The Bible Throughout Africa " (pp. 33–99), proceeds regionally. Maps are provided.

The Book of a Thousand Tongues: Being Some Account of the Translation and Publication of All or Part of the Holy Scriptures into More than a Thousand Languages and Dialects with over 1,100 Examples from the Text. By Eric M. North. Harper & Brothers for the American Bible Society. 1938.

Includes information concerning translators, their mission affiliation and publishing agencies.

Each in His Own Language. National Bible Society of Scotland. 1950.

Records the work of the N.B.S.S., stating what has been done in each language up to the date of publication.

The Hundred and Fiftieth Report of the British and Foreign Bible Society. British and Foreign Bible Society. 1956.

Provides a complete " Table of Languages " of B.F.B.S. with much information included; also maps (five for Africa) with language distribution marked.

INDEX

376

377

Mutesa II, 267
Mvera, 200
Mwenzo, 40
Myklebust, O. G., 306 *n.*

NAIROBI, 274, 291, 310, 322, 330
Namaqua, 22, 23
Nandi, 95
Nassau, R. H., 48
Natal, 35, 197, 290, 306
National Lutheran Council of America,
 85 *n.*
National Missionary Society of India,
 187
National War Memorial Health Foun-
 dation of South Africa, 255
Native Administration, 273 and *n.*
Nazi, 147 *n.*
Ndanda, 178
Ndola, 227
Ndunge, 312
Neill, S. C., 302, 304, 320 *n.*, 321 *n.*, 336 *n.*
Neukirchen Mission, 28, 33–4, 85 *n.*,
 89 and *n.*, 242
Nganischo, M., 37
Ngoni, 61
Ngubane, J. K., 332–3, 338
Nguludi, 63
Nhlapo, J. M., 354 *n.*
Nielsen, E. W., 302 *n.*
Niger Delta Pastorate, 126
Niger Territory, 59
Nigeria, domestic slavery, 167; educa-
 tion, 106 *n.*, 115–17, 180, 277, 283,
 291; influenza epidemic, 72; Islam,
 189, 327 ; land, 92; leprosy, 177–8;
 marriage custom, 219, 345; missions,
 56, 106 *n.*, 115–17, 177–8, 180, 185,
 188–9, 197, 209, 216, 226, 229, 246,
 253, 283, 297, 299, 305, 306, 307,
 310, 311, 345, 349; political development, 53, 262–3, 299; separatist
 movements, 126, 353–4; war, 60–1,
 65, 66, 67, 76 *n.*; women's rising,
 172–3
Nightingale, E. G., 268 *n.*
Nkrumah, K., 262
North German (Bremen) Missionary
 Society, *See* Bremen M. S.
Northcott, C. H., 274 *n.*
Northern Rhodesia, education, 117,
 179–80, 283 *n.*, 291, 293, 294;
 missions, 133, 172, 179–80, 218 *n.*,
 226, 232 *n.*, 243, 248, 283 *n.*, 294,
 296, 305, 306, 308; political development, 164–6, 267–8; war, 15, 67, 71 *n.*,
 74 *n.*, 79 *n.*, 243; Watch Tower, 230
Norway's Free Evangelical Mission to
 the Heathen, 122

Norwegian Baptist Mission, 51 *n.*, 122,
 243
Norwegian Lutheran Church of
 America, 306
Norwegian Methodist Church, 190,
 243
Norwegian Missionary Society, 243,
 306
Notcutt and Latham, 185 *n.*
Nyasa Baptist Industrial Mission, 62 *n.*
Nyasaland, education, 117, 291; Ethiopianism, 62–3; influenza epidemic,
 73; leprosy, 179; migrant labour,
 169–71; missions, 63–4, 199–200,
 226, 247, 300 *n.*, 306, 344 *n.*, 345;
 political development, 164–6, 267–8;
 war, 15, 29–30, 32, 61, 67

OBLATES OF MARY IMMACULATE,
 23, 246
Oblates of St. Francis of Sales, 23
Œchsner de Coninck, 21
Ogowe, 48, 347 *n.*
Oksas, F., 21
Oldham, J. H., 96 *n.*, 97 *n.*, 99 and *n.*,
 107, 111, 113, 115, 159
Oldrieve, F., 177 *n.*
Oliver, R., 97 *n.*, *et seq.*, 115 *n.*, 119 *n.*,
 134 *n.*, 203 *n.*
Omdurman, 178, 321
Ongino, 178
Ondo, 305, 353
Onitsha, 305
Opon, S., 124
Oppenheimer, E., 154 *n.*
Ormsby-Gore, W. G. A., 93 *n.*, 111 *n.*,
 158 *n.*
Orr and Gilks, 176 *n.*
Oukuambi, 191
Ovakuanjama, 191
Ovambo, 22, 23, 191, 243
Ovimbundu, 250
Owerri, 305
Oyo, 246

PALLOTTINE FATHERS, 20 *n.*, 21
Pan-African Congress, 89
Paris Evangelical Missionary Society,
 21, 41, 48, 85 *n.*, 87, 133, 200–1, 212,
 243–4, 246–7, 310 *n.*, 347 *n.*
Parker, K., 219
Parrinder, G., 325
Parsons, E. C., 349 *n.*
Passfield, S., 159–60
Paul, Apostle, 211, 225, 315, 347,
 356
Pauw, J. C. C., 256 *n.*
Peabody, F. G., 114 *n.*
Penn School, S. C., 113, 114 *n.*